Photographs & Text:
Flurina Rothenberger

Proofreading:
Eric Rosencrantz
Design, editing and illustrations: Hammer/ Sereina Rothenberger & David Schatz

Lithography: Stefanie Stroh
Printed and bound by Offsetdruckerei Karl Grammlich GmbH Pliezhausen, Germany

Edition Patrick Frey
Limmatstrasse 268
CH–8005 Zurich
editionpatrickfrey.com
mail@editionpatrickfrey.ch

ISBN 978-3-905929-73-7

With the kind support of

Dr. Georg und Josi Guggenheim-Stiftung, Erna und Curt Burgauer Stiftung

Stadt Zürich Kultur

Kanton Zürich Fachstelle Kultur

Distribution

Switzerland:
AVA Verlagsauslieferung
CH–Affoltern am Albis
ava.ch

Germany, Austria:
GVA Gemeinsame Verlags-auslieferung, D–Göttingen
gva-verlage.de

France, Luxembourg, Belgium:
Les presses du réel, F–Dijon
lespressesdureel.com

United Kingdom:
Antenne Books, GB–London
antennebooks.com

Japan:
Marginal Press, JP–Tokyo
marginal-press.com

Australia, New Zealand:
Perimeter Distribution
perimeterdistribution.com

USA:
RAM publications & distribution
USA–Santa Monica
rampub.com

Rest of the world:
Edition Patrick Frey
CH–Zurich
editionpatrickfrey.com

First edition
Edition Patrick Frey, 2015
Printed in Germany

Acknowledgements

My deepest gratitude goes to the people portrayed in this book. To my parents and Judith Wyder, to Barbara Achermann, Martina Böhler, Flavio Karrer and Andrea Gohl. I thank Maggy Lawson, the Wilson and Mbaye families. Special thanks to Patrick Frey, Andrea Kempter and Stephanie Rebonati. Thanks to Sereina Rothenberger and David Schatz for their tireless commitment, critique and sensitive handling of the editing and design.

Quotes

"I love to dress like I am coming from somewhere and I have a place to go." Oyebamire Bola, Nigerian student

"No aid! Shut the doors and start talking business." James Shikwati, Kenyan economist

"We are a continent, not a country." Catherine Phiri of Media 365, Zambia

"Don't worry about my life, it's my talent!" Taxi sticker in Ghana

"I'm a black samurai, bright light in your black night!" Alpha Blondy, Ivorian musician

"We face neither east nor west; we face forward." Dr. Kwame Nkrumah, first president of Ghana

"Democracy¿ Dem all crazy!" Fela Kuti, Nigerian musician

"Le coeur n'est pas un genou pour qu'on le plie." Nash, Ivorian musician

For the people whose lives I portray:
I owe them everything.

Flurina Rothenberger

I love to dress like I'm coming from somewhere and I have a place to go

Images from the African Continent 2004–2014

Edition Patrick Frey
N° 173

RÉPUBLIQUE DE COTE D'IVOIRE

CARTE D'IDENTITE SCOLAIRE

ANNEE 198 .5..... 198 ..6.....

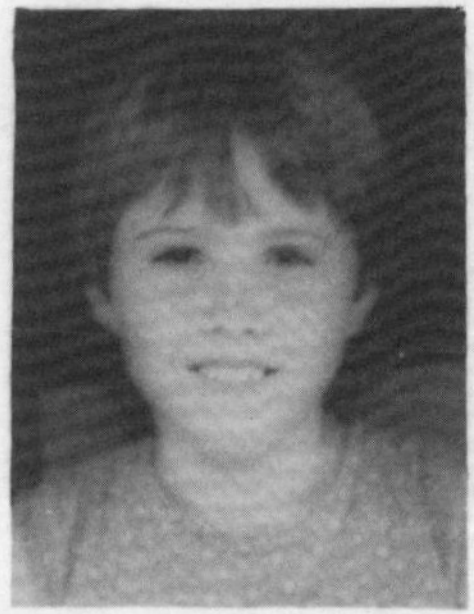

Nom: ROTHENBERGER

Prénoms: Flurina

Né le 29.03.77

à Switzerland

Domicile: Zuenoula

Signature de l'Elève:

Flurina Rothenberger

Nom de l'Etablissement: Vavoua International School

Je soussigné Mlle.J.E. Barnicoat certifie que

M lle. ROTHENBERGER, Flurina

est Elève dans mon Etablissement.

CACHET

Mission Evangélique de l'Afrique Occidentale – VAVOUA INTERNATIONAL SCHOOL

SIGNATURE

Jean E. Barnicoat

Directrice

Introduction

"The single story creates stereotypes, and the problem with stereotypes is not that they are untrue, but that they are incomplete. They make one story become the only story." (Chimamanda Ngozi Adichie, novelist)

I grew up in Zuénoula, a rural town in the center of Côte d'Ivoire. Since then my memories of this stage in my life have been rounded out by experiences in very different parts of Africa. And yet many of my first adventures remain special and vivid in my mind to this day. I am still reluctant to ride in a four-wheel drive – owing to a heavy dose of nostalgia for the Renault 12 of my childhood: a vehicle bolted together on Ivorian soil with that special extra, namely an added base plate under the chassis for "challenging" roads. One day in 1985 we were on our way back home from a visit to the town of Tabou. It was the rainy season and the track had turned into a soft muddy field. We got stuck, the engine of the R12 went dead and my parents exchanged a funny glance. After we'd spent hours shoving tree branches under the slippery tires, a relaxed, elegant man in a very shiny car drove up and stopped. He made a joke about the *poto-poto* (local term for mud) before calling in help on his walkie-talkie. He then got out of the car, skillfully sidestepping the mud to keep his leather loafers clean, and swept my rain-soaked sisters and me into the soft backseat of his vanilla-scented car. The man, who owned a rubber plantation, invited us to stay in his guest apartment on the compound while he had the car fixed. It was the classiest place we had ever been to. We spent the afternoon splashing around in a big blue chlorinated pool, thrilled at this rare opportunity. The next morning we climbed into our now spotless, vacuumed car, scented with a Little Tree air freshener dangling from the rear-view mirror. The cleanliness didn't last long, though. A few days later, a neighbor delivered her baby on the backseat of the vehicle while being rushed to the clinic. So she named the boy Renault.

This book is a tribute to ordinary life. No spectacular or sensational incidents, just selected daily observations from countries in Africa I have worked or stayed in over the past ten years. These pictures are a modest personal selection of glimpses of Africa that cannot possibly reflect the huge diversity of such a vast continent, comprising 55 independent countries and a correspondingly wide range of peoples, lifestyles and cultures. Conflicting facts, opportunities, intentions and events often closely co-exist here, stitched together to form a multilayered backdrop to daily life in Africa. Against such a diverse backdrop, the job of keeping the story simple can easily lead to misconceptions. Most settings I have worked in unmask stereotypes not as being untrue but–precisely as novelist Ngozi Adichie puts it–incomplete. Trying to single out a statement from a place of such contrasting truths is comparable to tackling the traffic in a city like Accra in Ghana or Dar es Salaam in Tanzania. As the situation evolves around you, you're constantly forced to reconsider your judgment and focus–or else you get stuck and left behind. This is one of the edifying and refreshing challenges I love about working in Africa: it is a strong and constant reminder that a particular image is always an intentional choice of one perspective from among many. The questions this continent raises and casually places in my path make me stop and think about what I actually understand.

"Home isn't a place where you just show up. It is a place you're invested in." (Frances M. Williams, business consultant)

It is precisely the many lingering uncertainties that boost my thinking process and ultimately leave me more invested here than elsewhere. I was lucky enough to grow up in an environment which had no preset ground rules, but instead provided sufficient social skills that you implicitly learned and applied and expected from others. This created an atmosphere of relaxed self-awareness. One in which I was greeted, looked in the eye, called *toubab* (term for Westerner in West Africa) to my face–and welcomed. To this day I am openly tagged as an outsider and have without exception felt accepted everywhere I've been, welcomed not with jittery self-consciousness, but with genuine hospitality. It is this liberty I've been granted to feel complete while remaining in-between worlds that fills me not only with serenity but with what is closest to a feeling of home. The way people choose to engage with my work has inevitably influenced how I capture an image and why. Most of my stories are set south of the Sahara, and the choreography of life there is often both carefully arranged and extremely improvised. This is a very generalized description, but one that reflects a widespread talent that African societies seem to share: an uncanny ability to reconcile contrasts. This ability is at the conceptual core of the present book. I hope Africans living in and outside the continent will recognize fragments of their own past or present reality and tie-ins to their own admiration for the richness that life on this continent has to offer. There is a precious quality we can learn from a majority of Africans: there is always a reason to greet people properly, exchange a few words and thoughts, regardless of how we're dressed, where we are coming from or headed to. Ultimately, it is a sense of comfort that reawakens the moment I step onto African soil. It is the conviction and peace at heart that things will work out one way or another. By surprise or as promised.

Flurina Rothenberger,
February 2015

The photographs shown in this book, drawn from both independent and commissioned stories and projects I've worked on in Africa over the past ten years, were shot in the following countries:

Maroc
Tunisie

Mali

Sénégal
Burkina Faso
Sierra Leone
Ghana Togo Ethiopia
Côte d'Ivoire

Tanzania

Angola
Madagascar

Moçambique

South
Africa

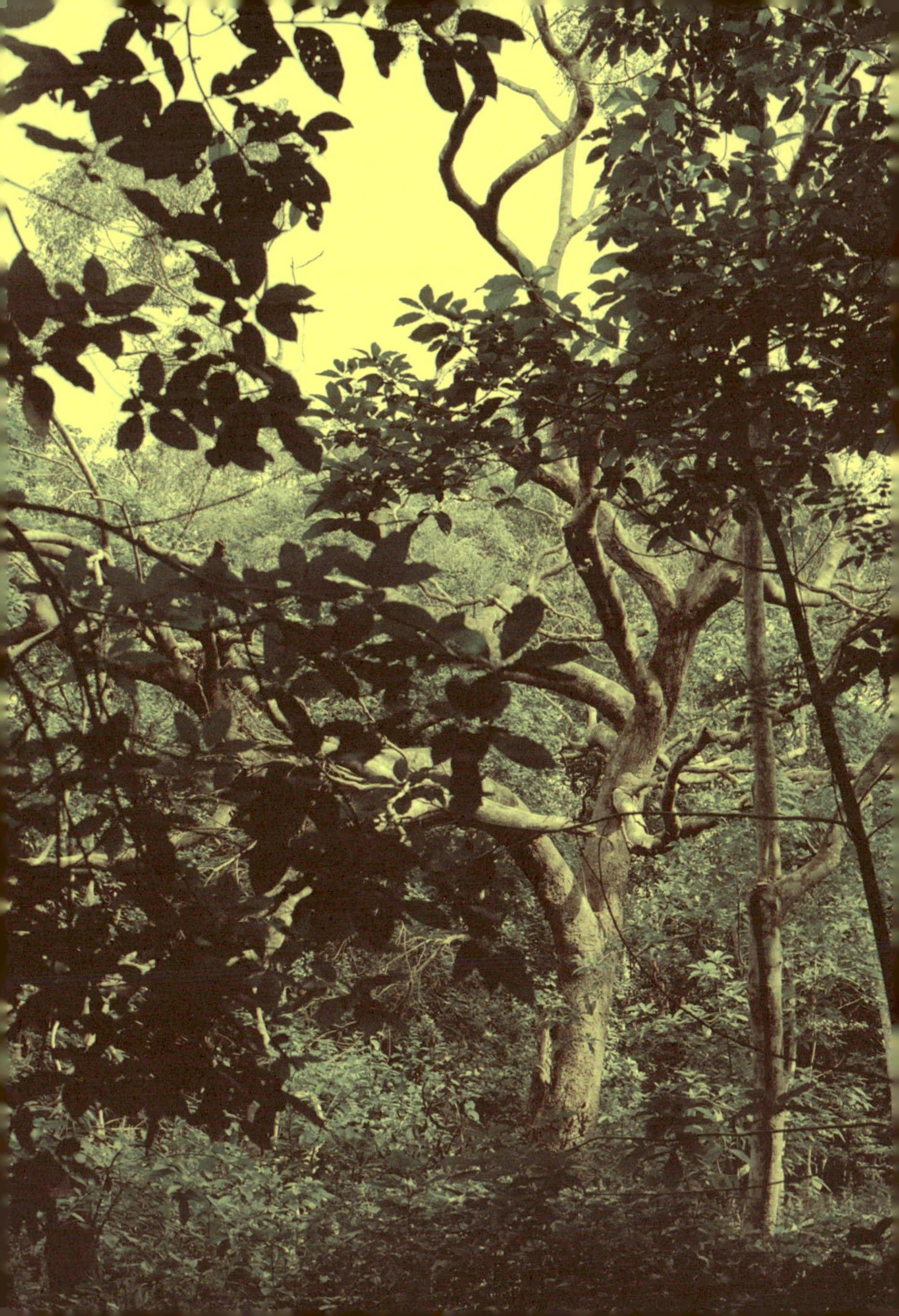

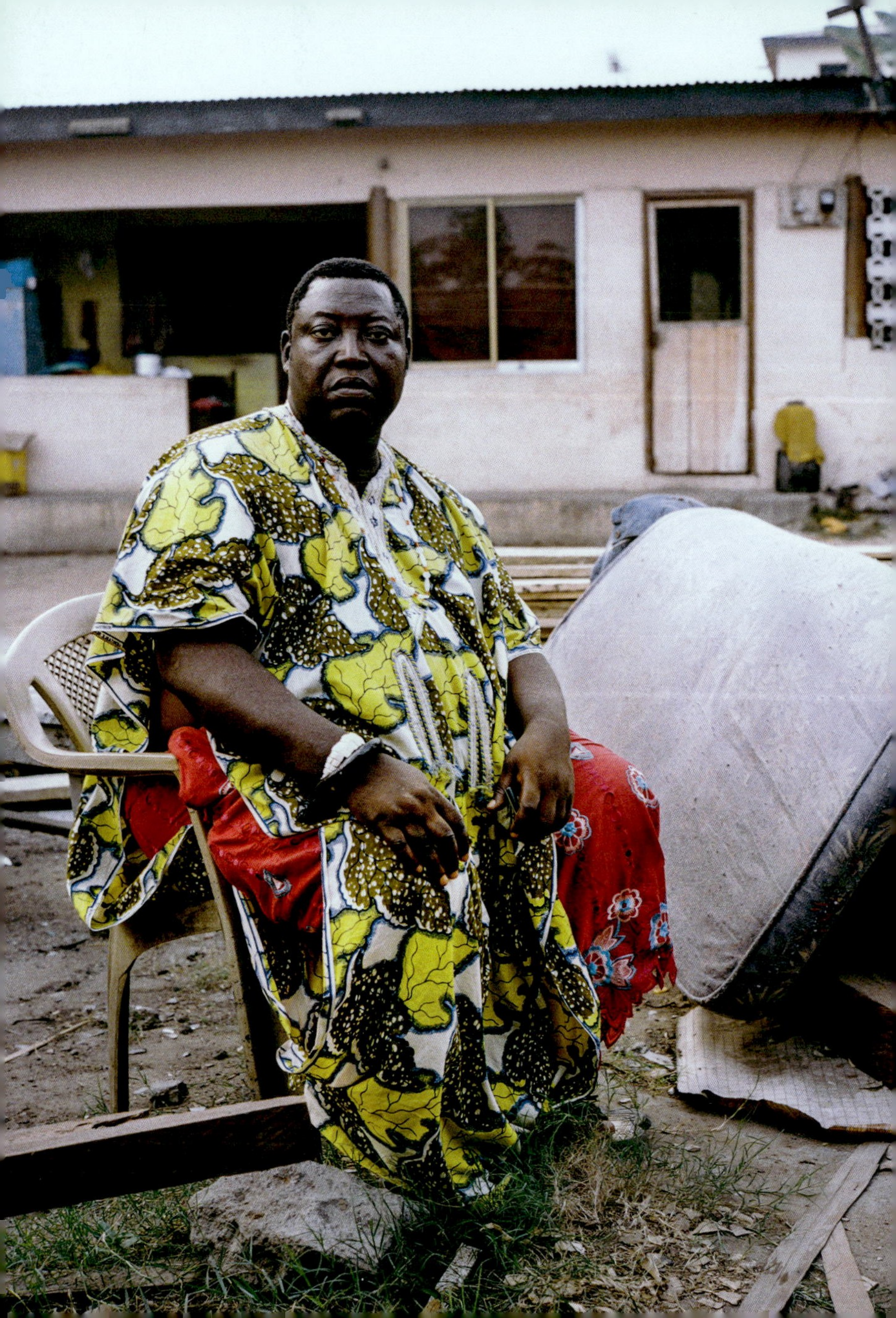

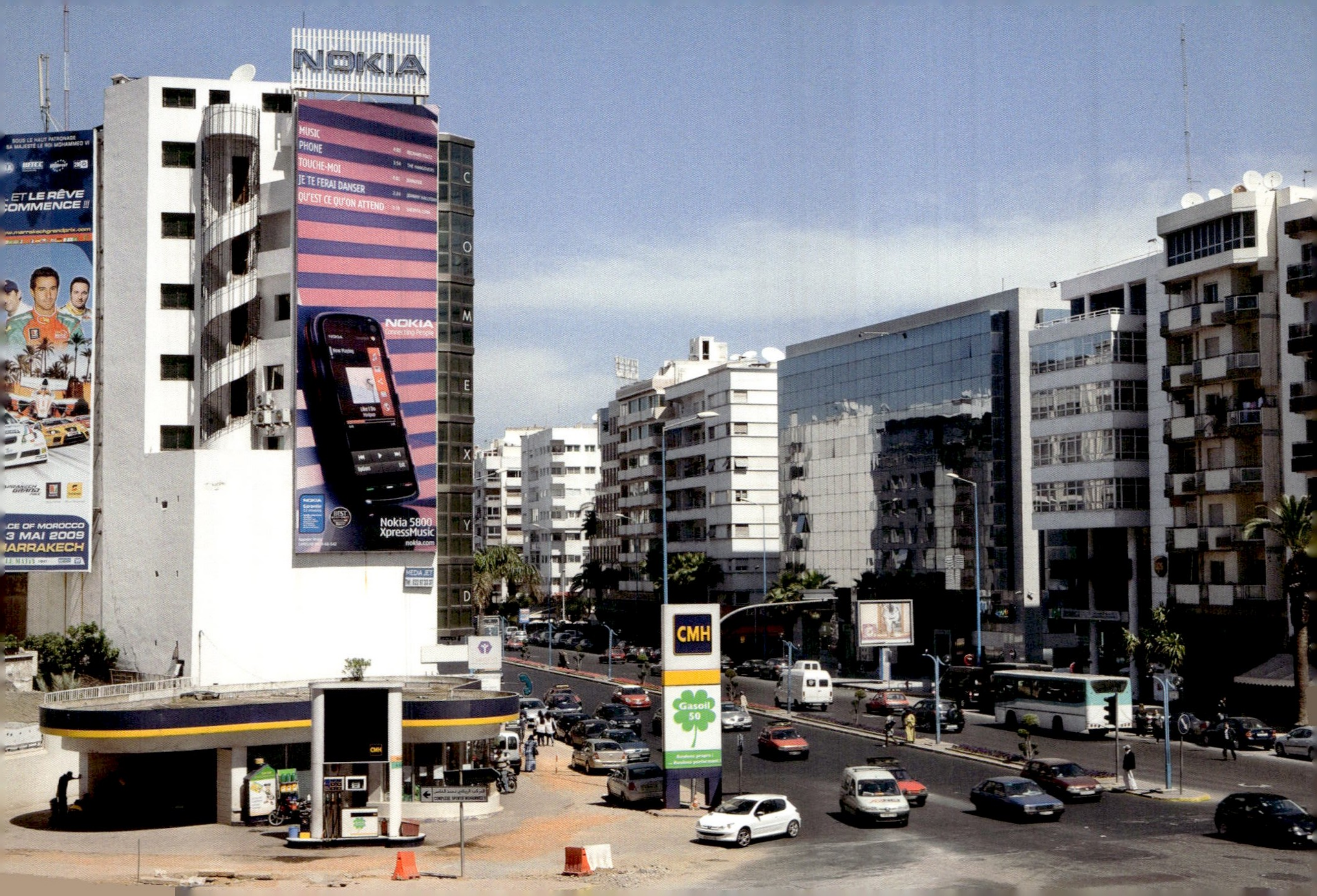
NOKIA
MUSIC
PHONE
TOUCHE-MOI
JE TE FERAI DANSER
QU'EST CE QU'ON ATTEND
NOKIA
Connecting People
Nokia 5800
XpressMusic
nokia.com
C
O
M
E
X
Y
D
ET LE RÊVE
COMMENCE !!
3 MAI 2009
MARRAKECH
CMH
Gasoil
50

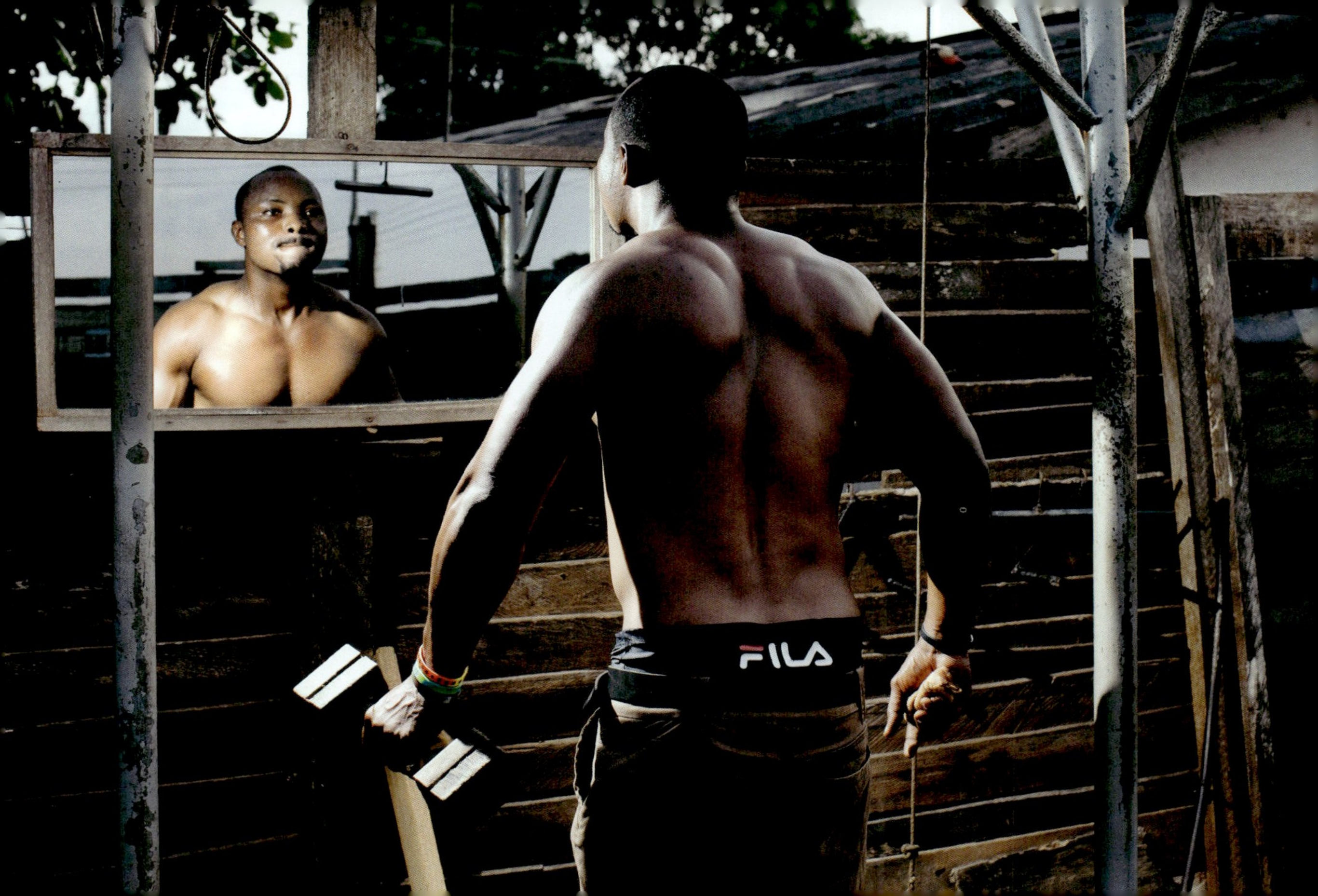
FILA

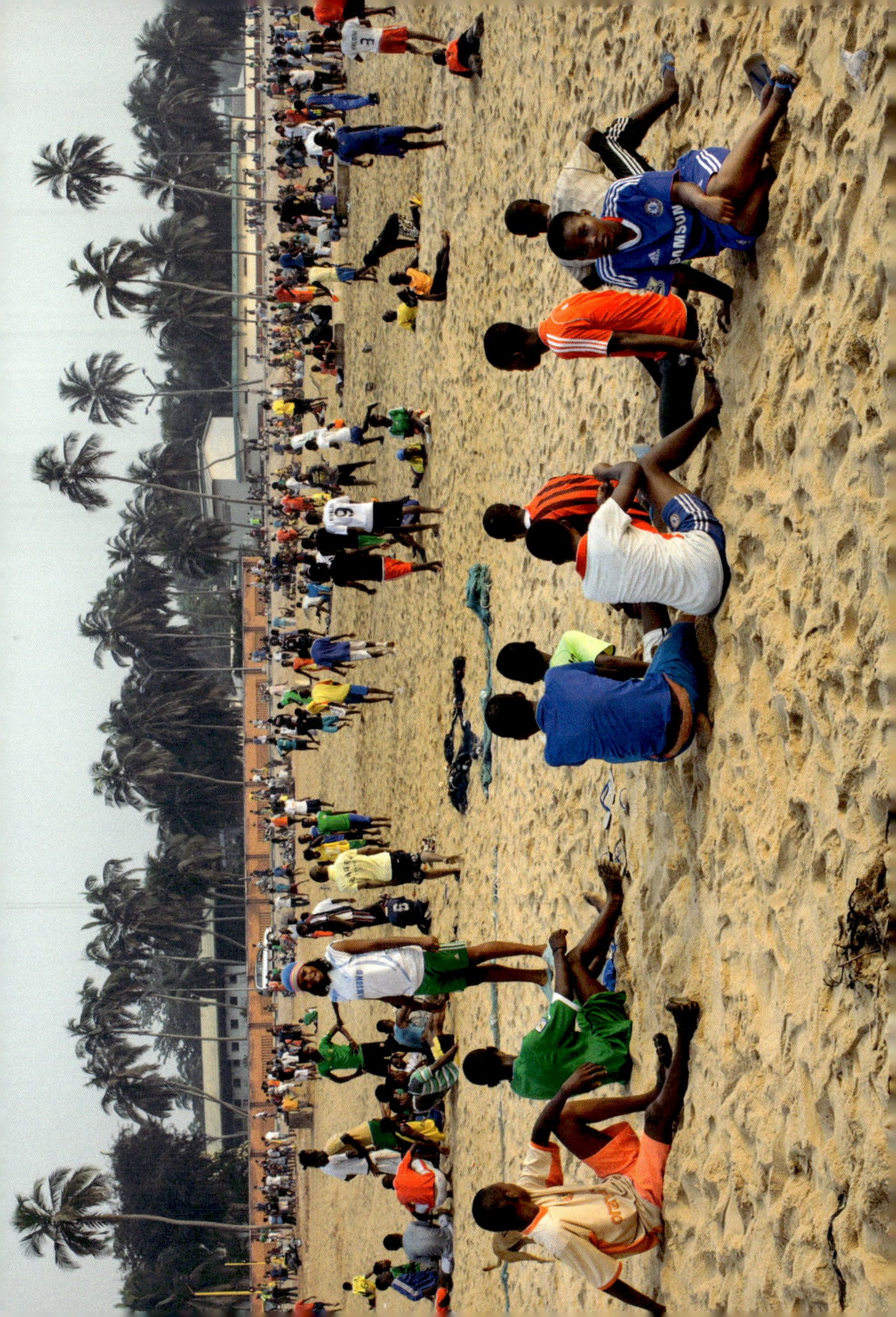

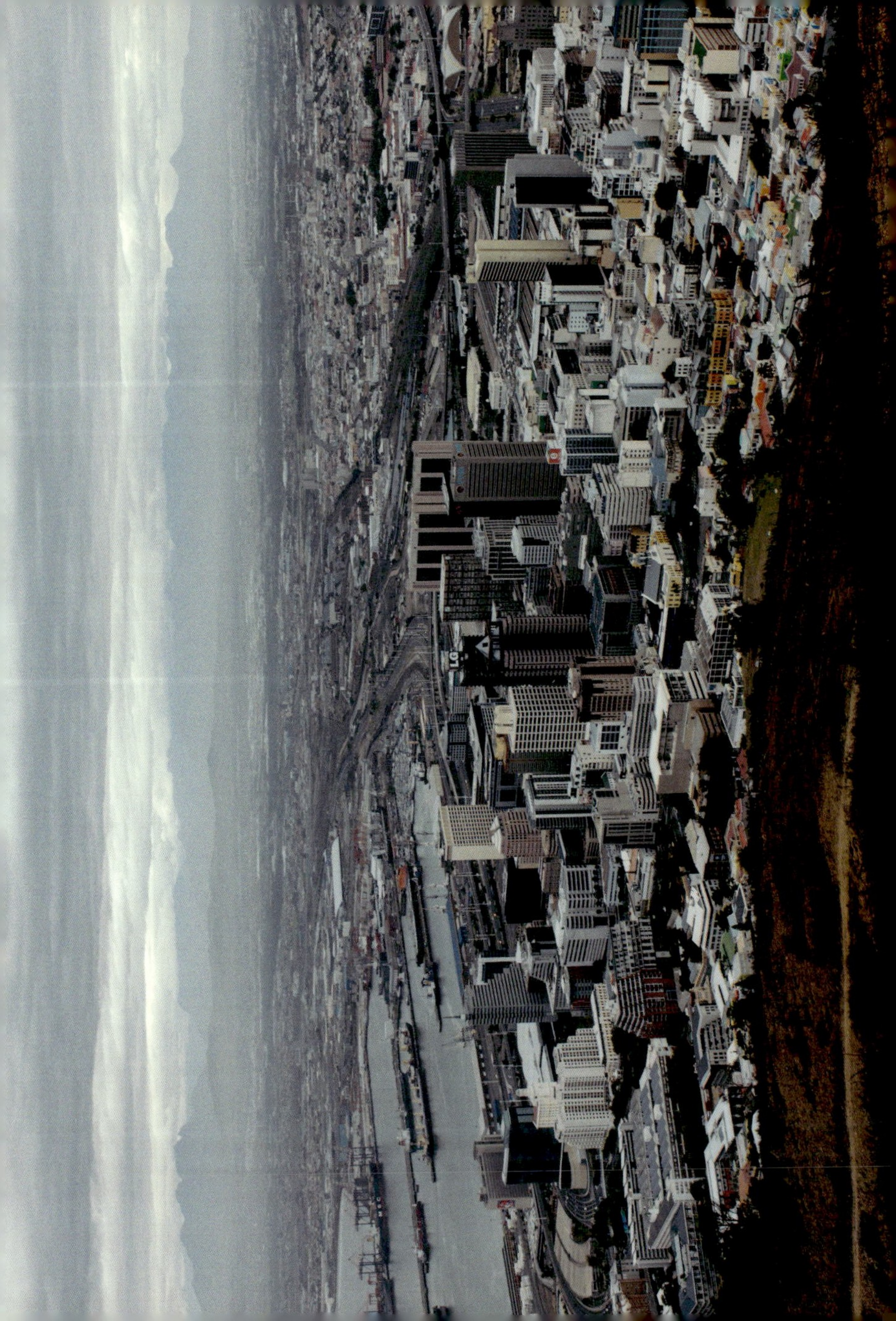

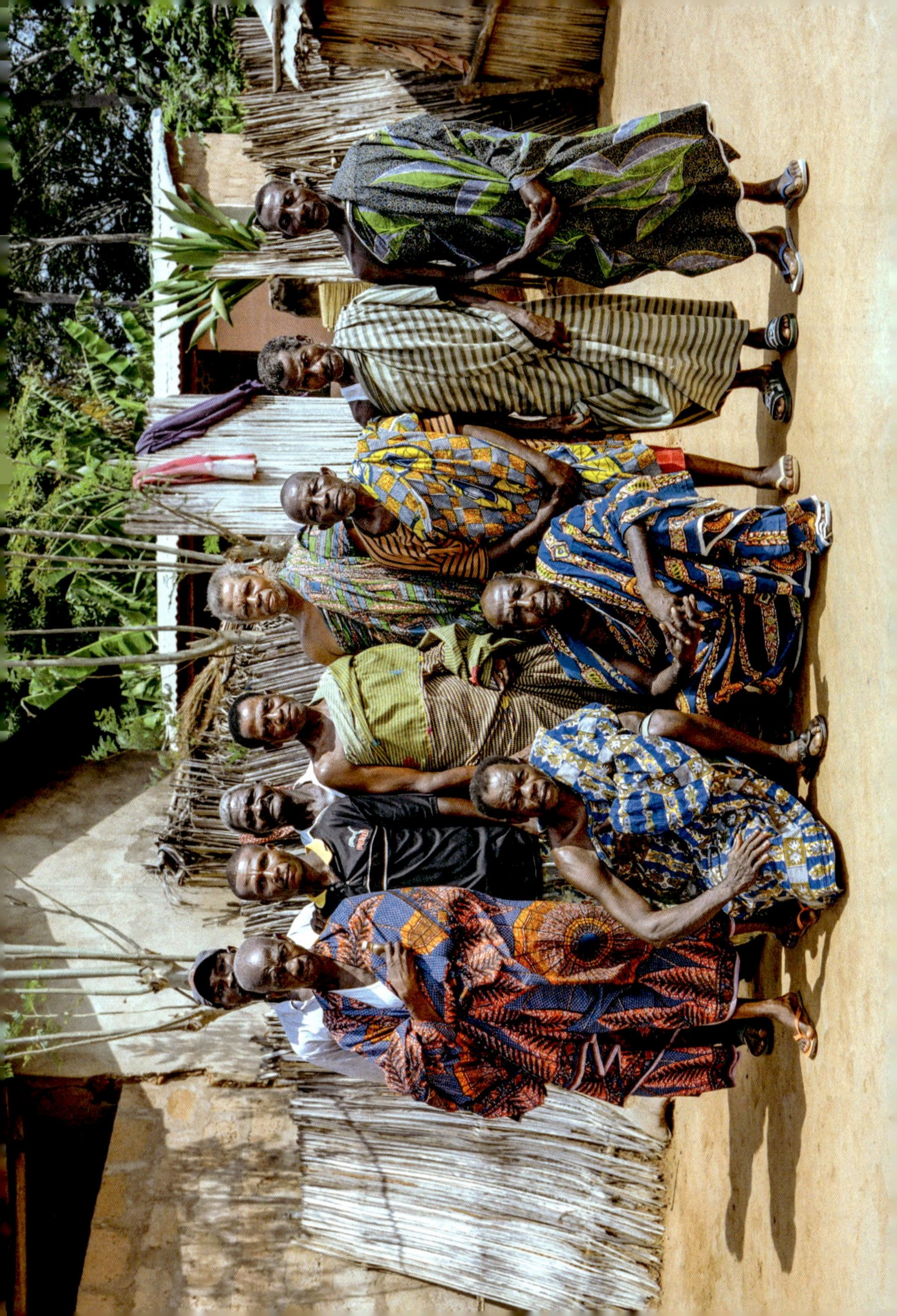

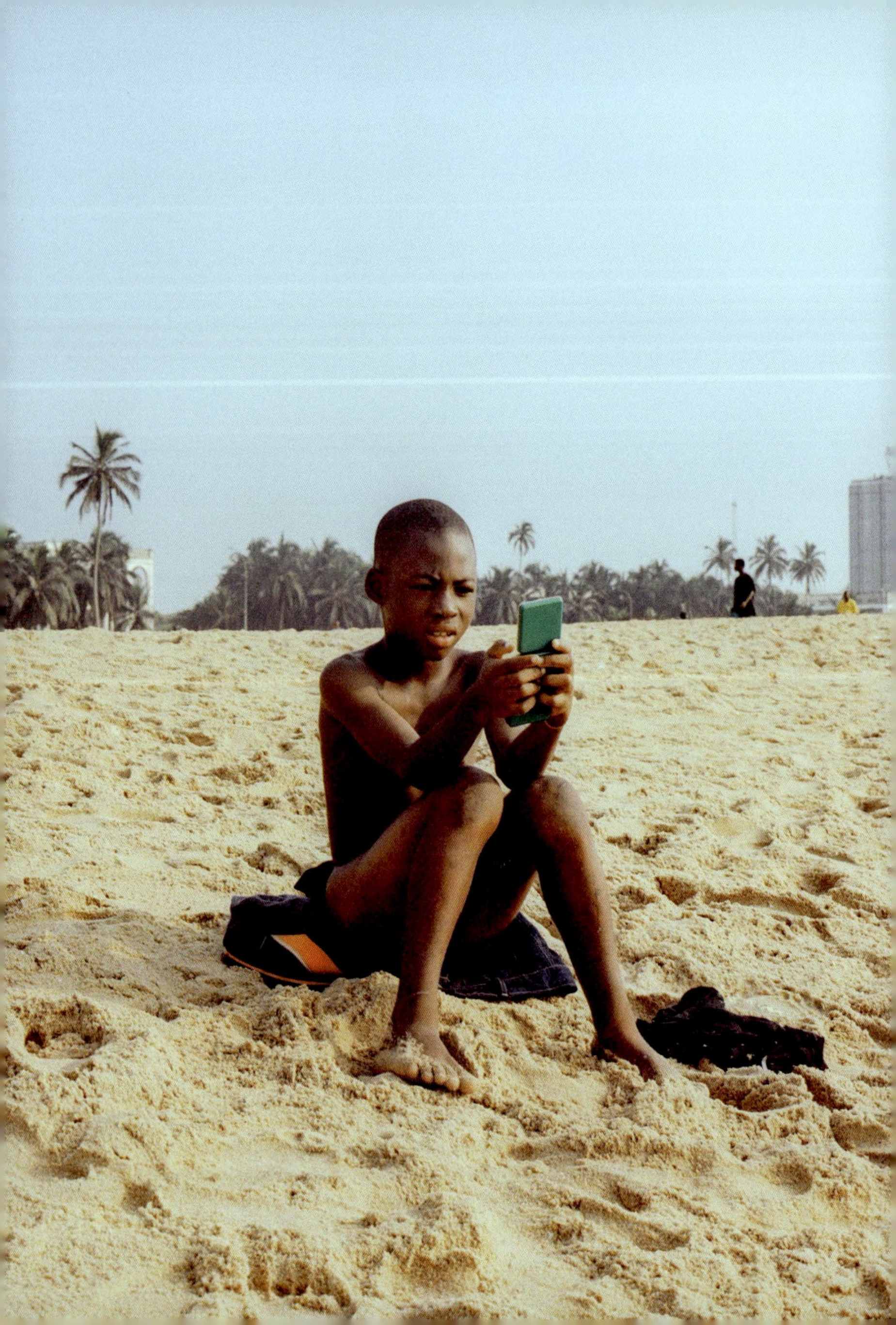

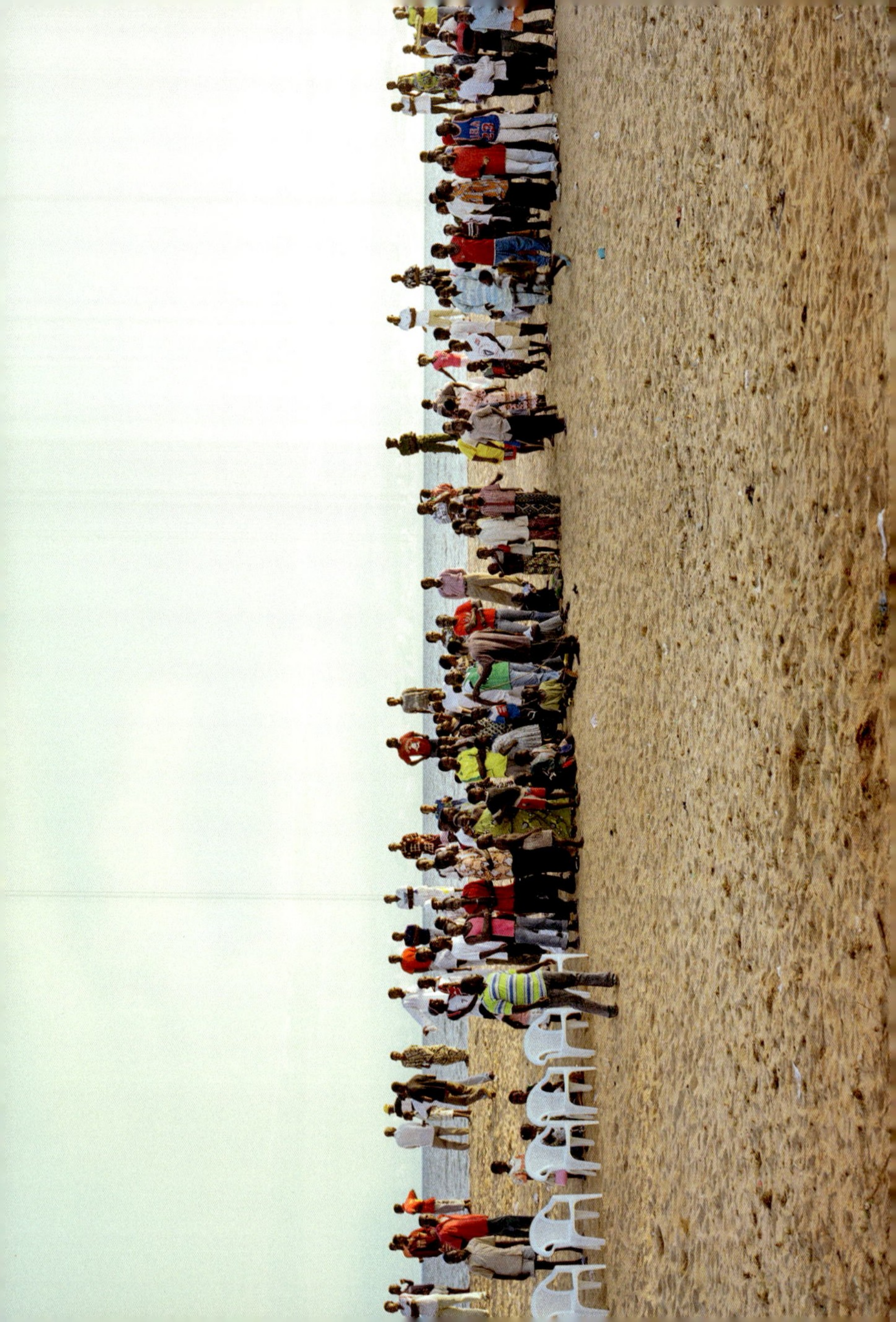

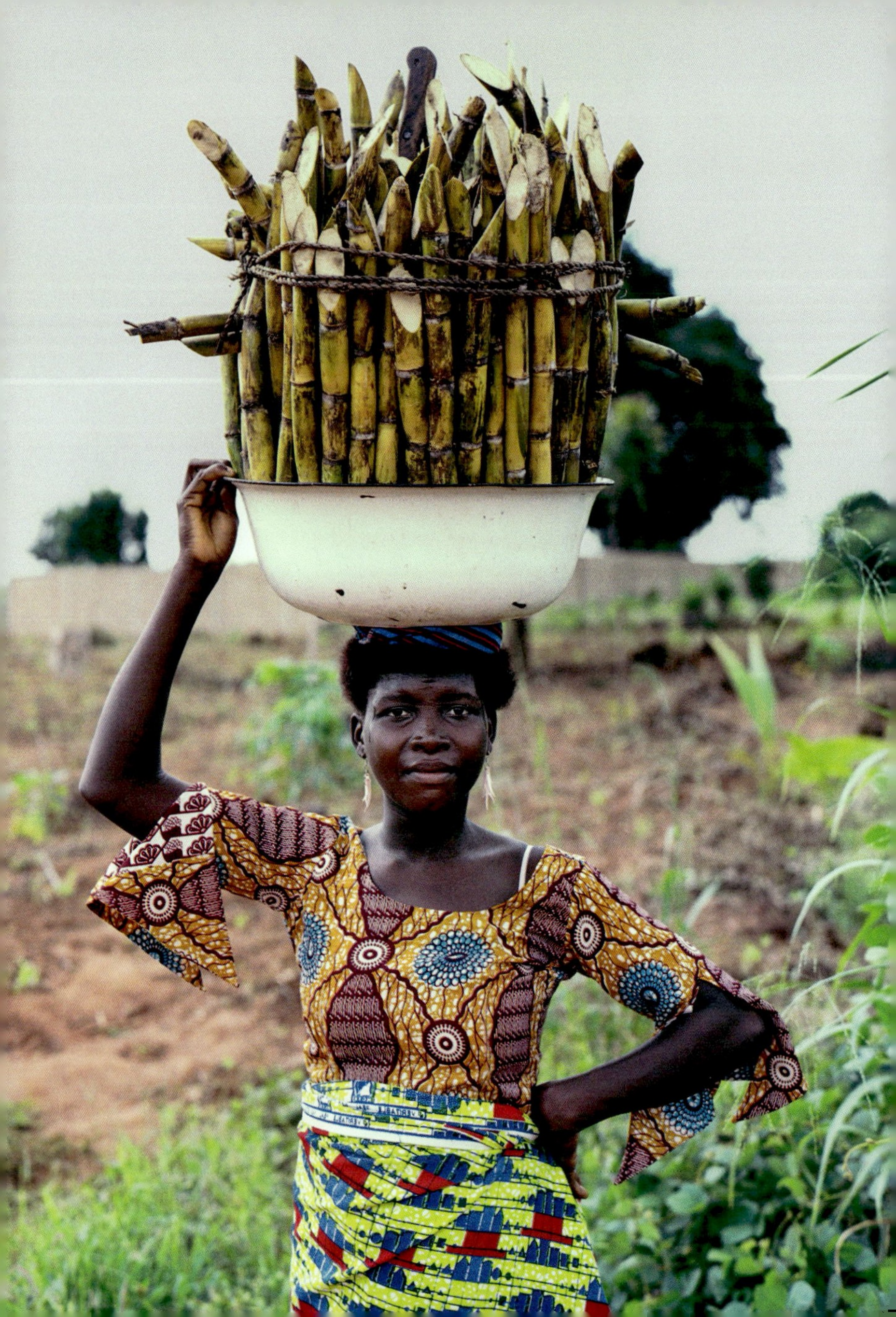

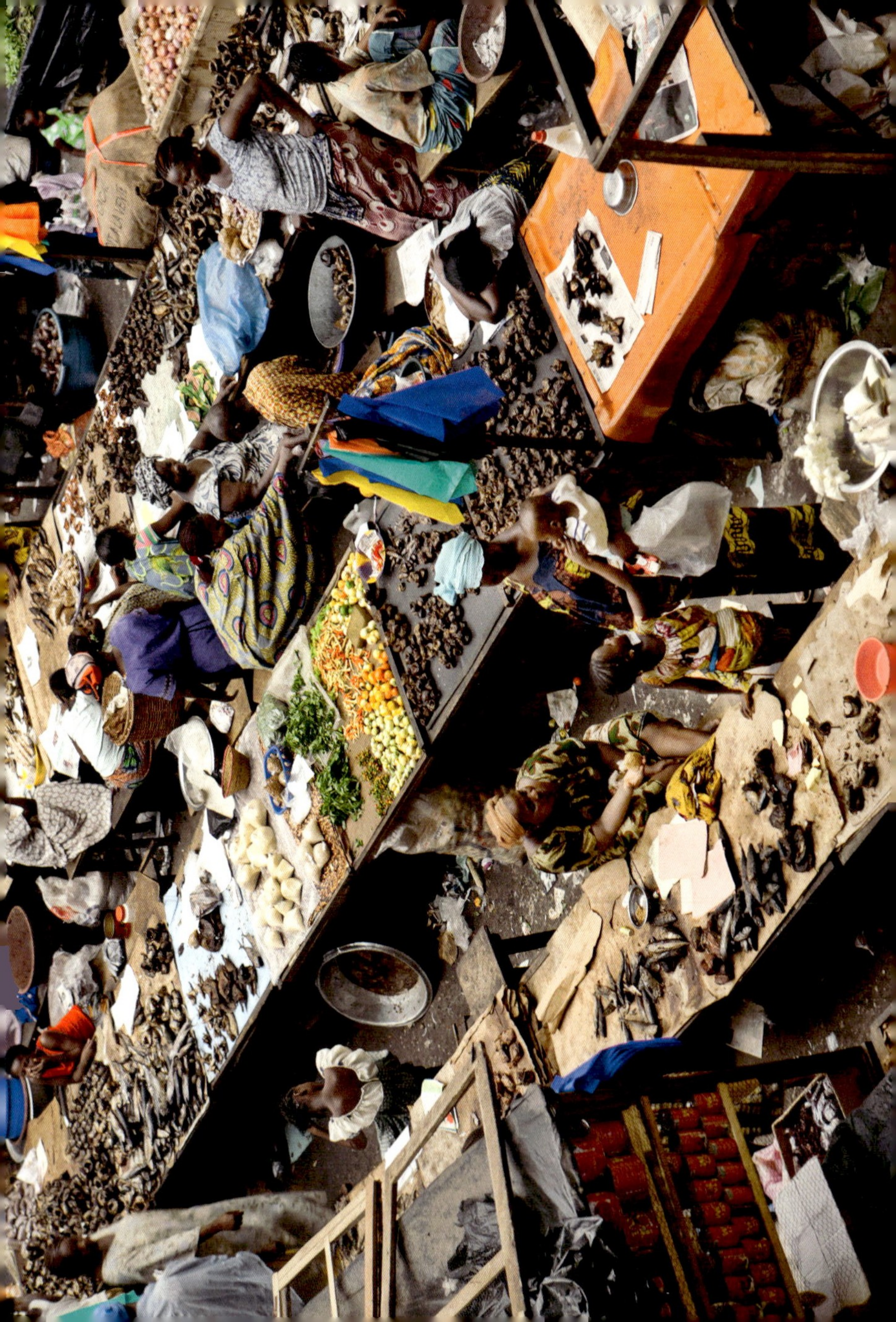

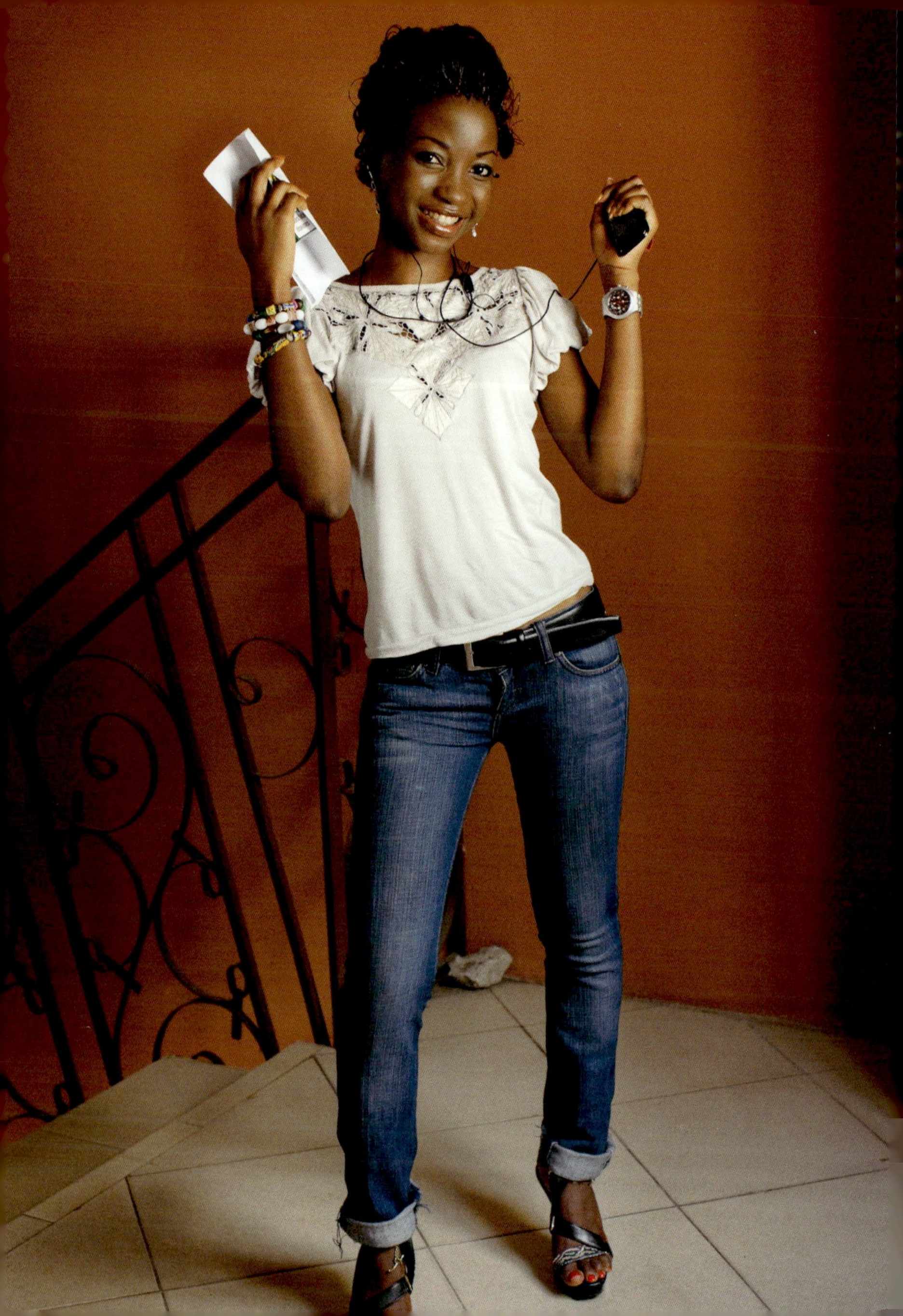

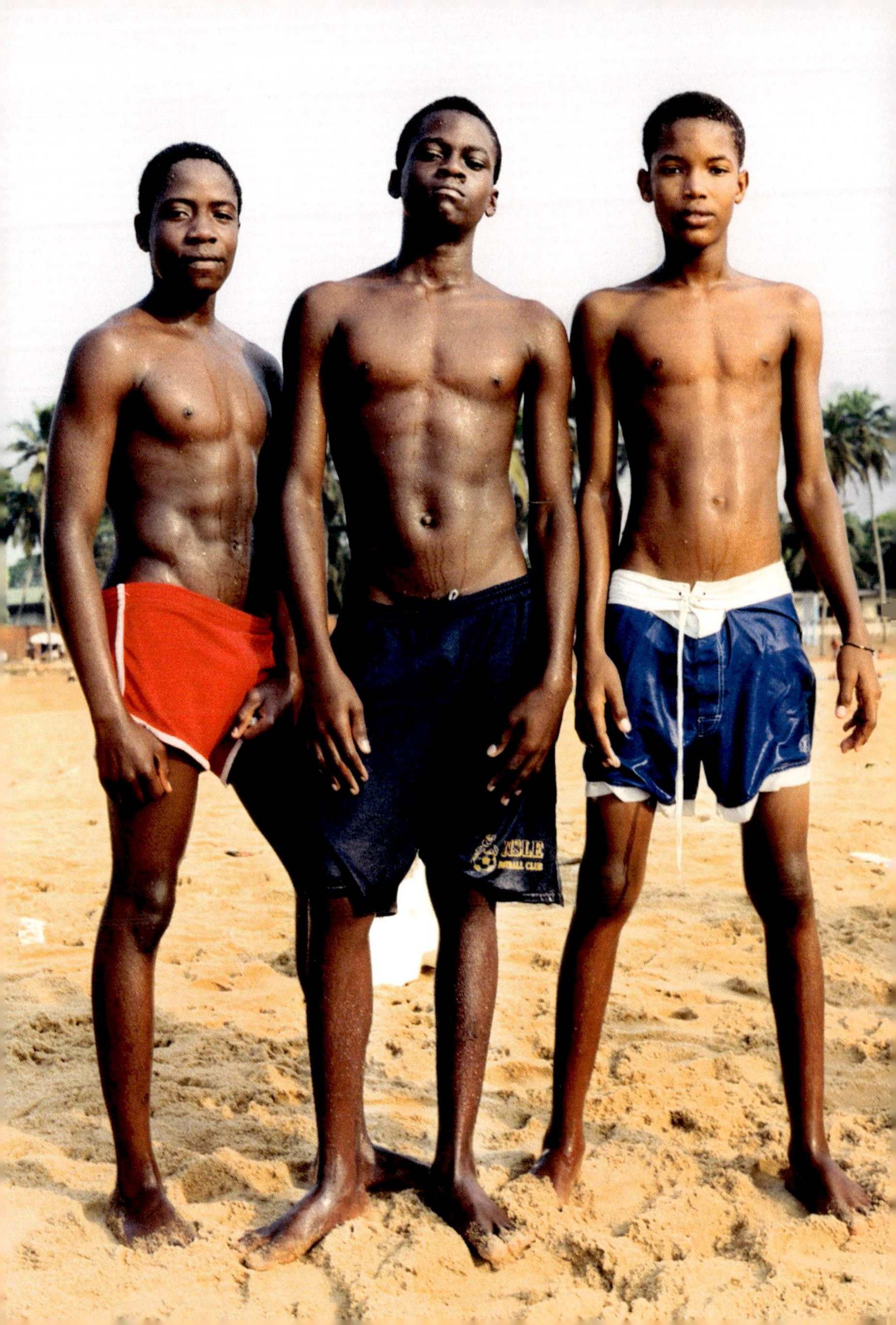

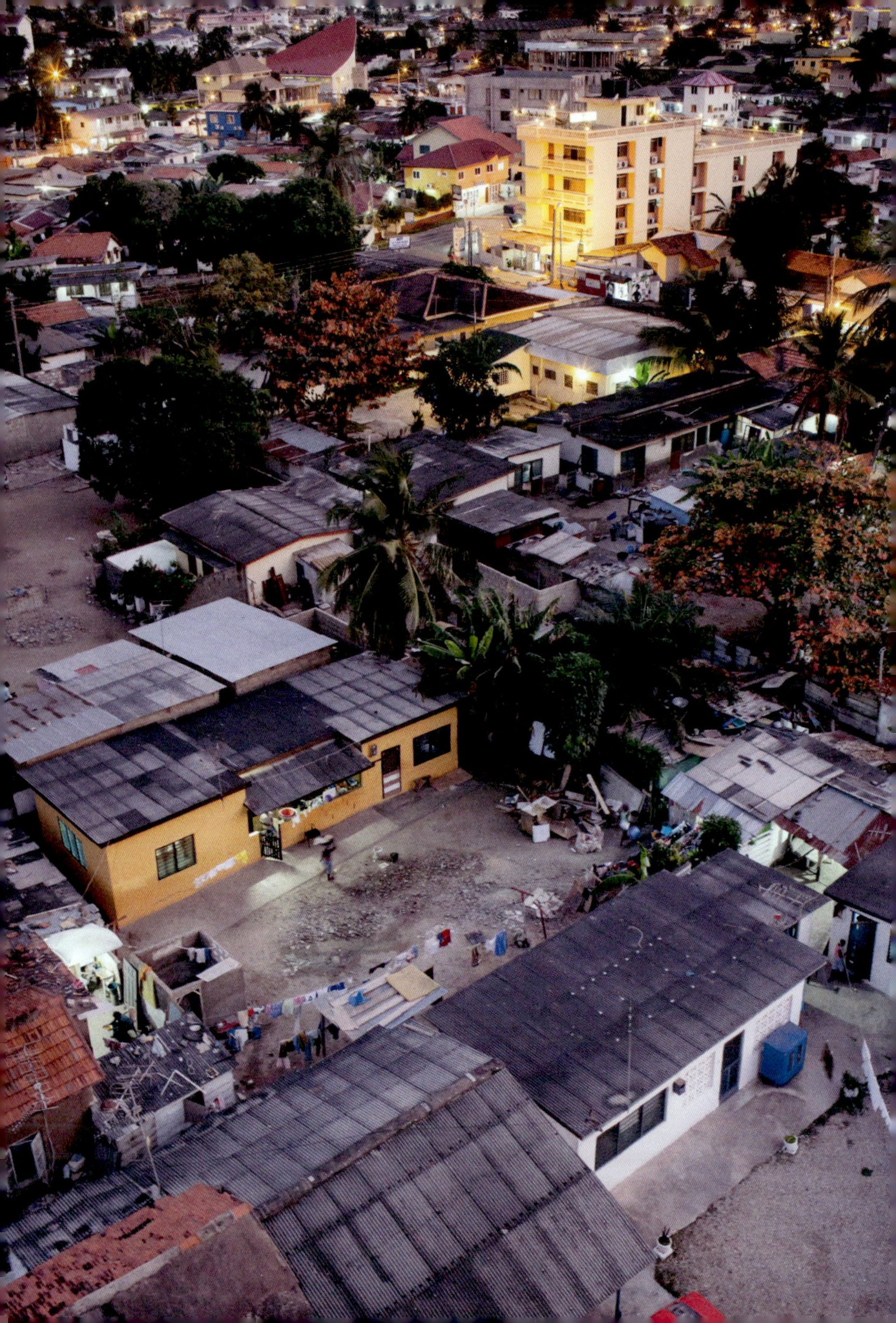

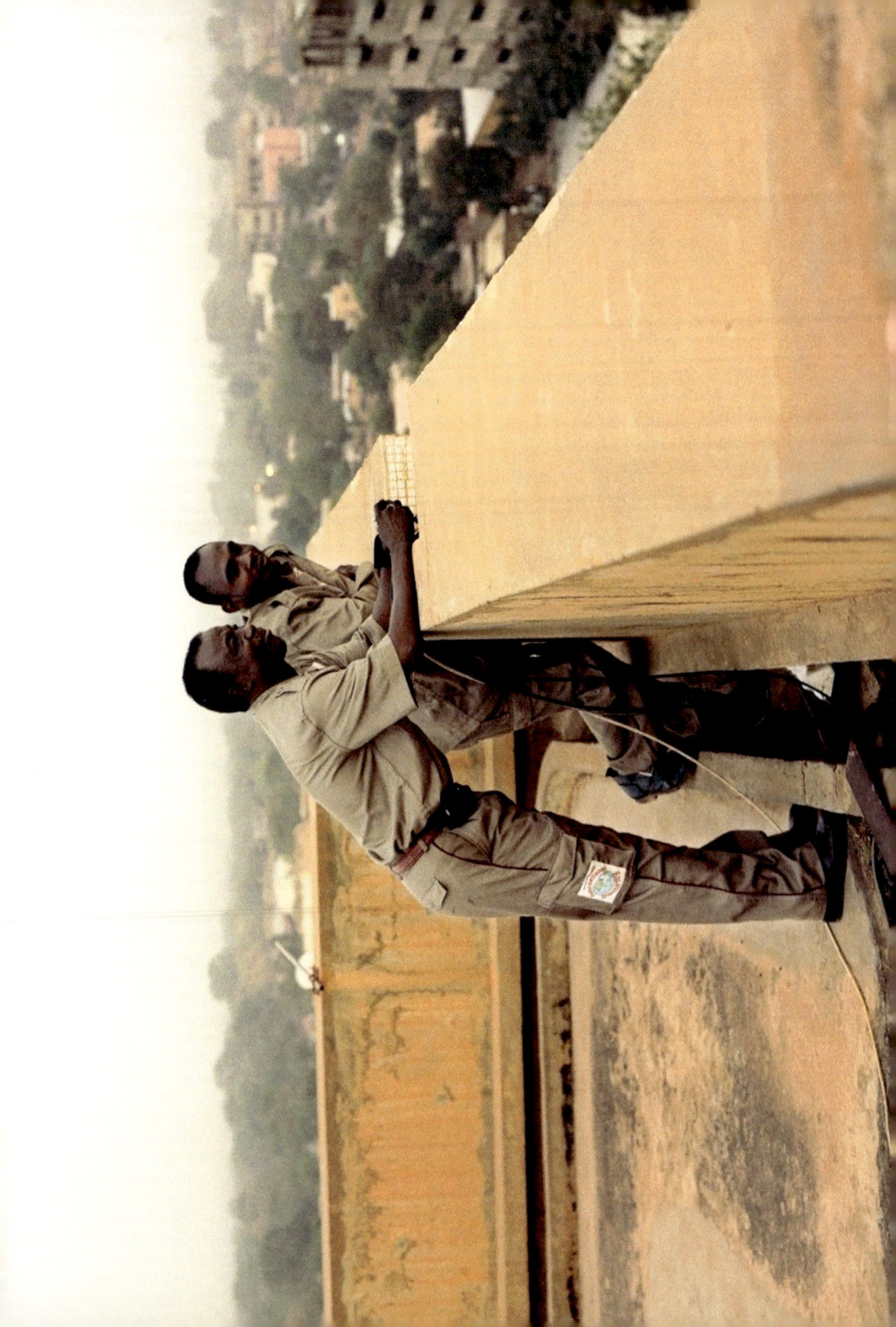

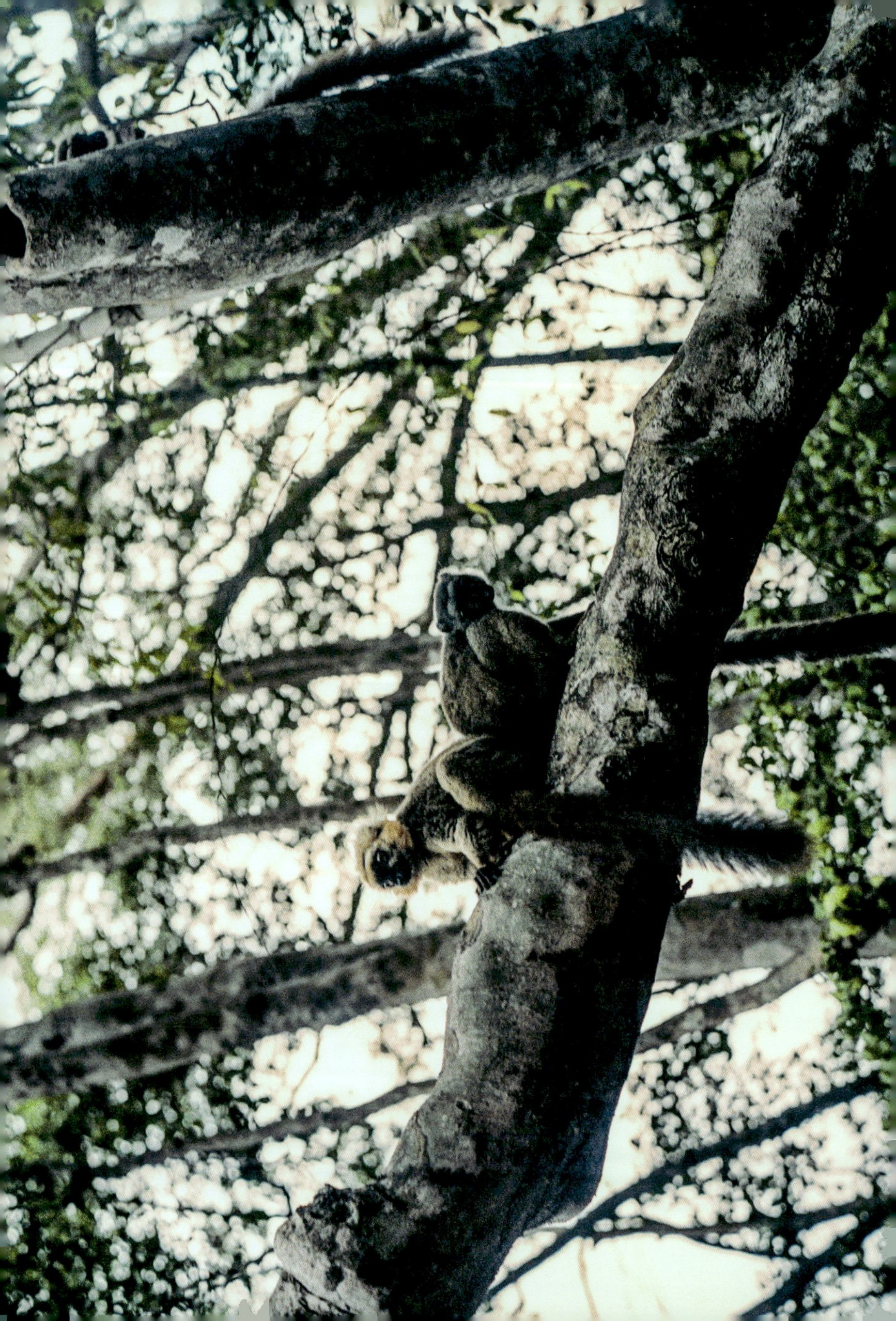

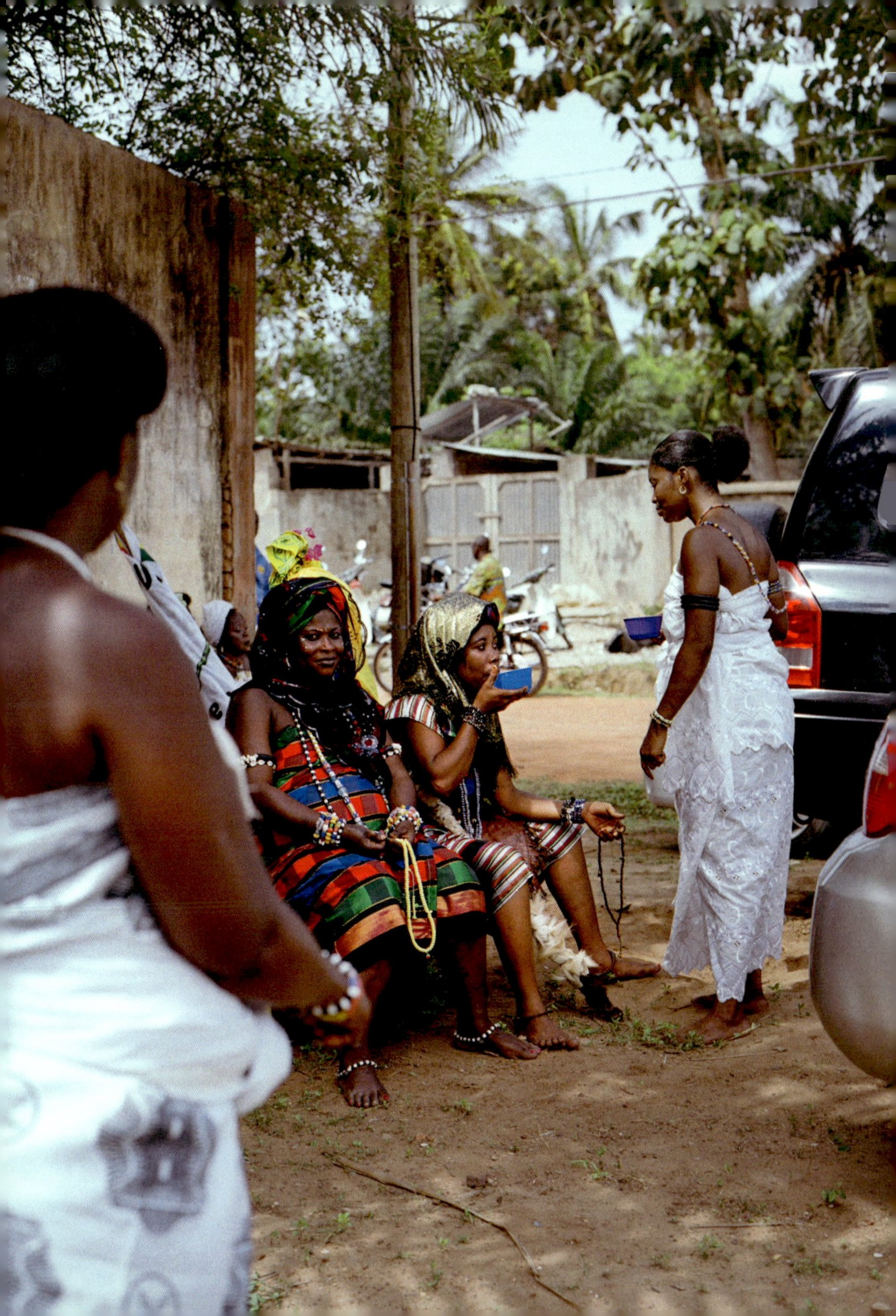

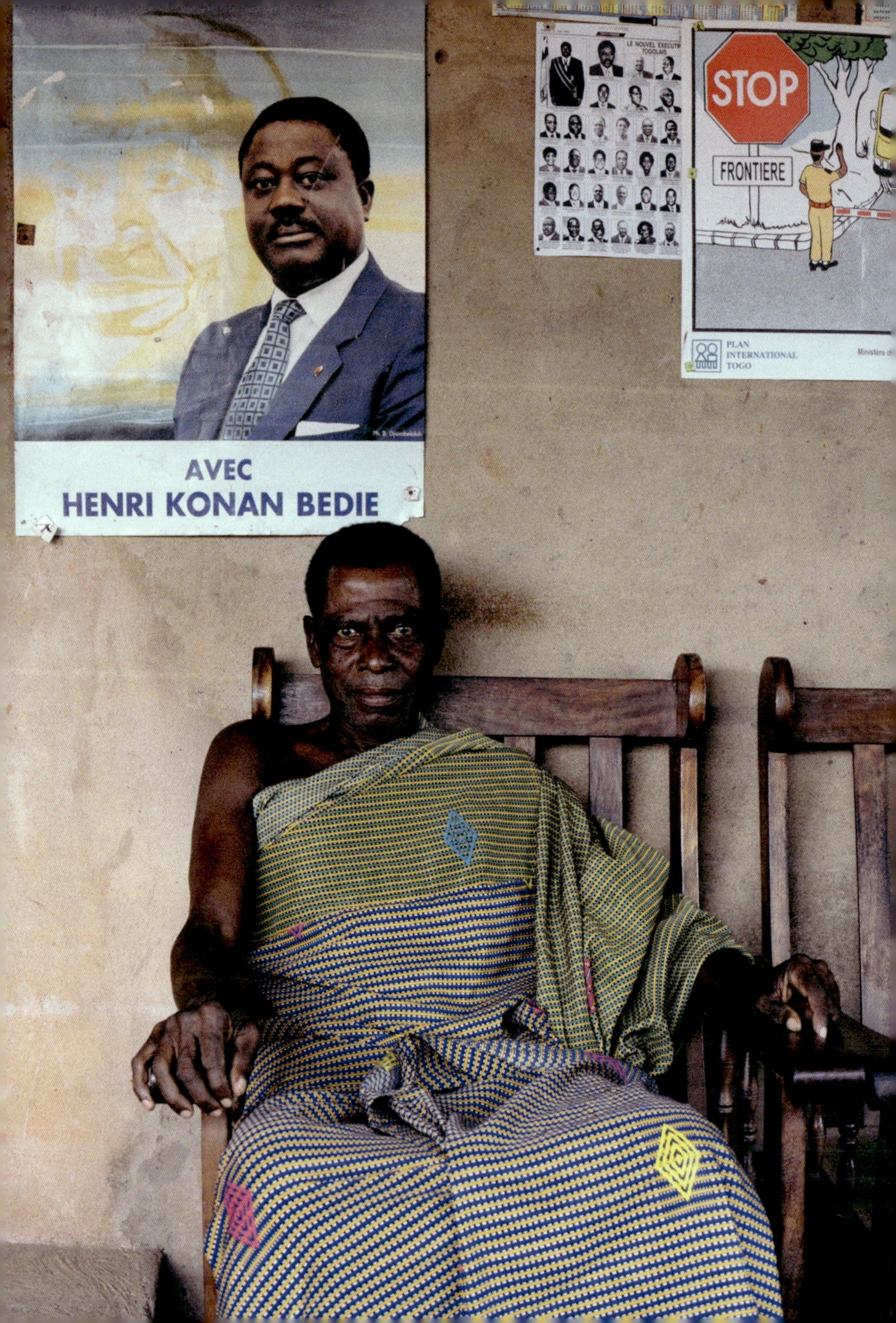

AVEC
HENRI KONAN BEDIE
STOP
FRONTIERE
PLAN
INTERNATIONAL
TOGO

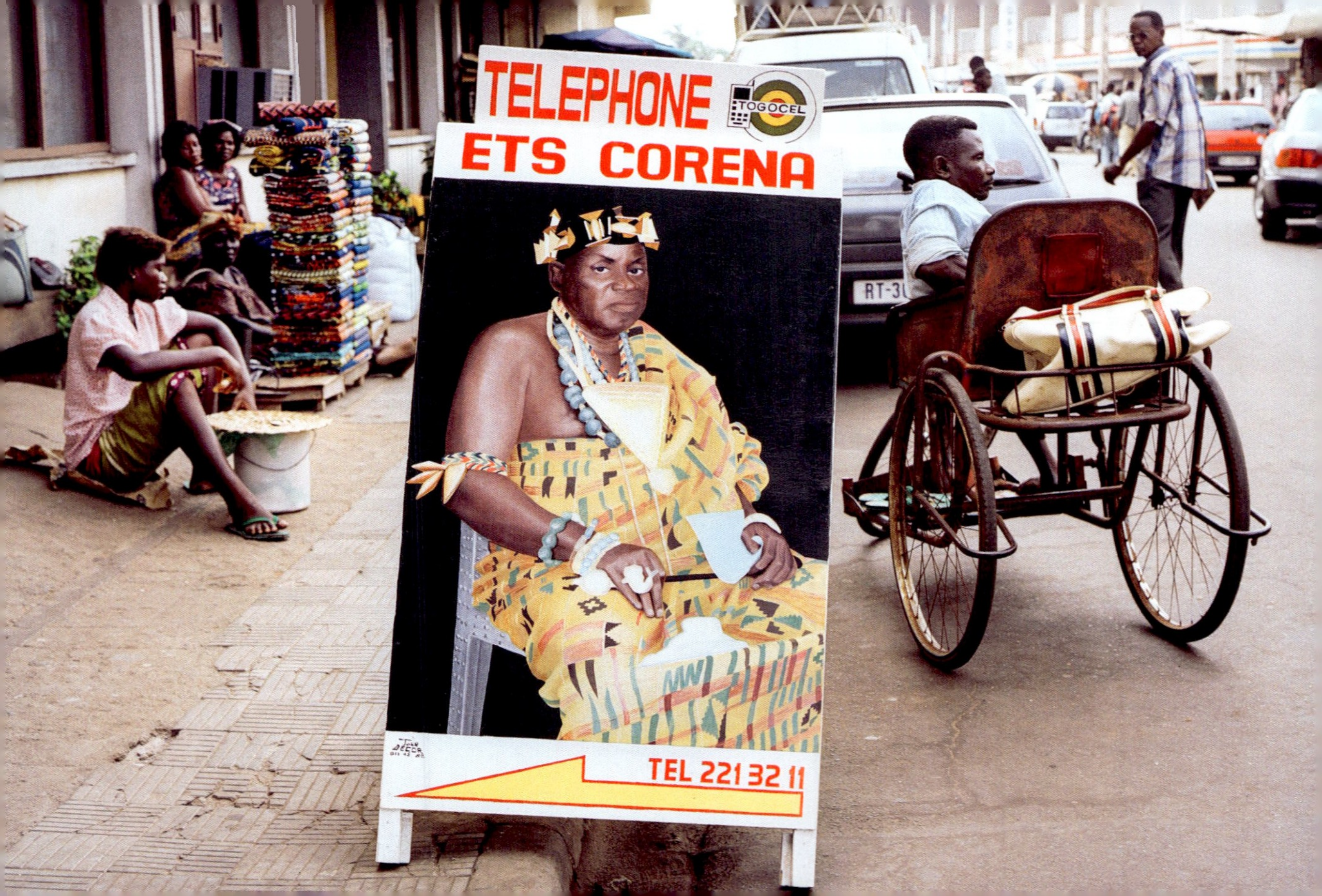
TELEPHONE
TOGOCEL
ETS CORENA
TEL 221 32 11

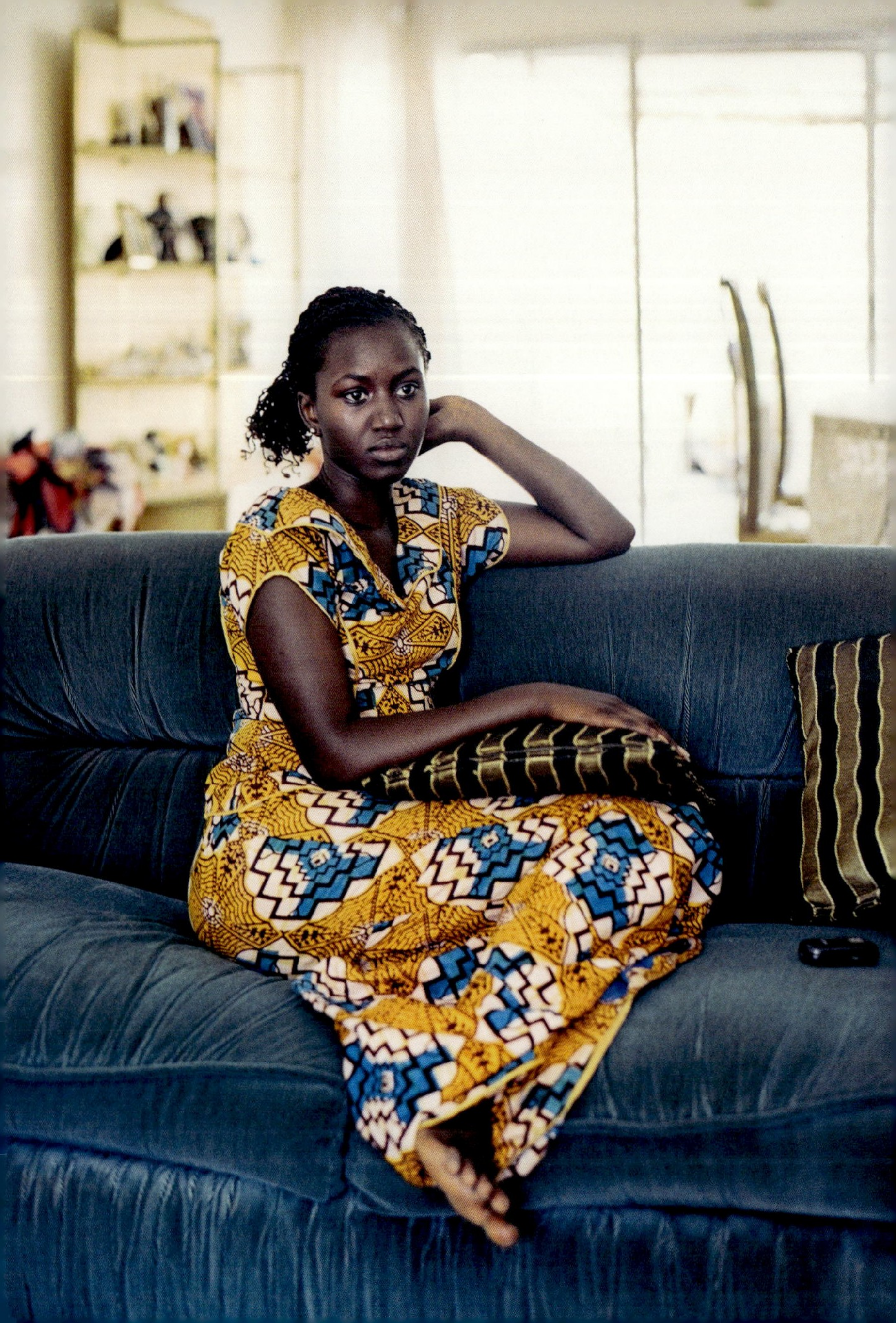

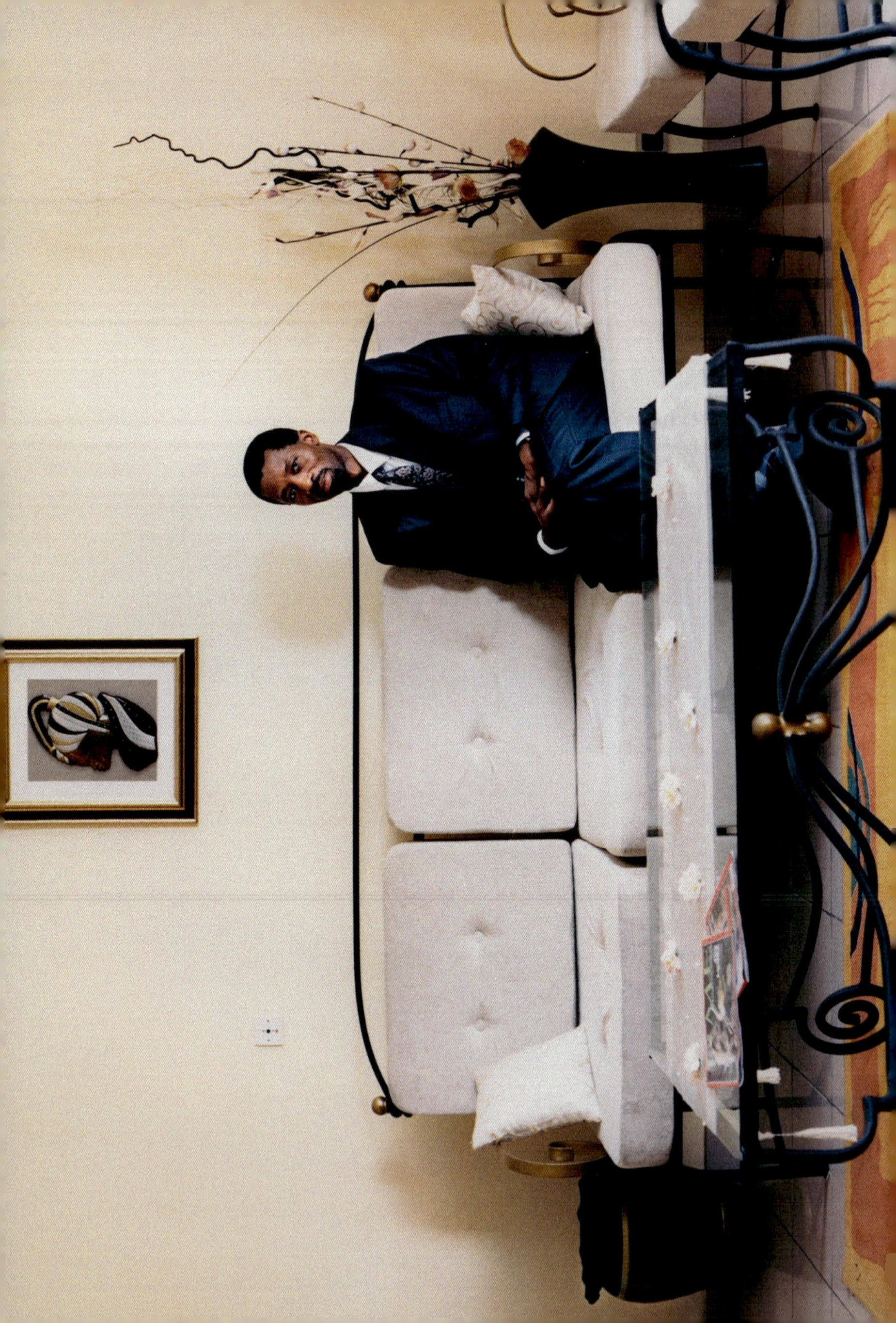

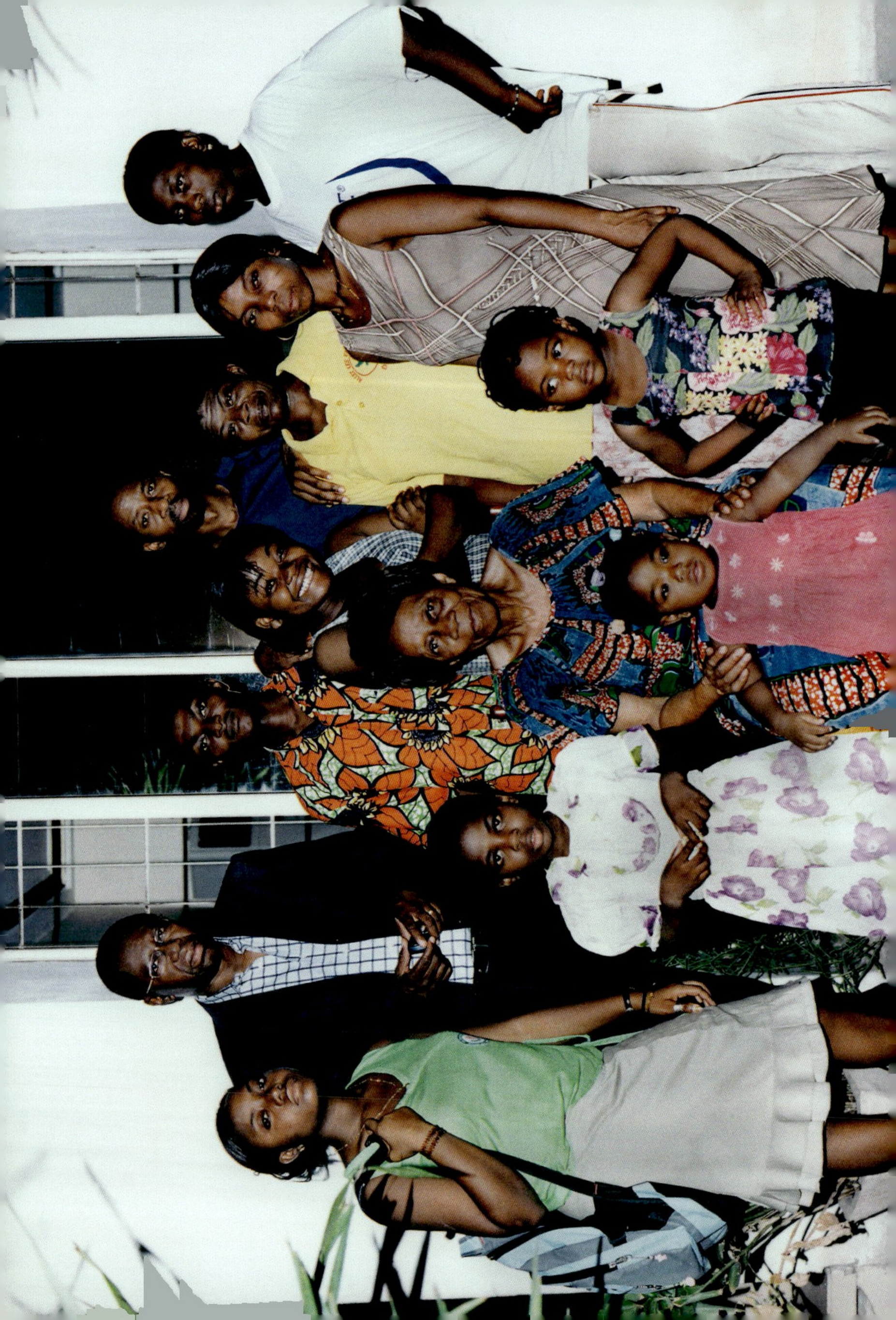

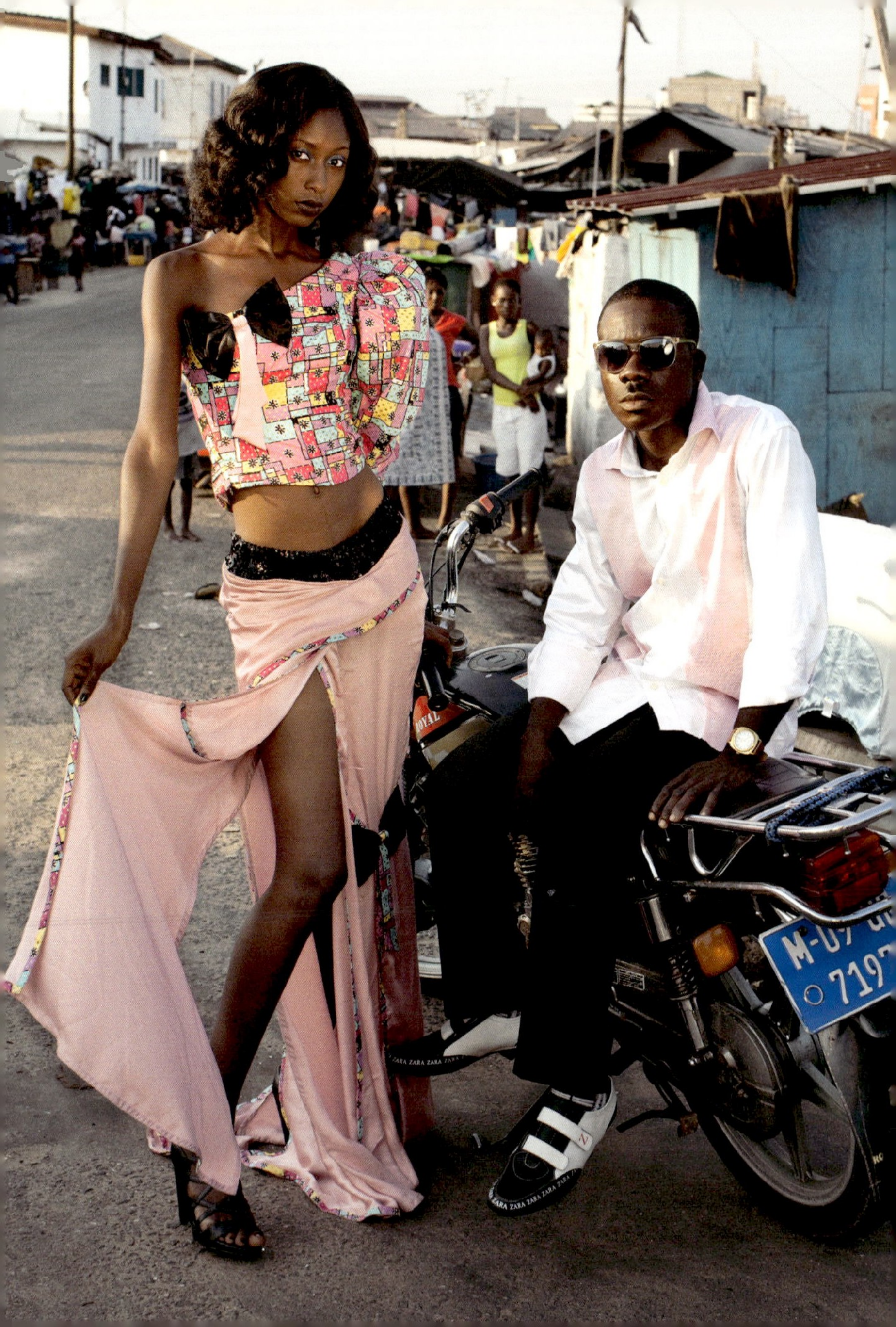
ROYAL
ZARA ZARA ZARA ZARA

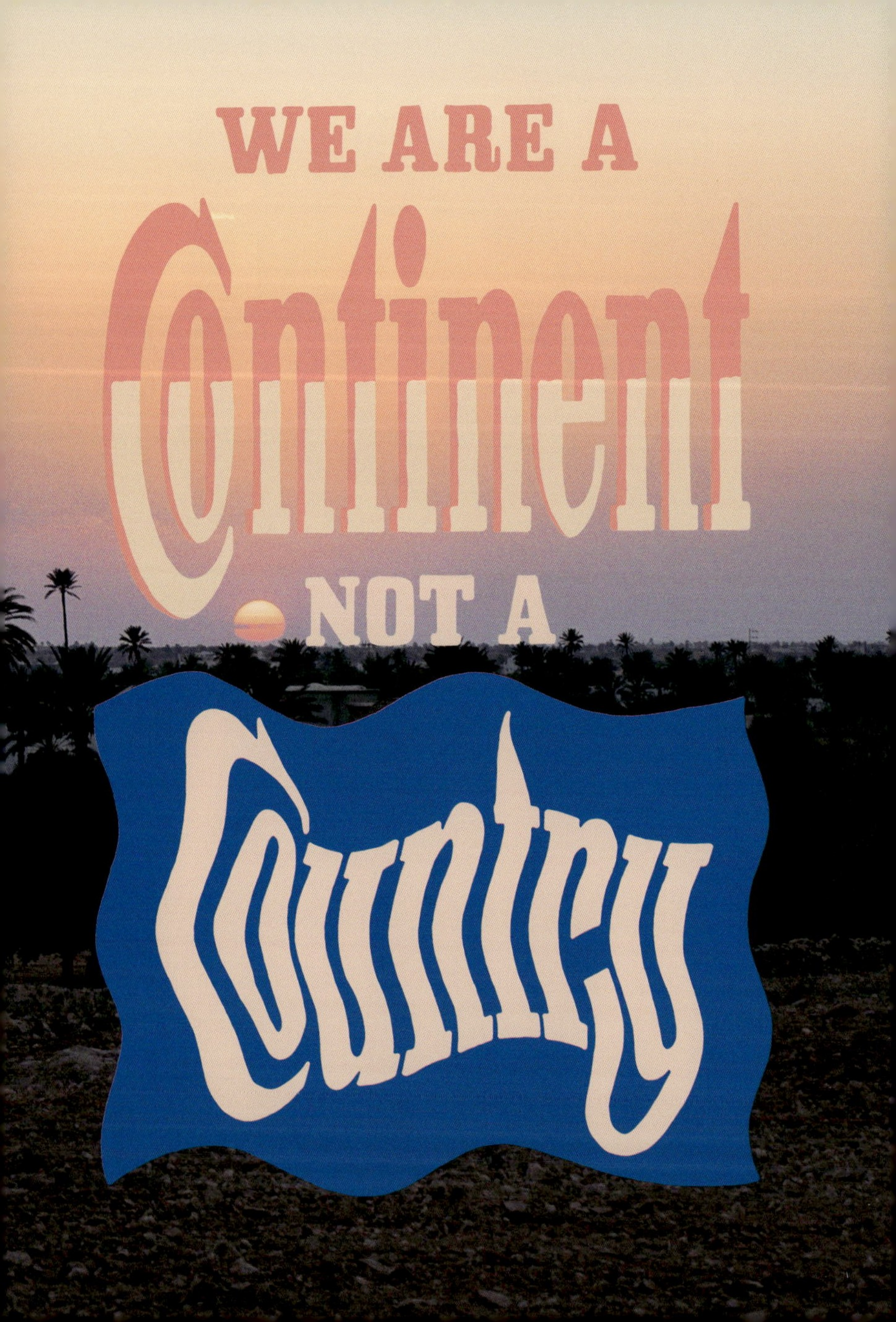
WE ARE A
Continent
NOT A
Country

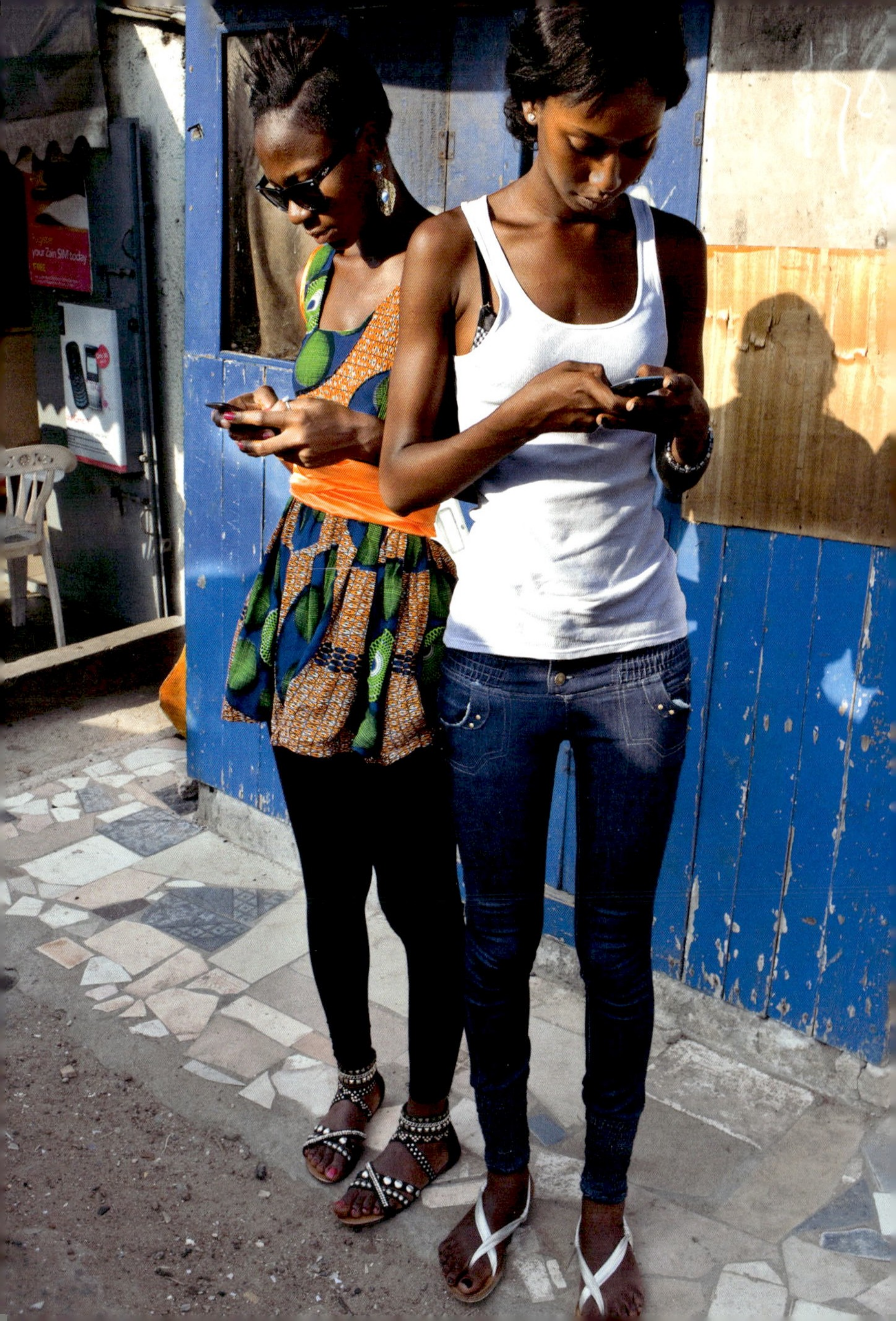

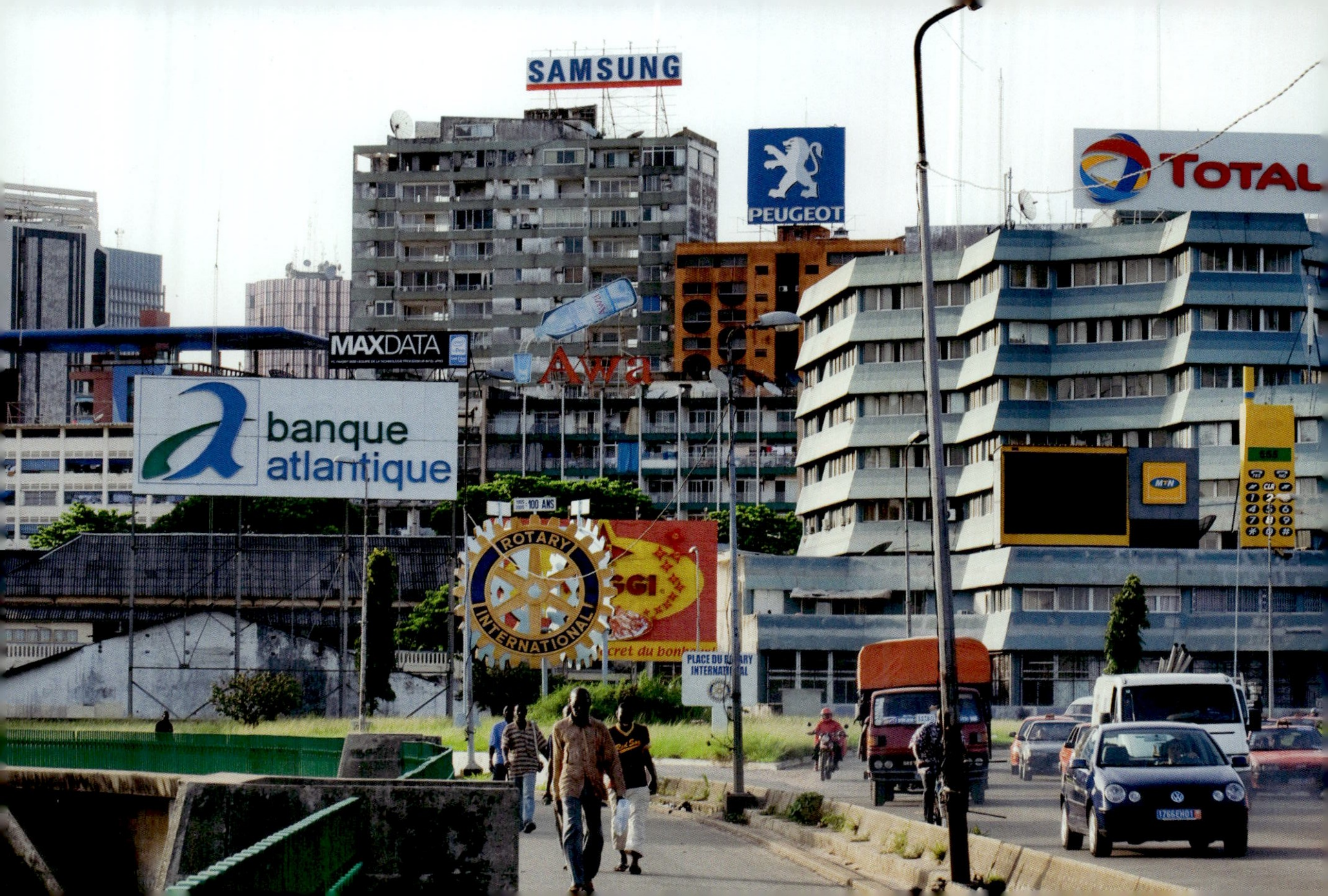
SAMSUNG
PEUGEOT
TOTAL
MAXDATA
Awa
banque
atlantique
100 ANS
ROTARY
INTERNATIONAL
cret du bon
PLACE DU R
INTERNAT

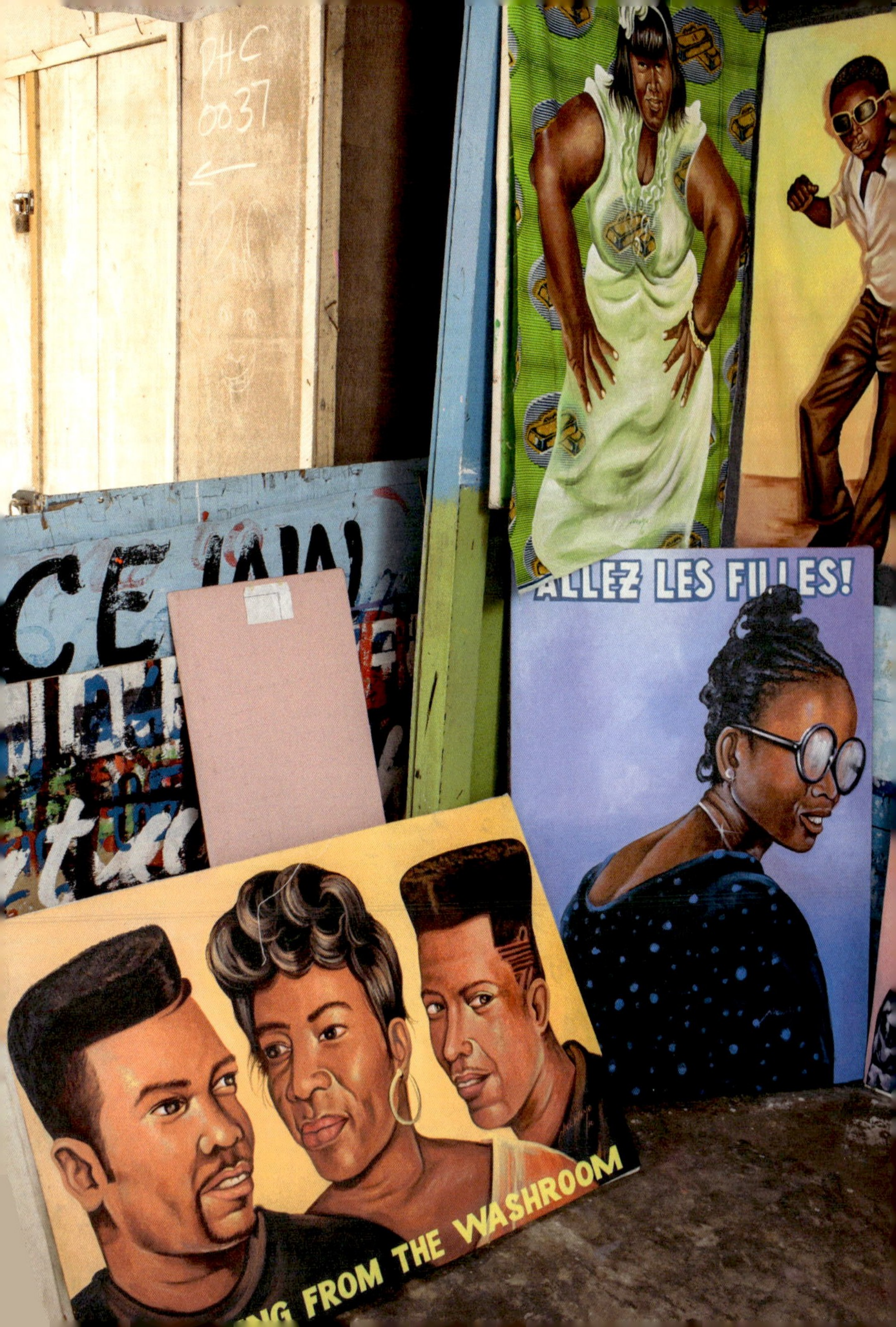
PHC
0037
ALLEZ LES FILLES!
NG FROM THE WASHROOM

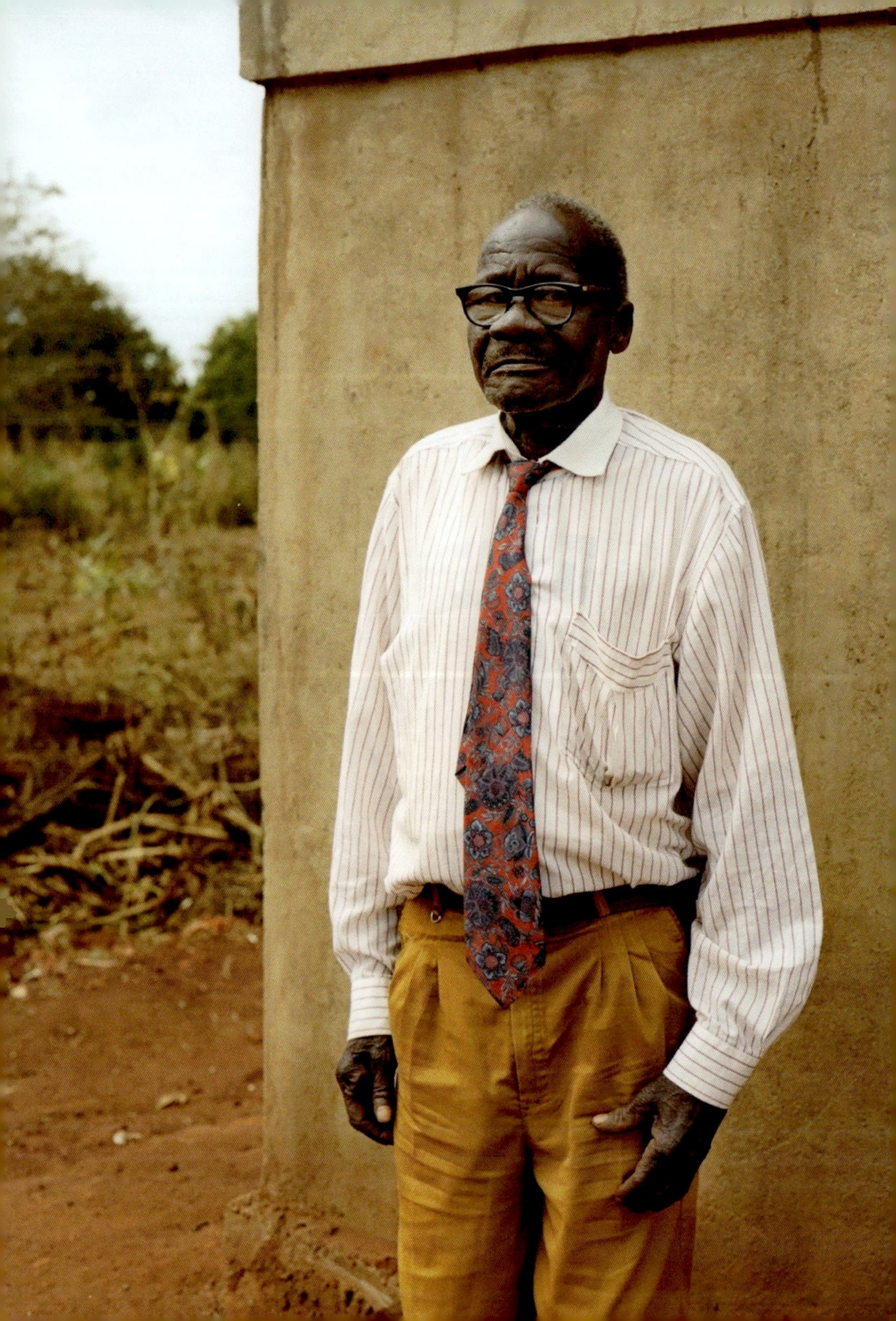

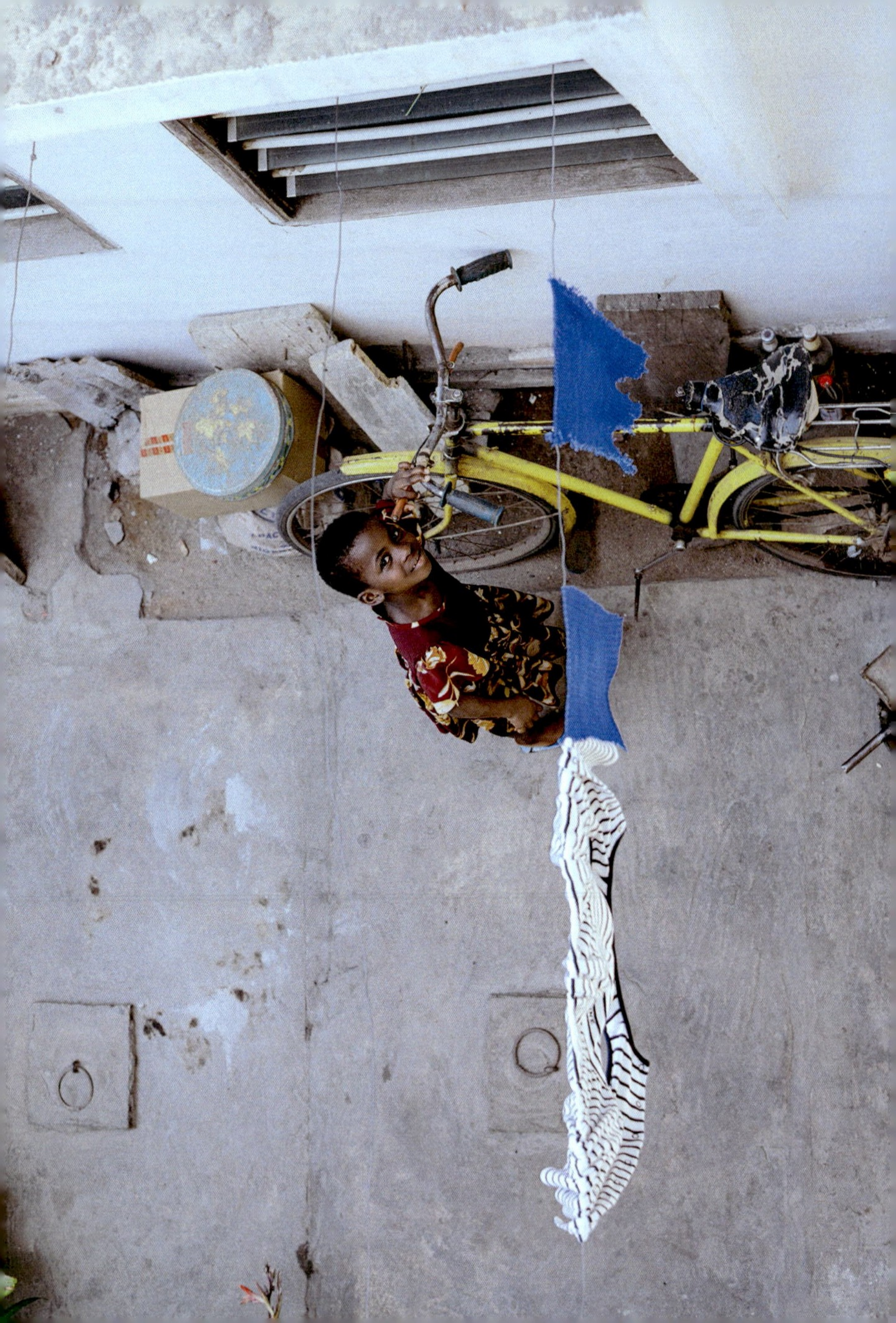

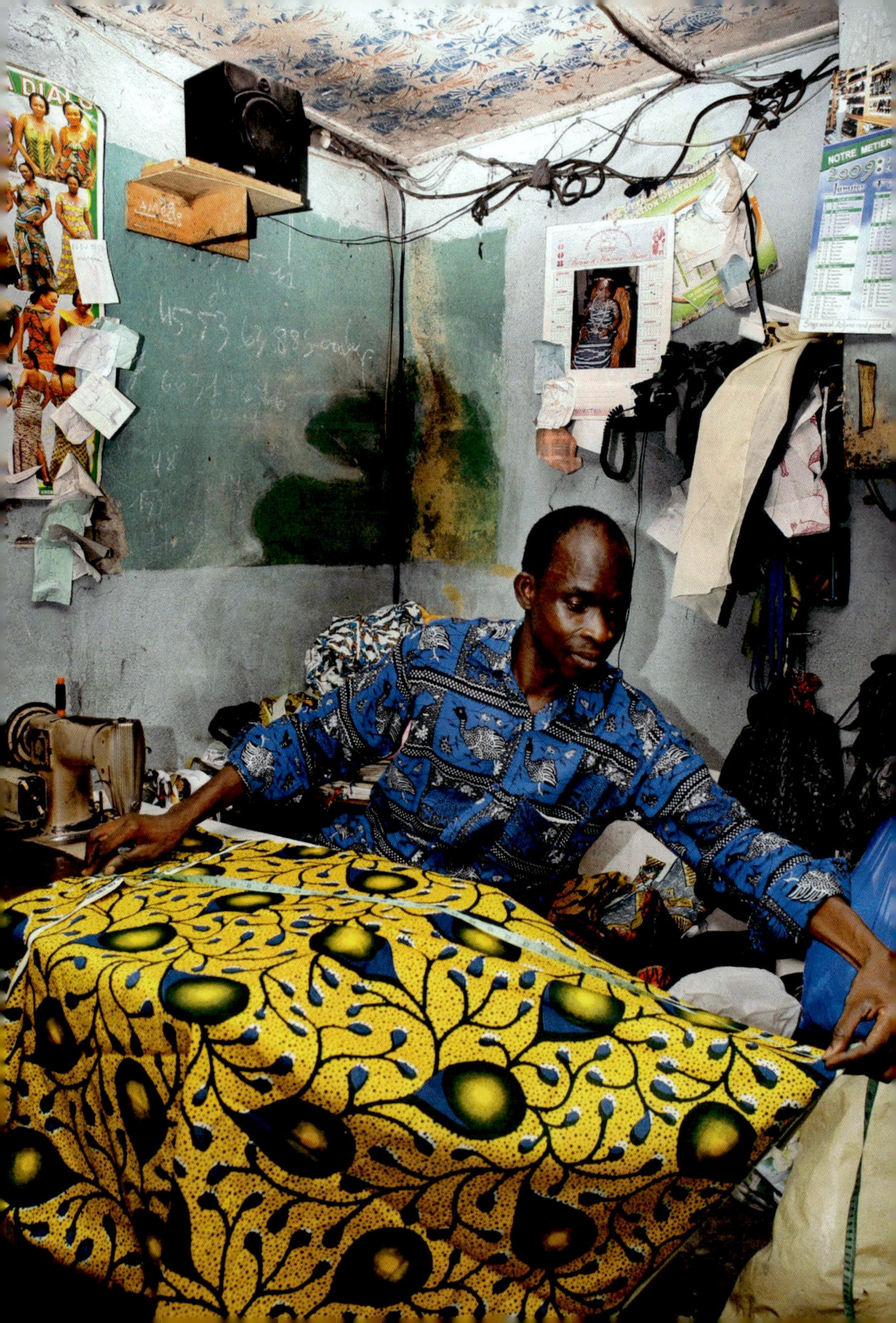
NOTRE METIER
2009

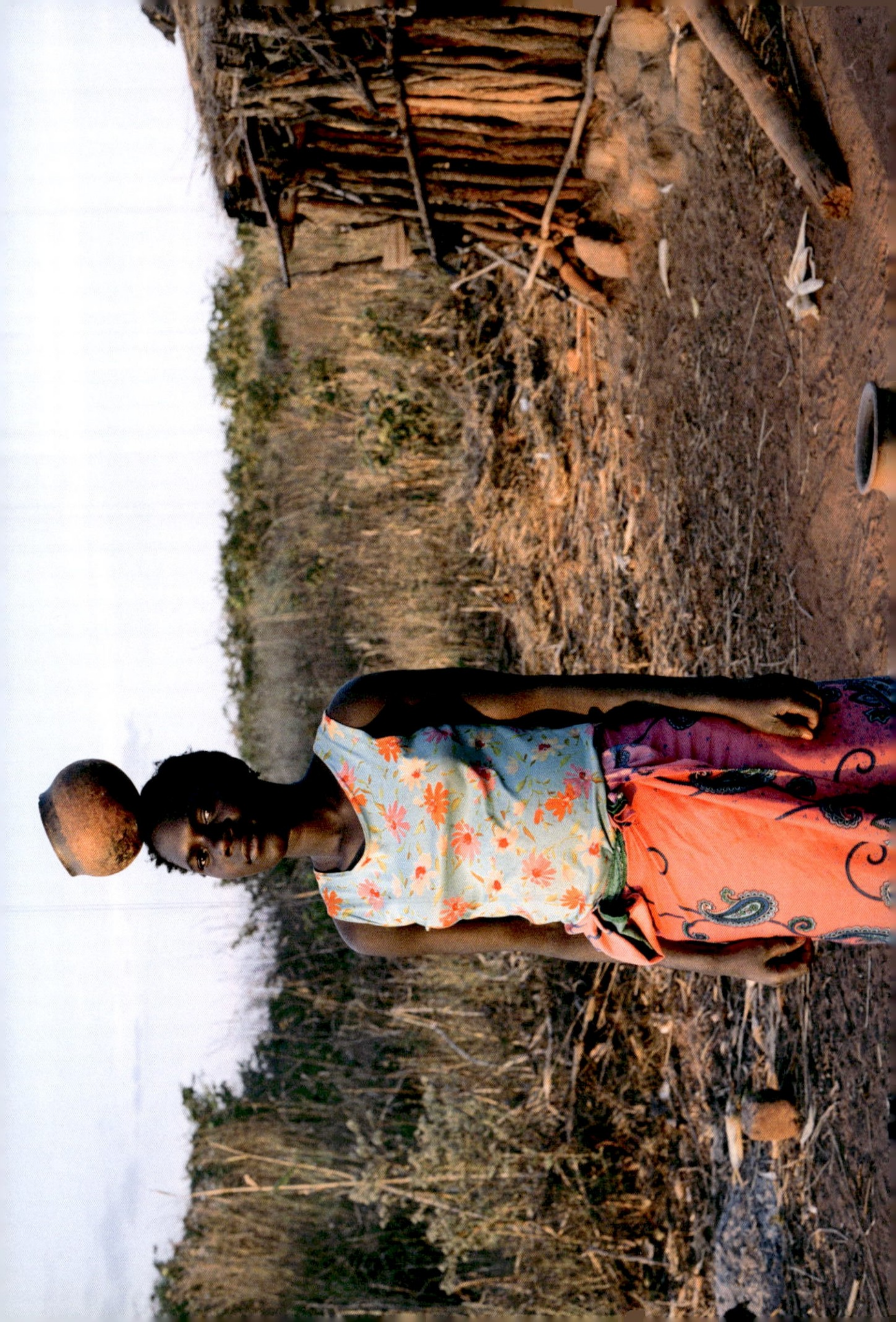

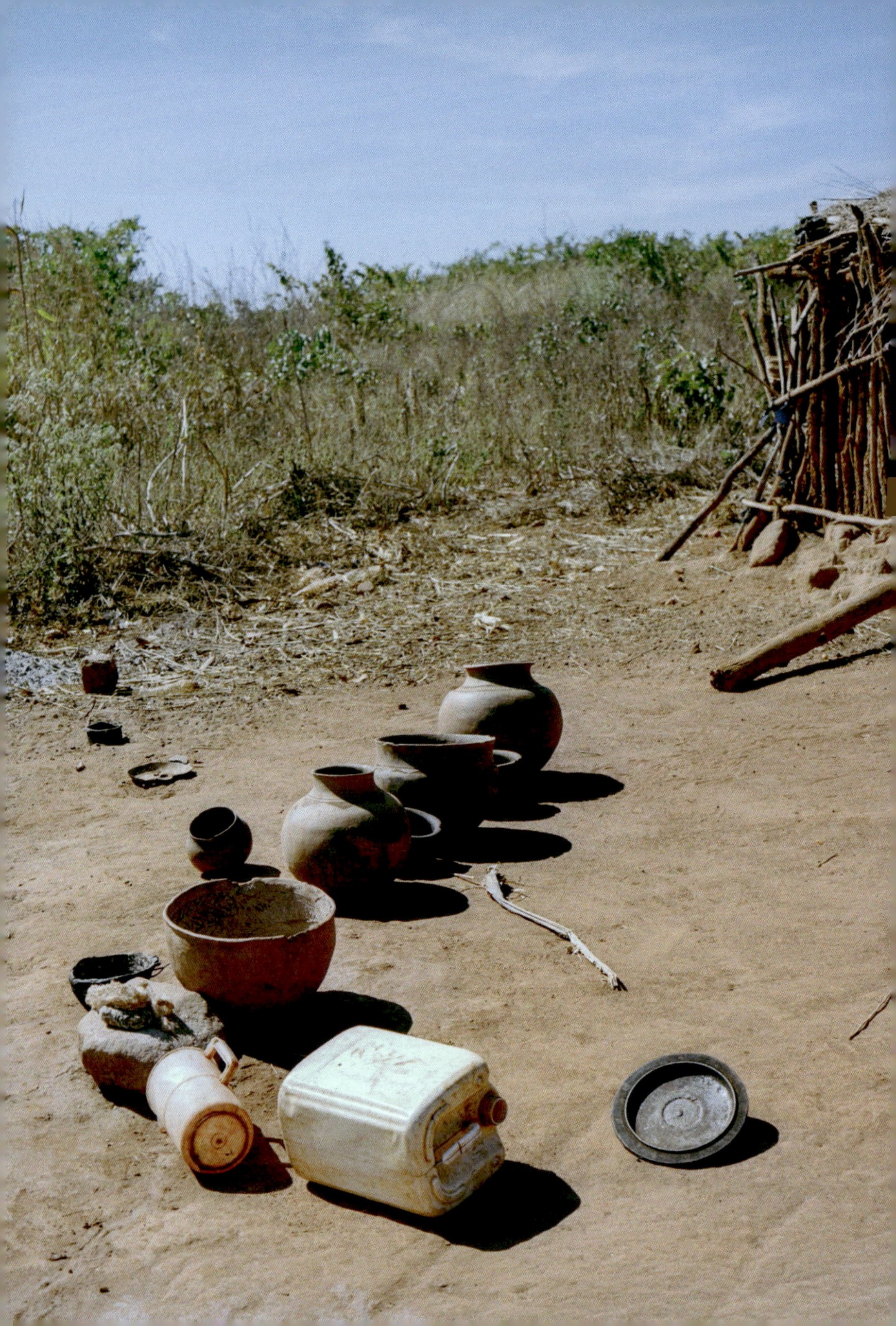

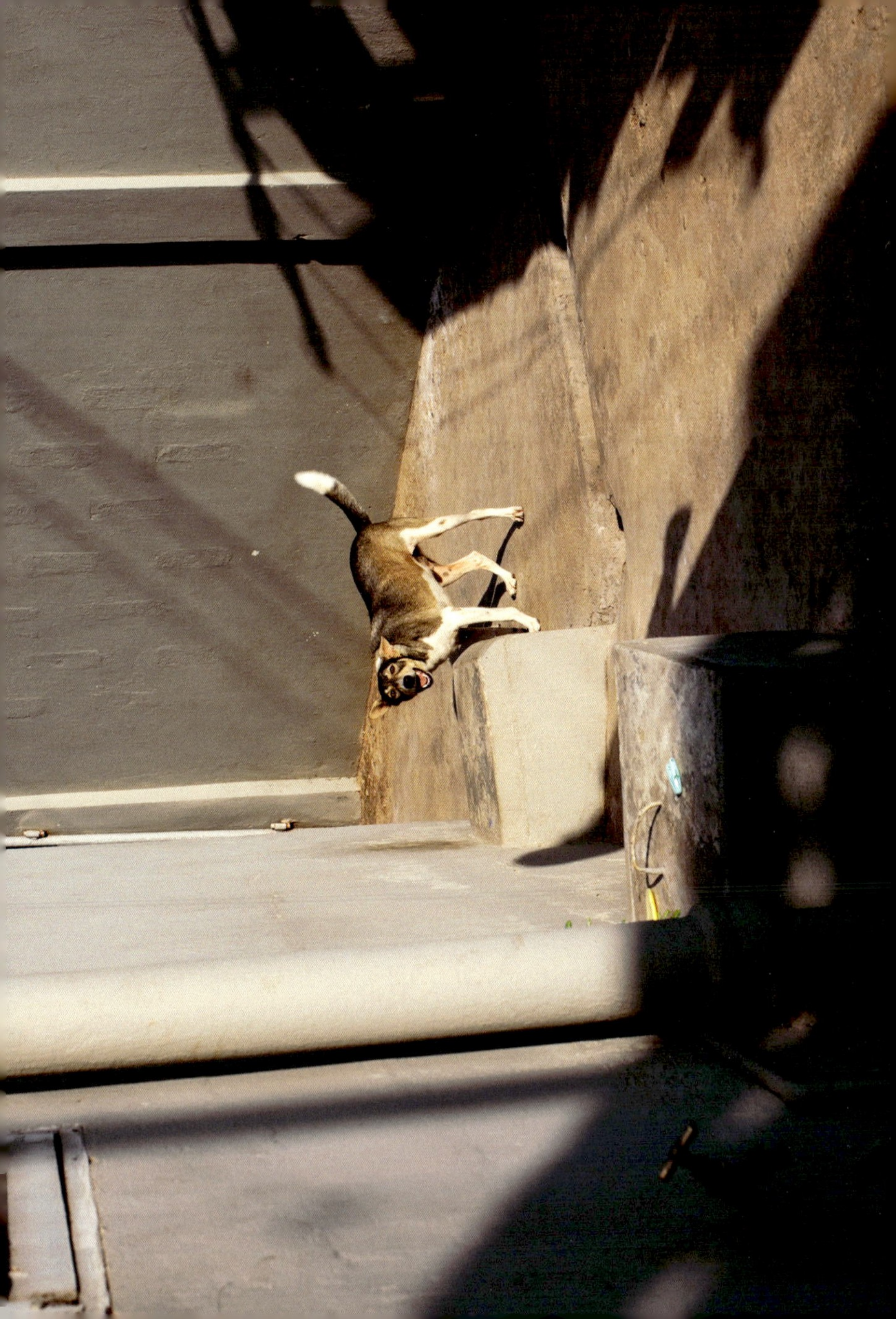

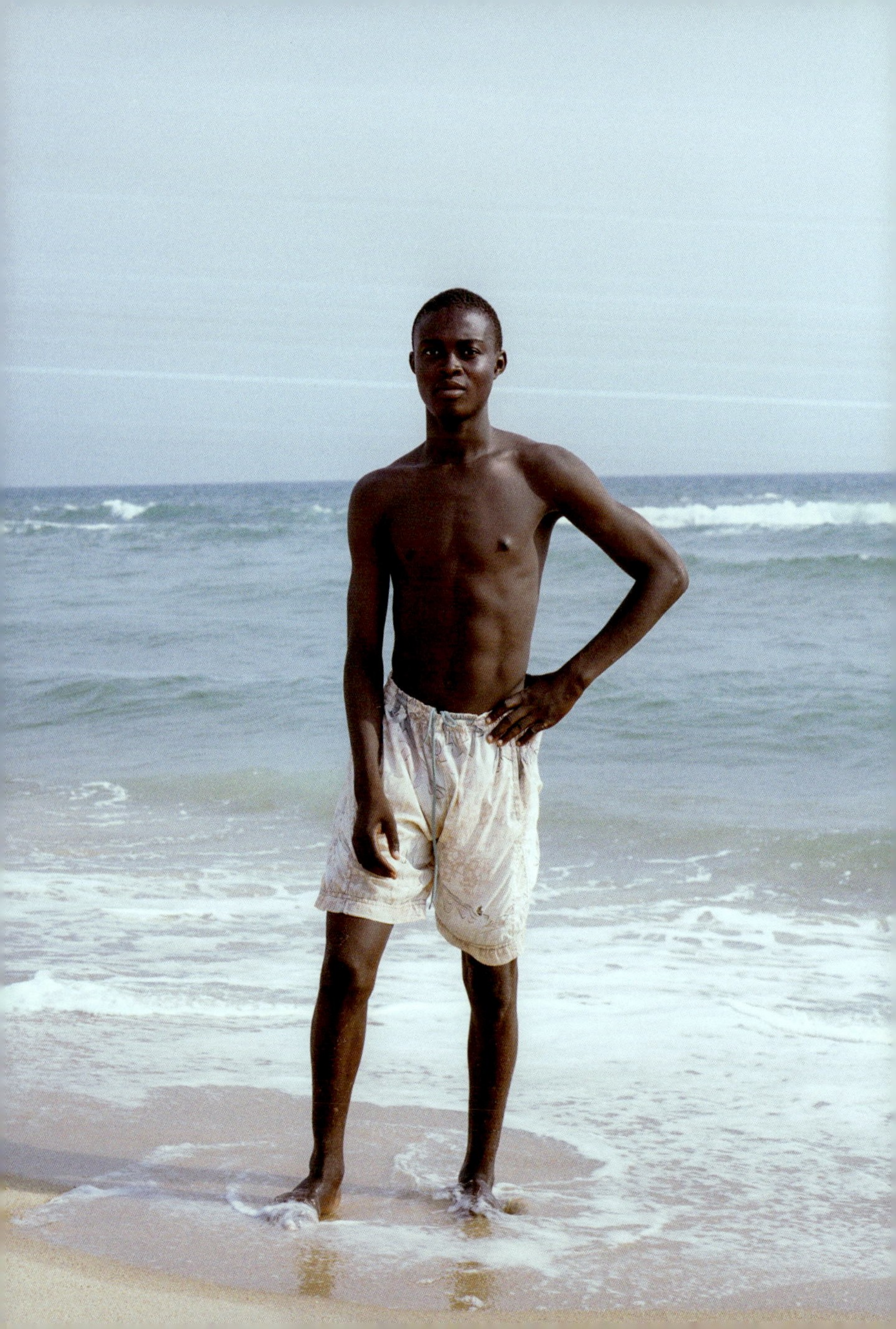

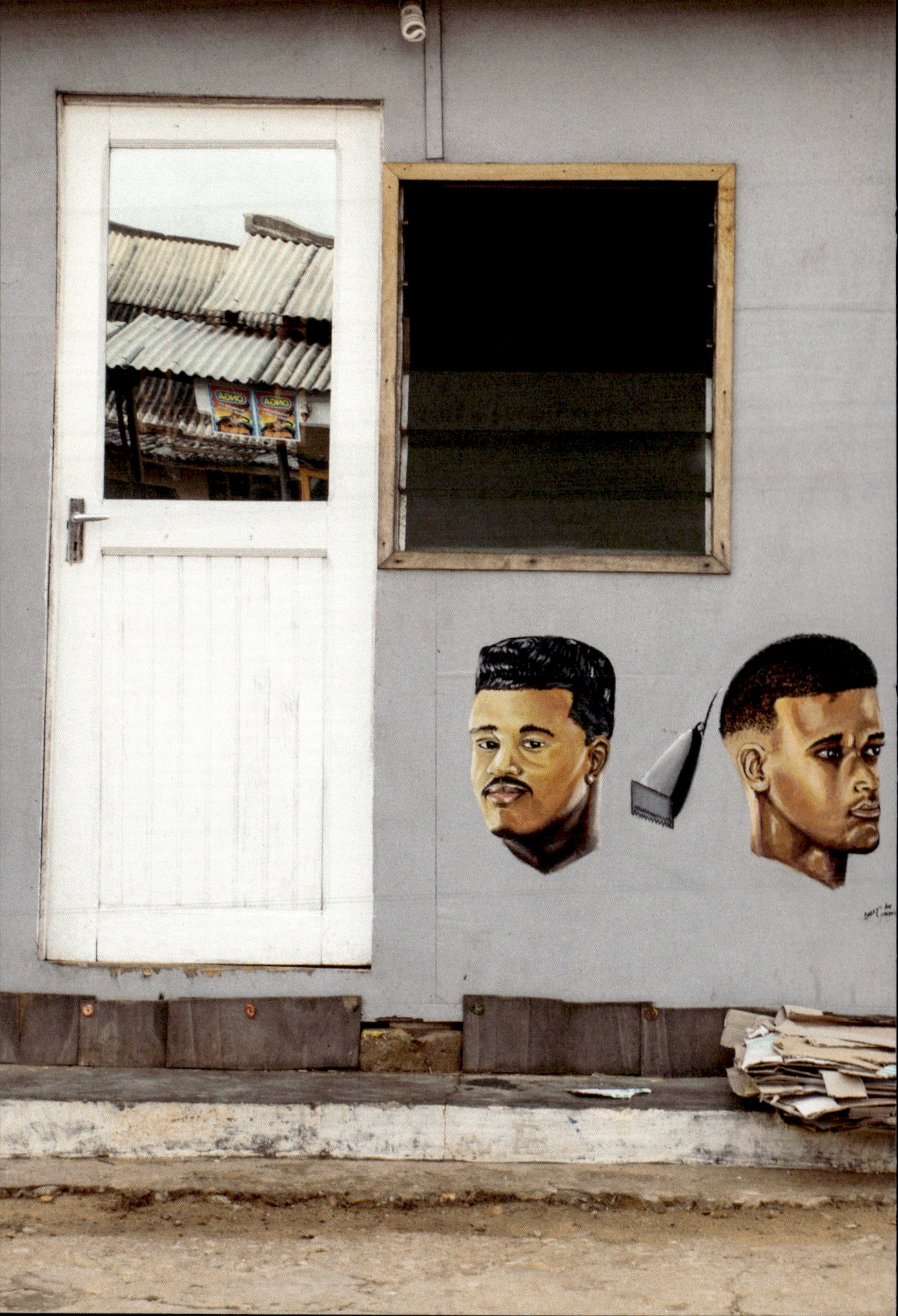

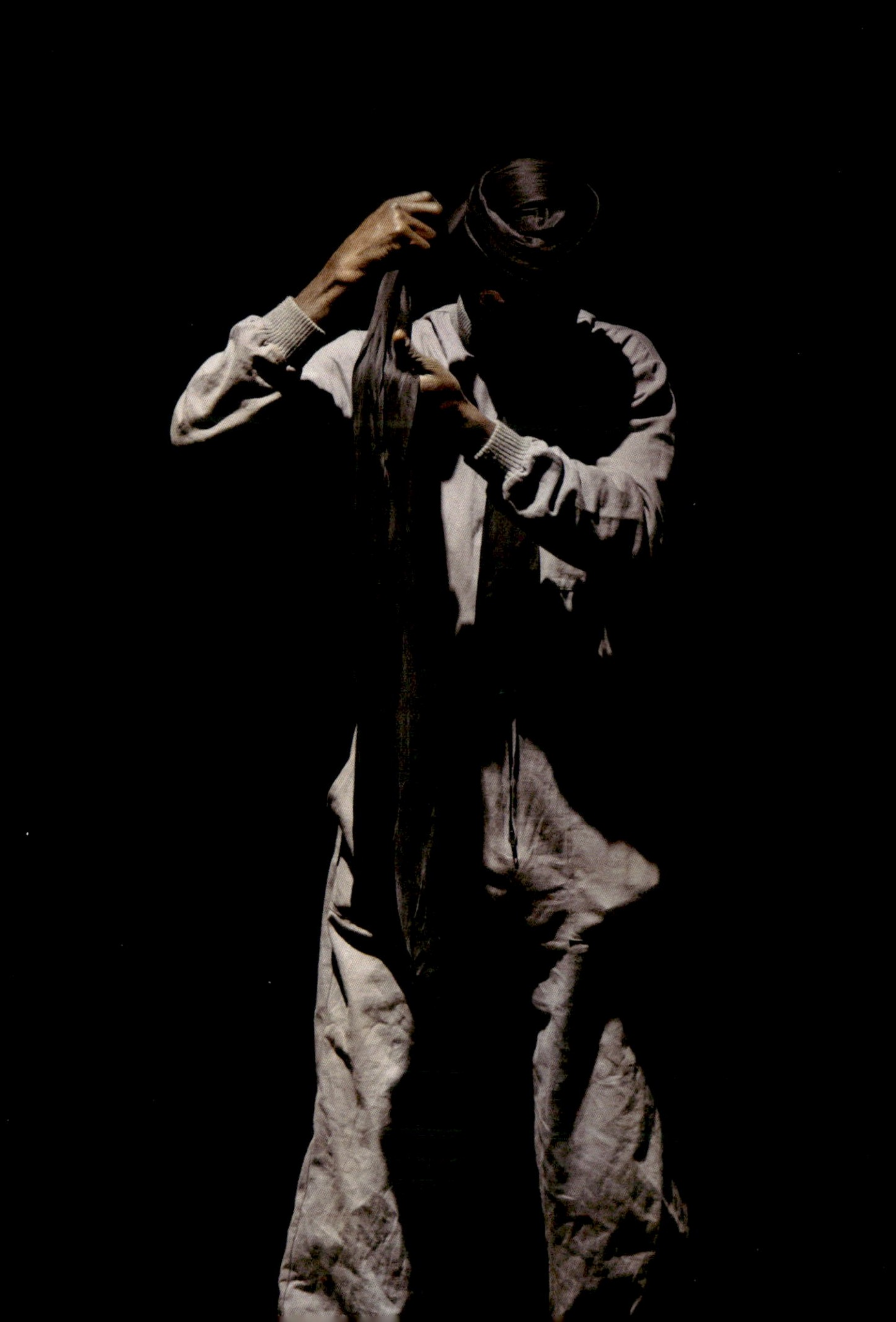

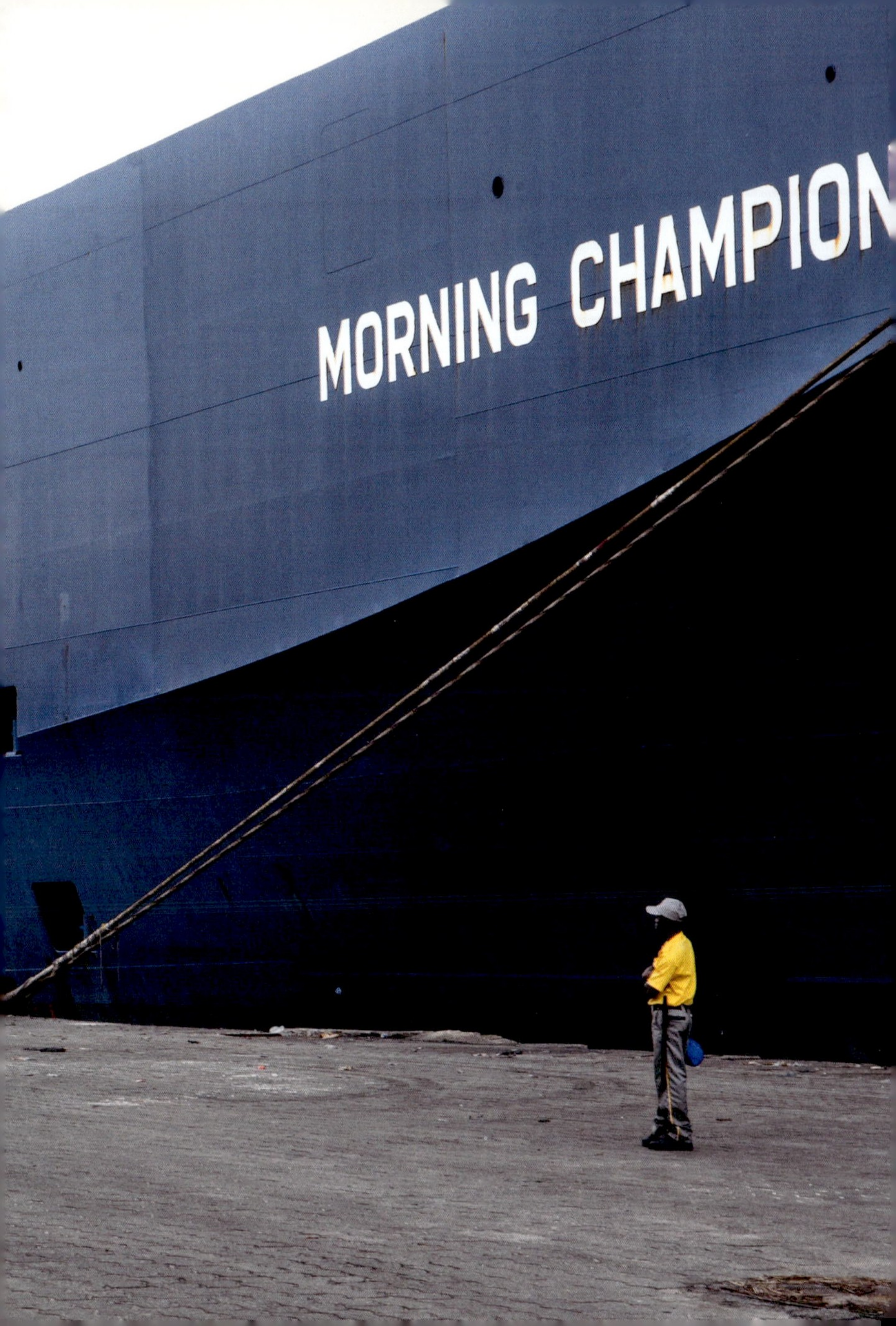
MORNING CHAMPION

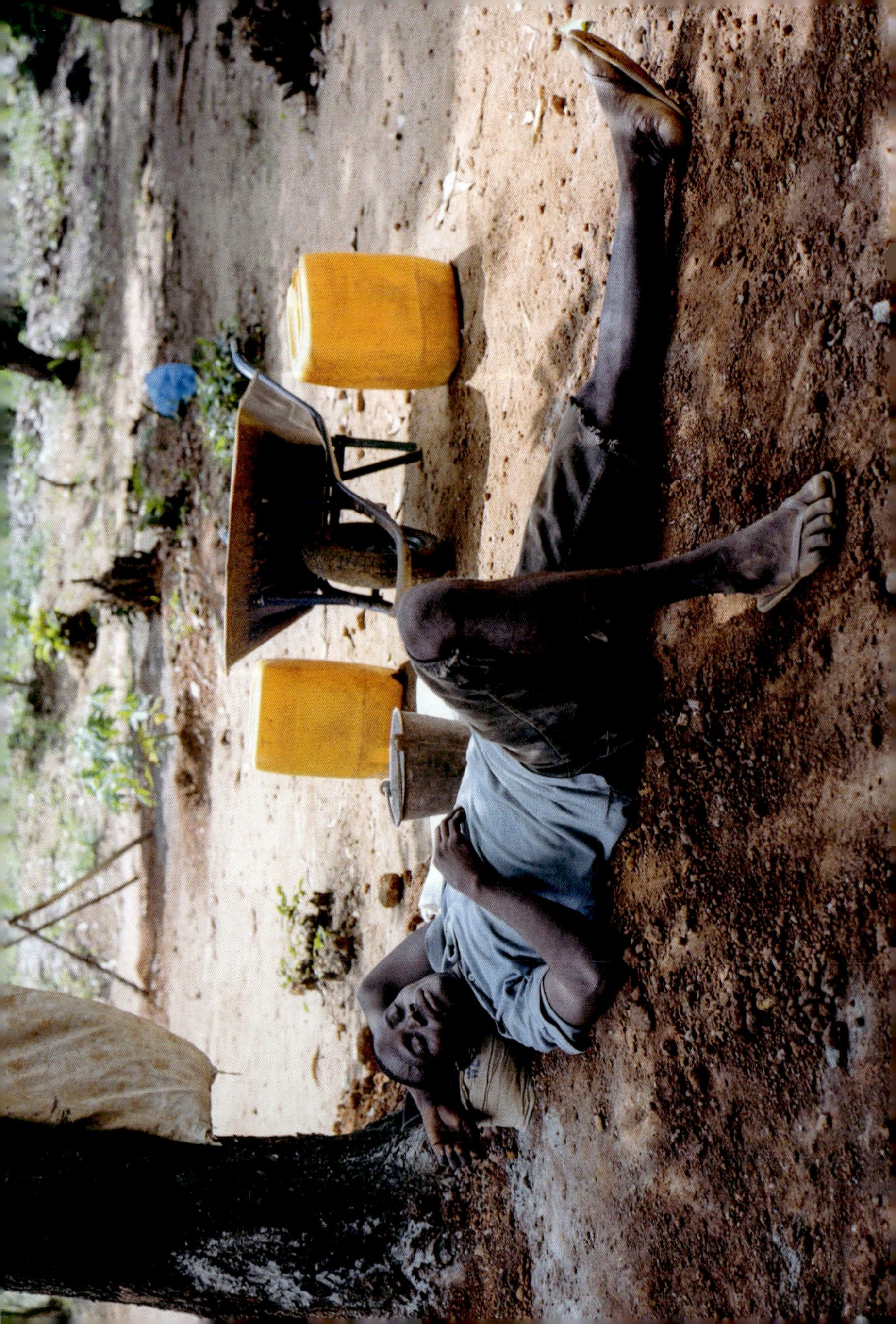

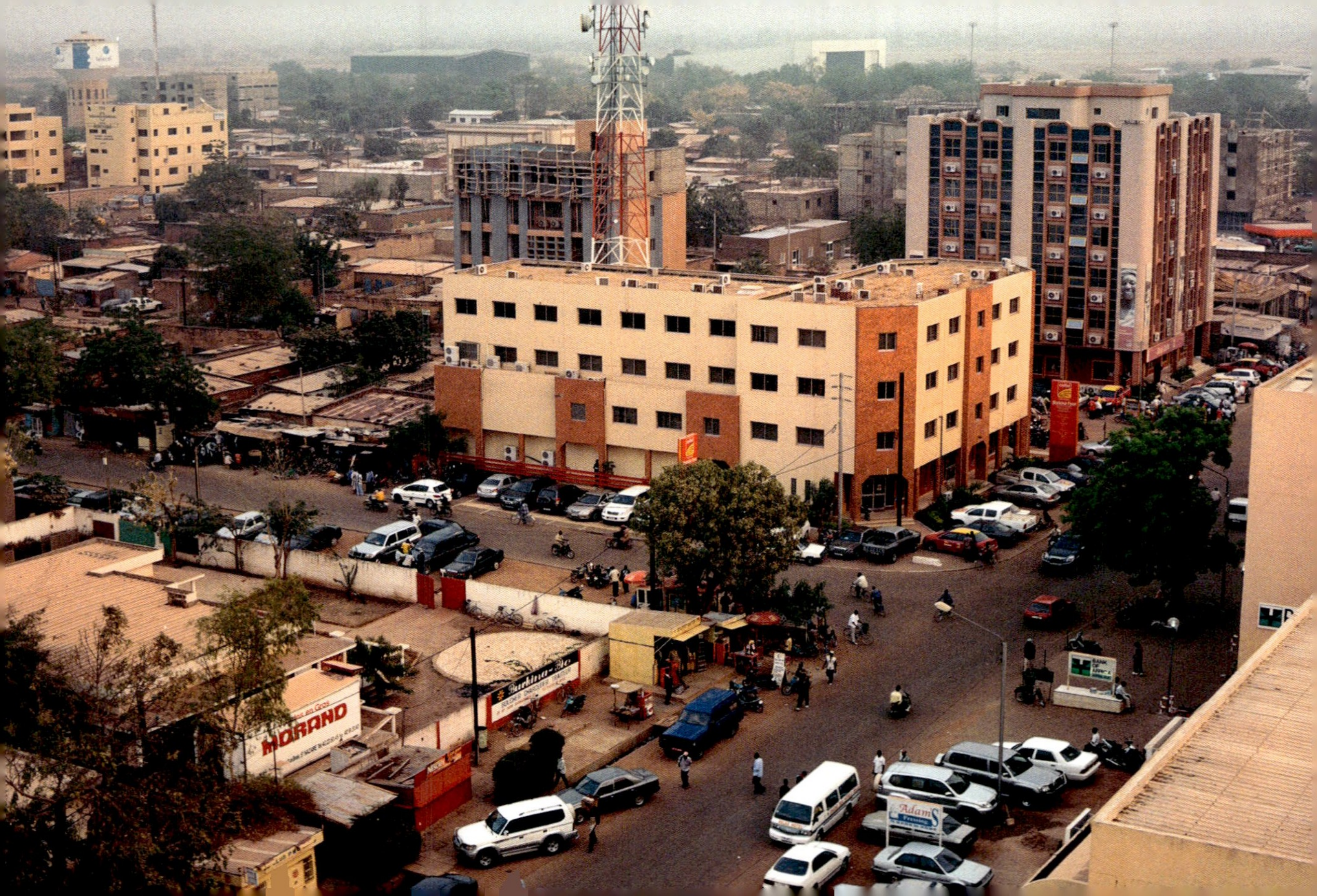
MORAND
Adams

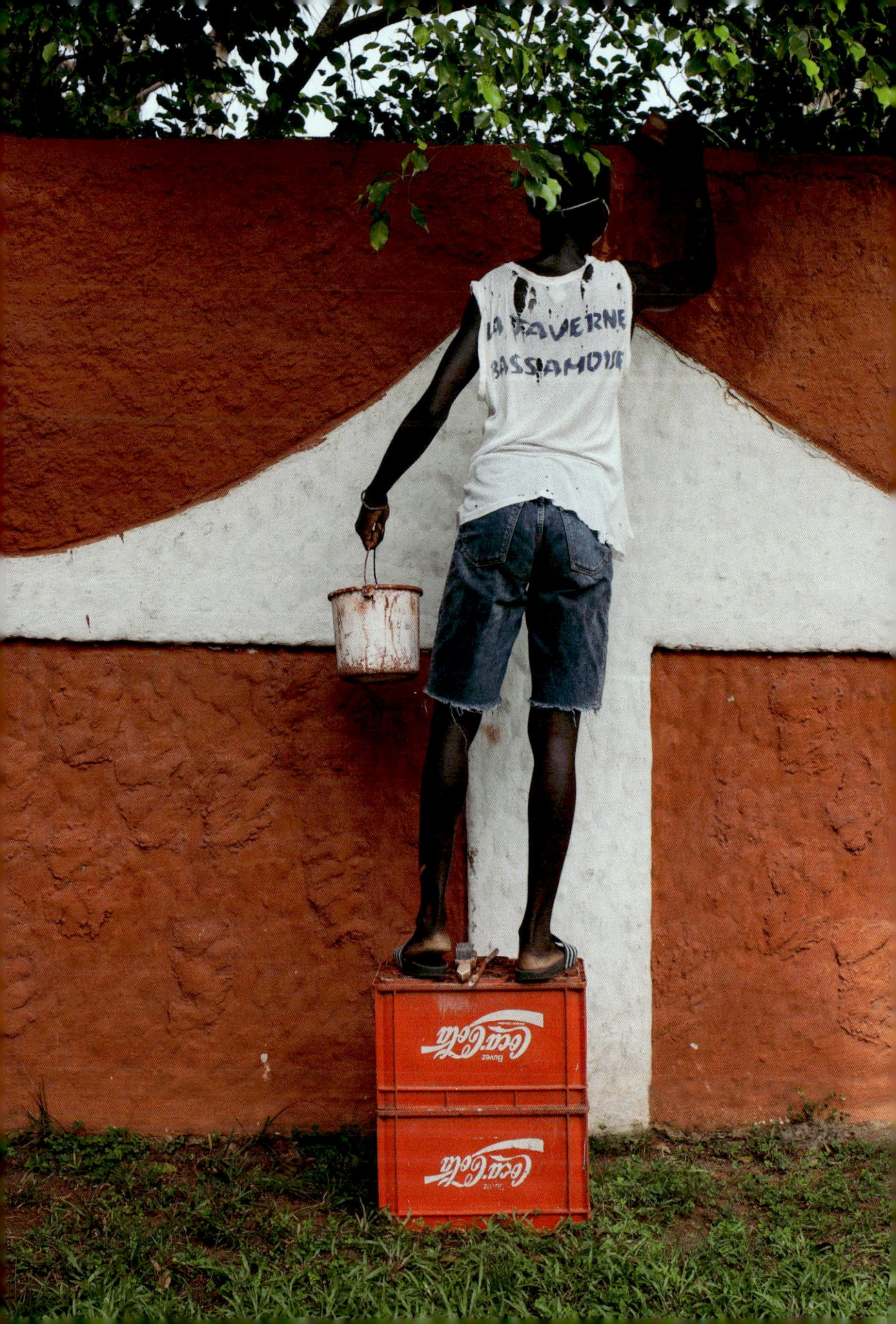
LA TAVERNE

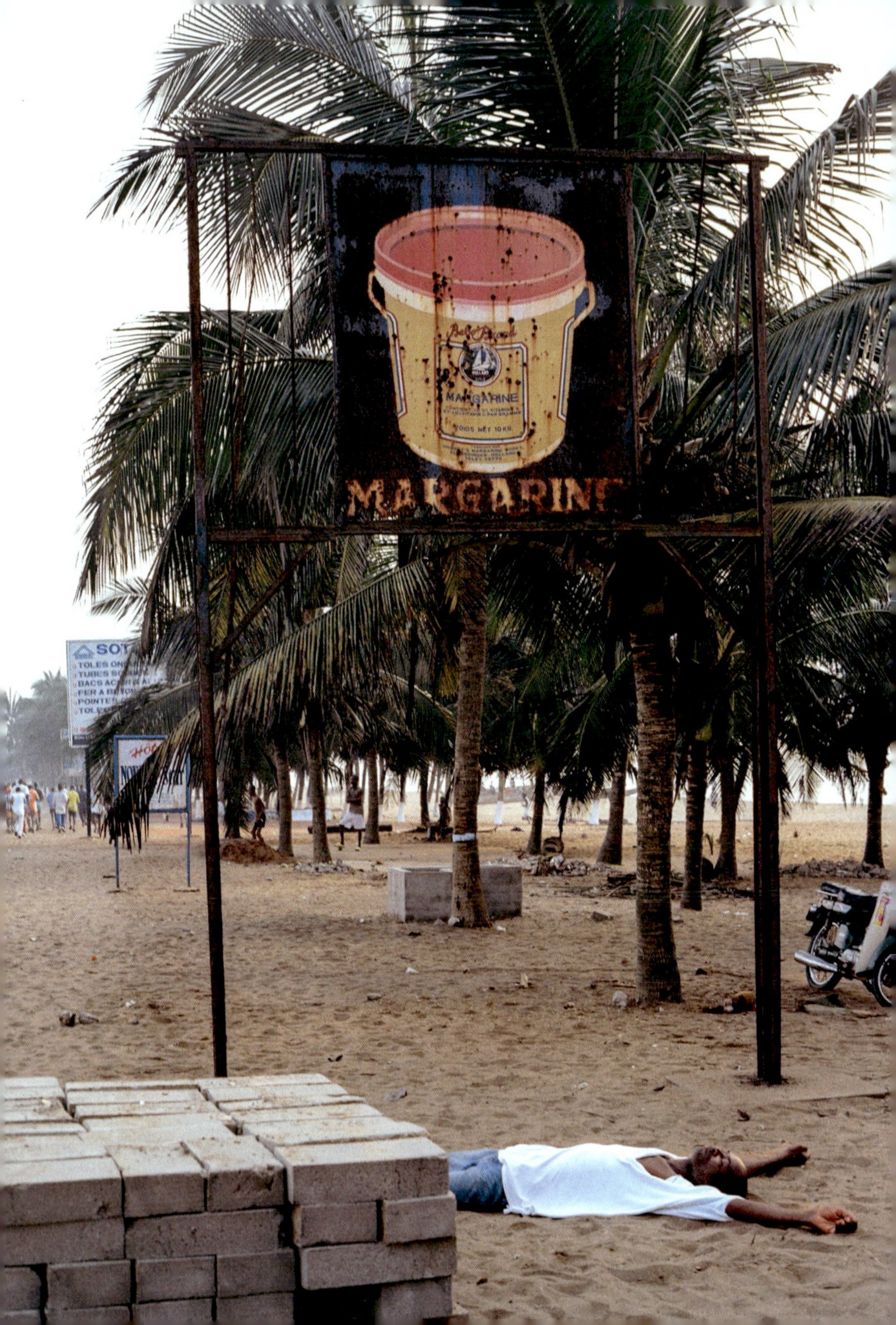
MARGARINE
MARGARINE

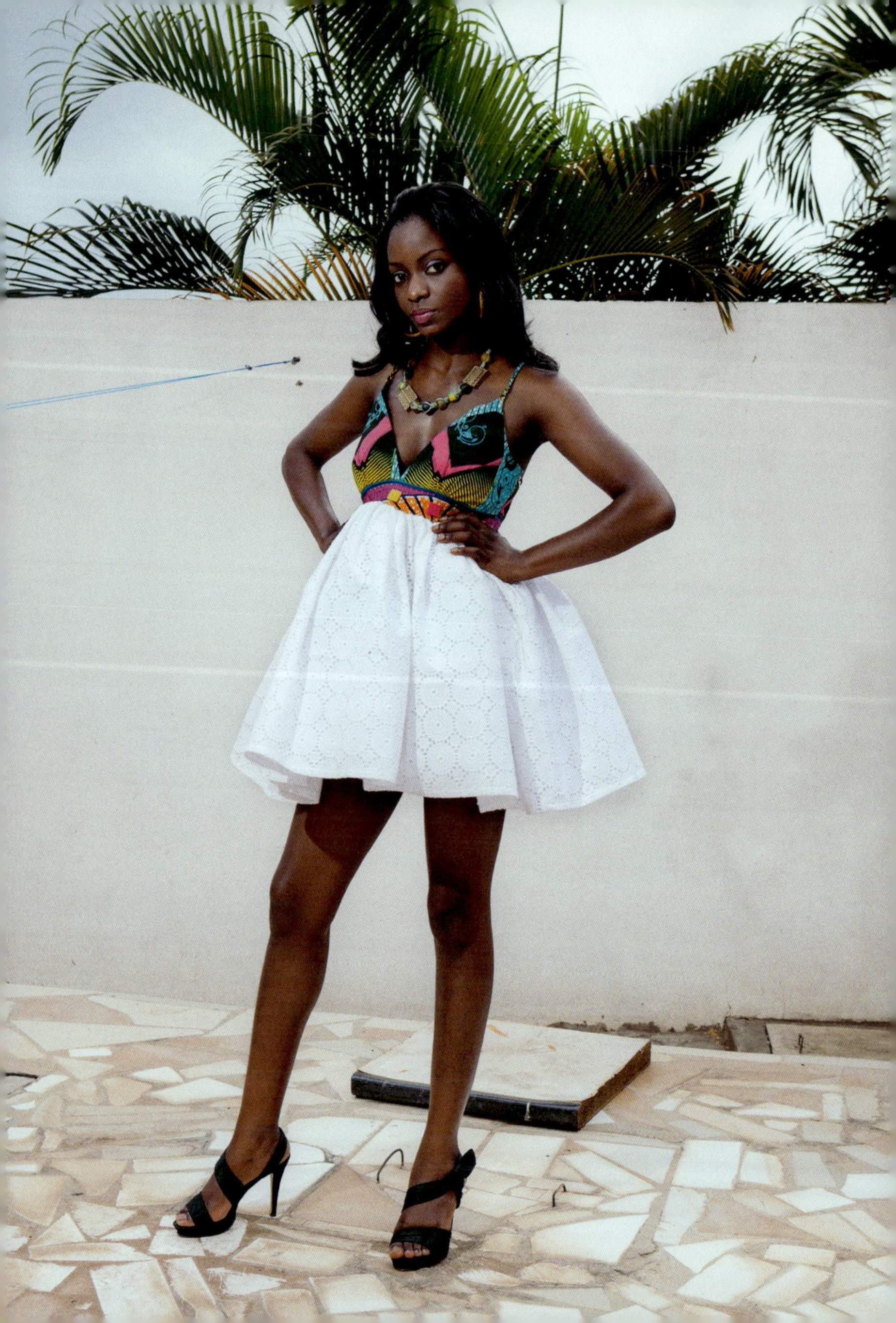

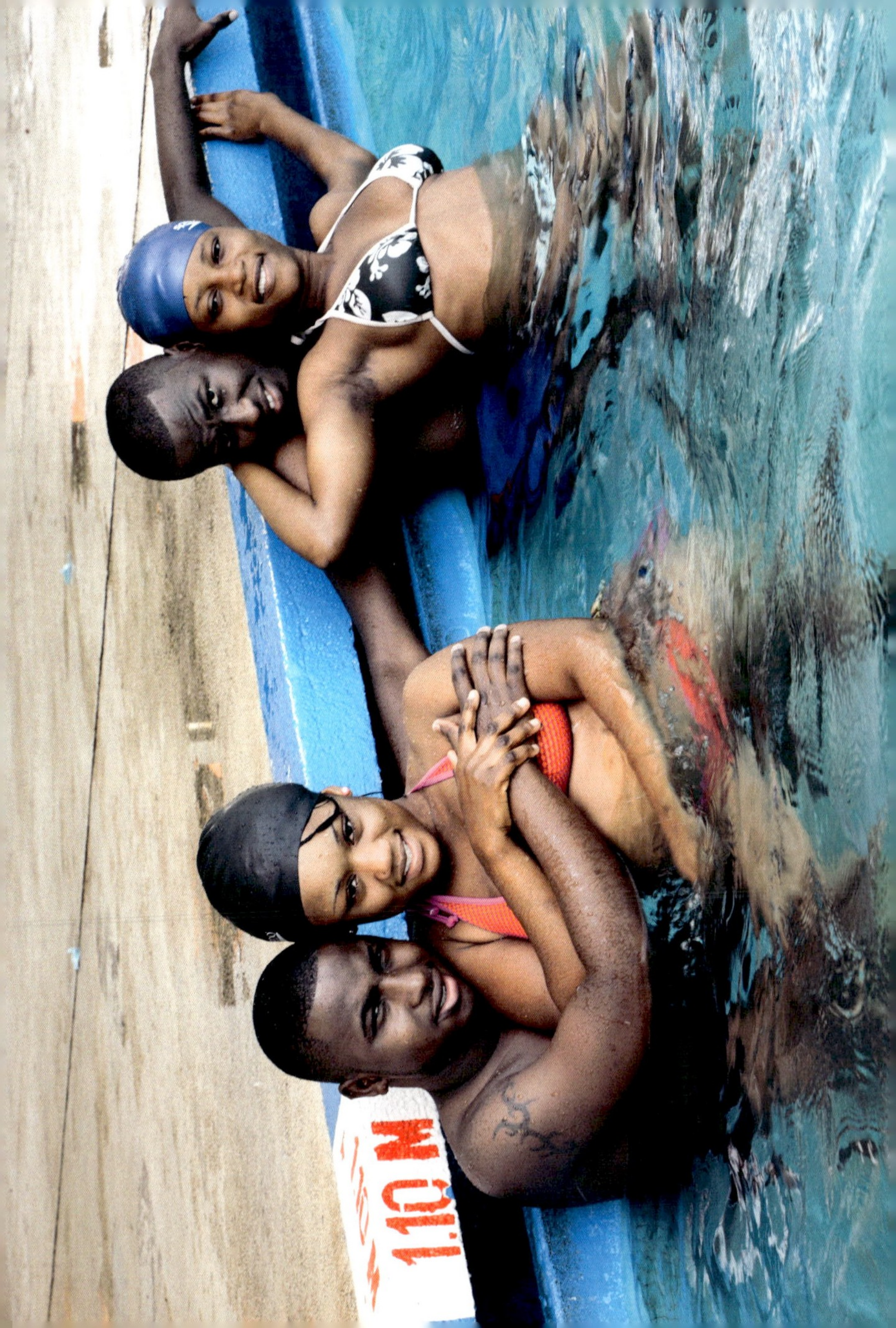
110 M

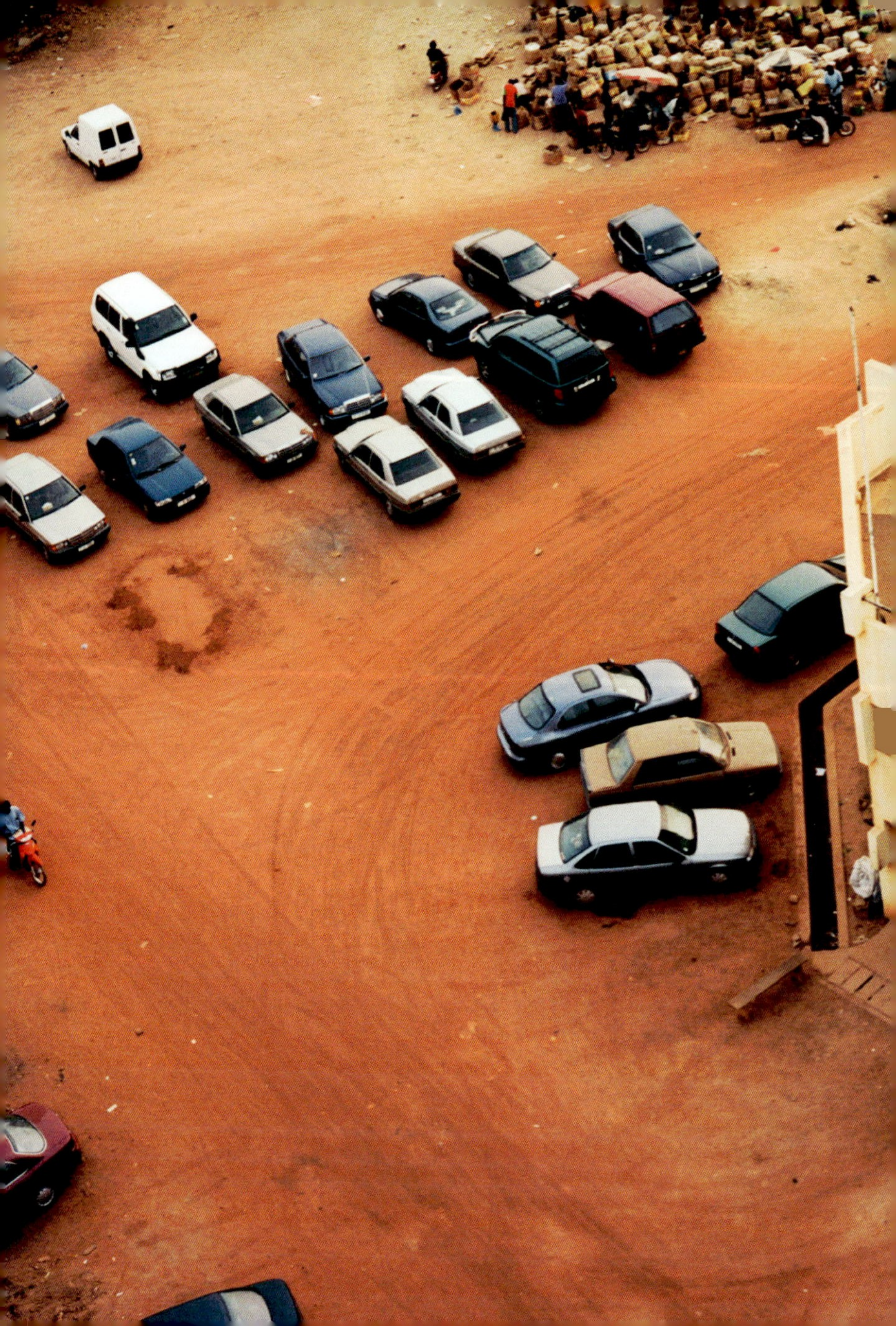

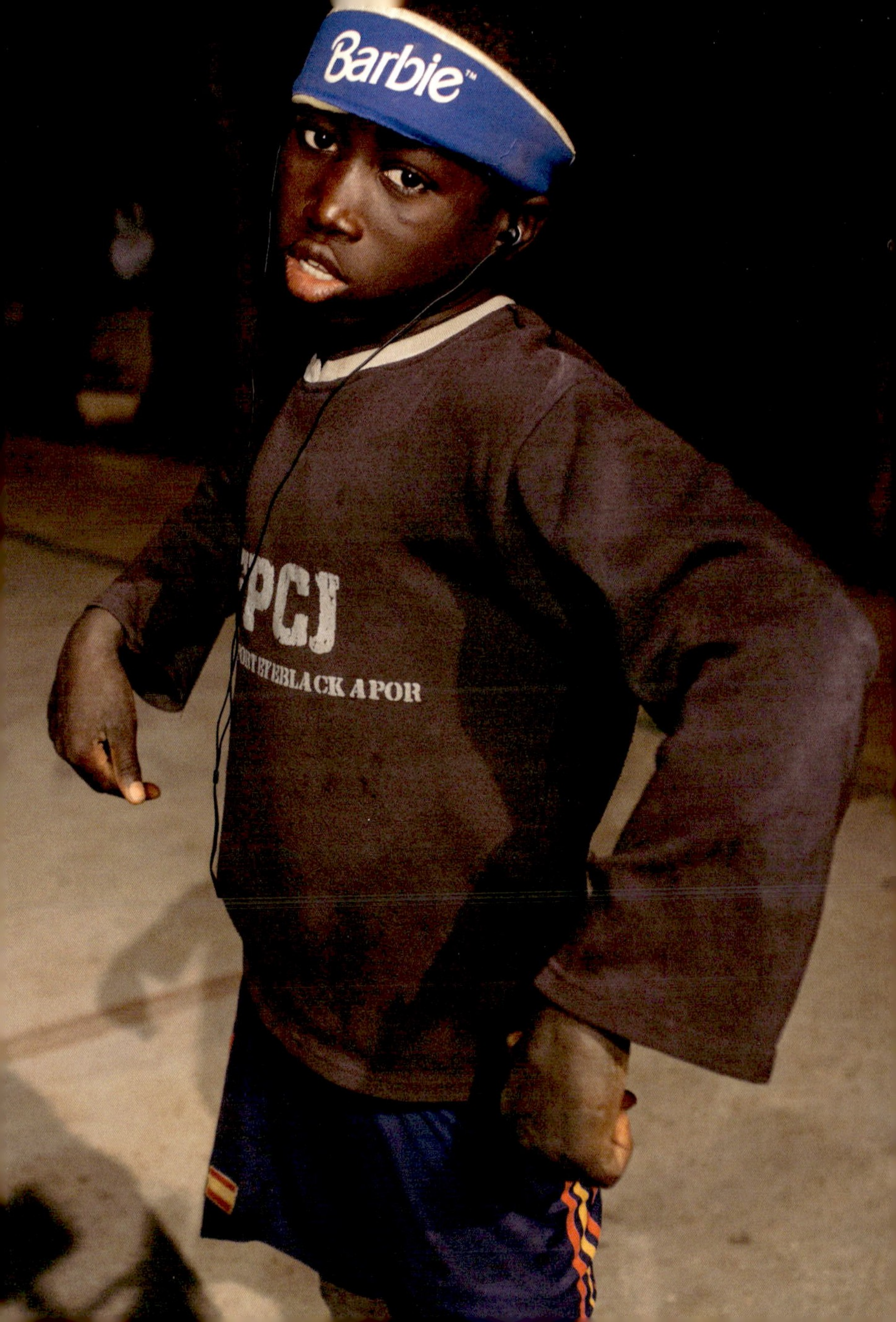
Barbie™
PCJ
EBLACK APOR

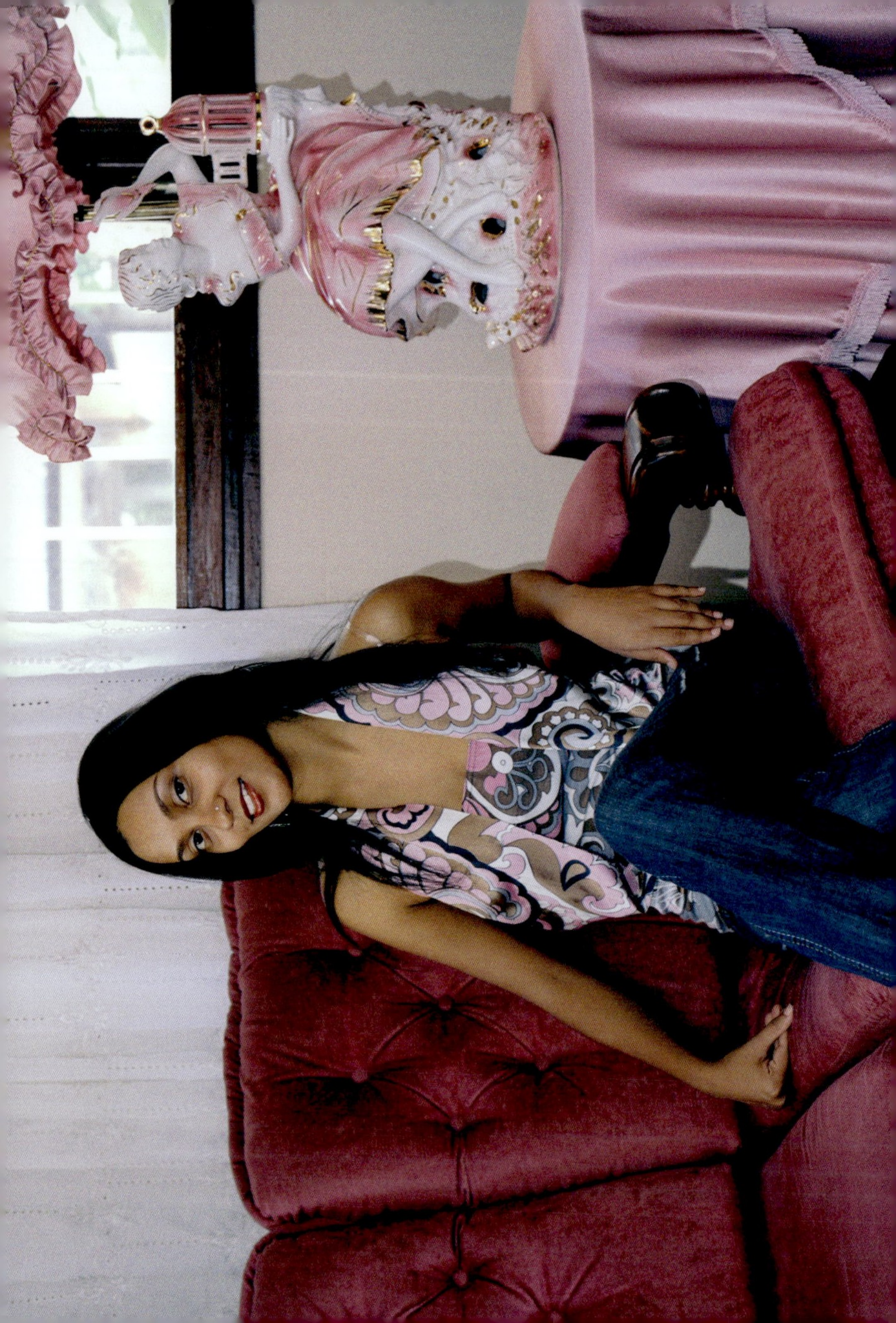

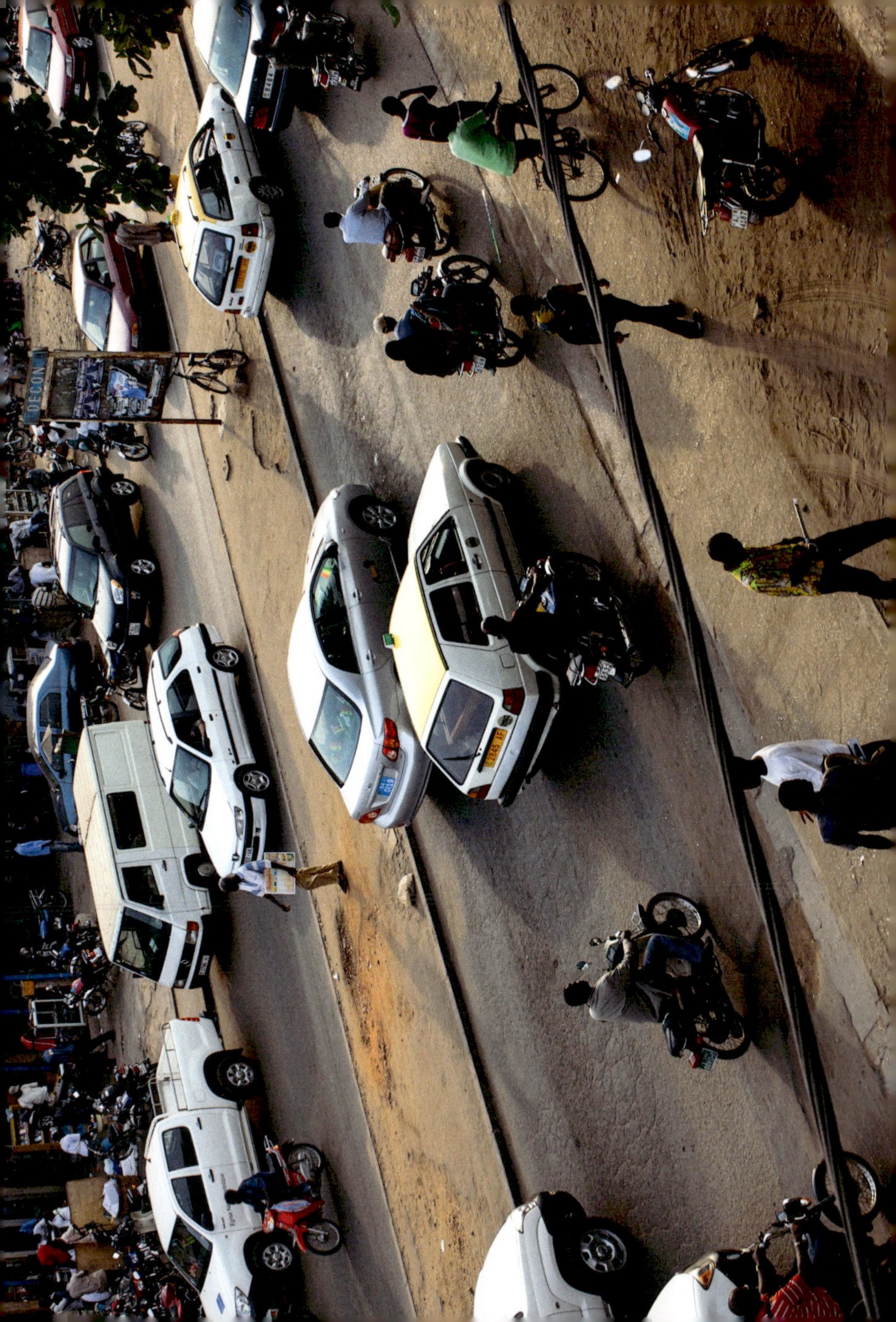

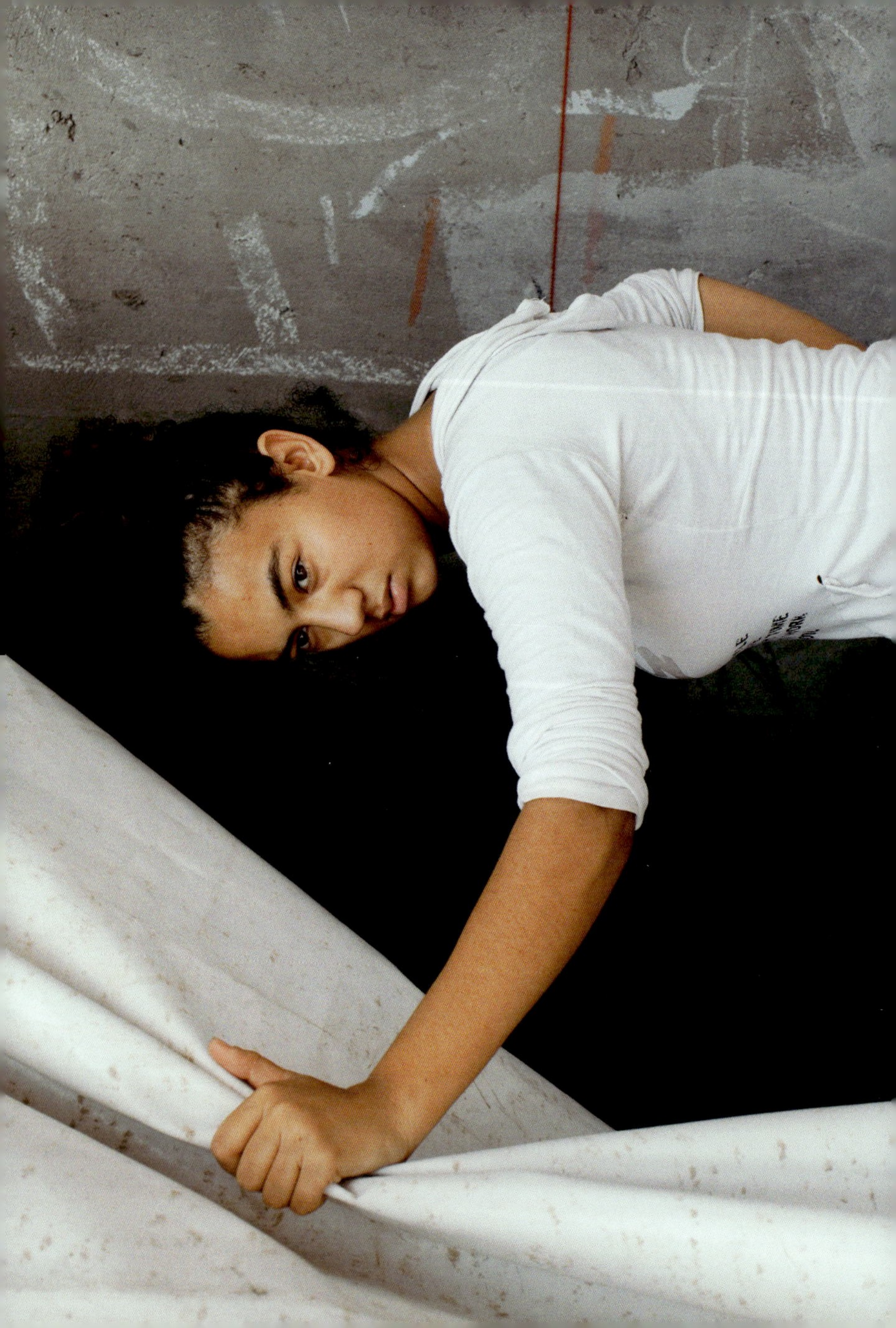

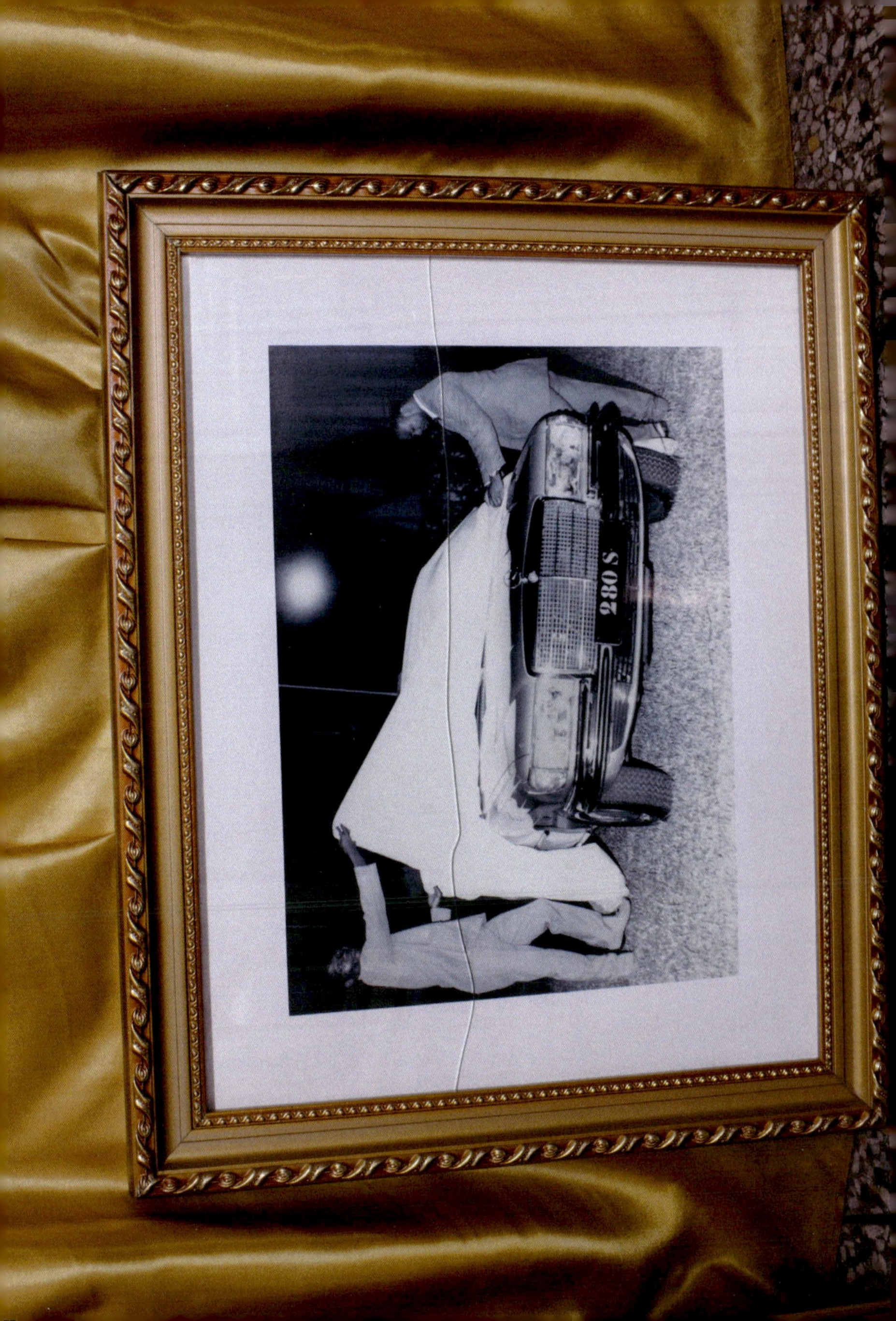
280 S

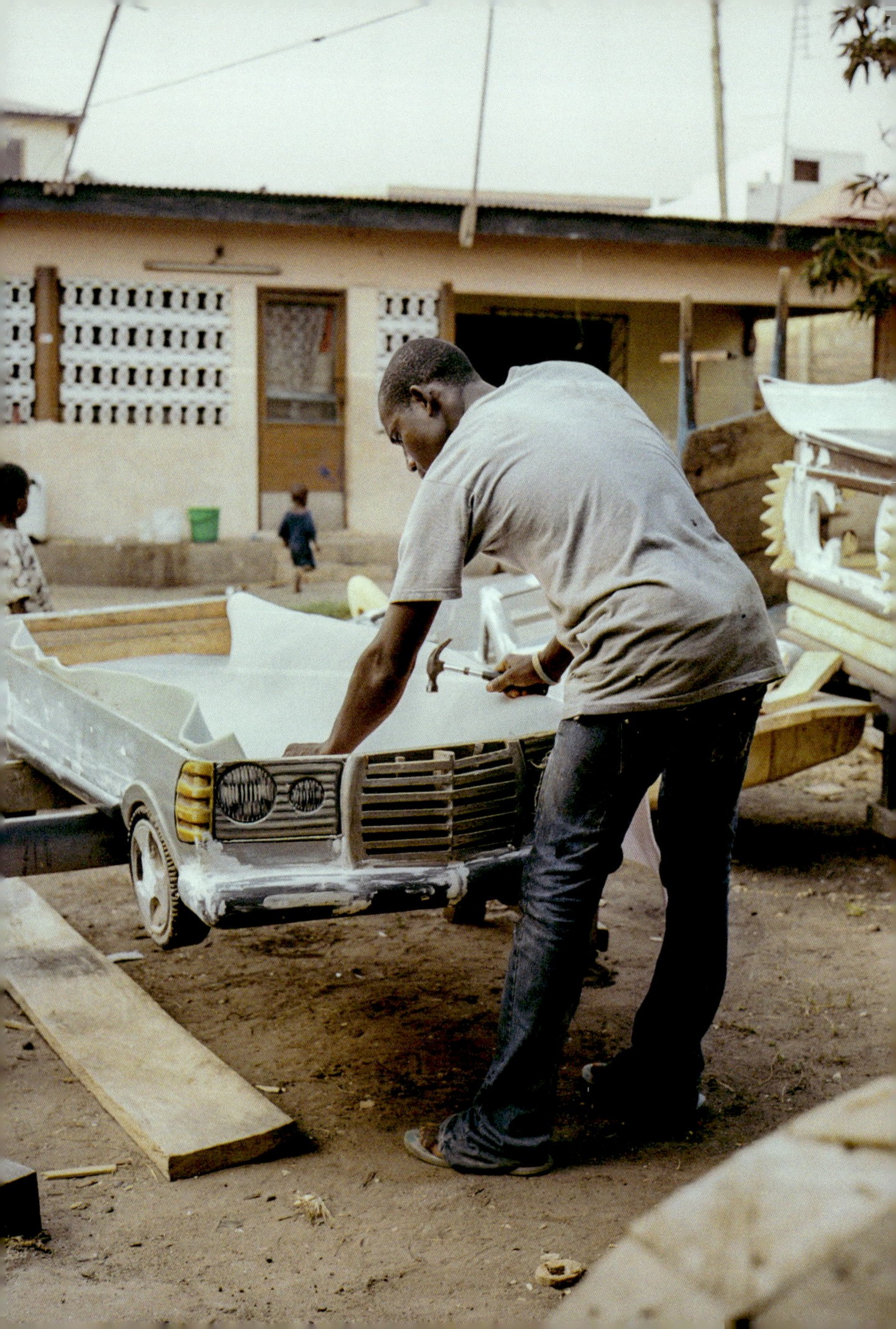

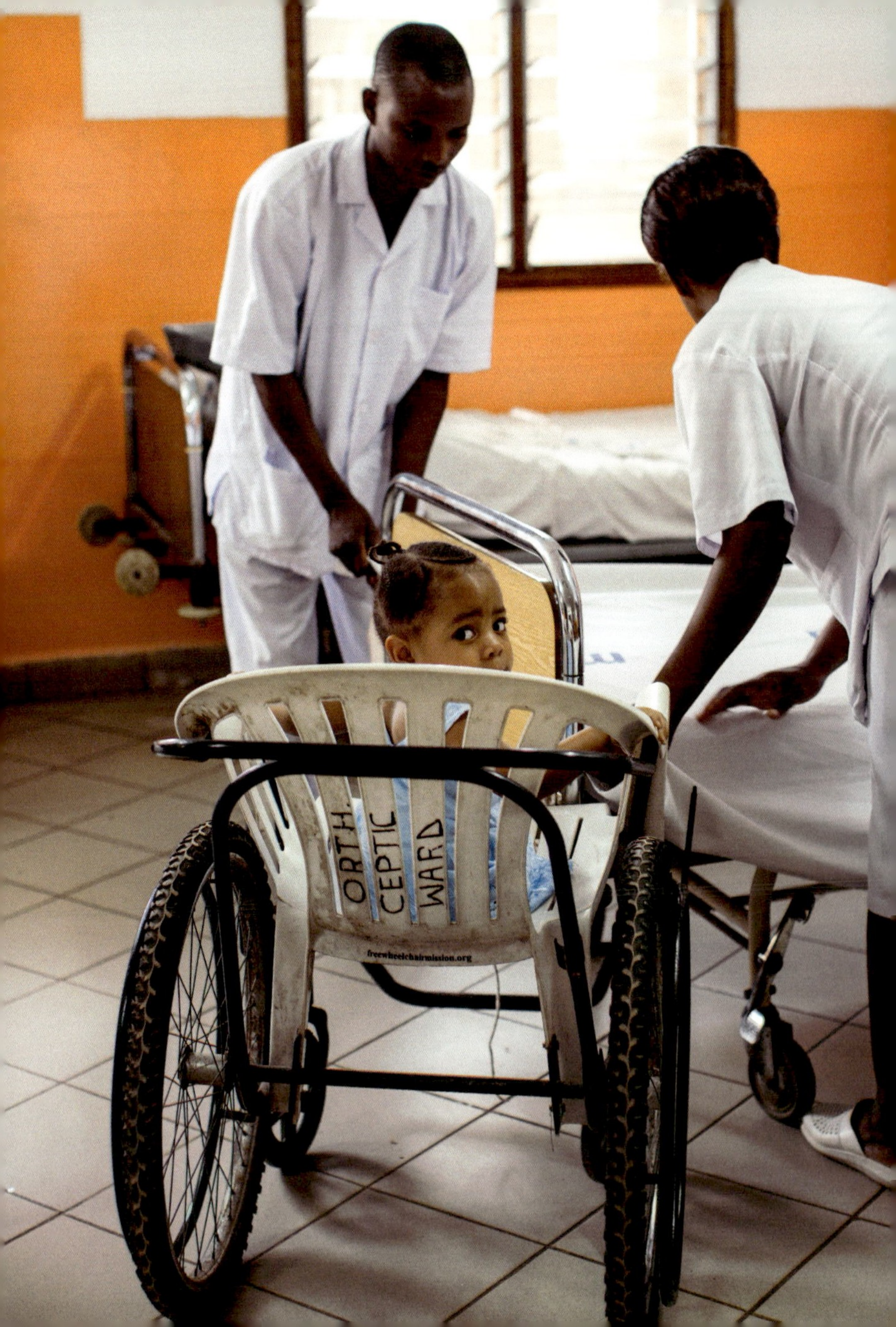
ORTH.
CEPTIC
WARD
freewheelchairmission.org

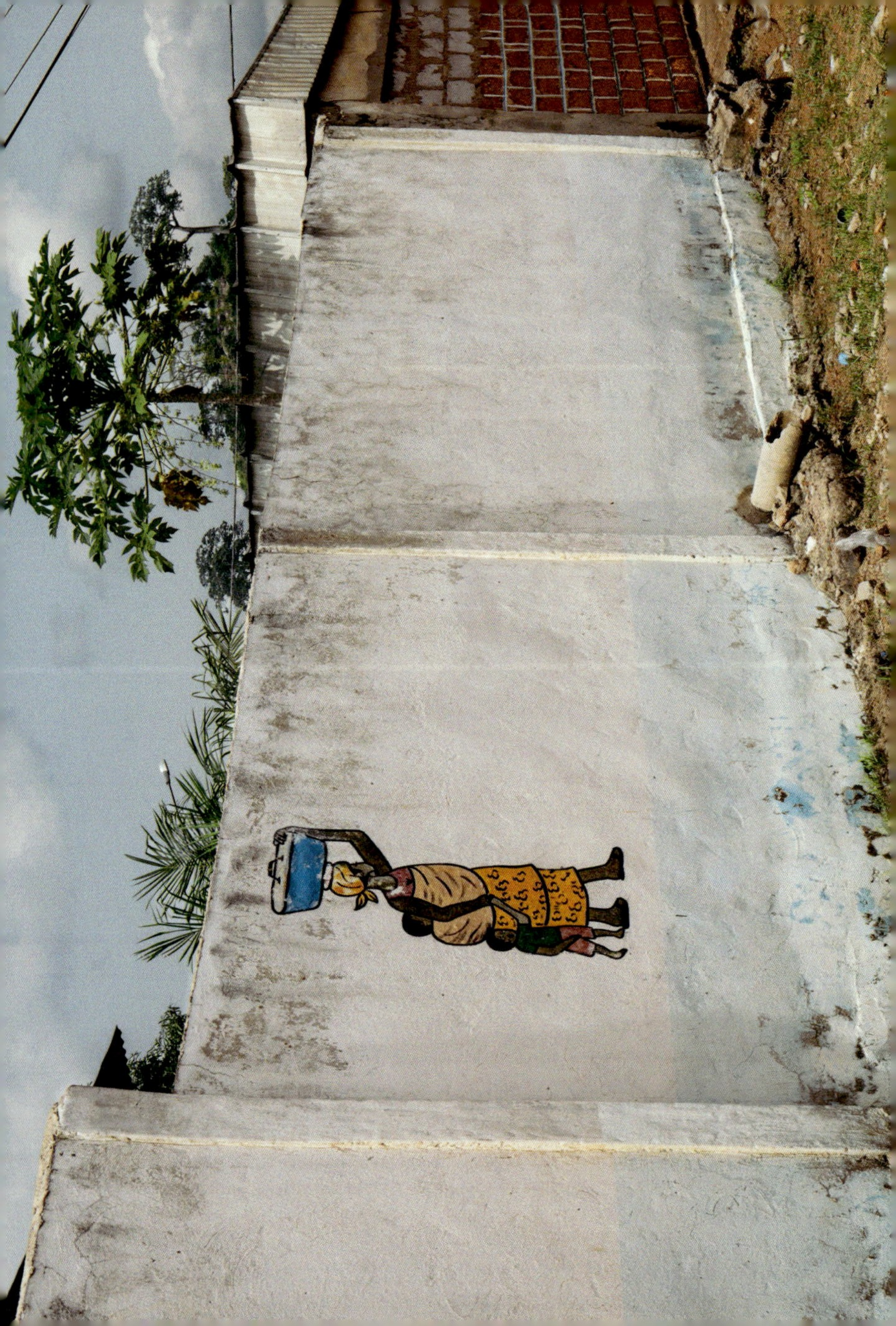

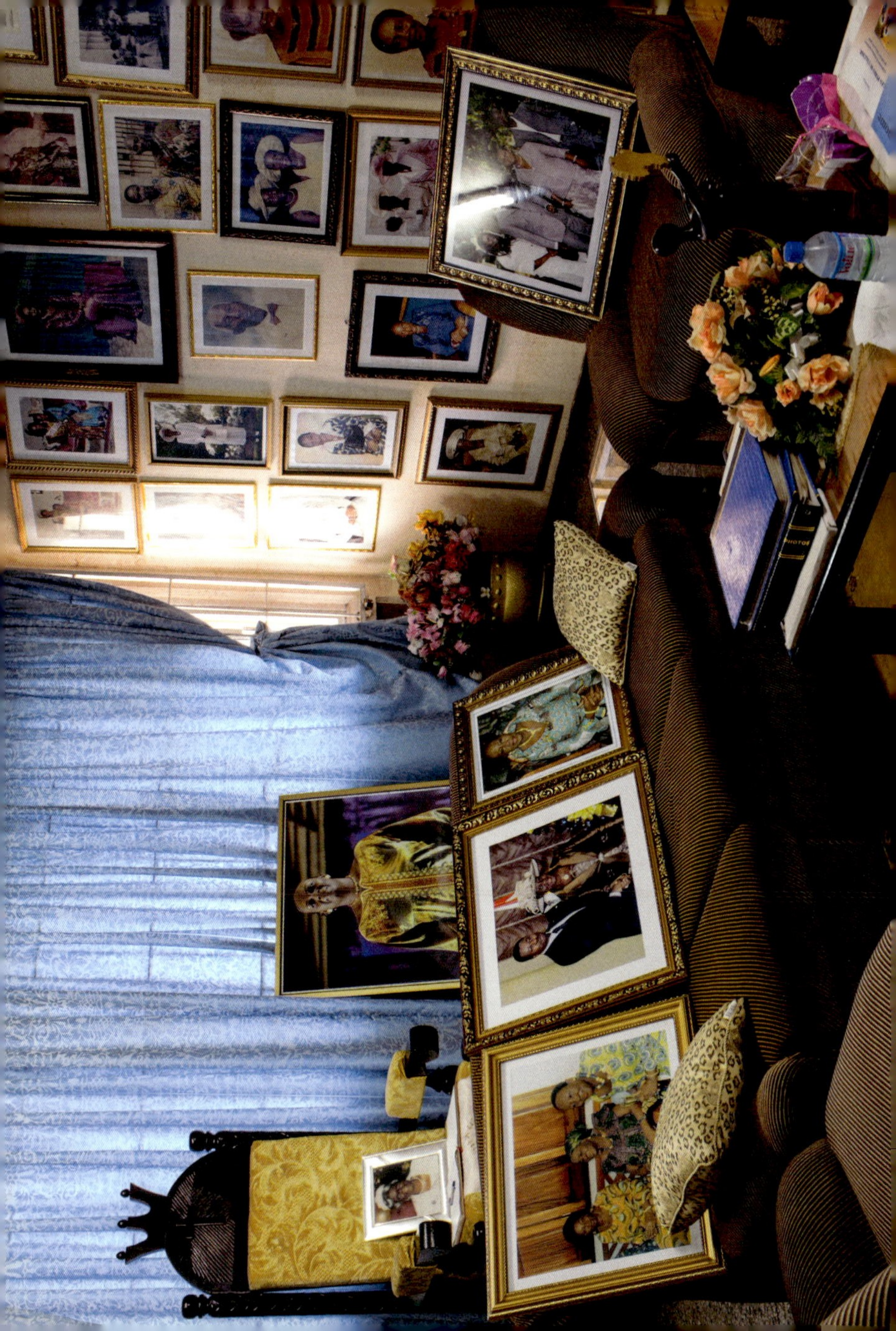

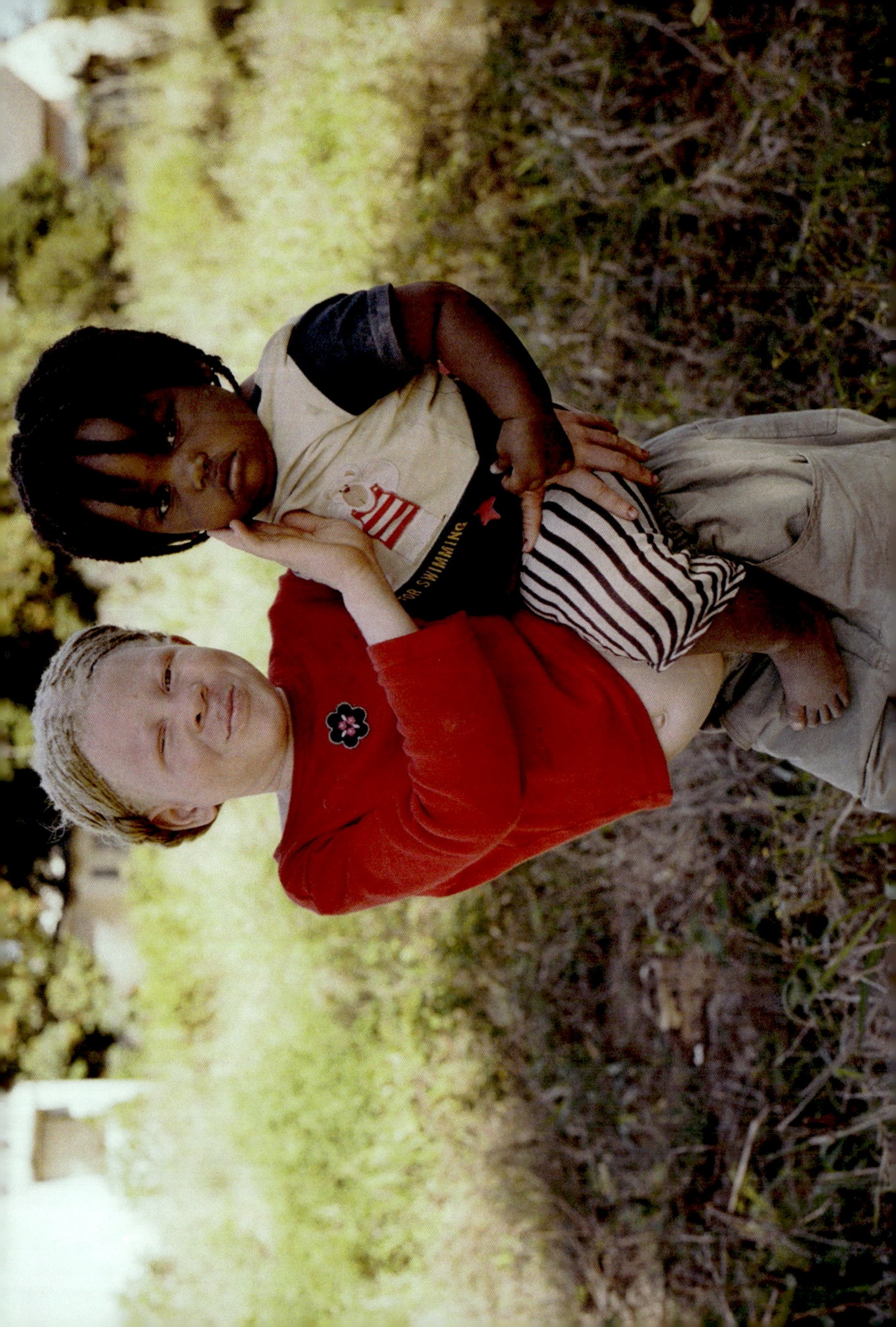
FOR SWIMMING

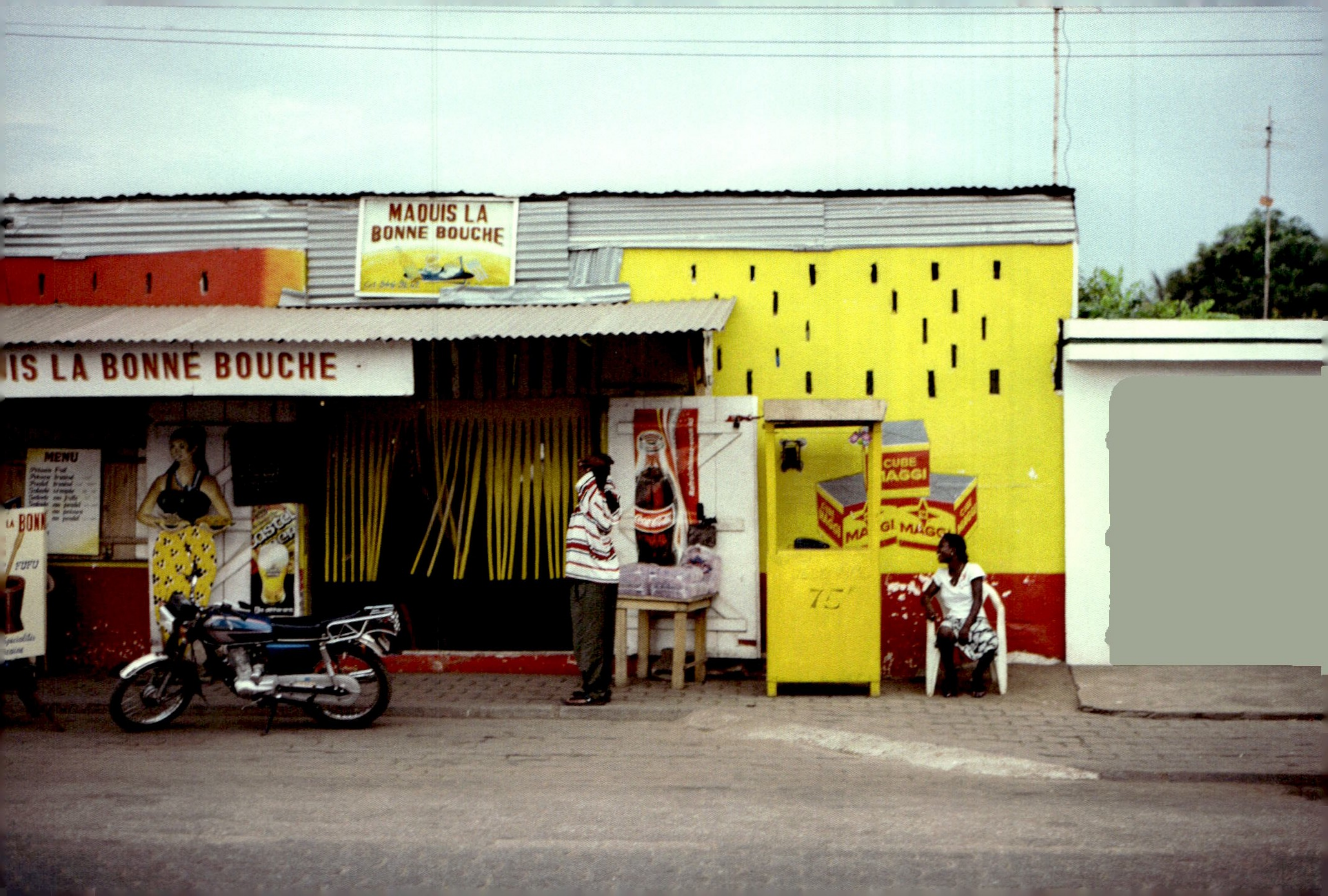
MAQUIS LA
BONNE BOUCHE
IS LA BONNE BOUCHE
MENU
LA BONN
FUFU
CUBE MAGGI
MAGGI
MAGGI
75

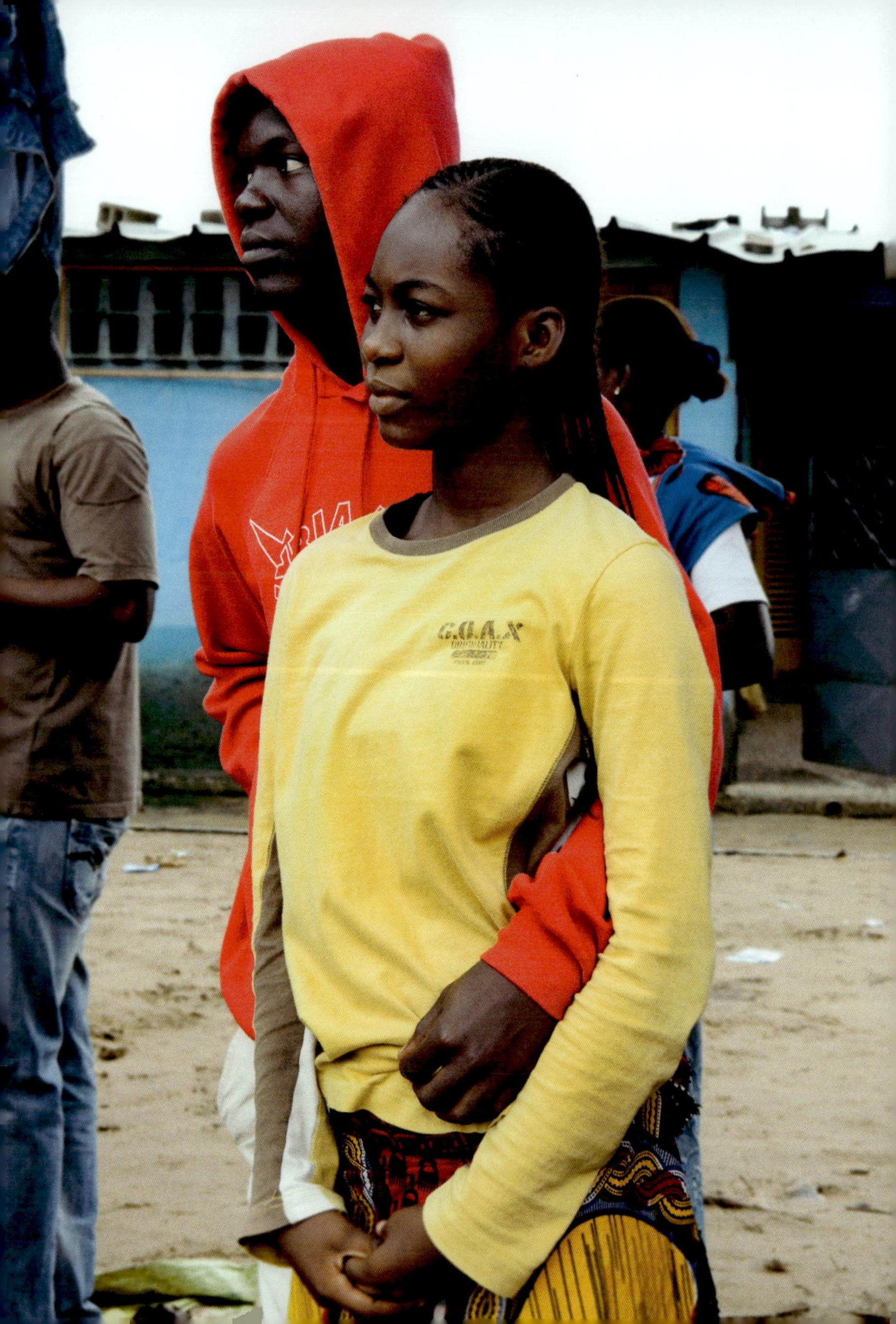

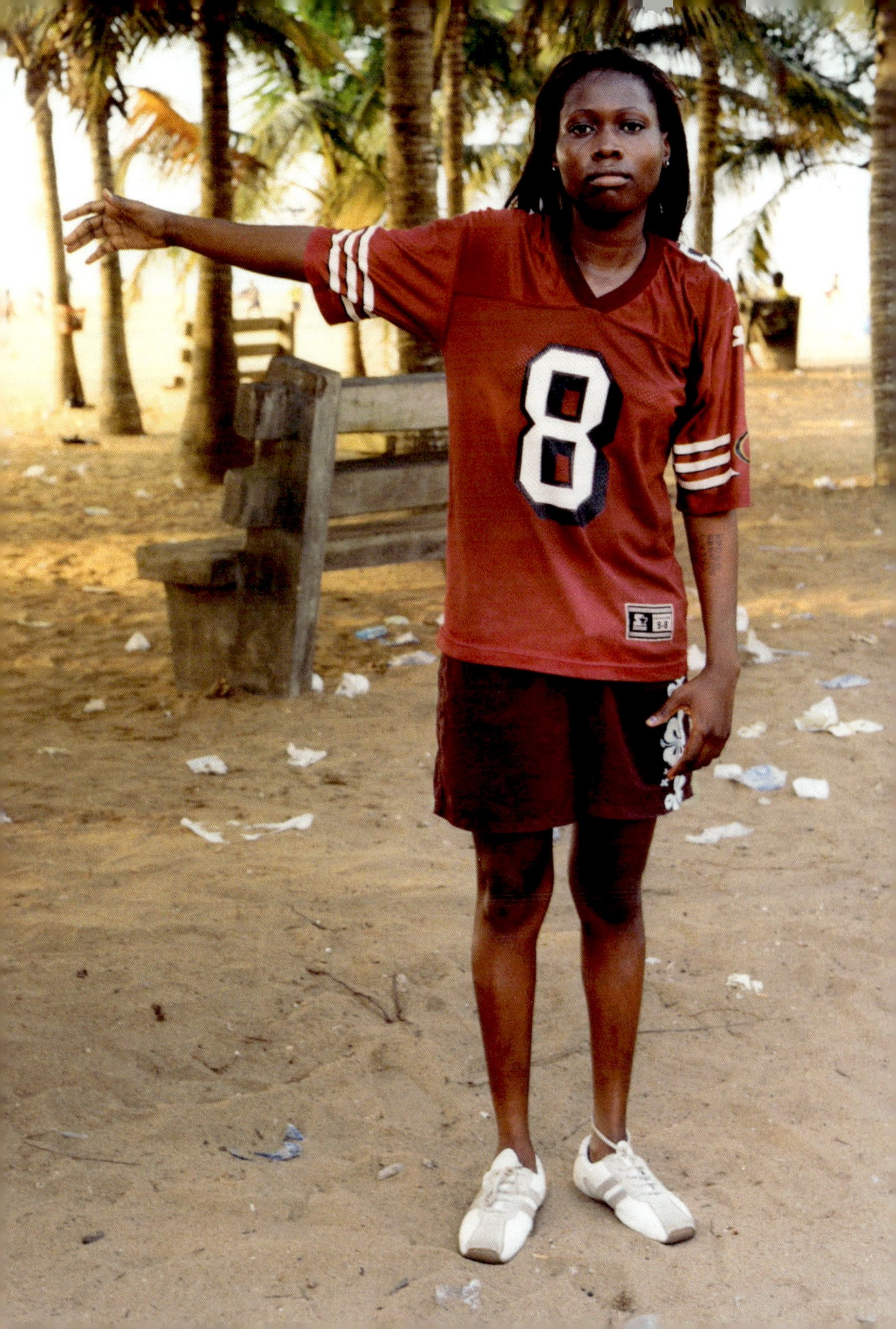
8

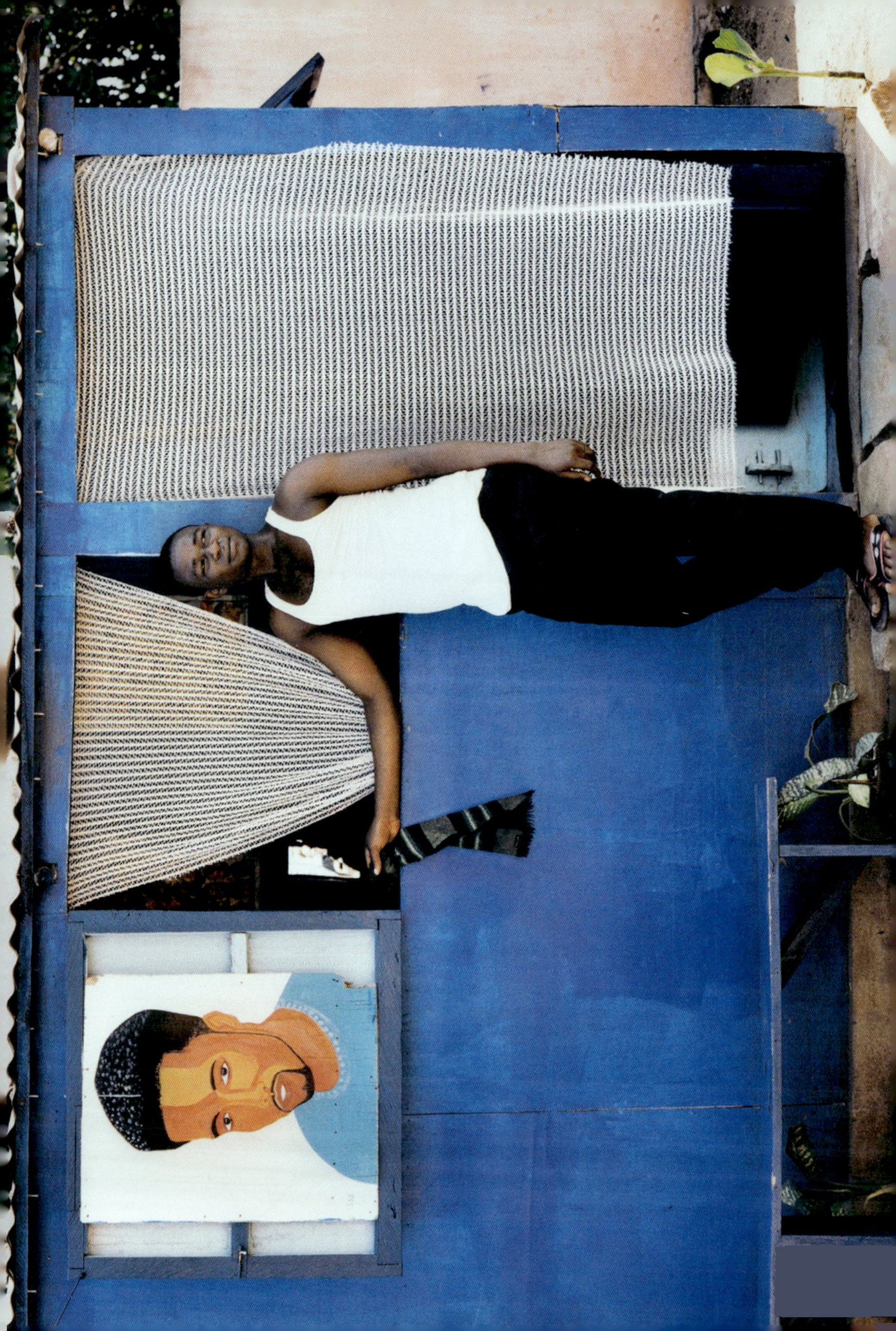

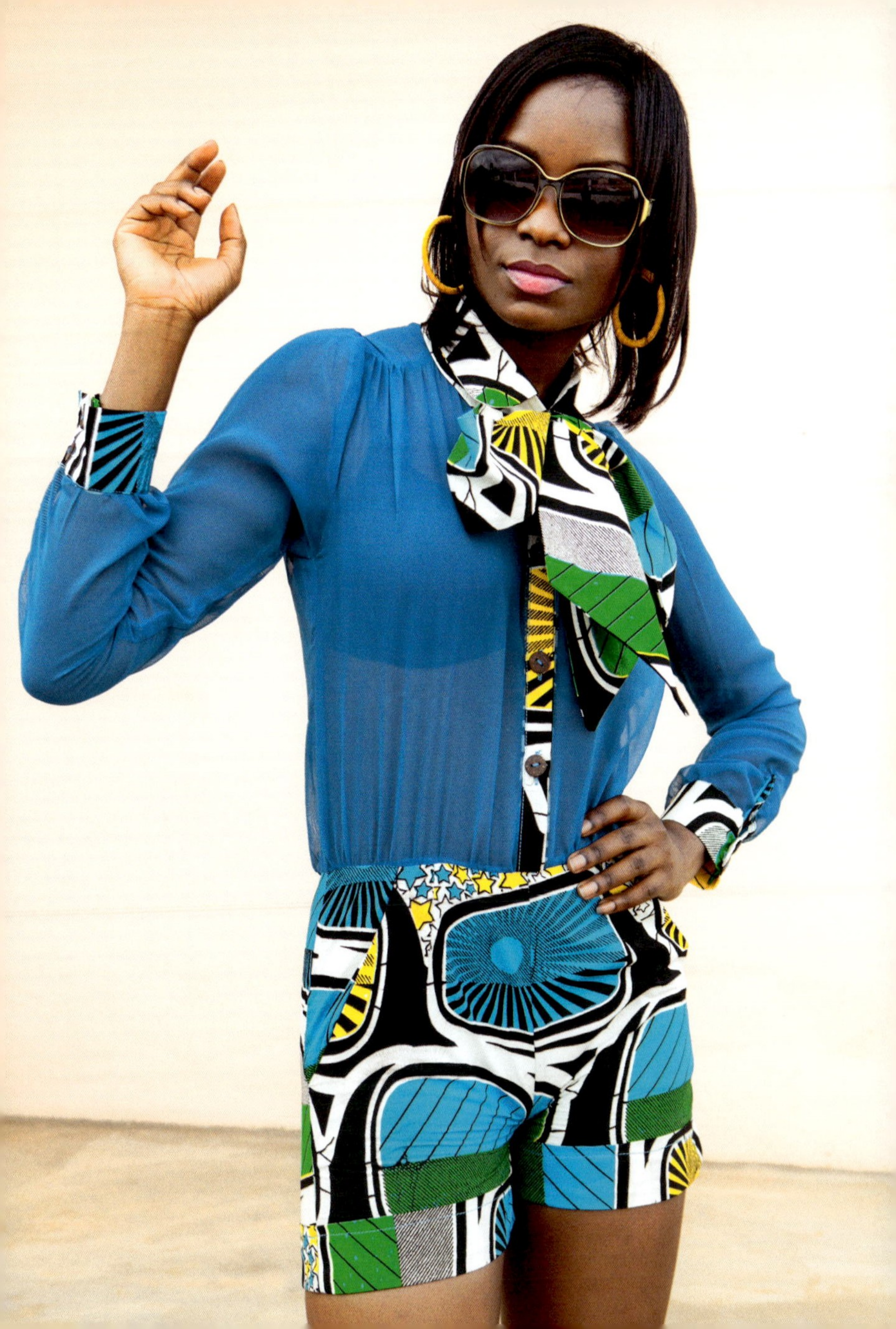

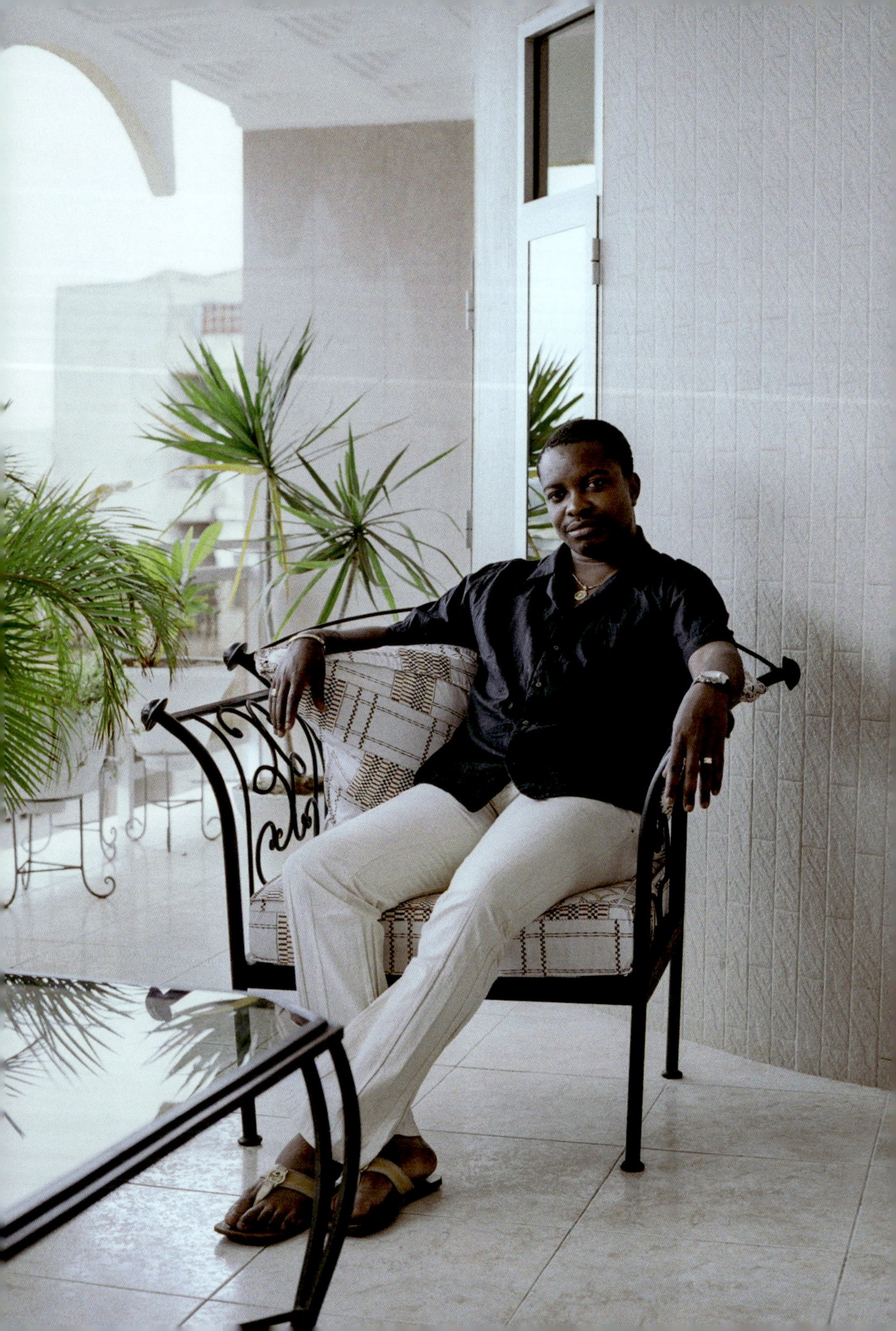

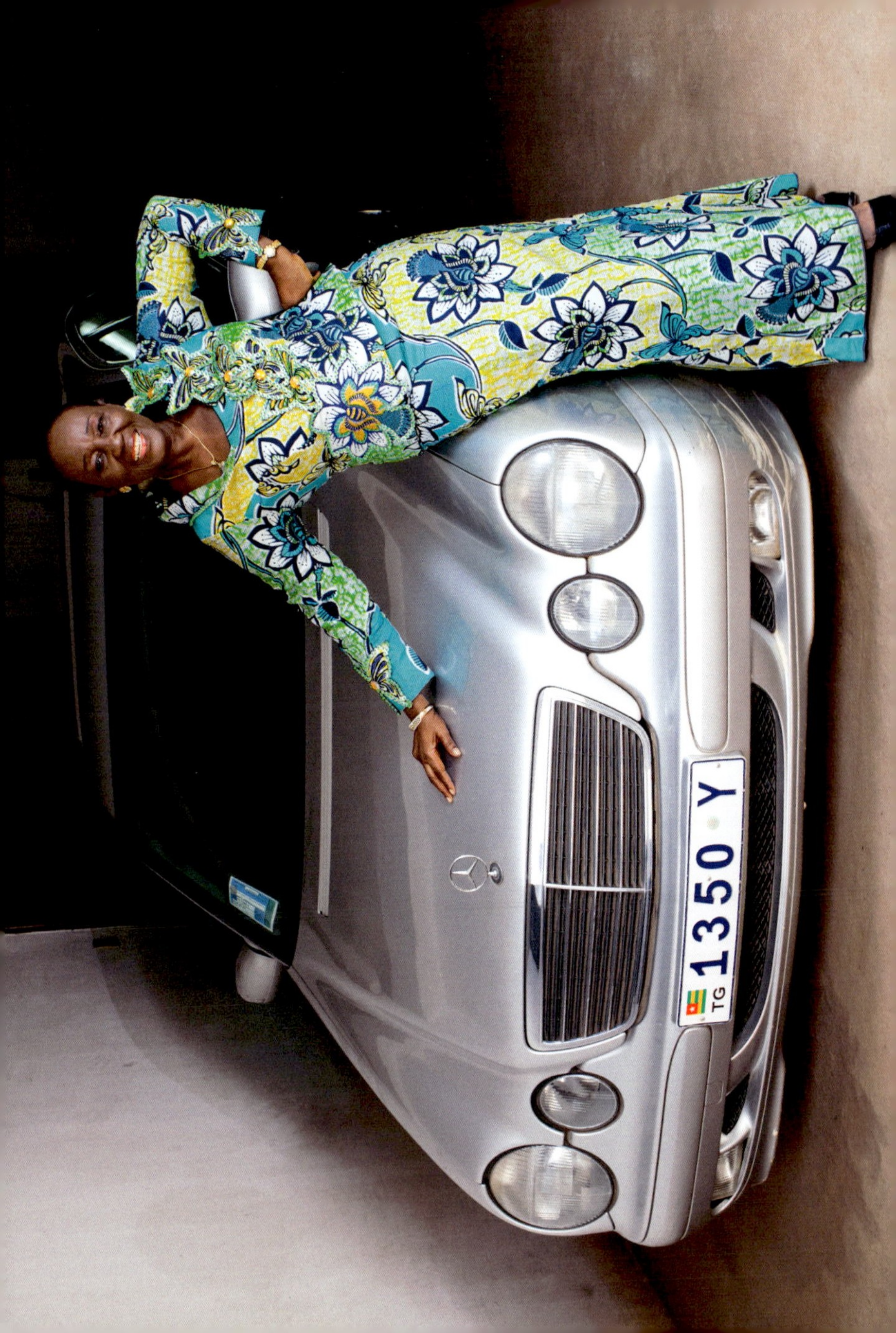
TG 1350 Y

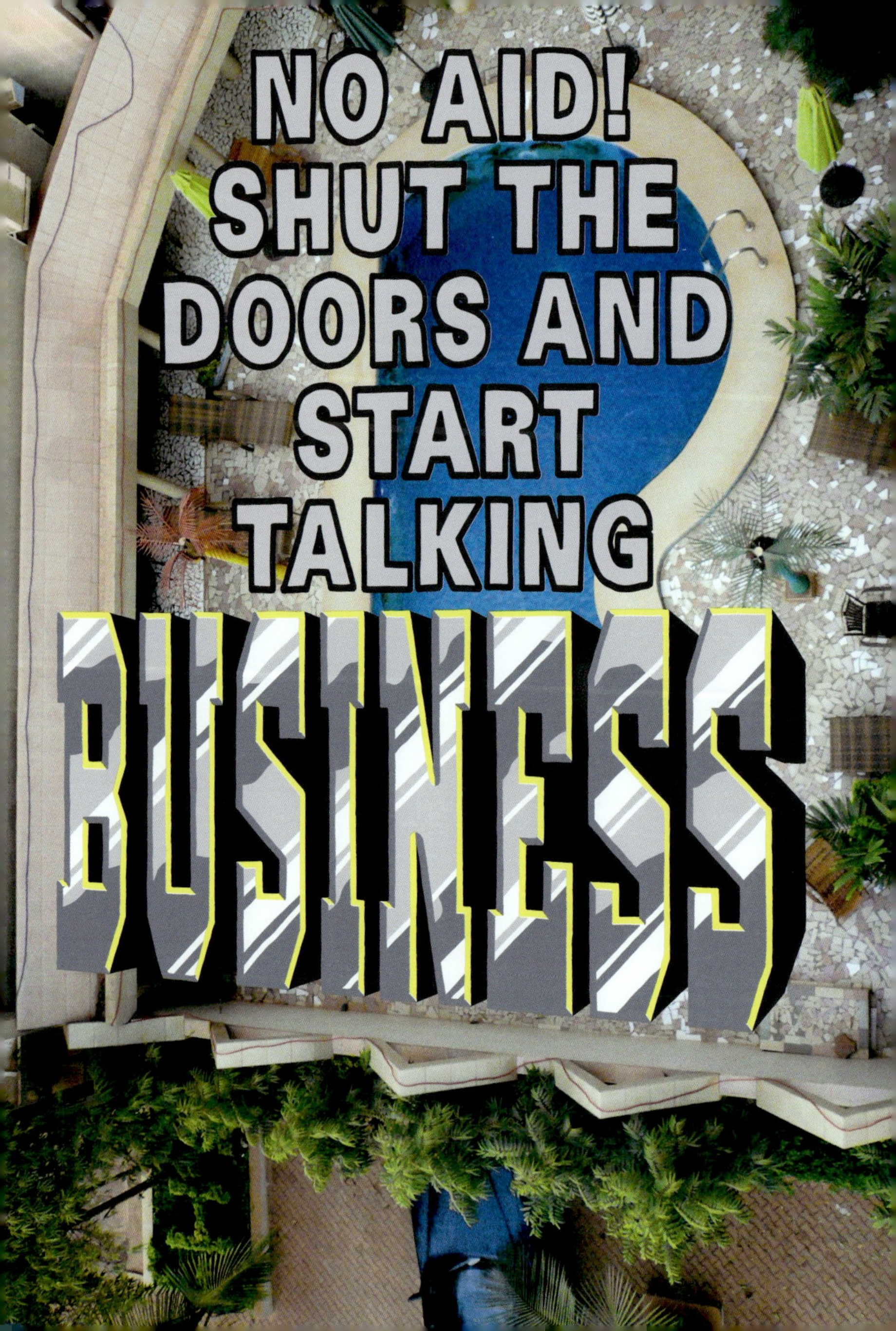
NO AID!
SHUT THE
DOORS AND
START
TALKING
BUSINESS

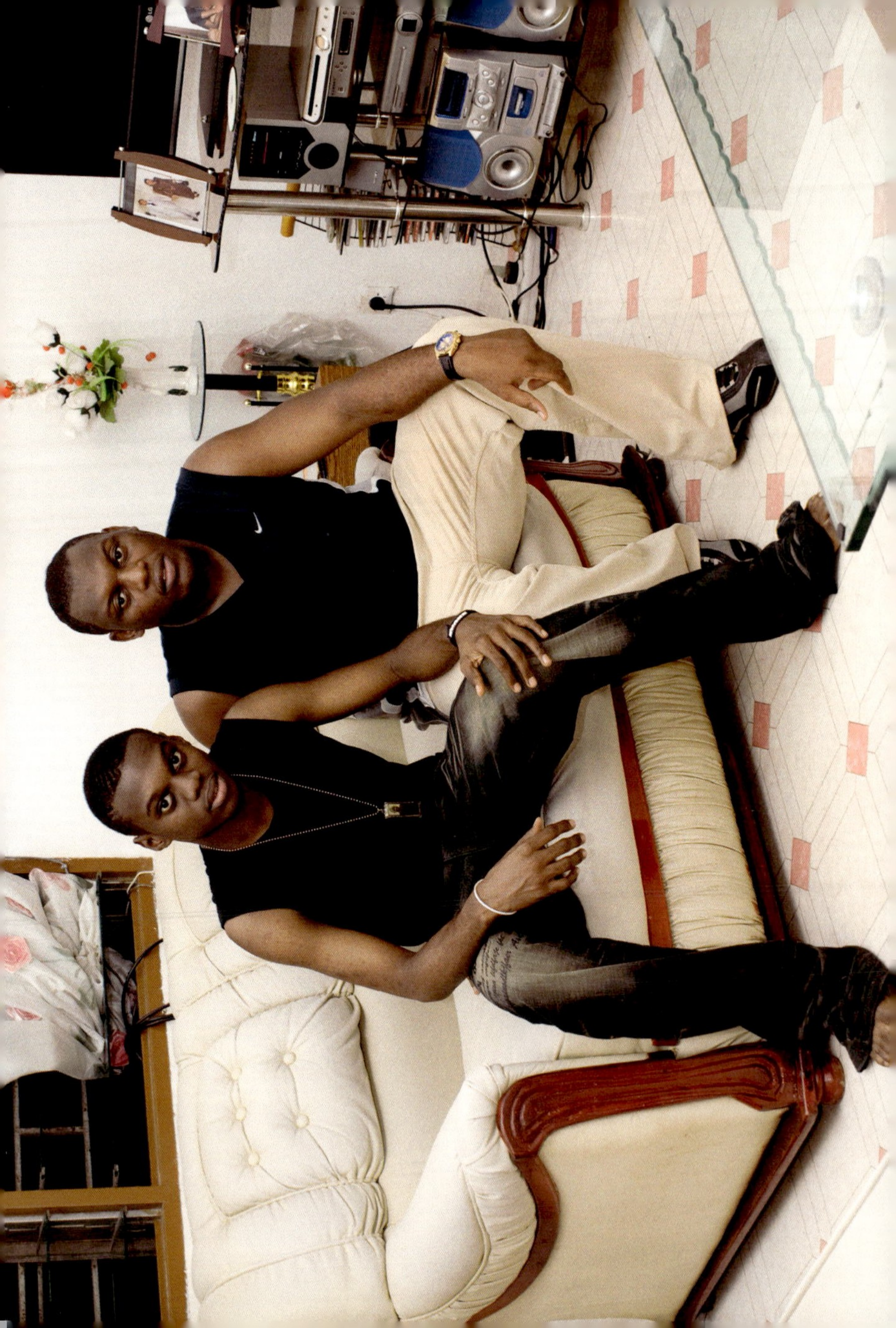

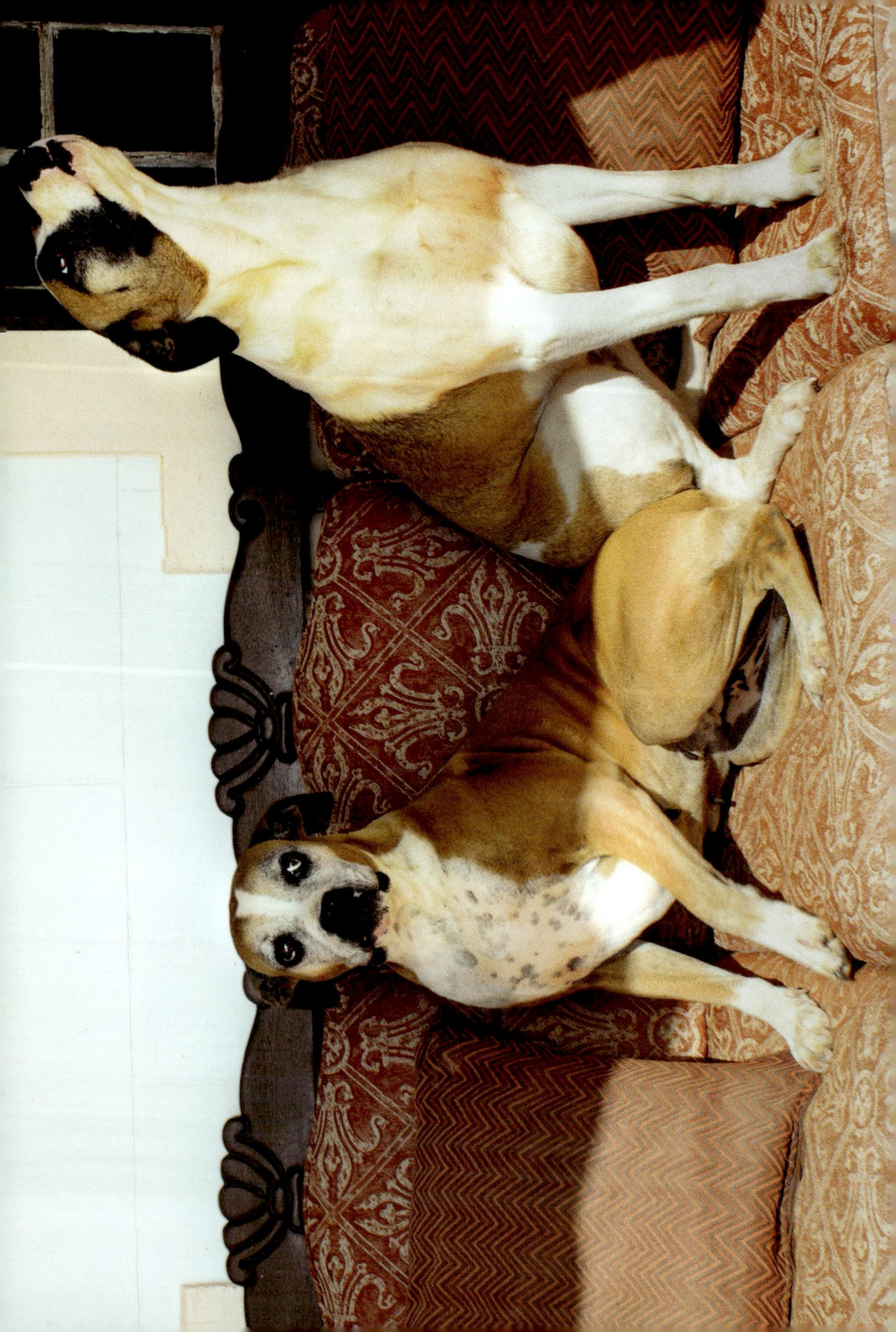

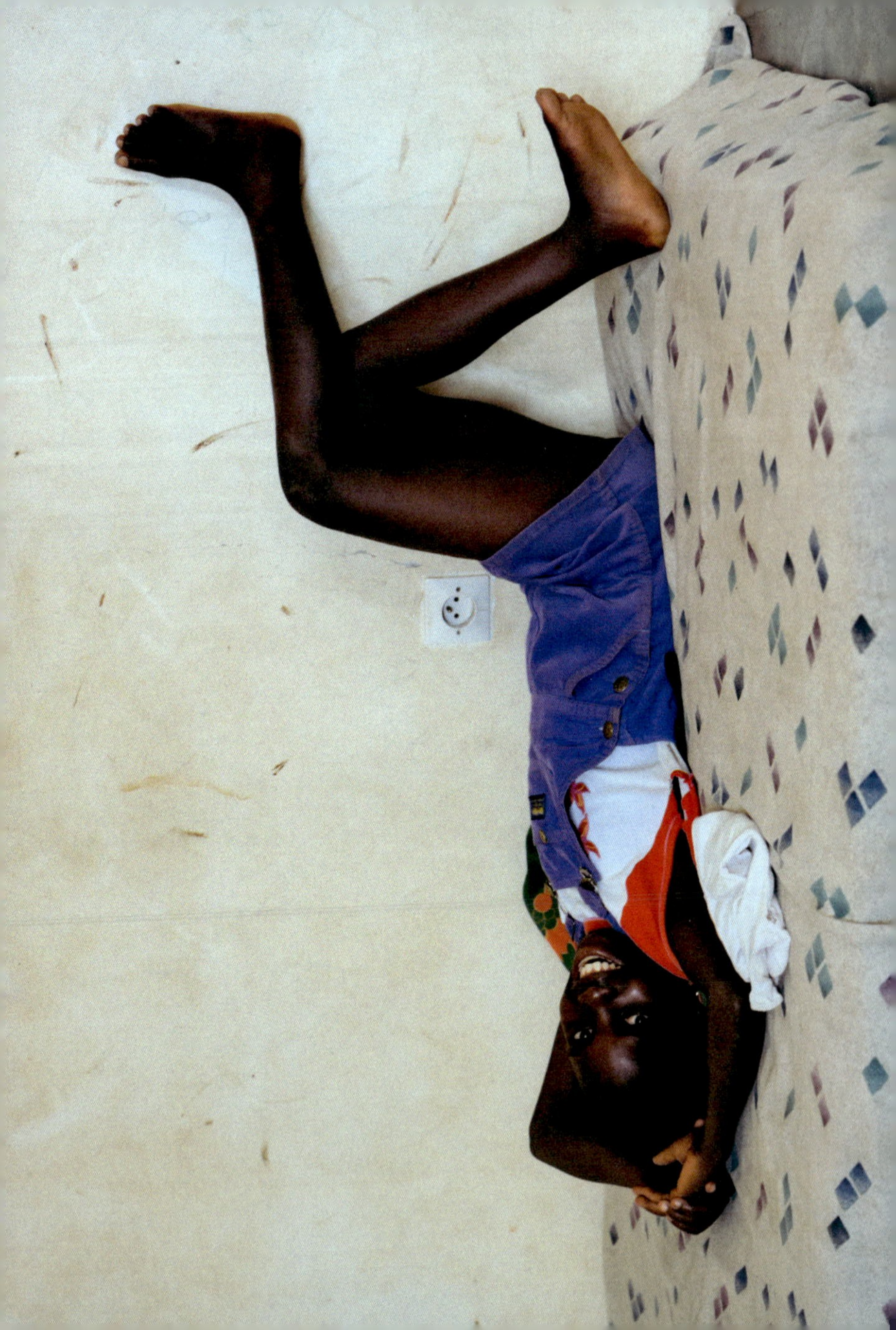

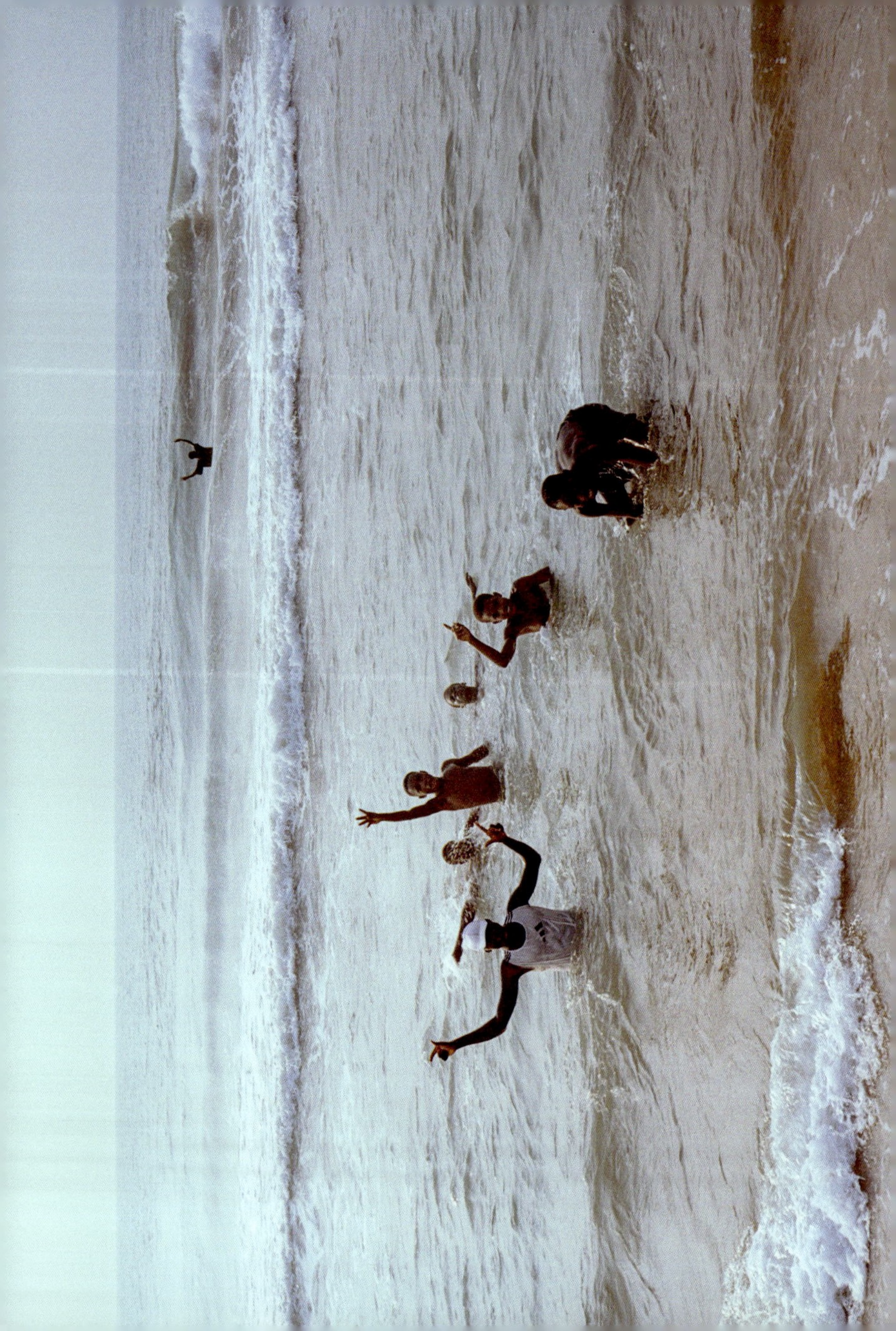

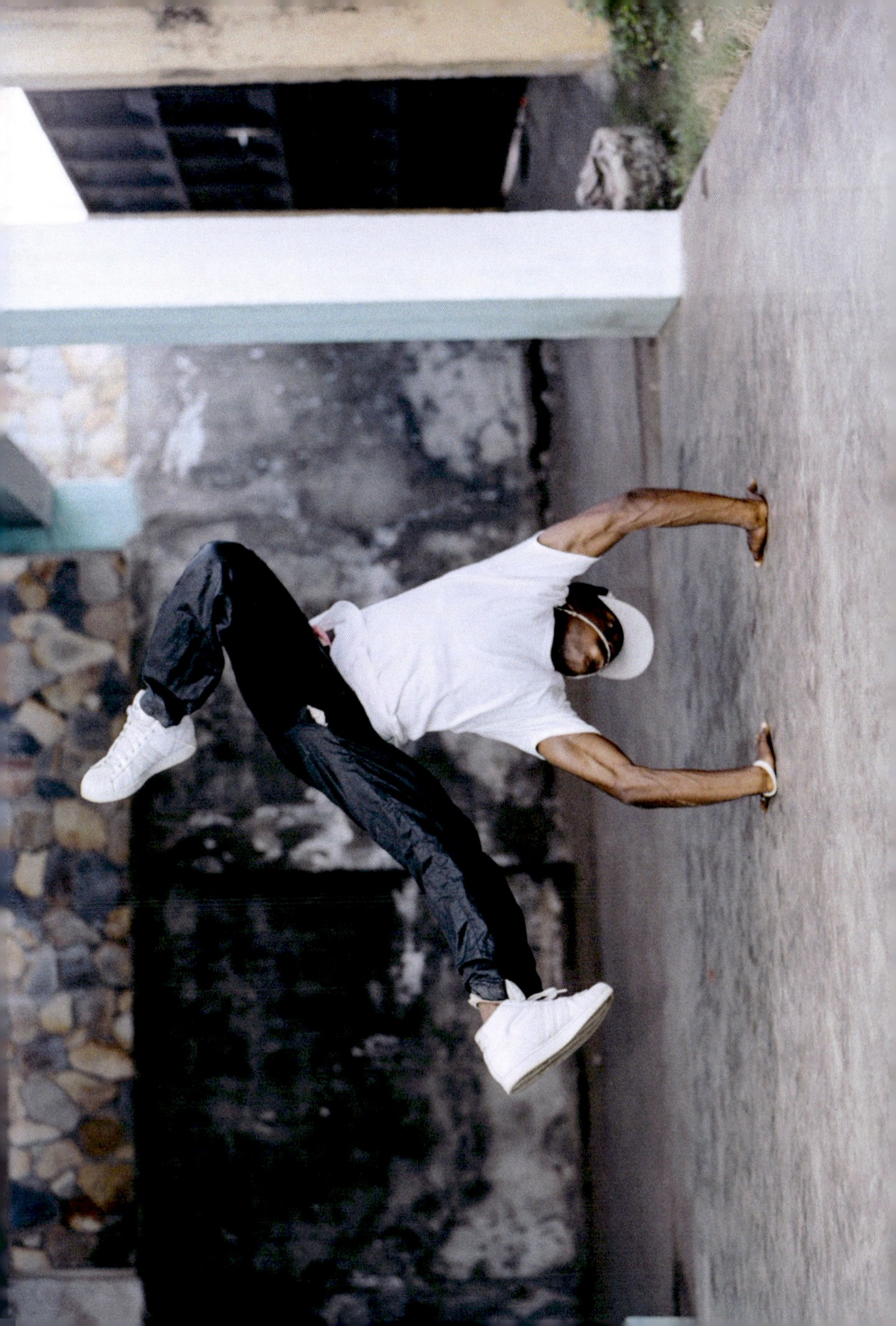

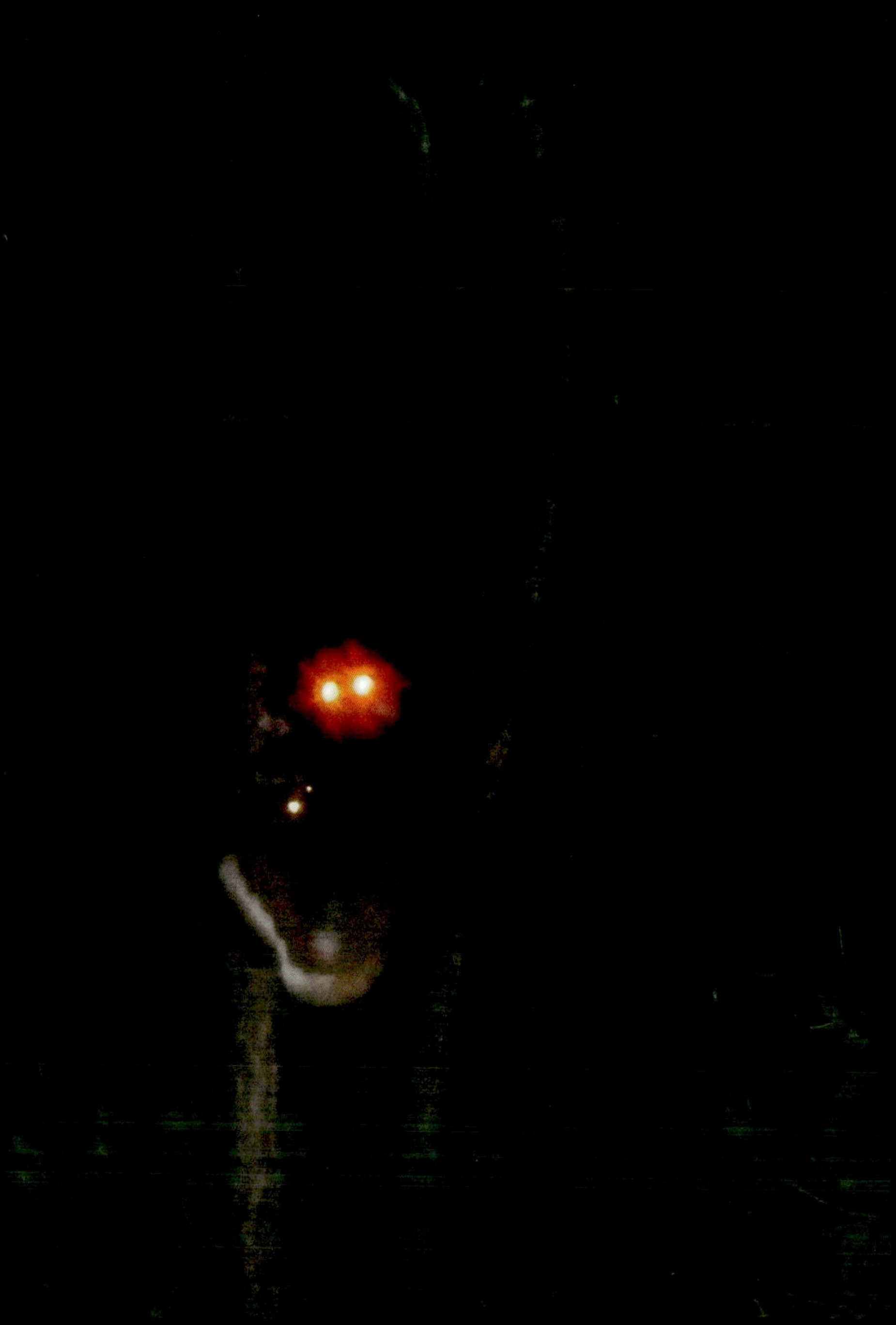

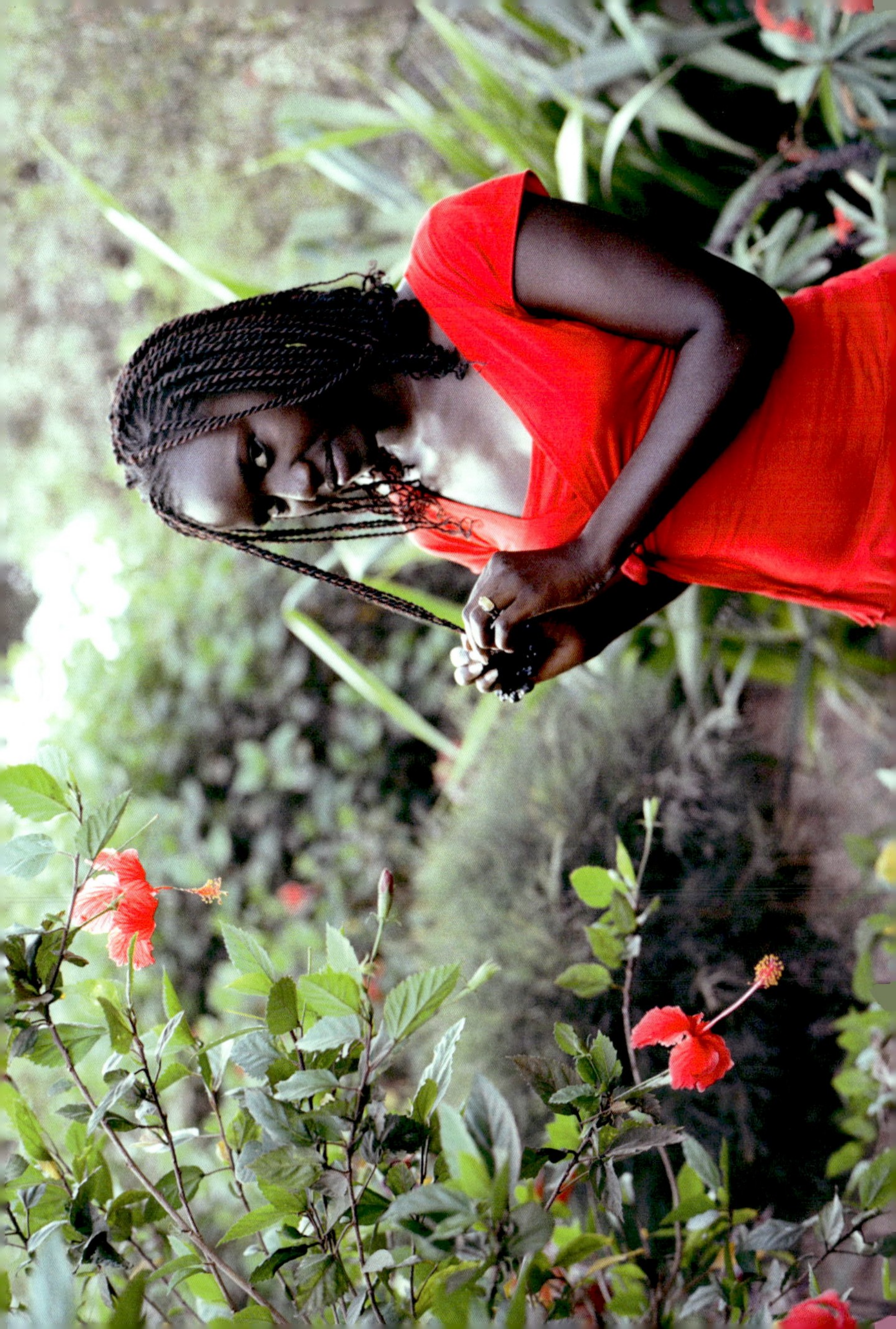

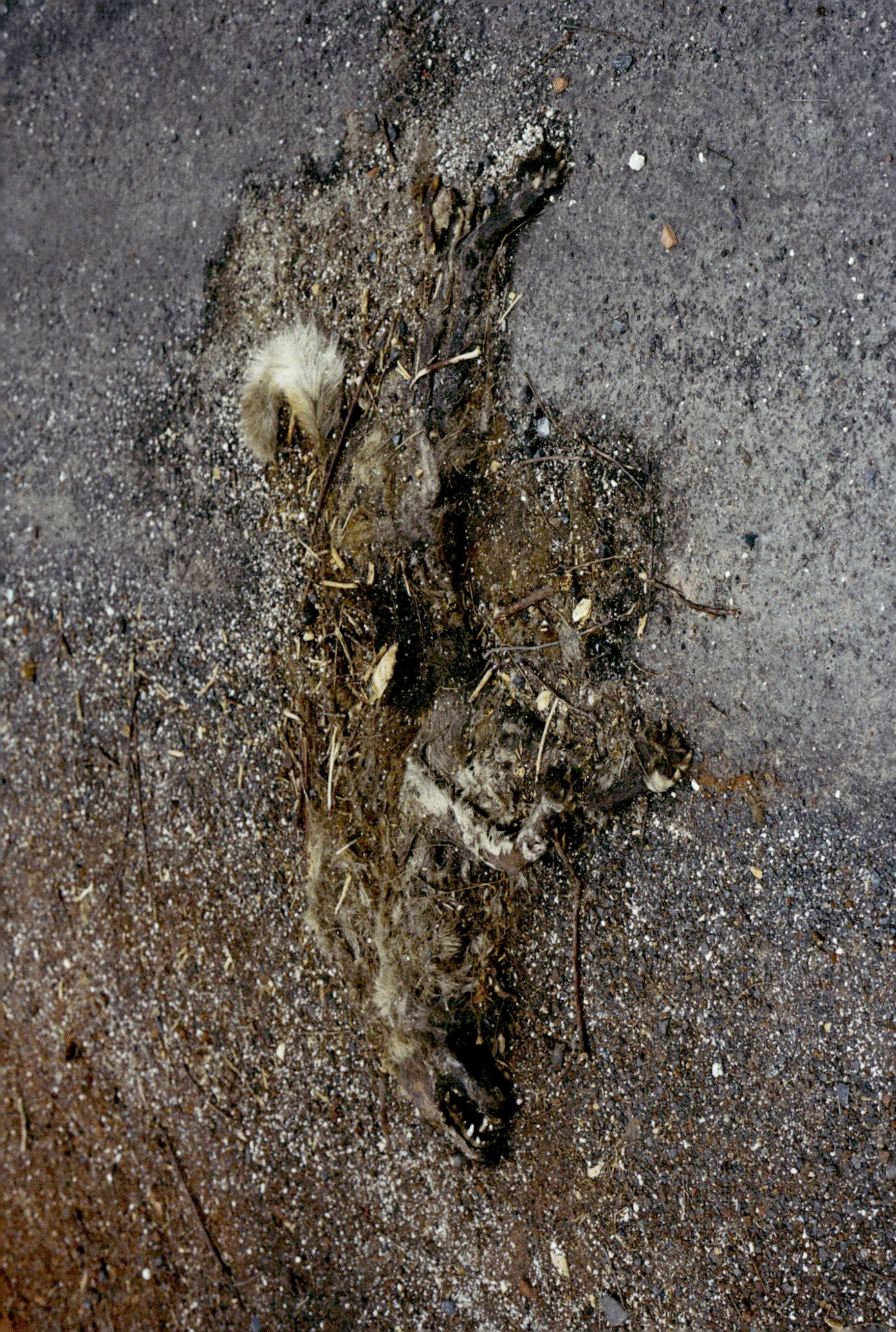

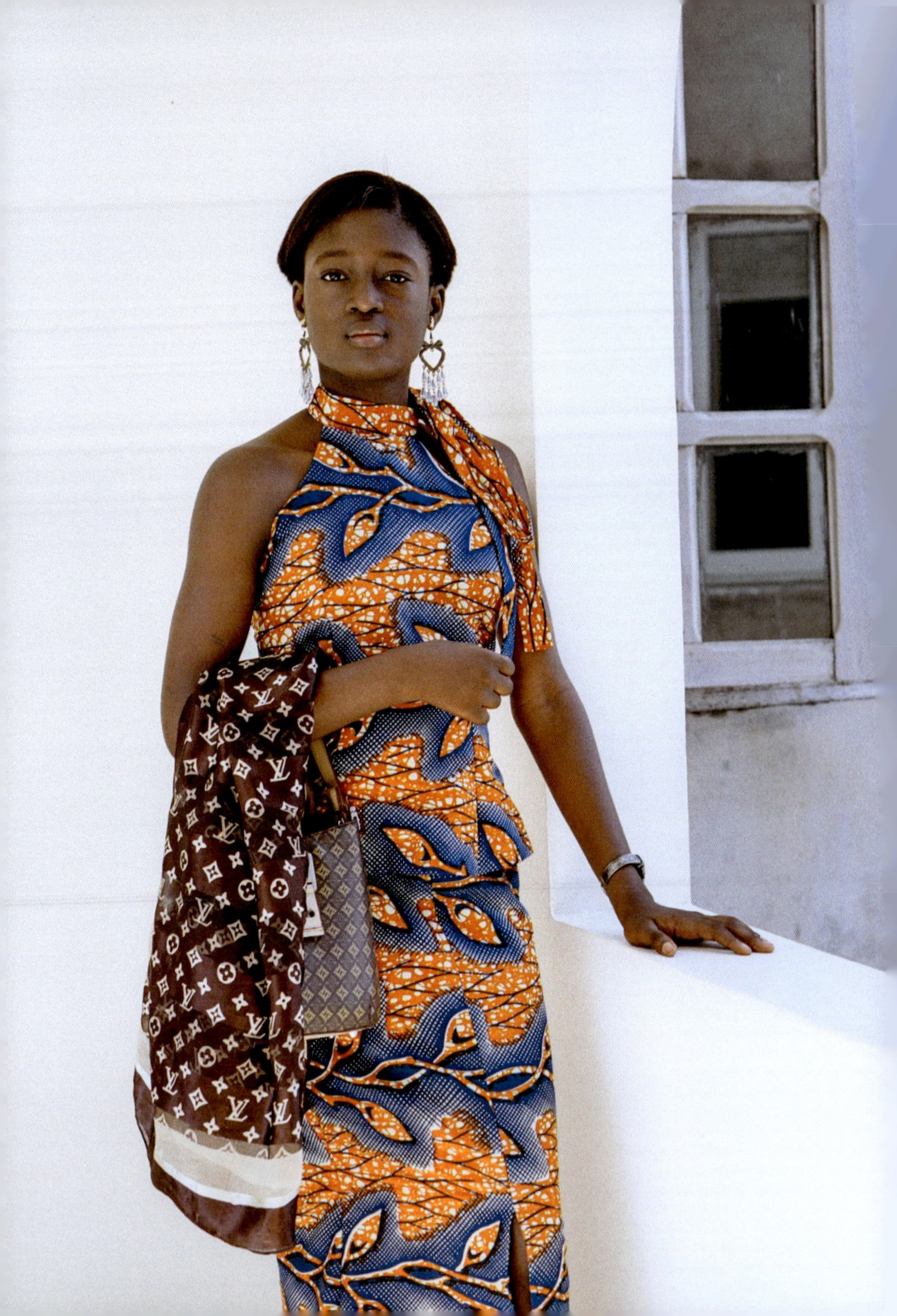

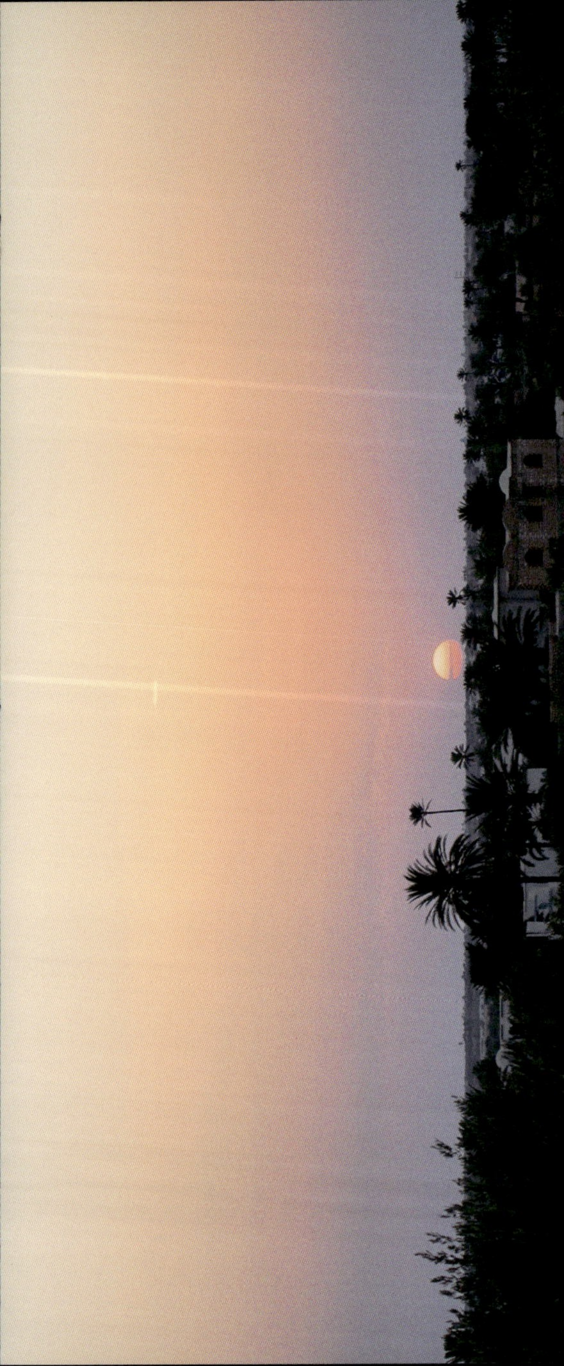

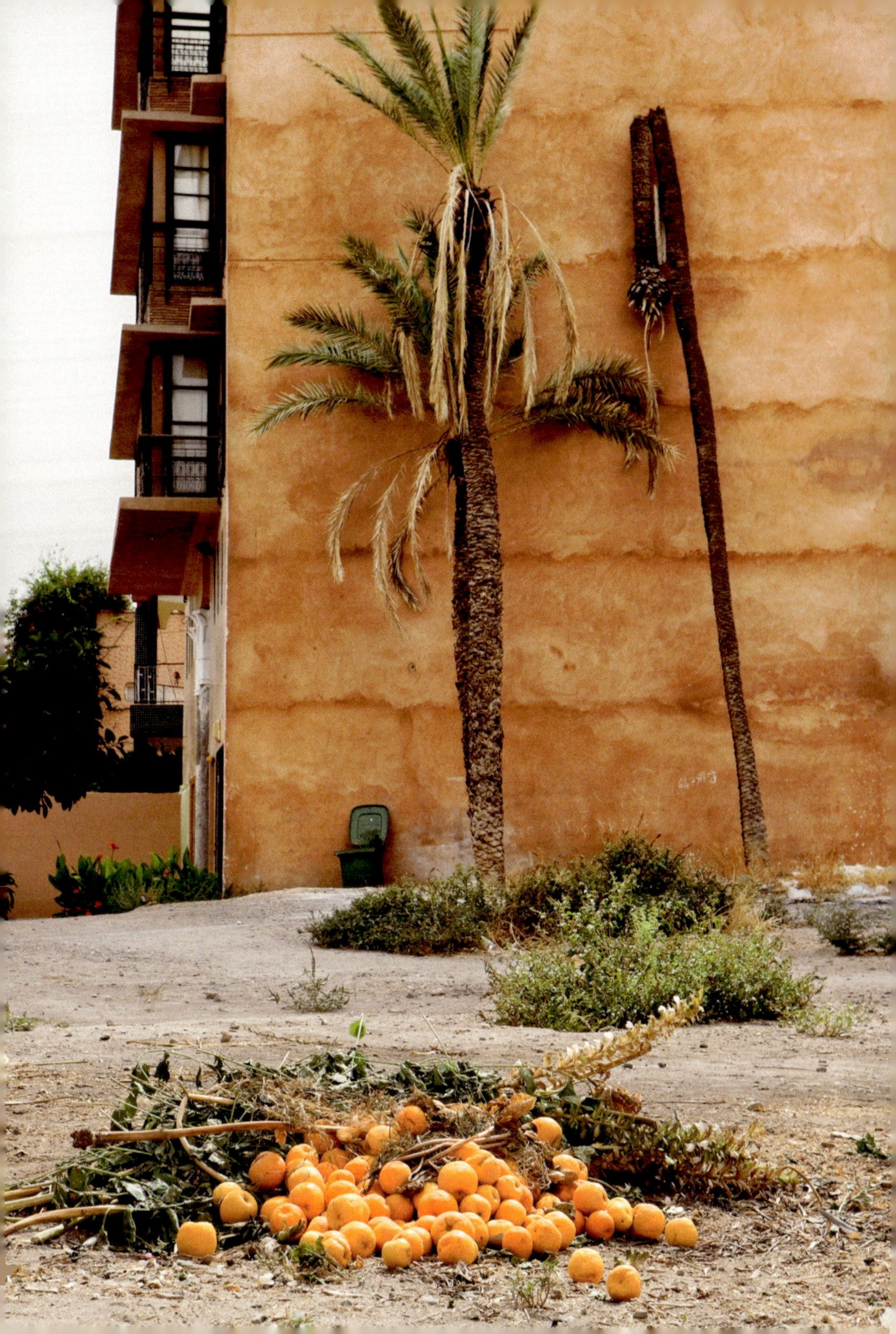

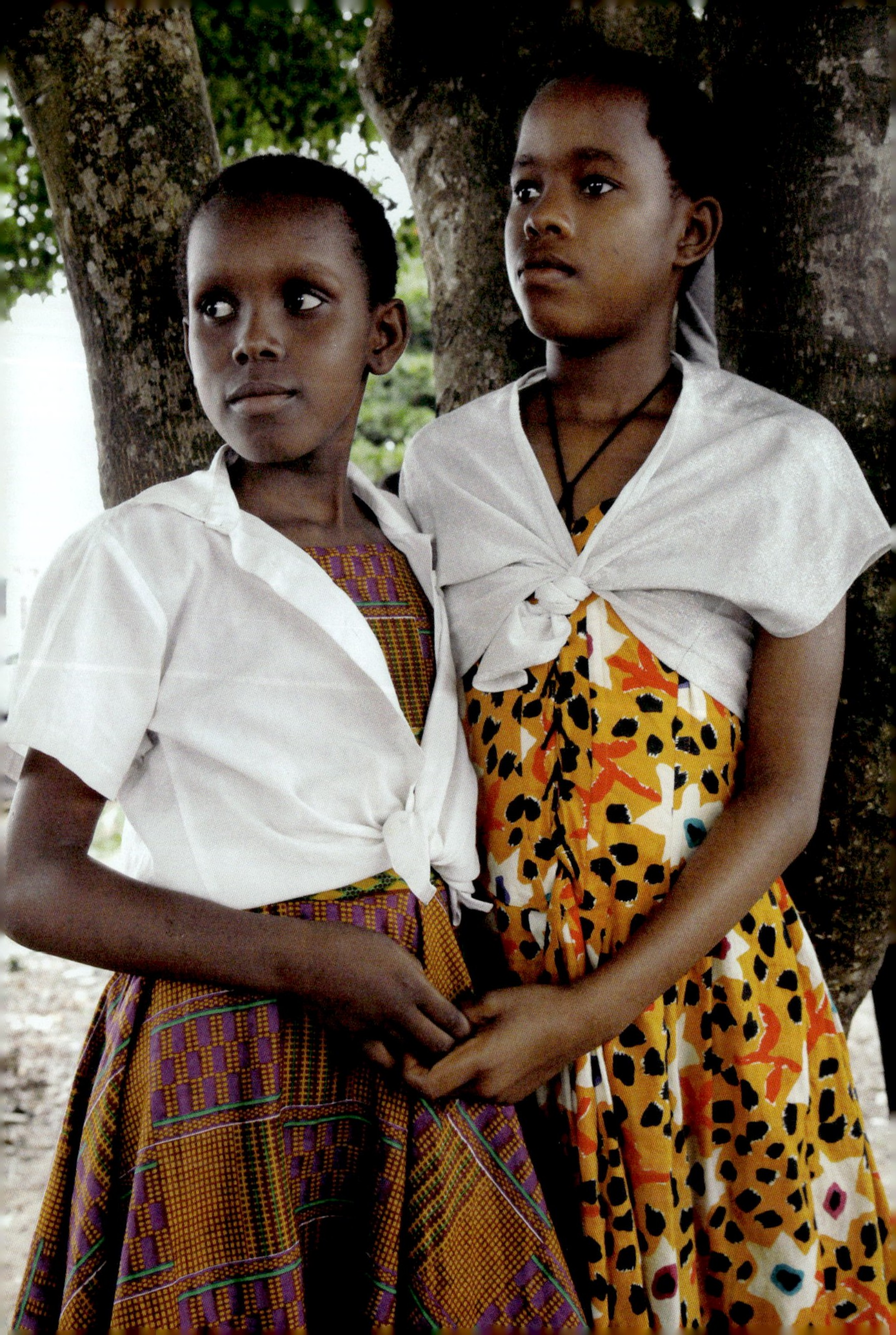

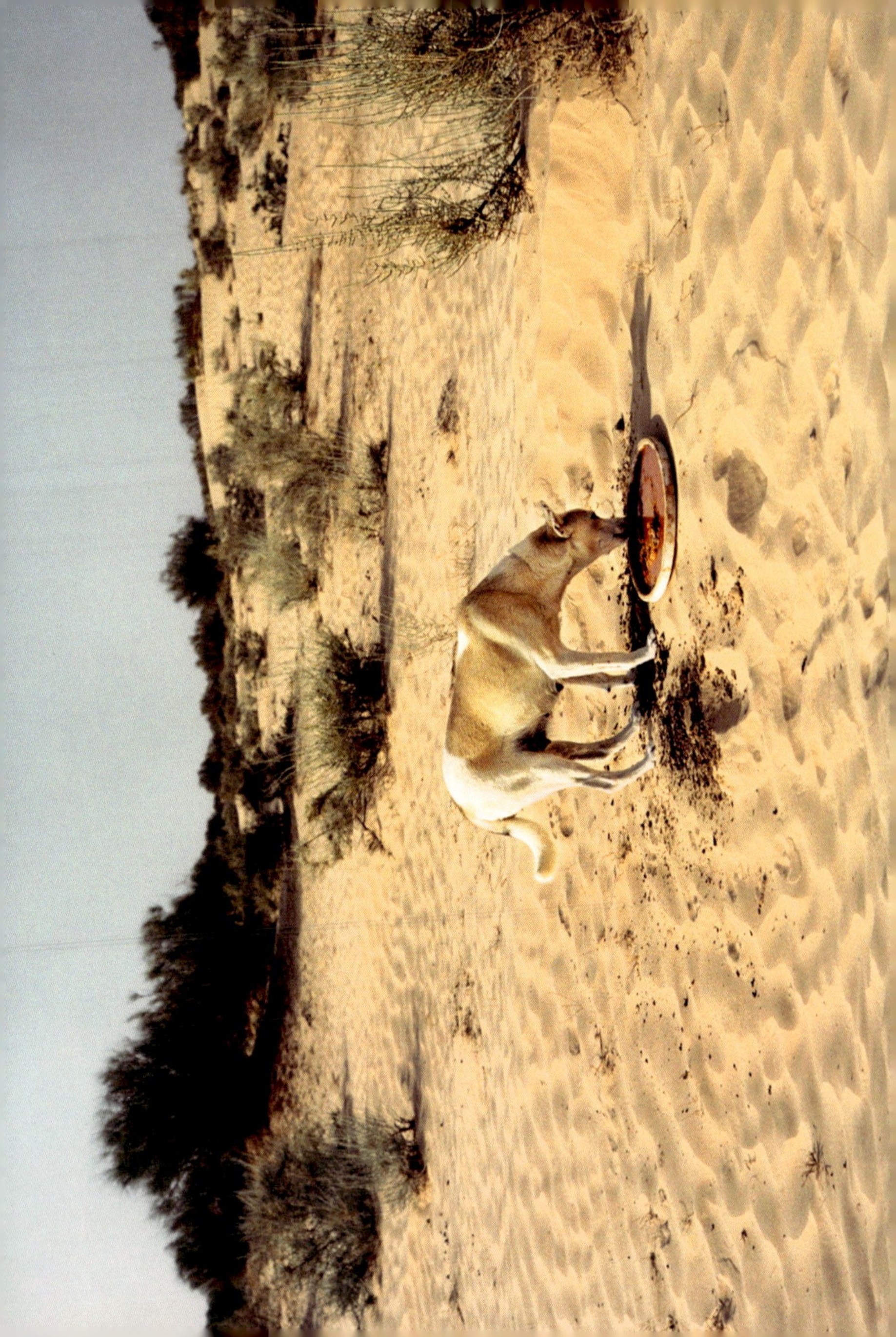

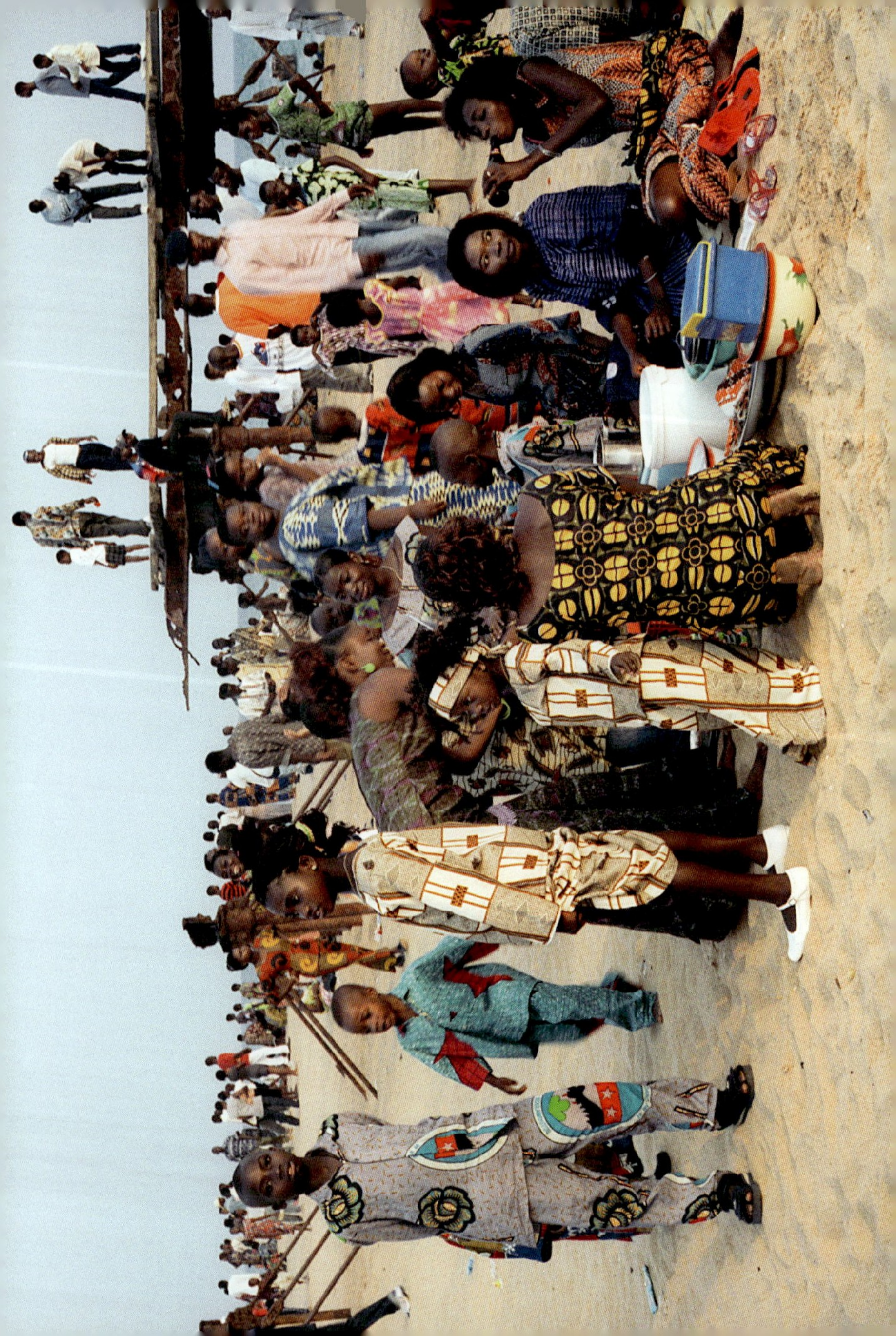

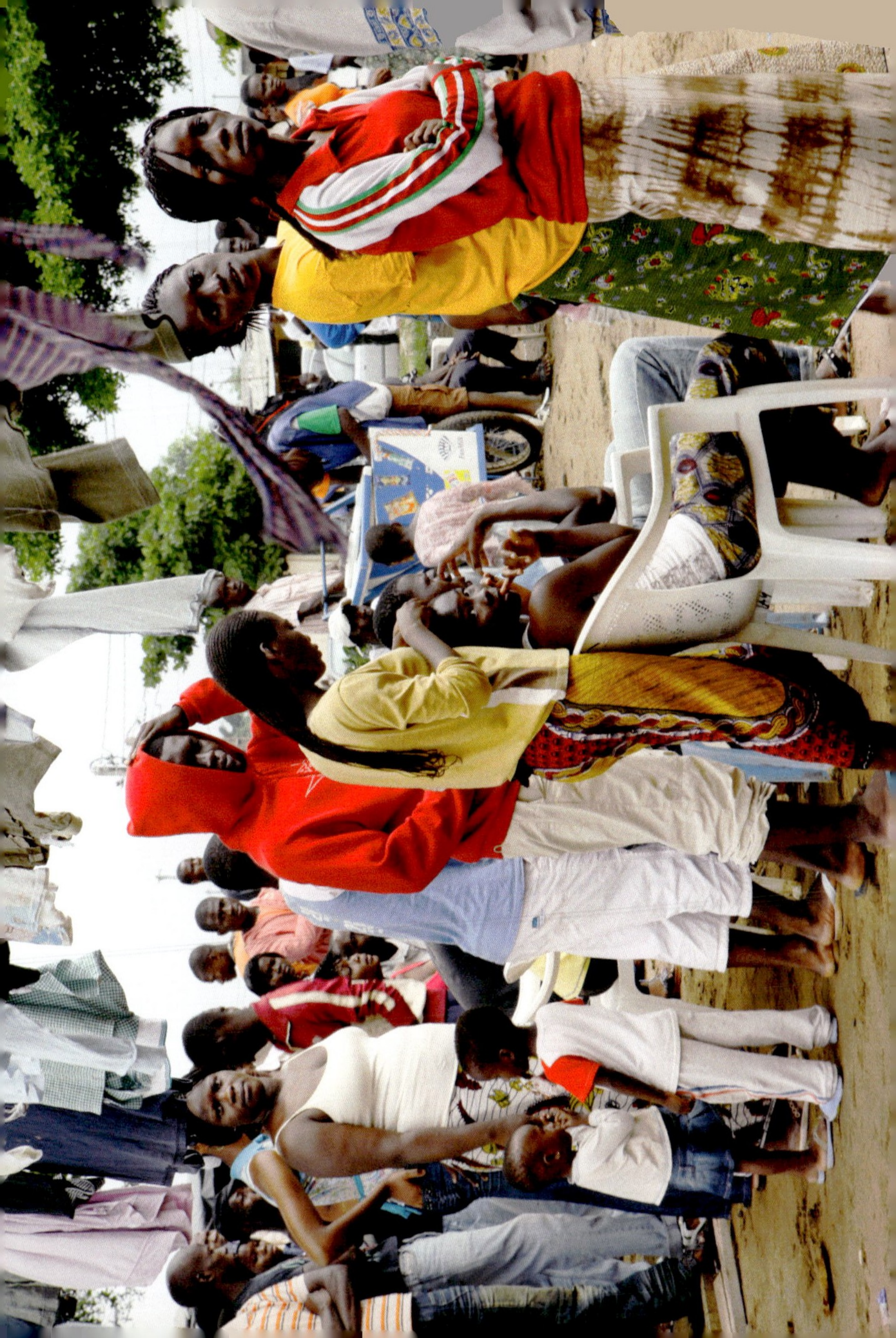

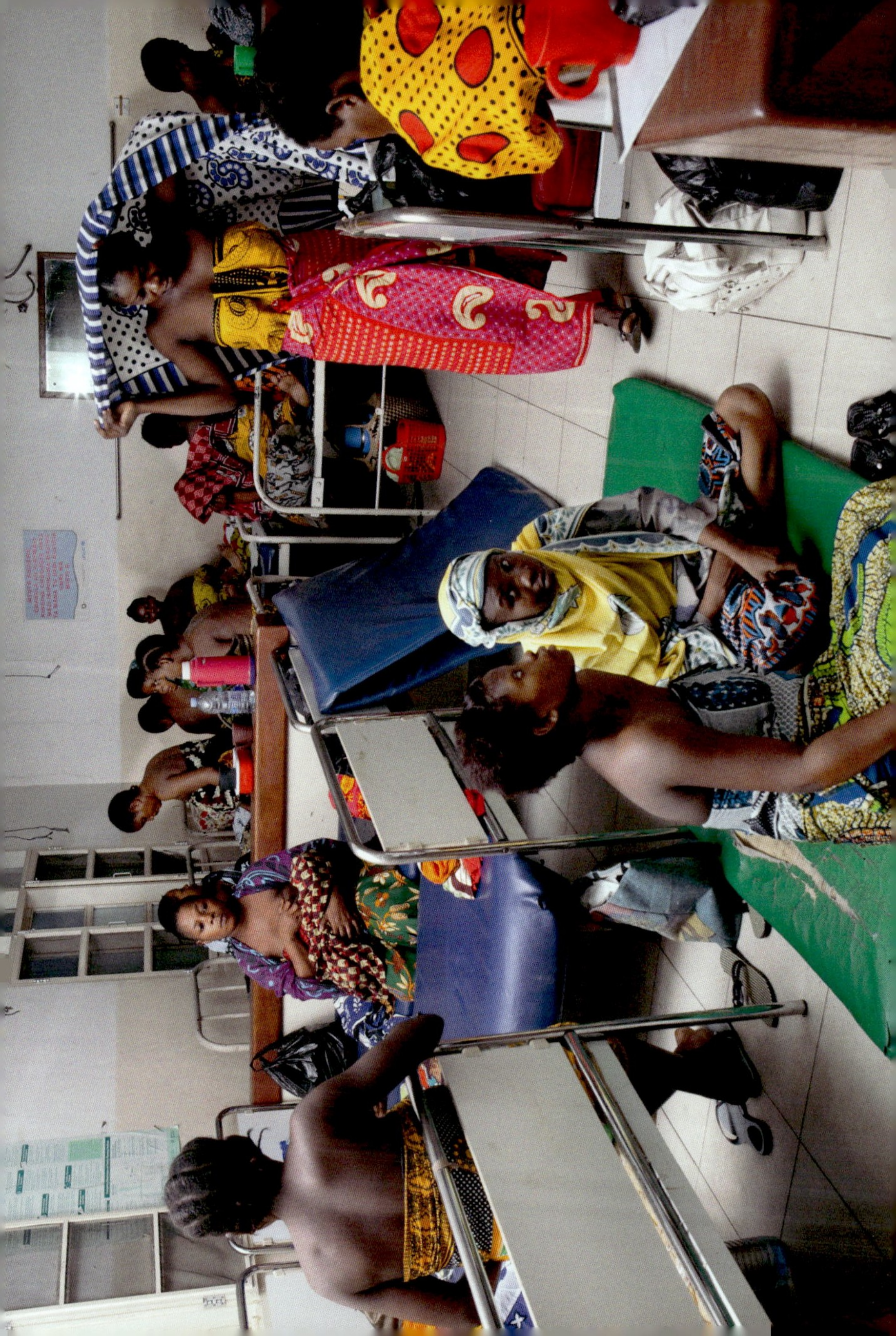

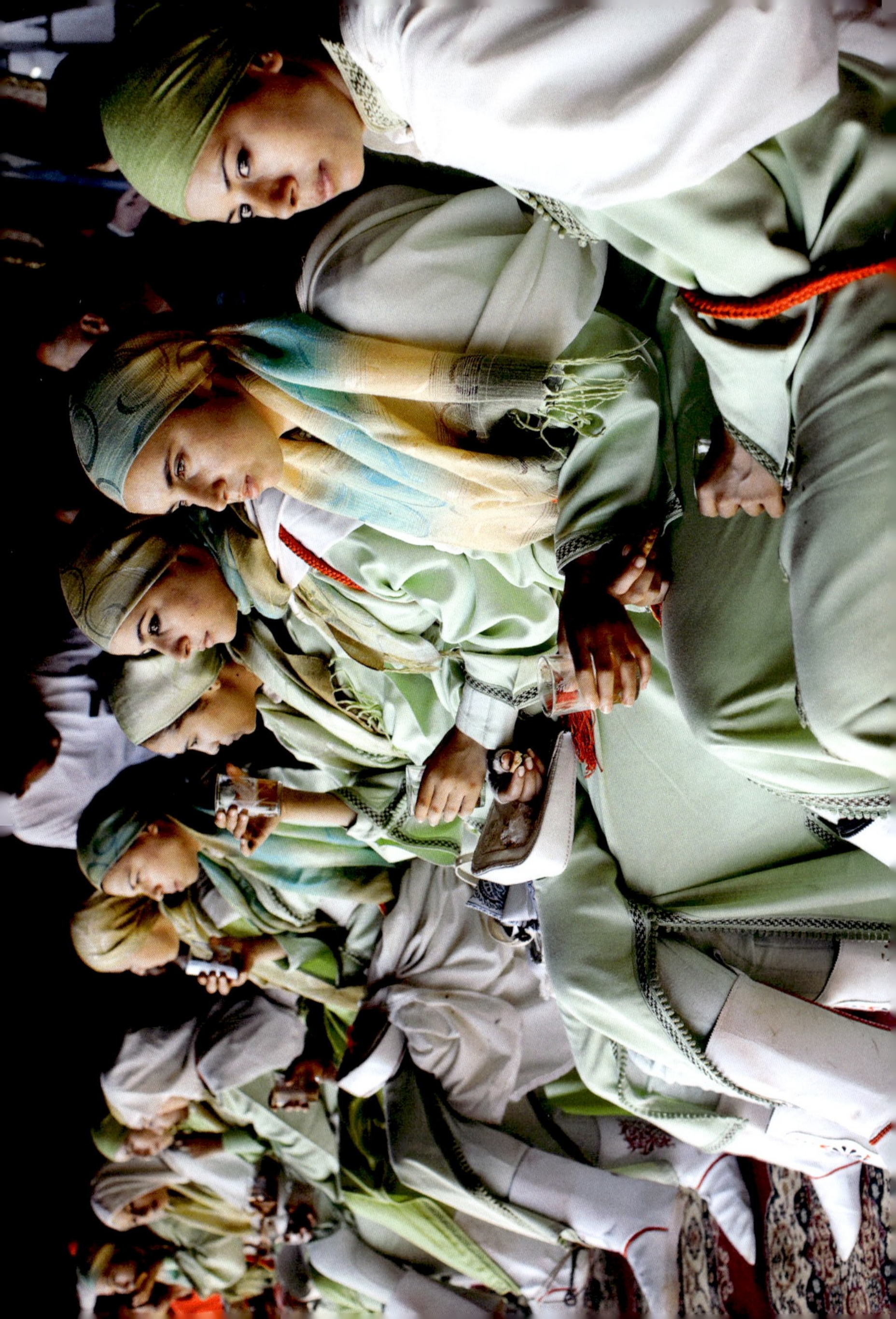

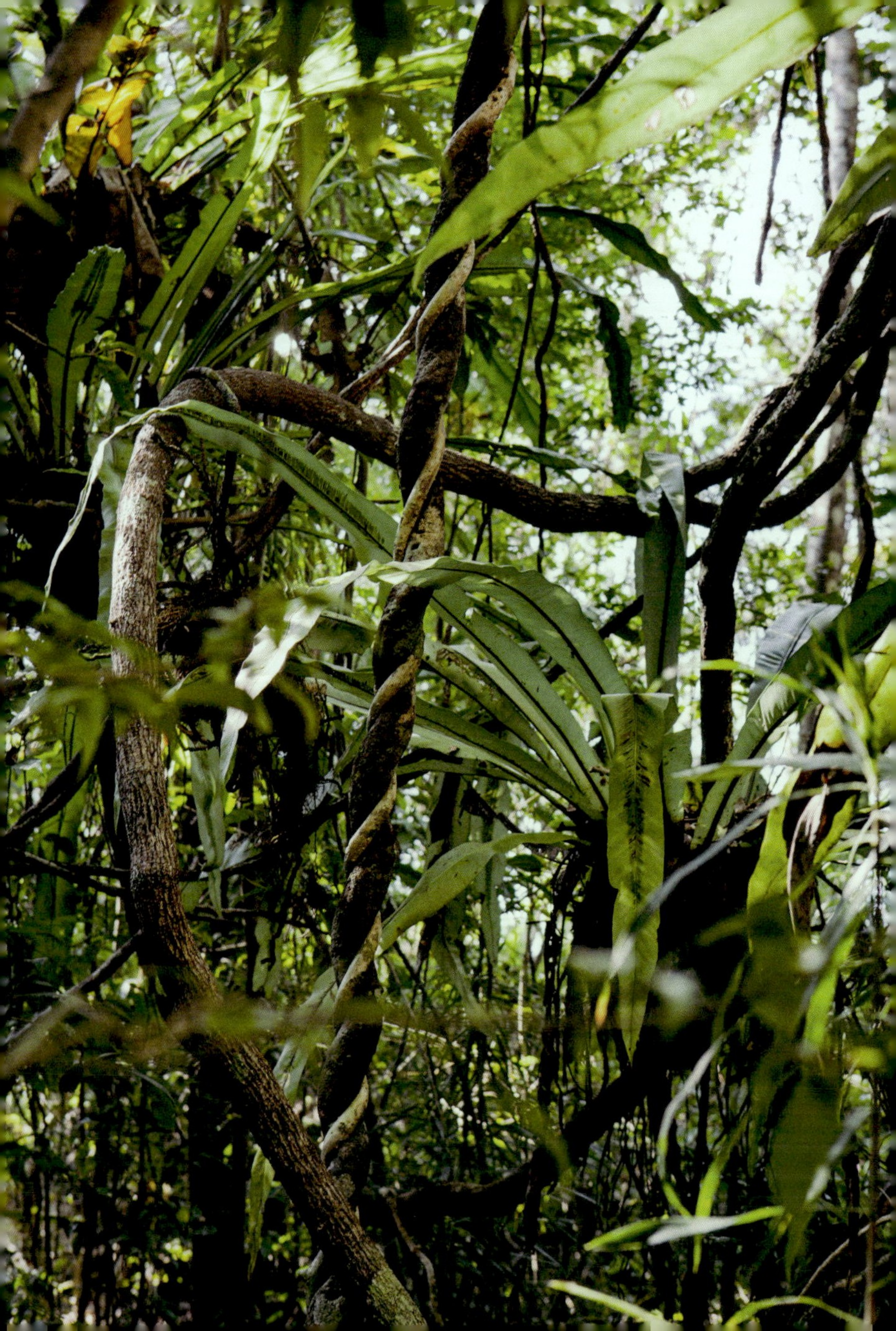

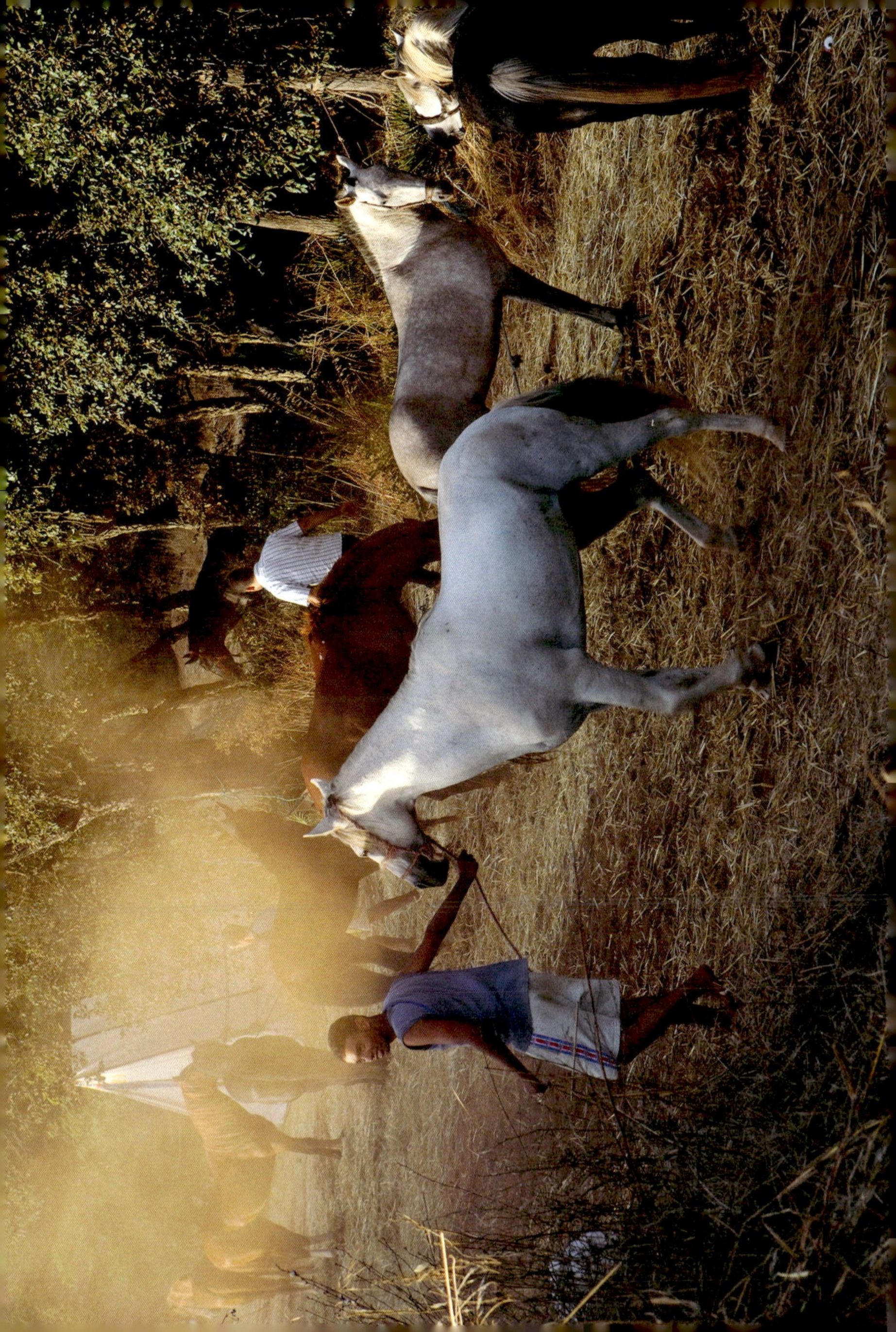

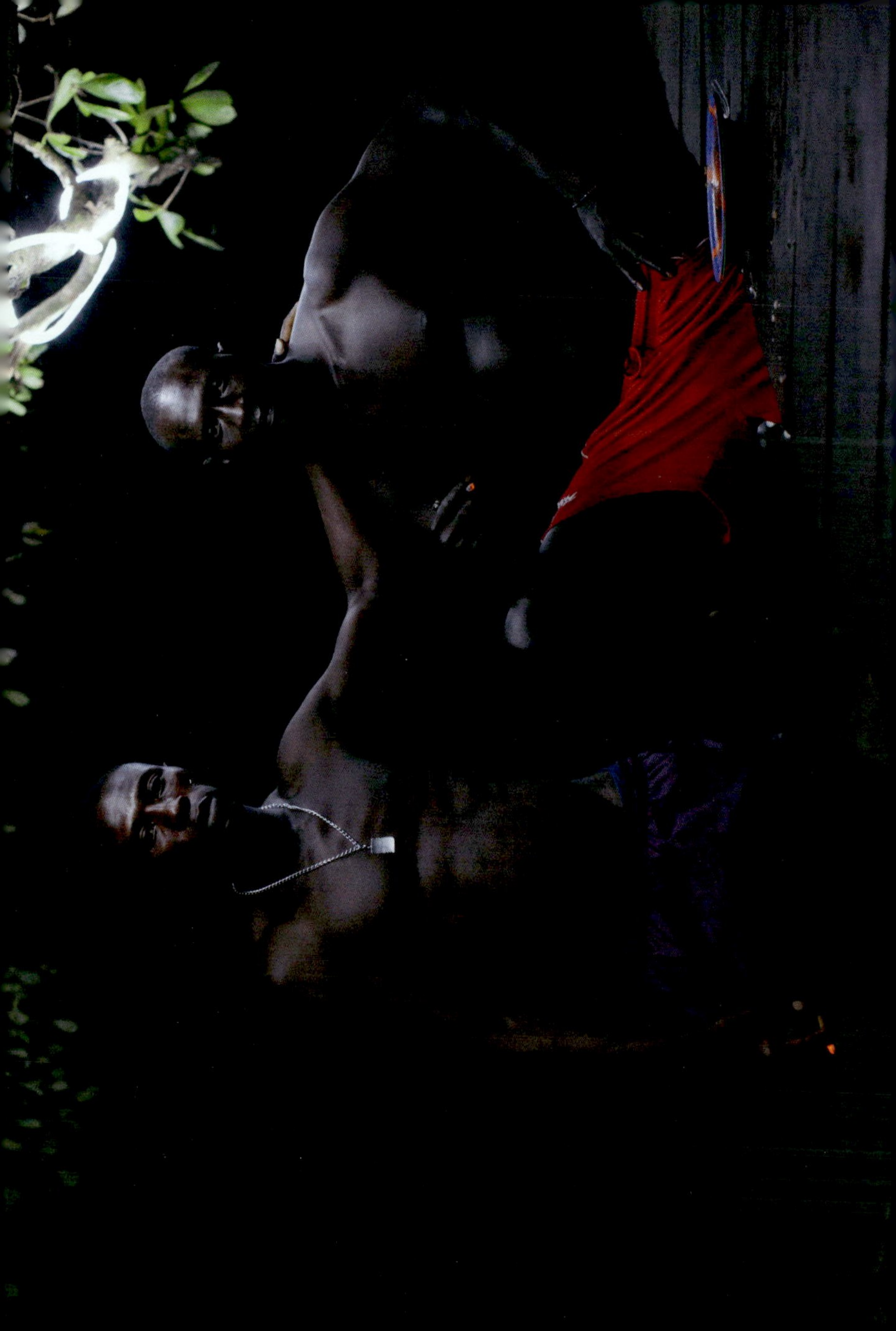

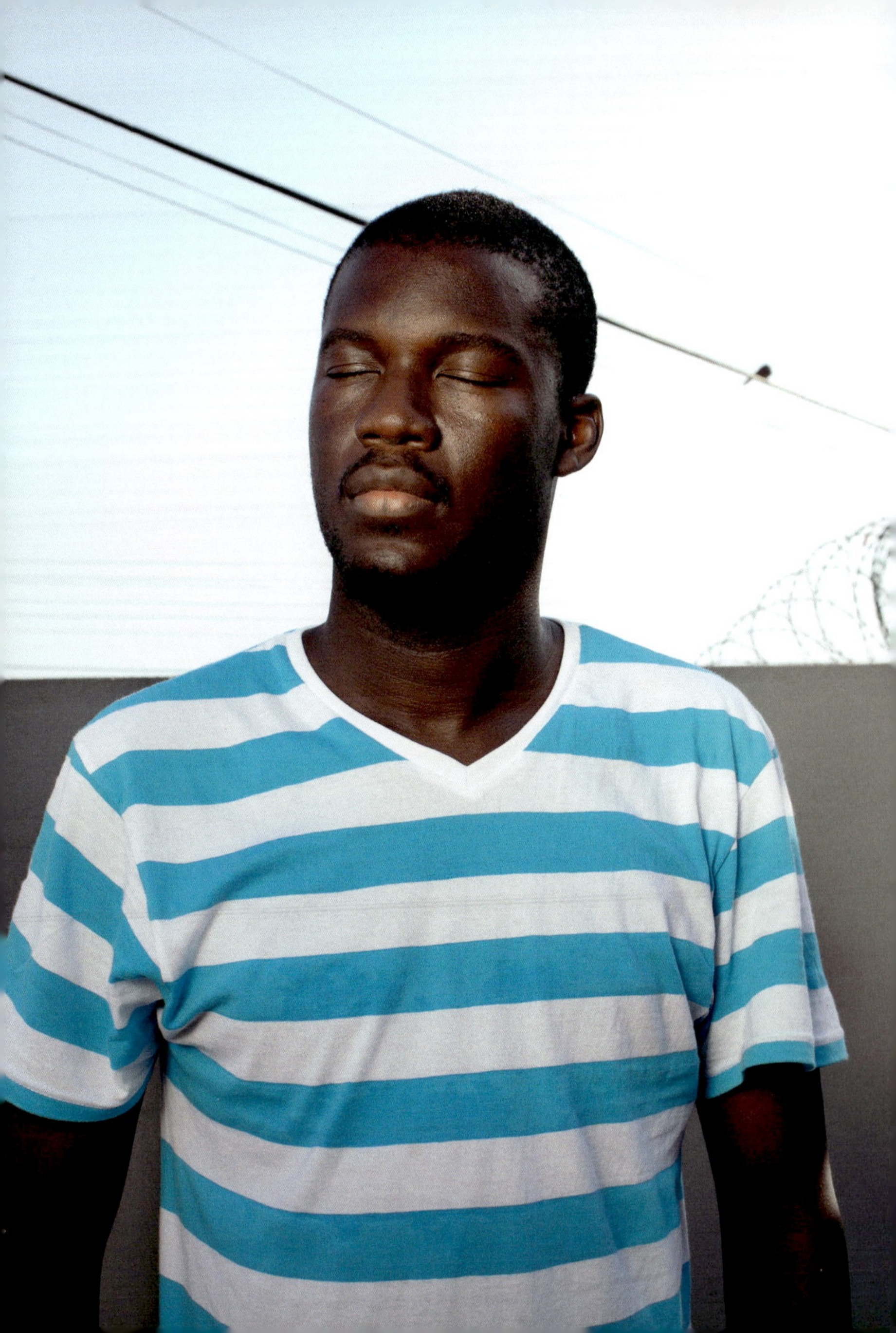

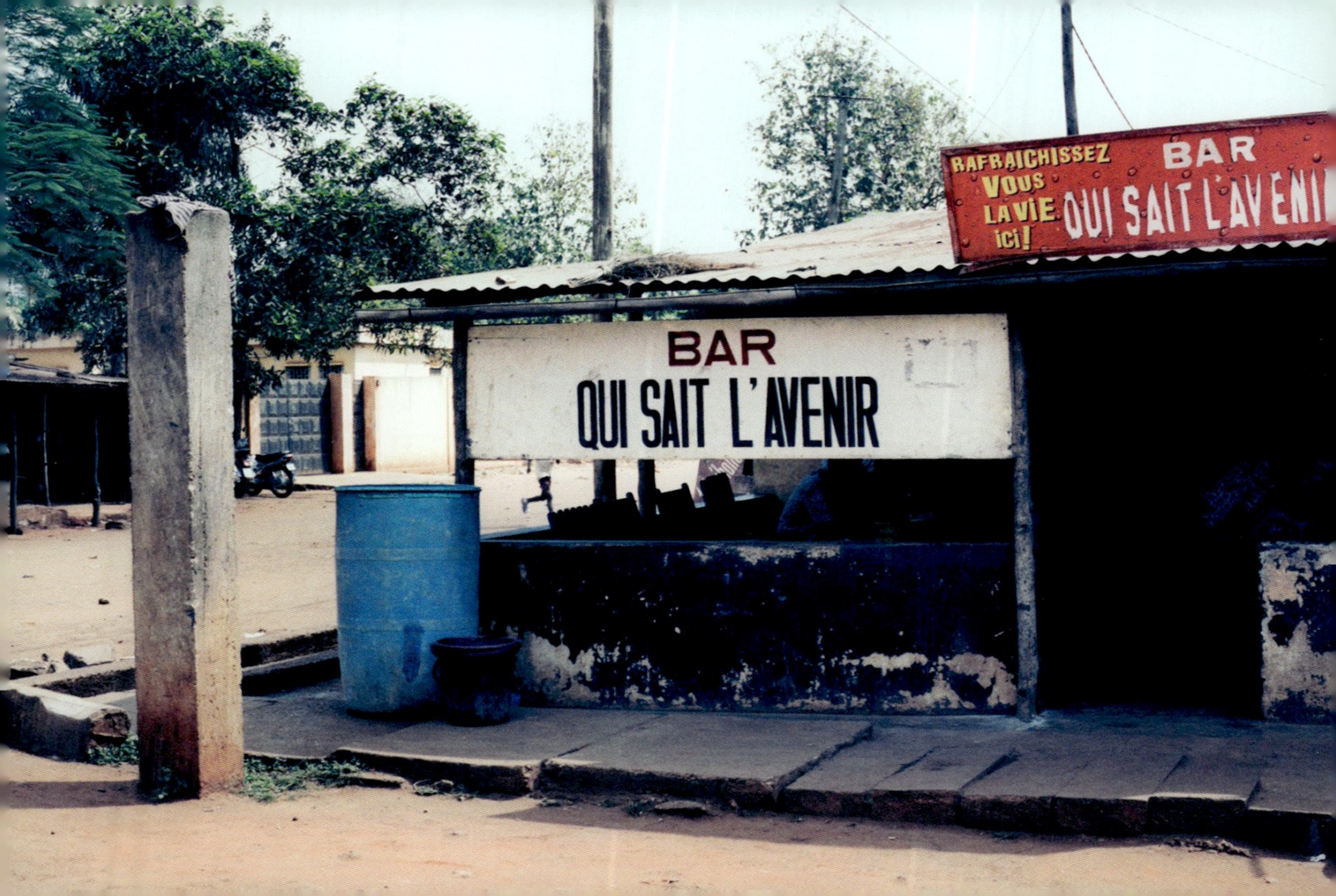
RAFRAICHISSEZ
VOUS
LA VIE
ICI!
BAR
QUI SAIT L'AVENI
BAR
QUI SAIT L'AVENIR

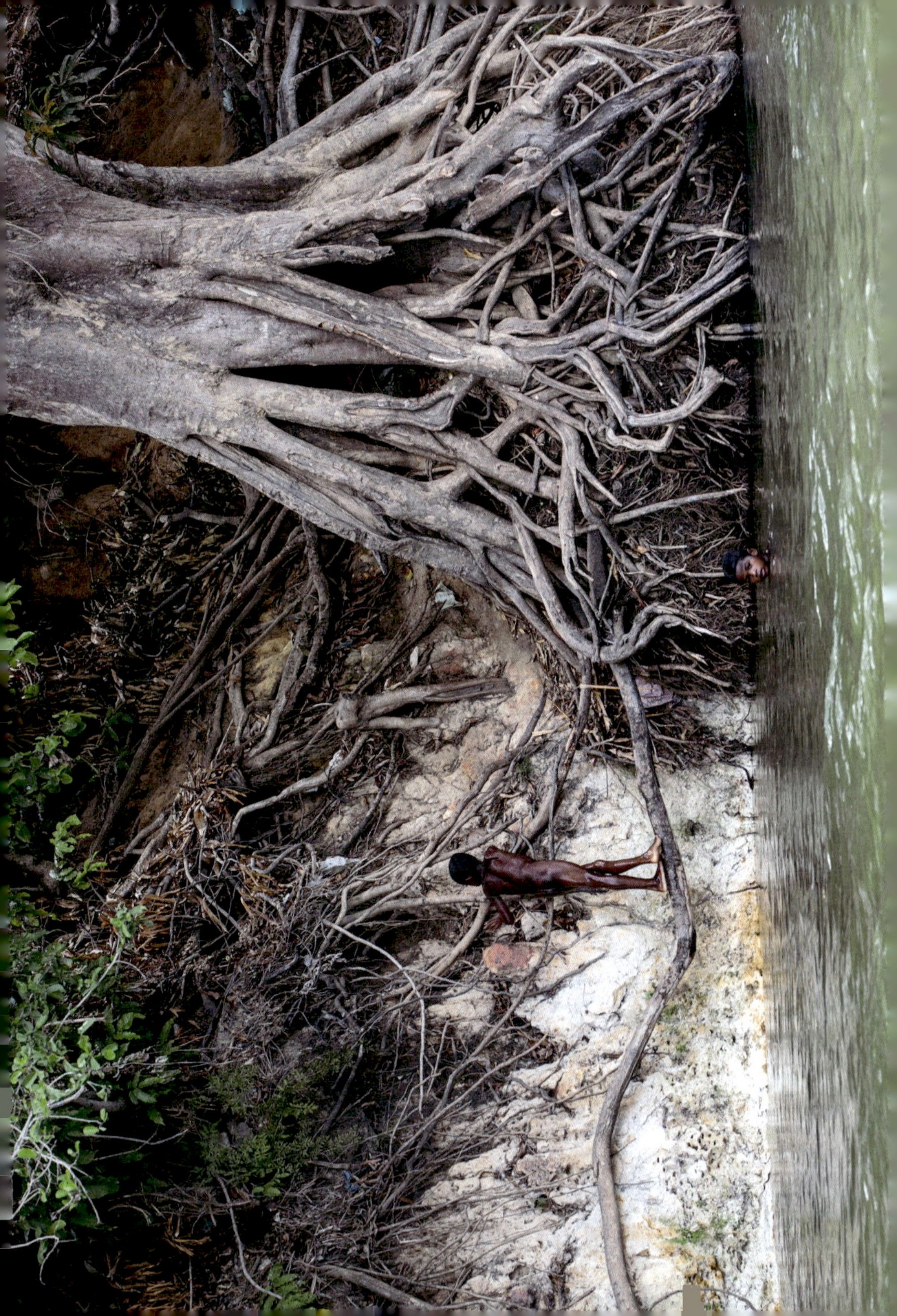

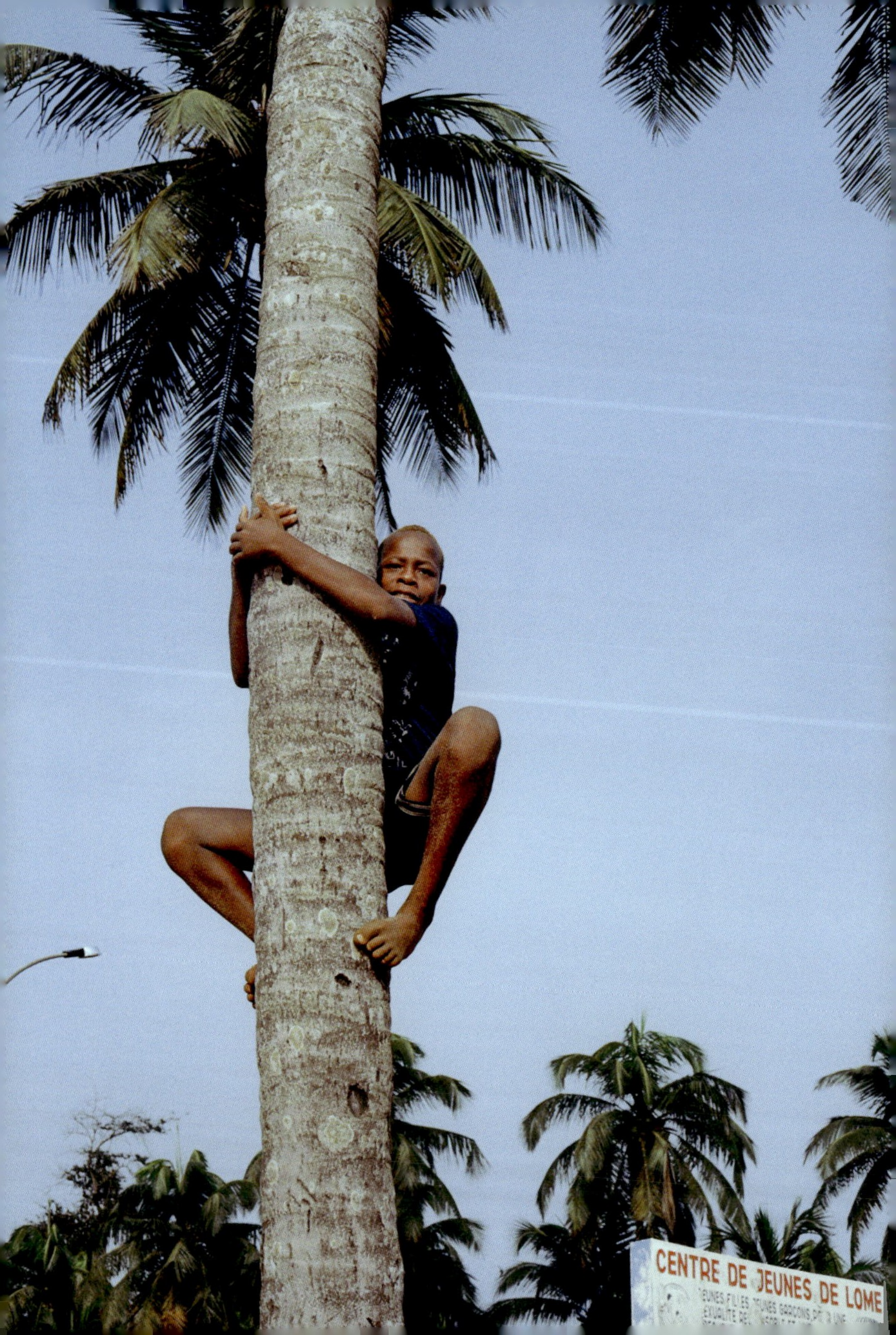
CENTRE DE JEUNES DE LOME

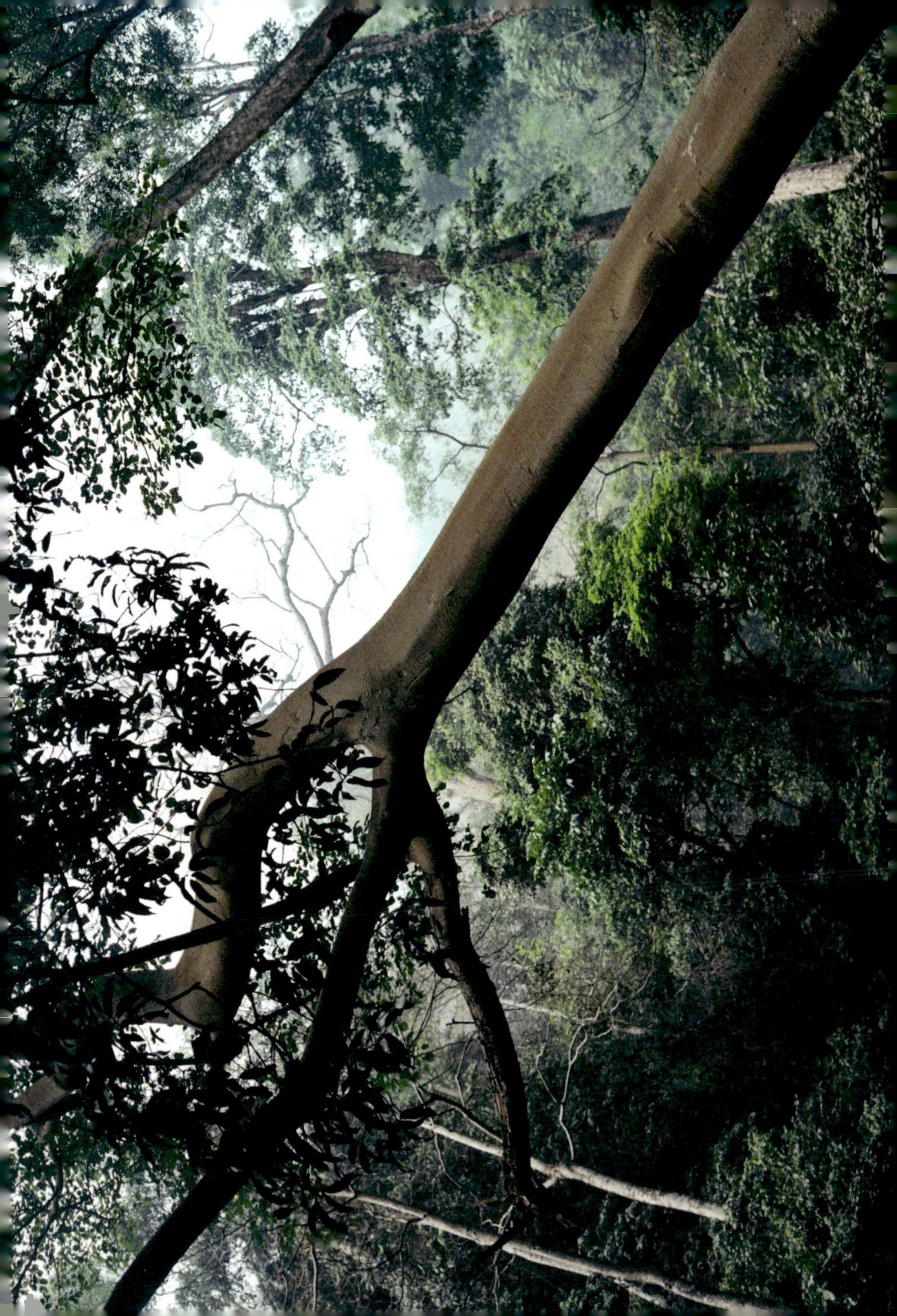

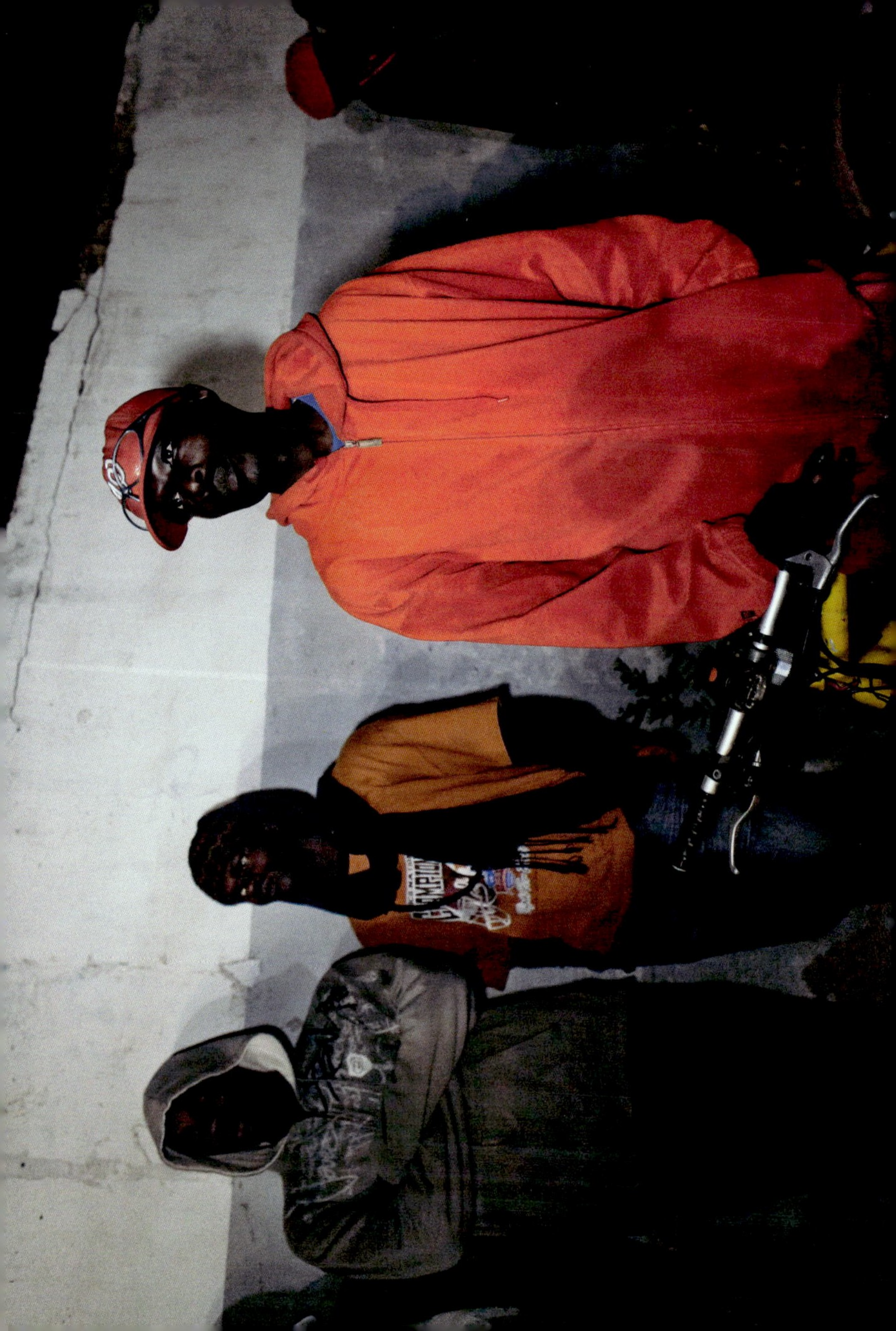

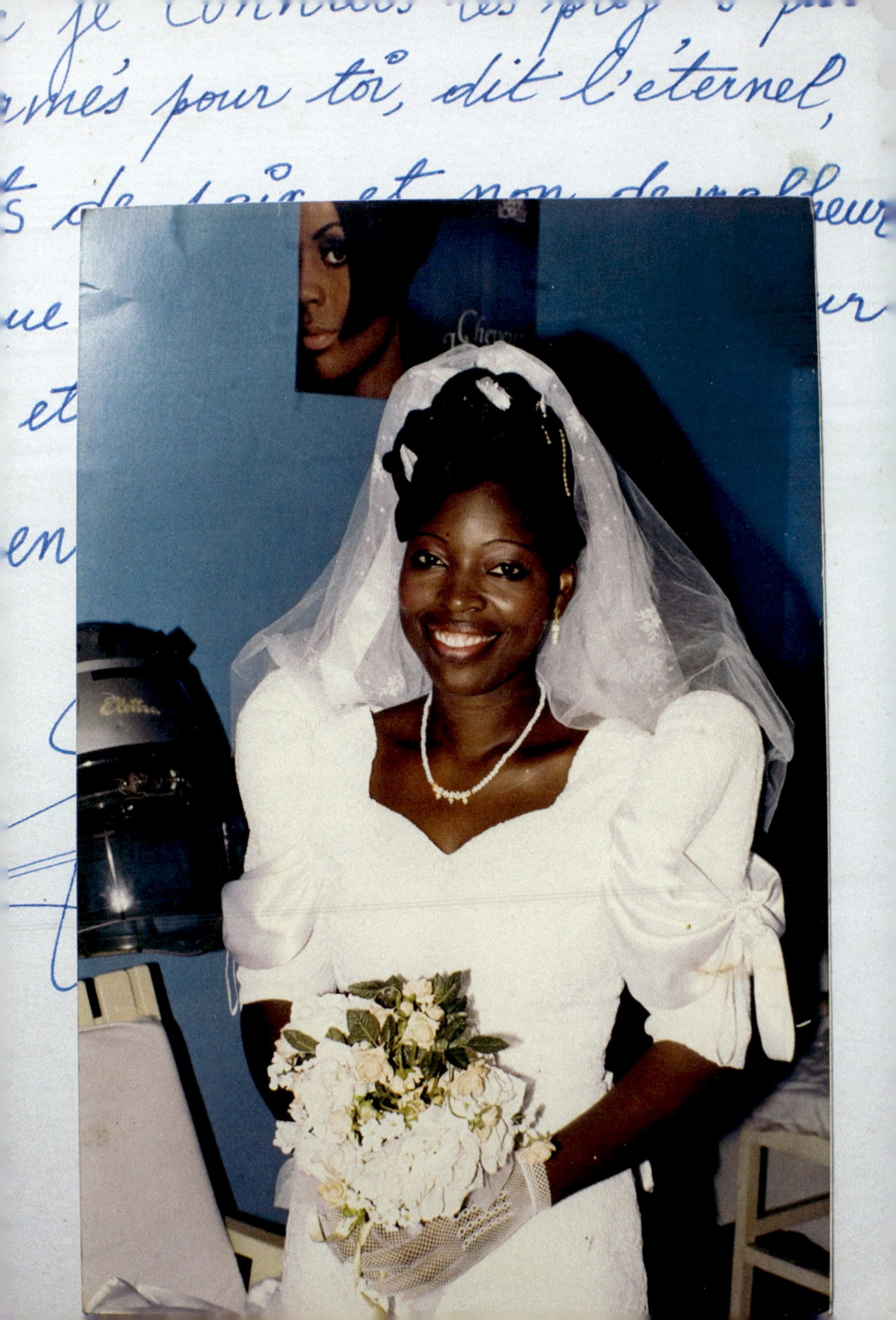
més pour toi, dit l'éternel,

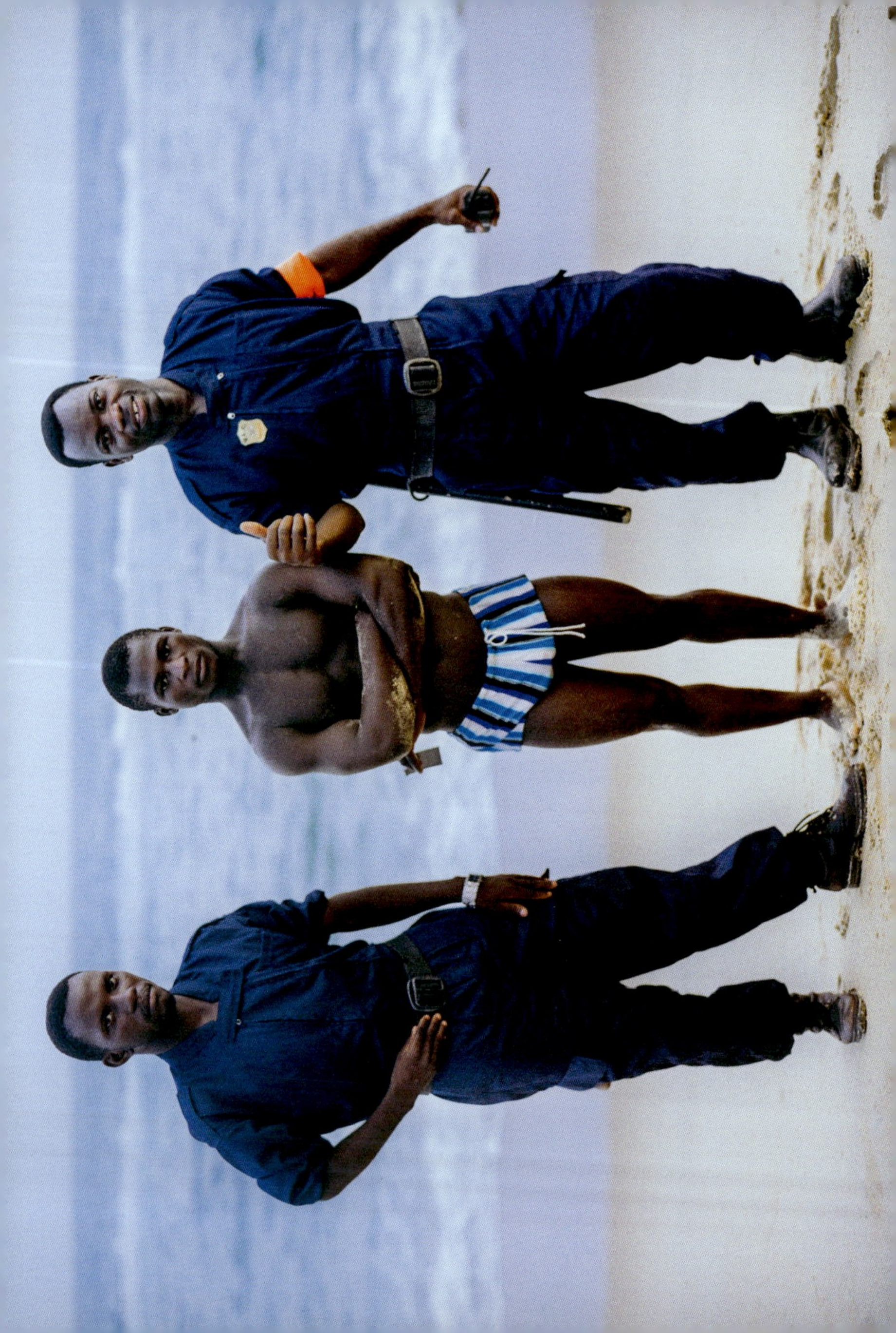

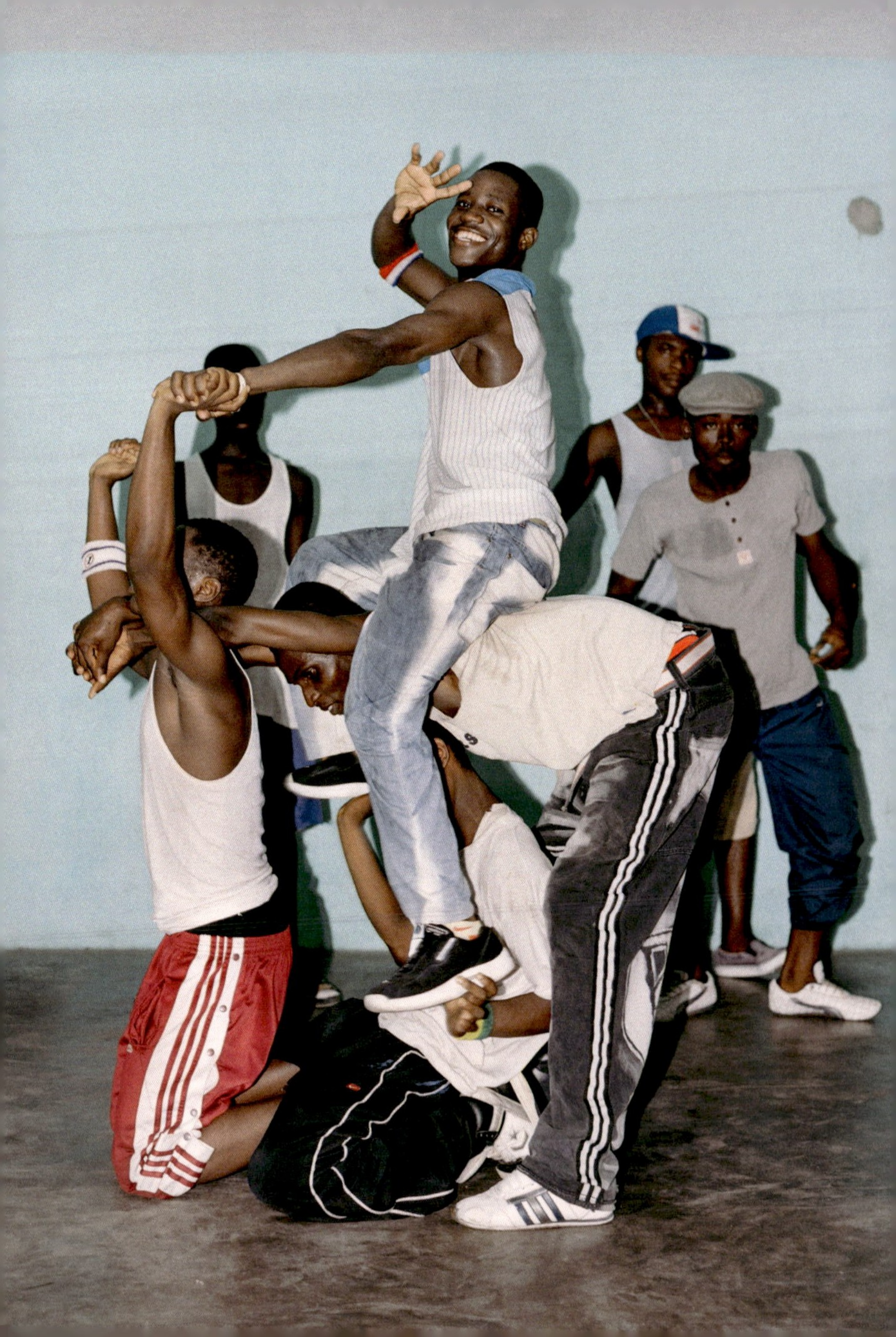

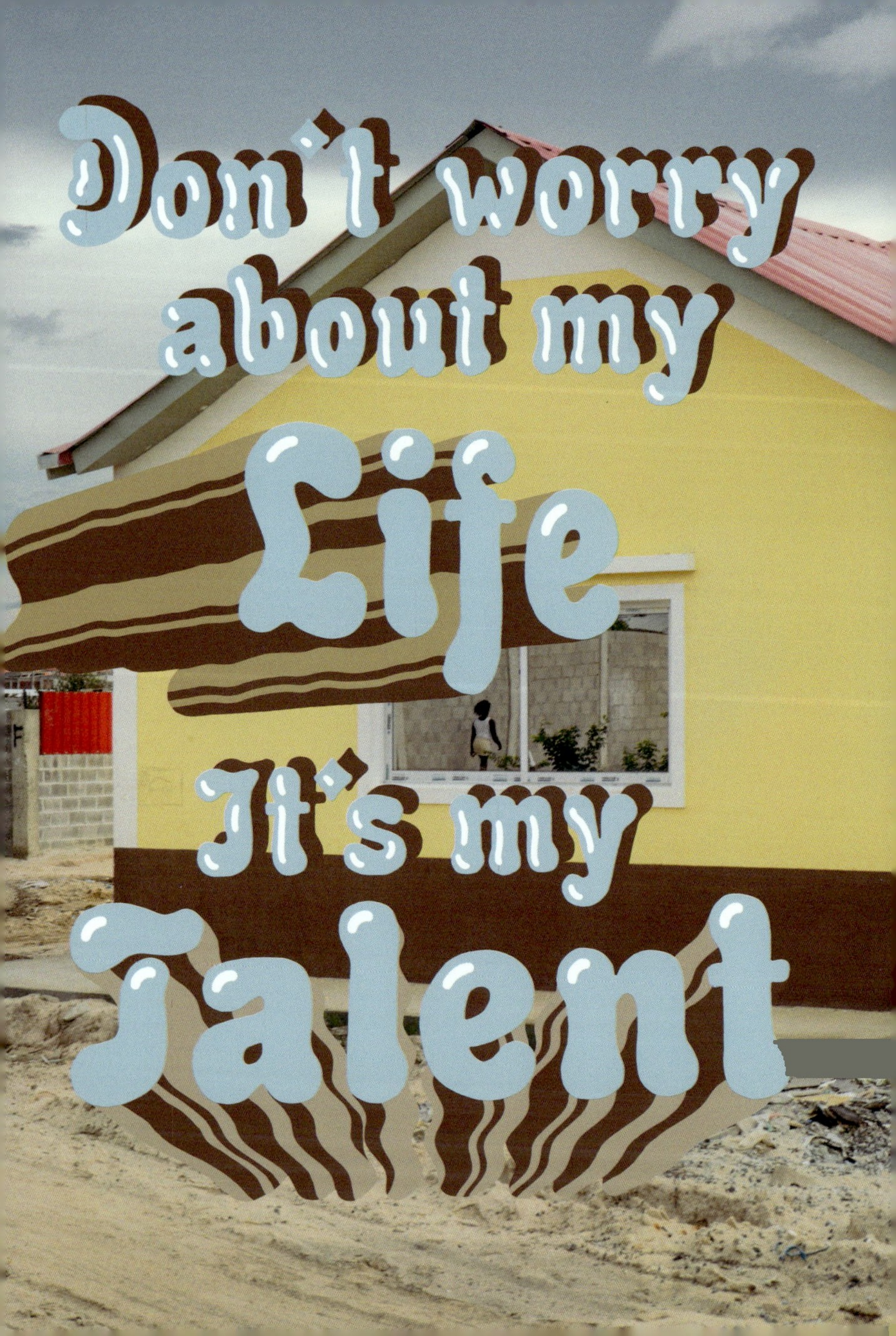
Don`t worry
about my
Life
It's my
Talent

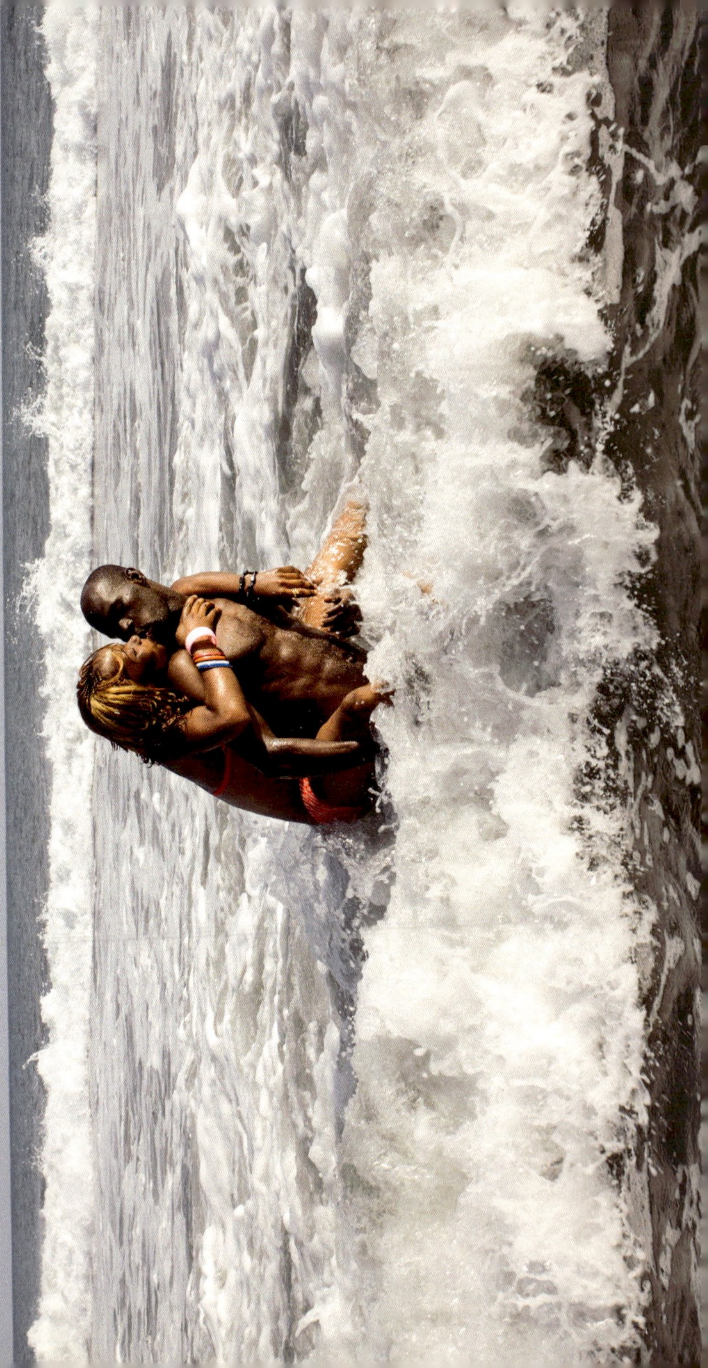

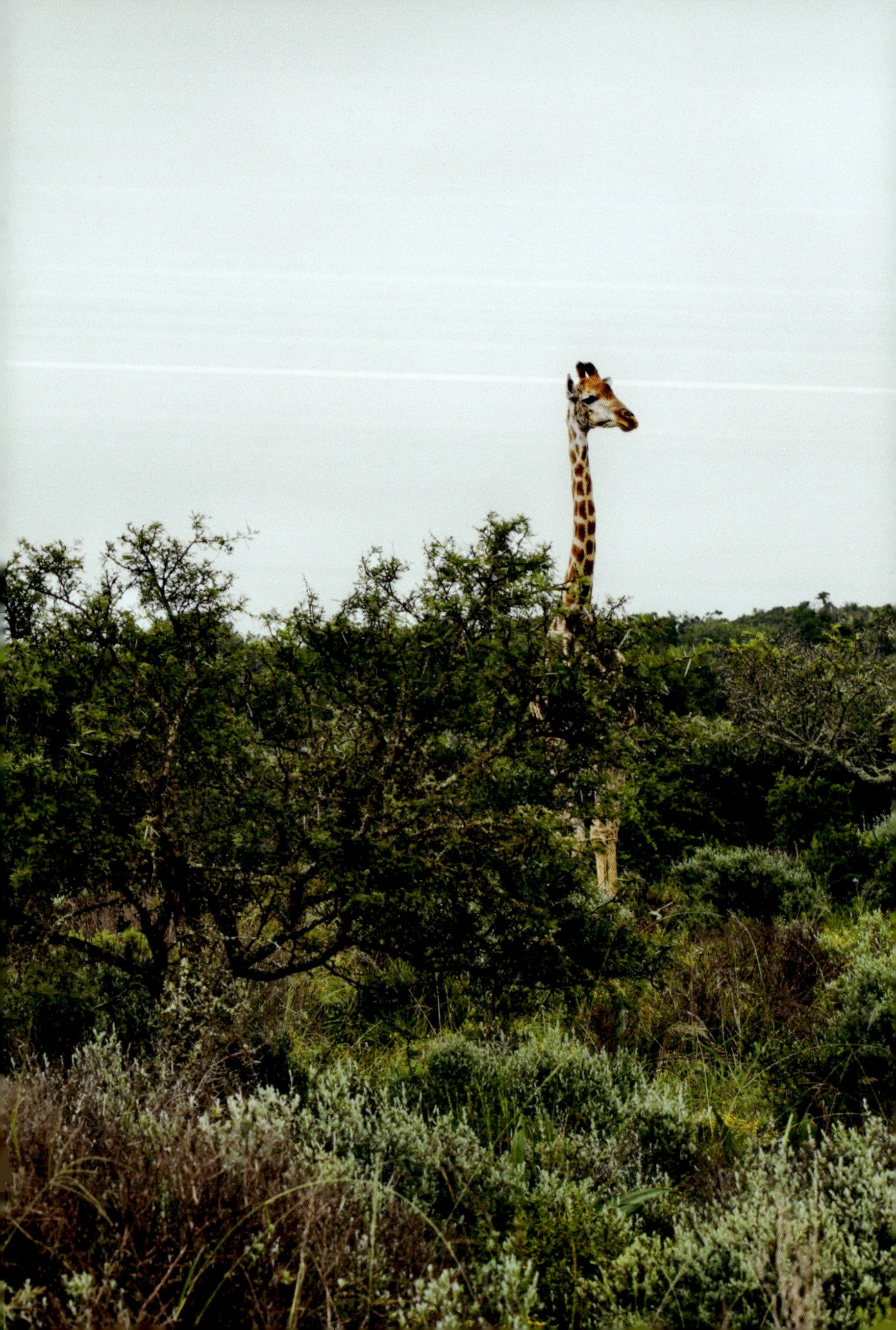

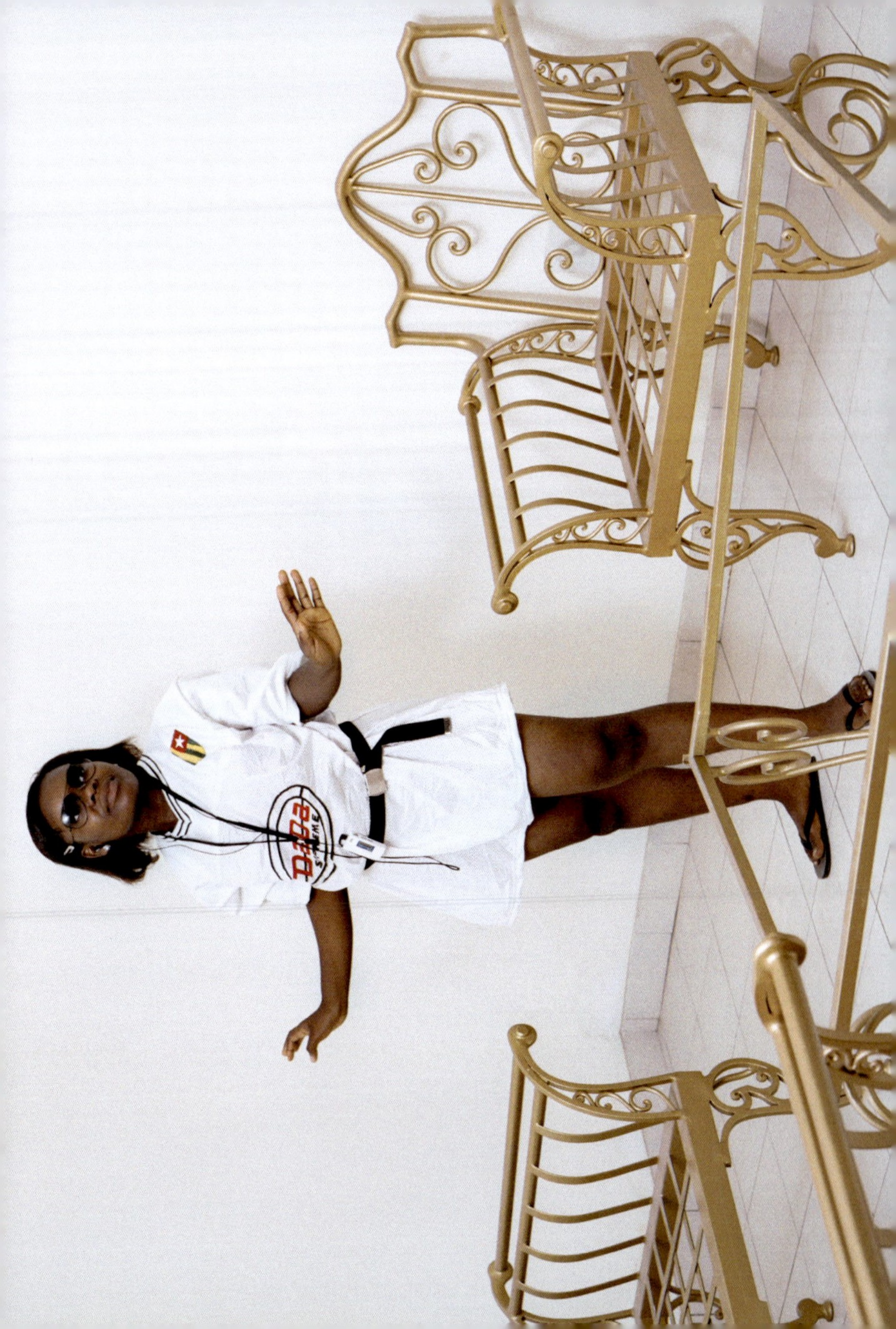
DaDa

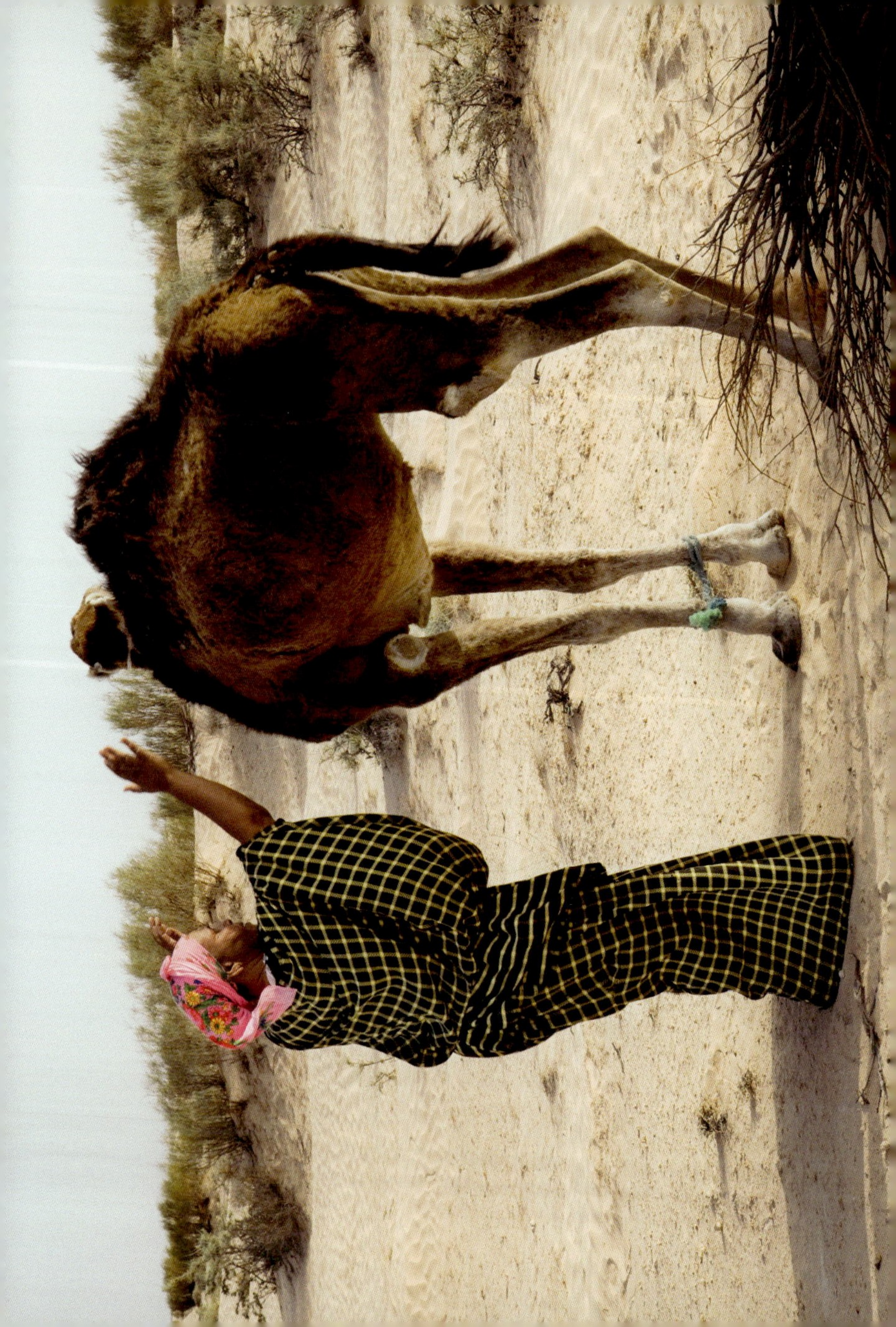

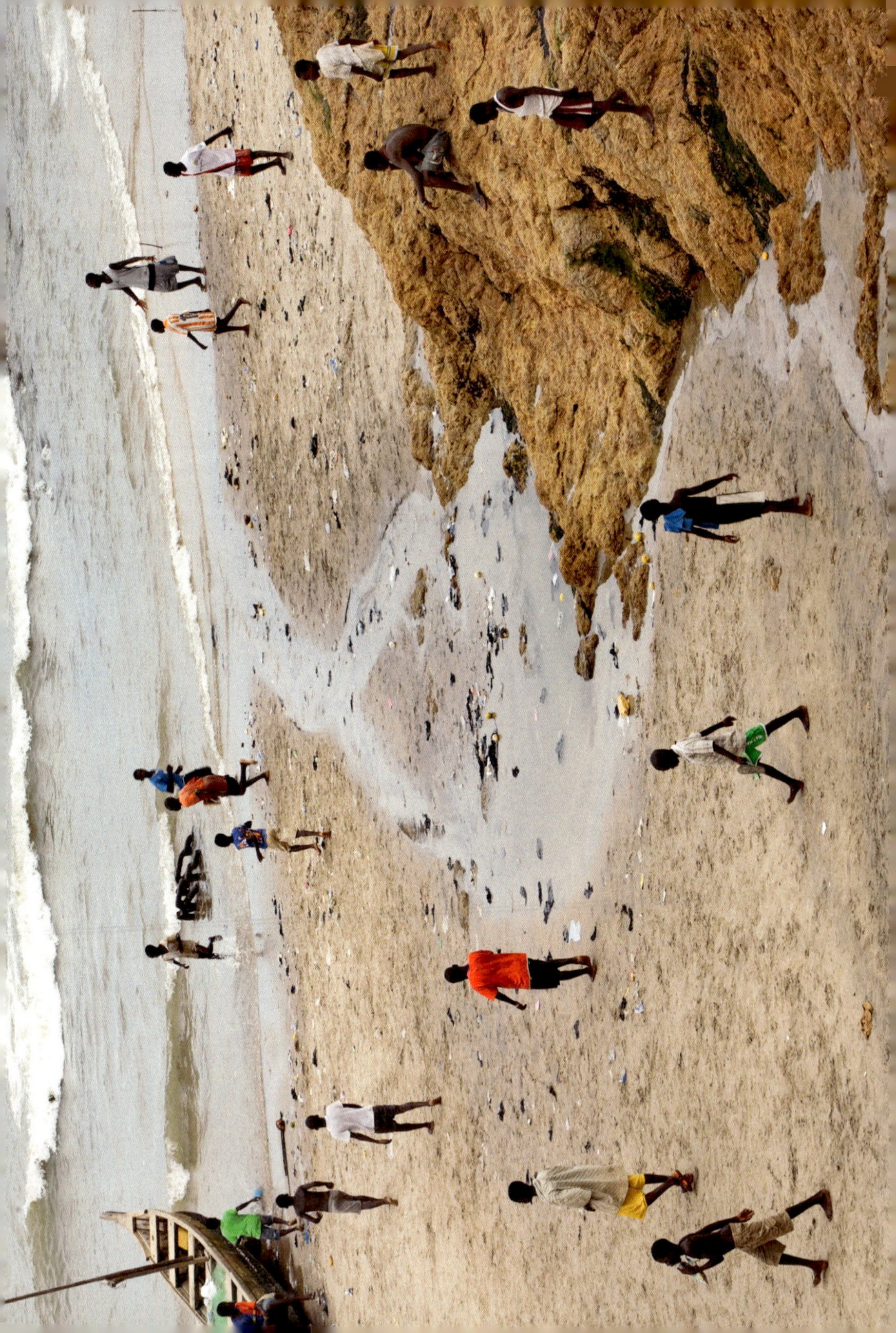

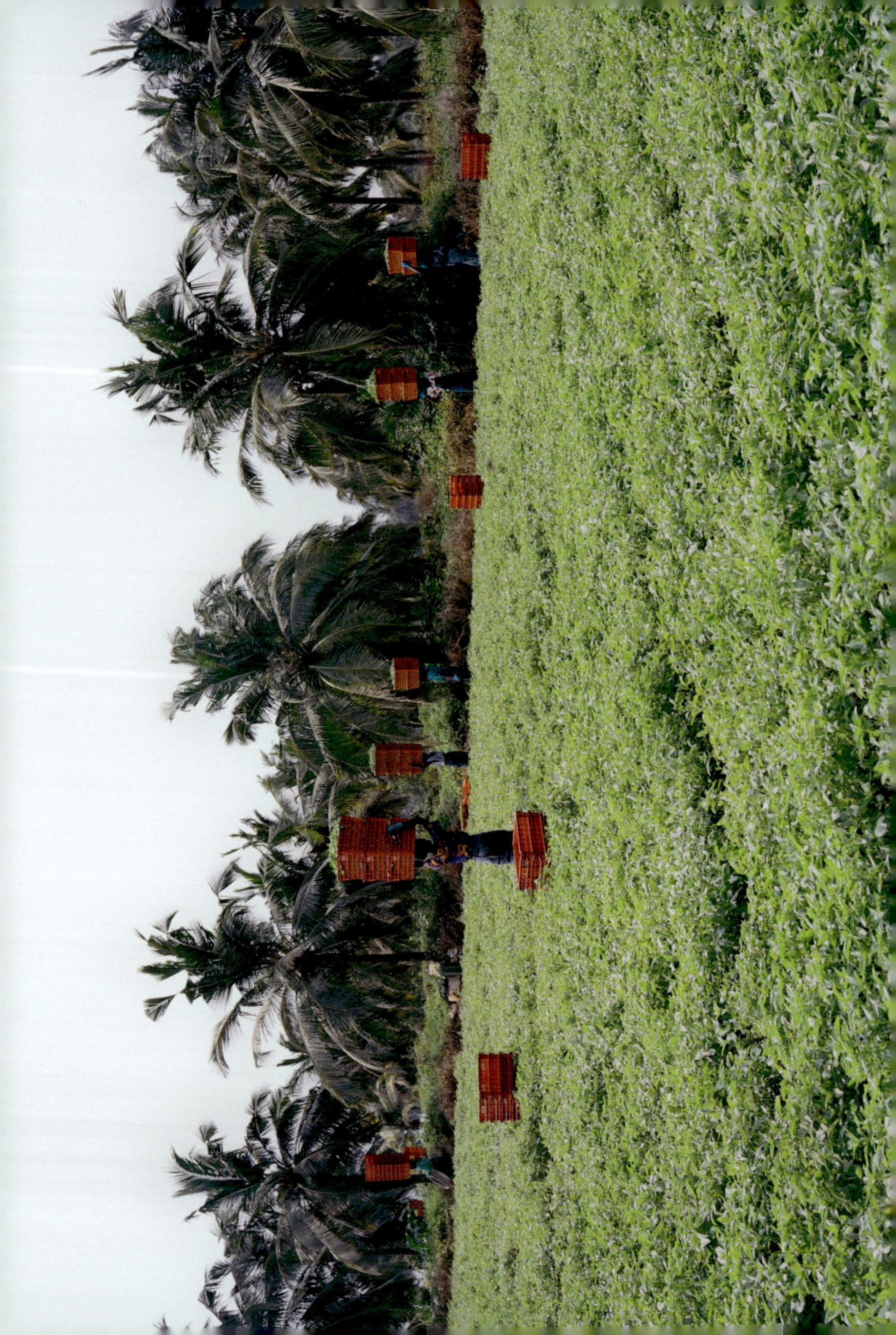

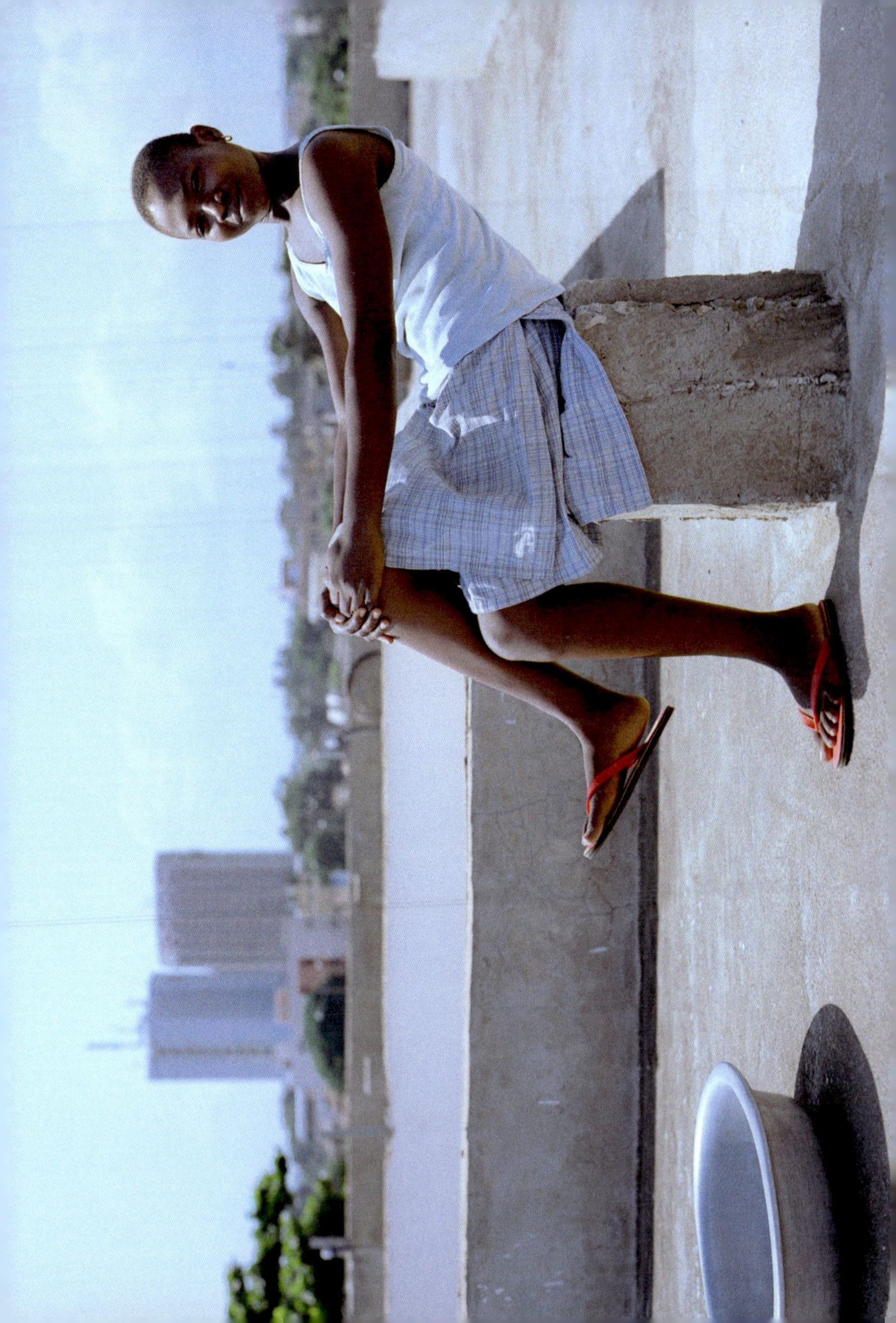

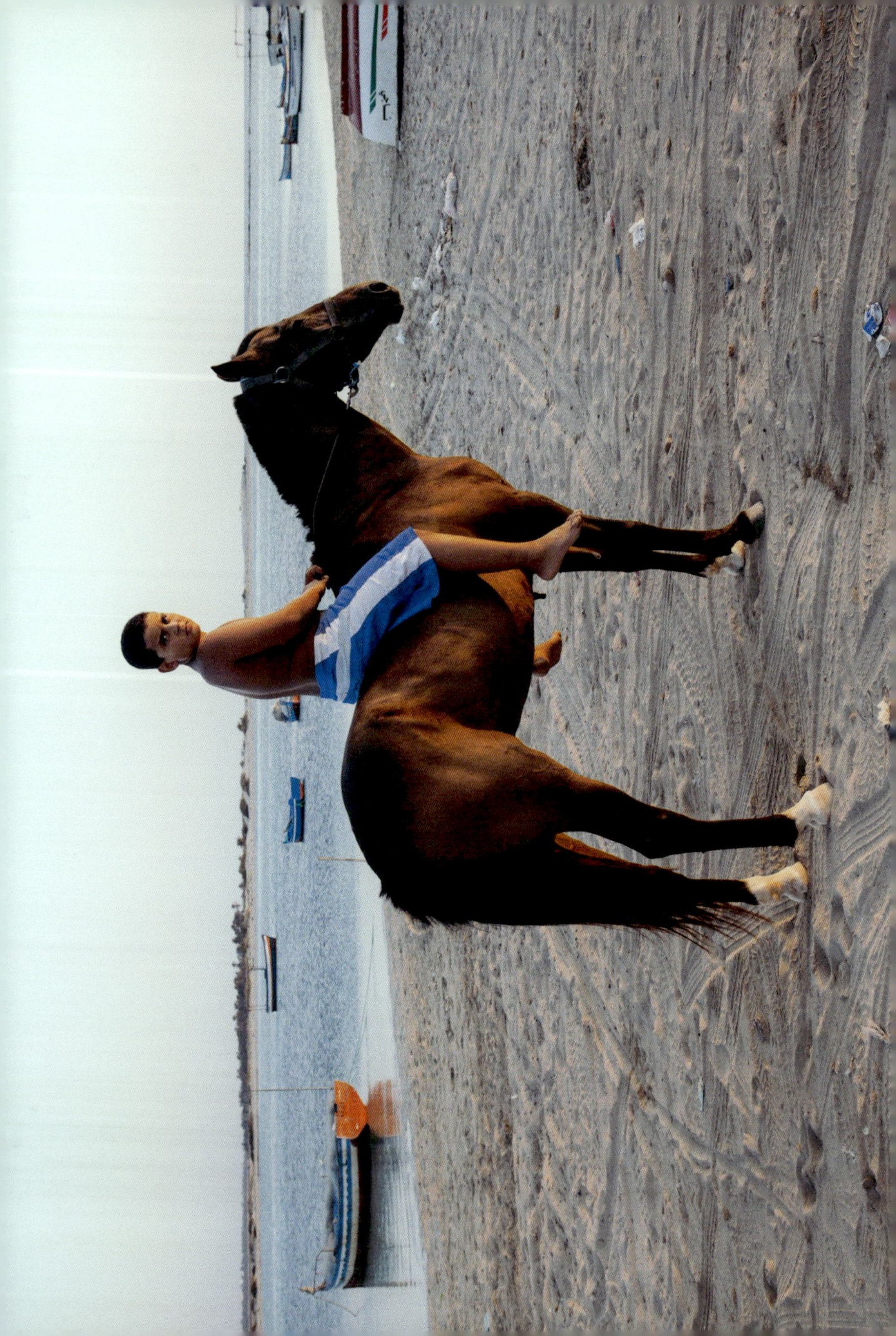

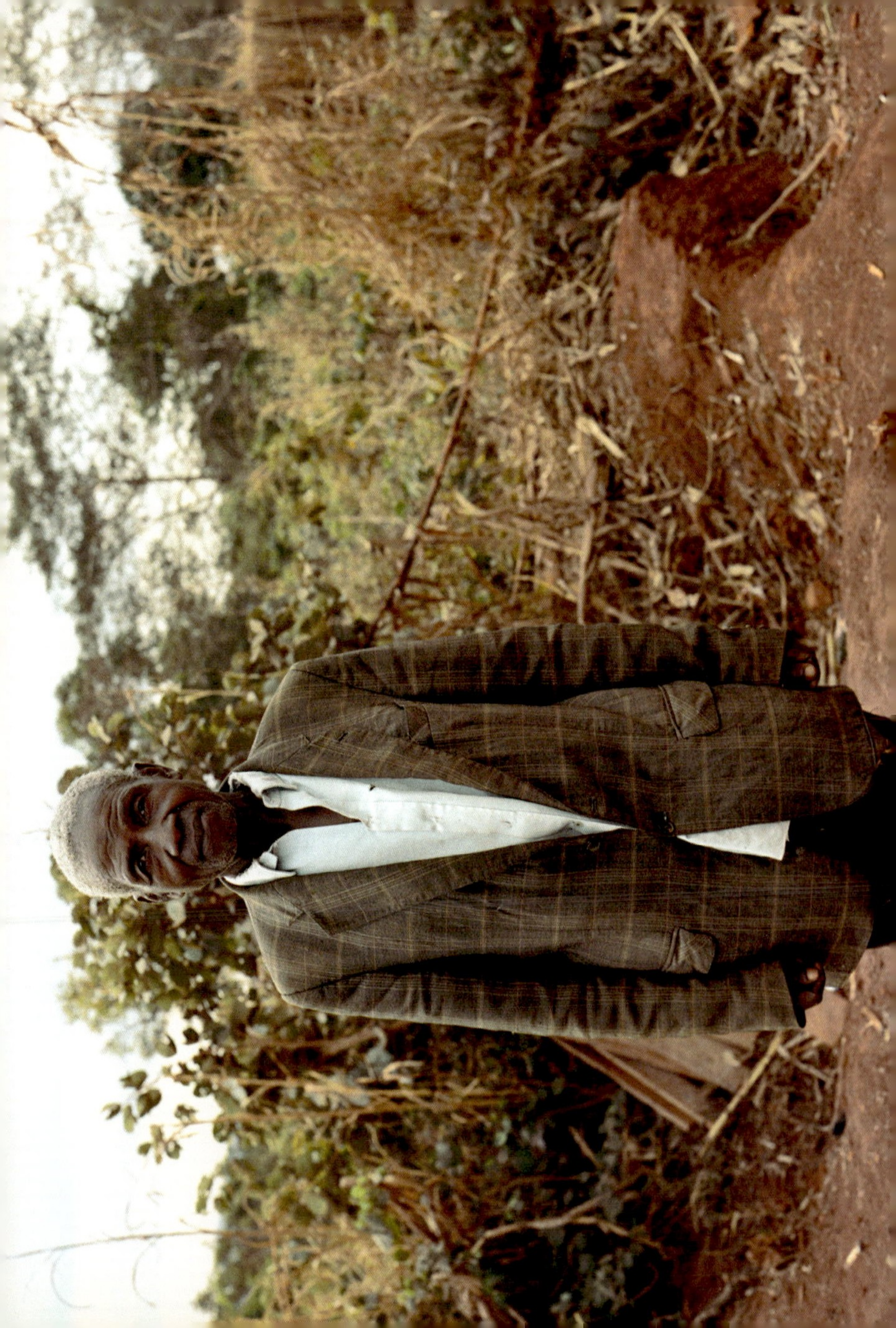

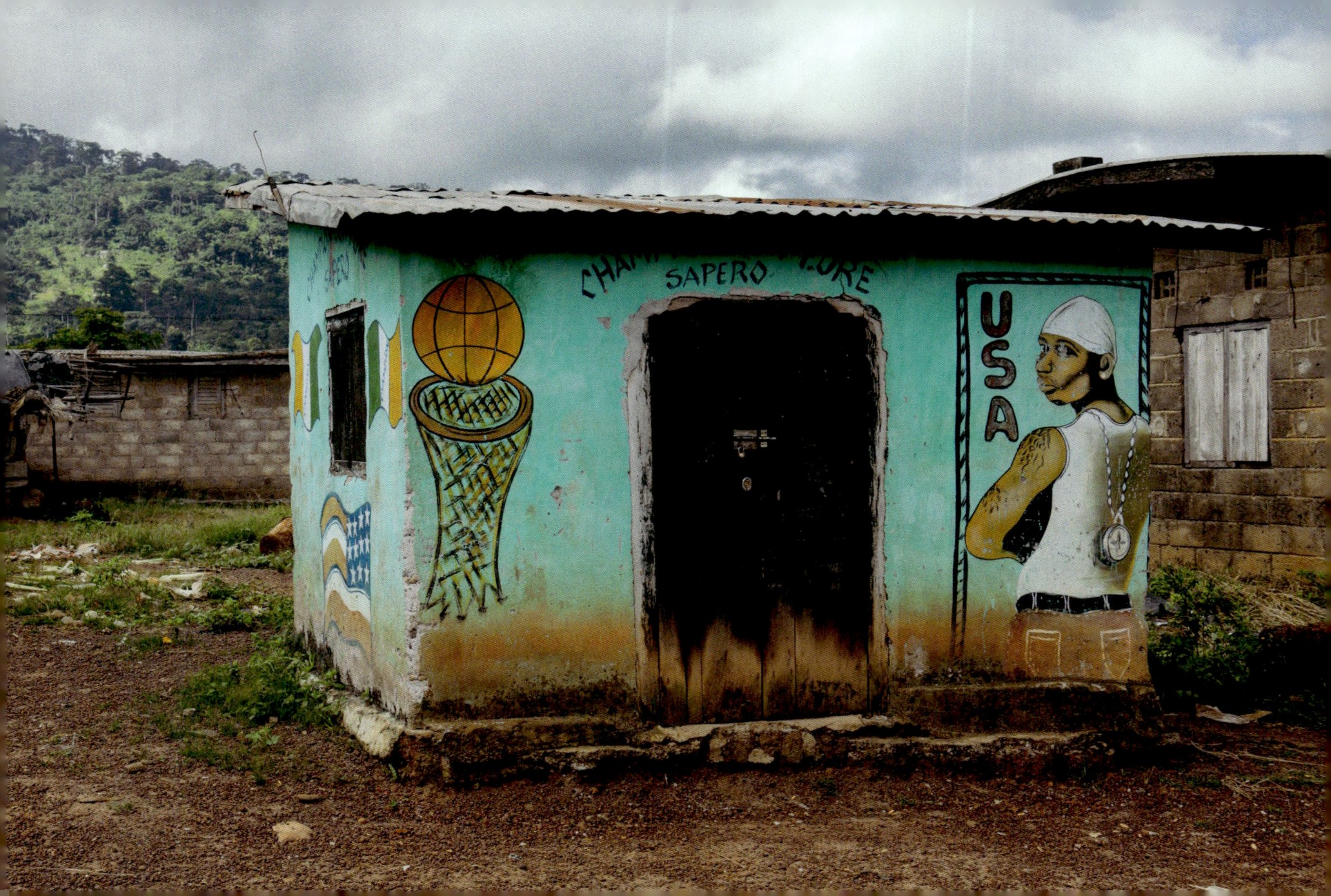
SAPERO
USA

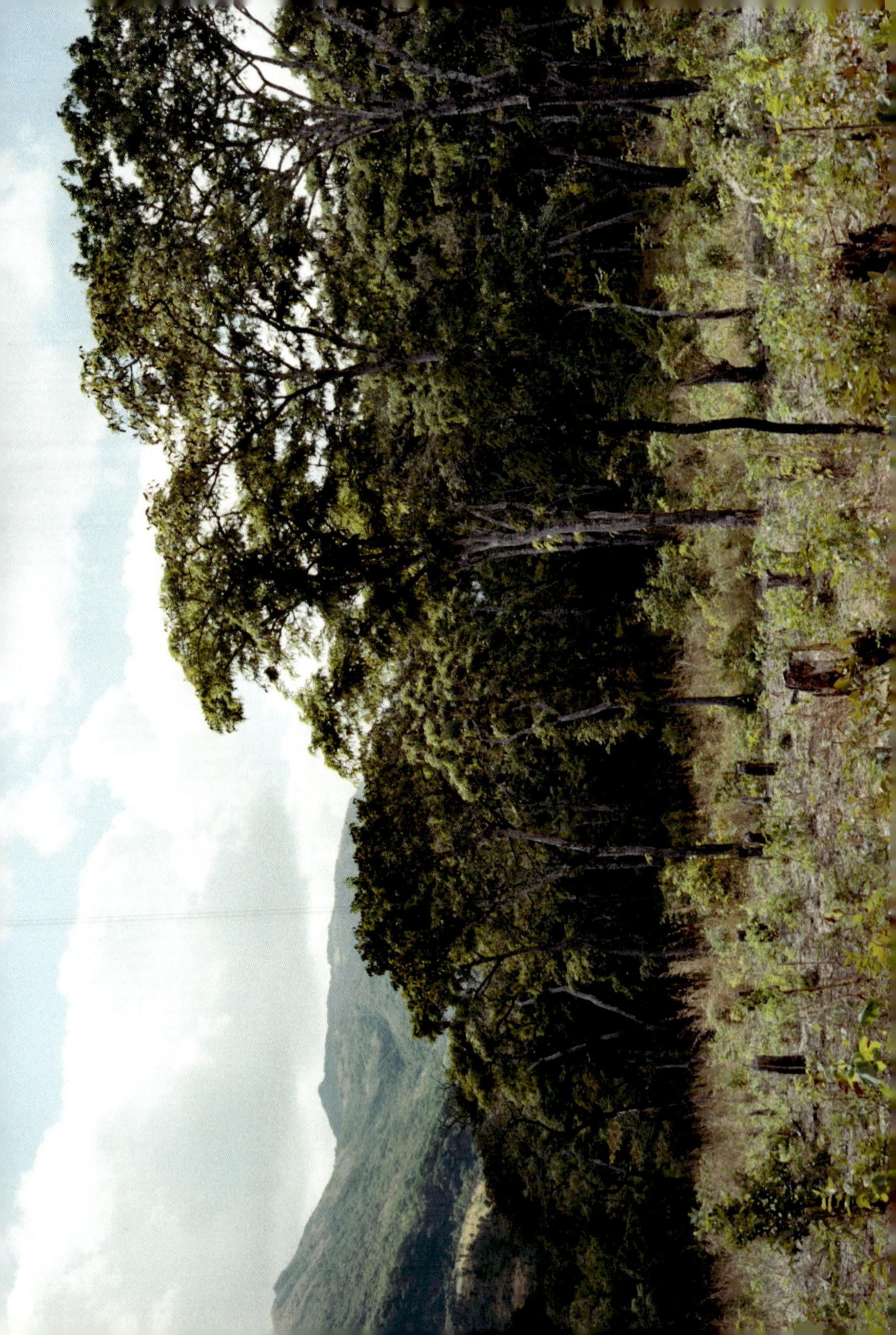

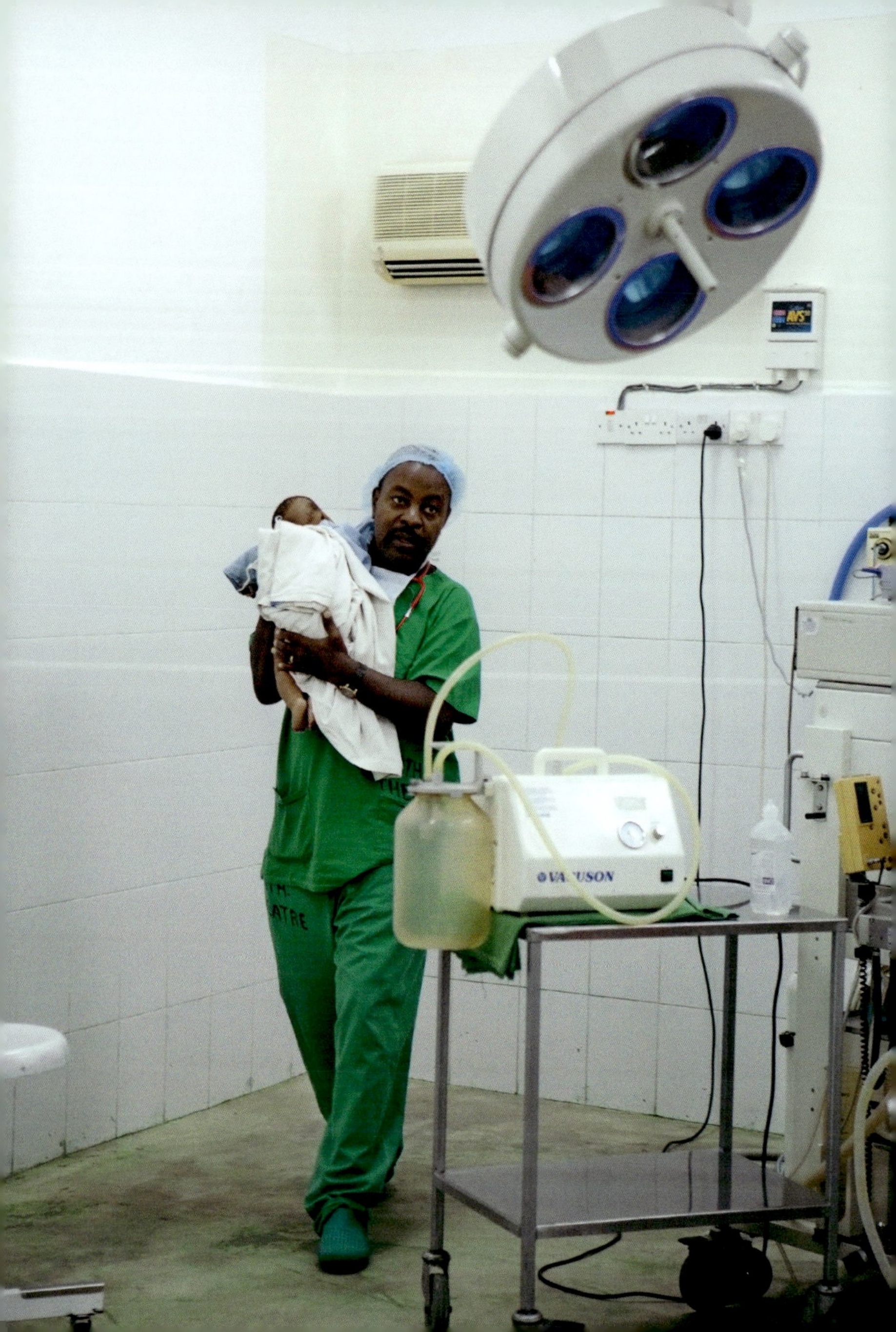

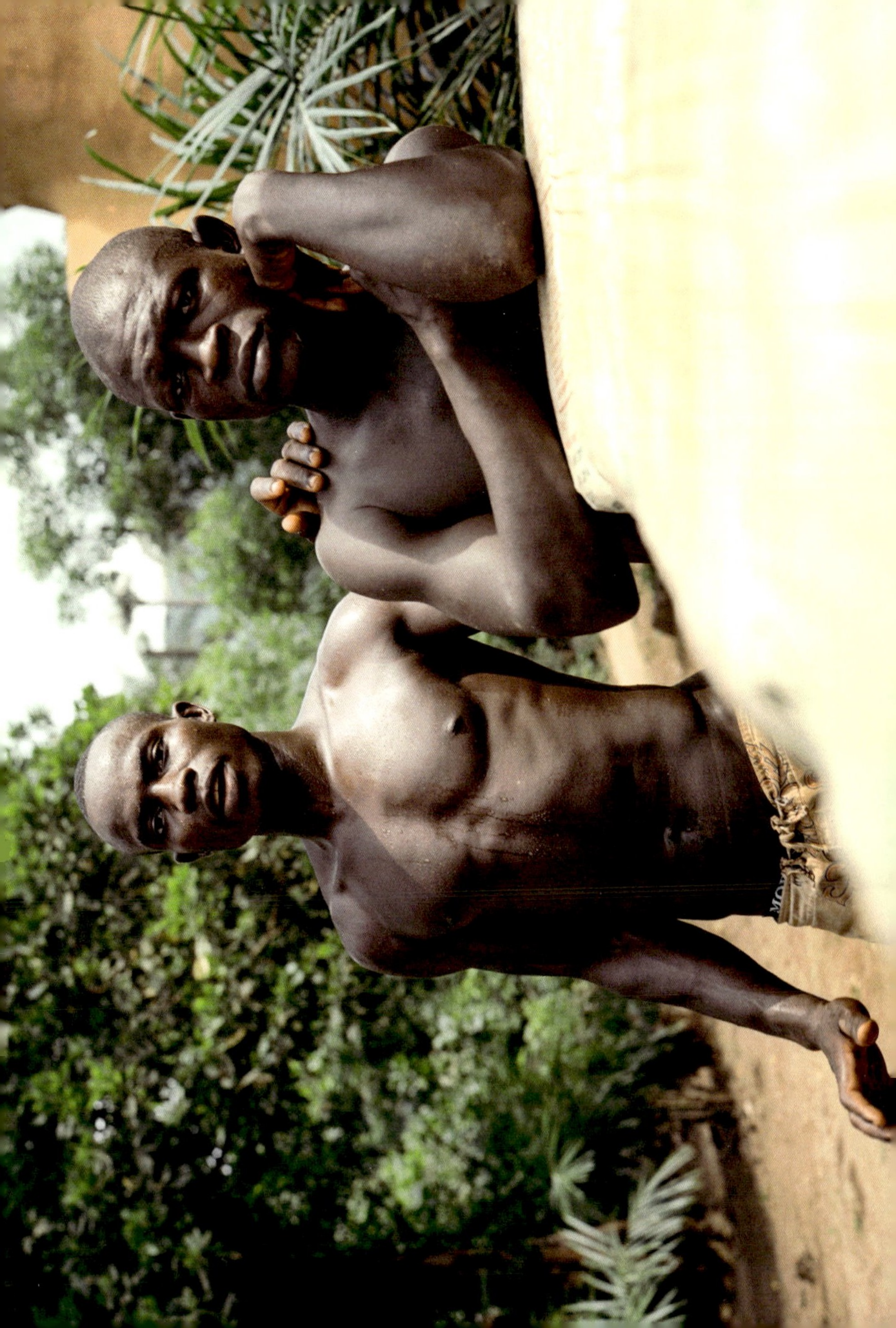

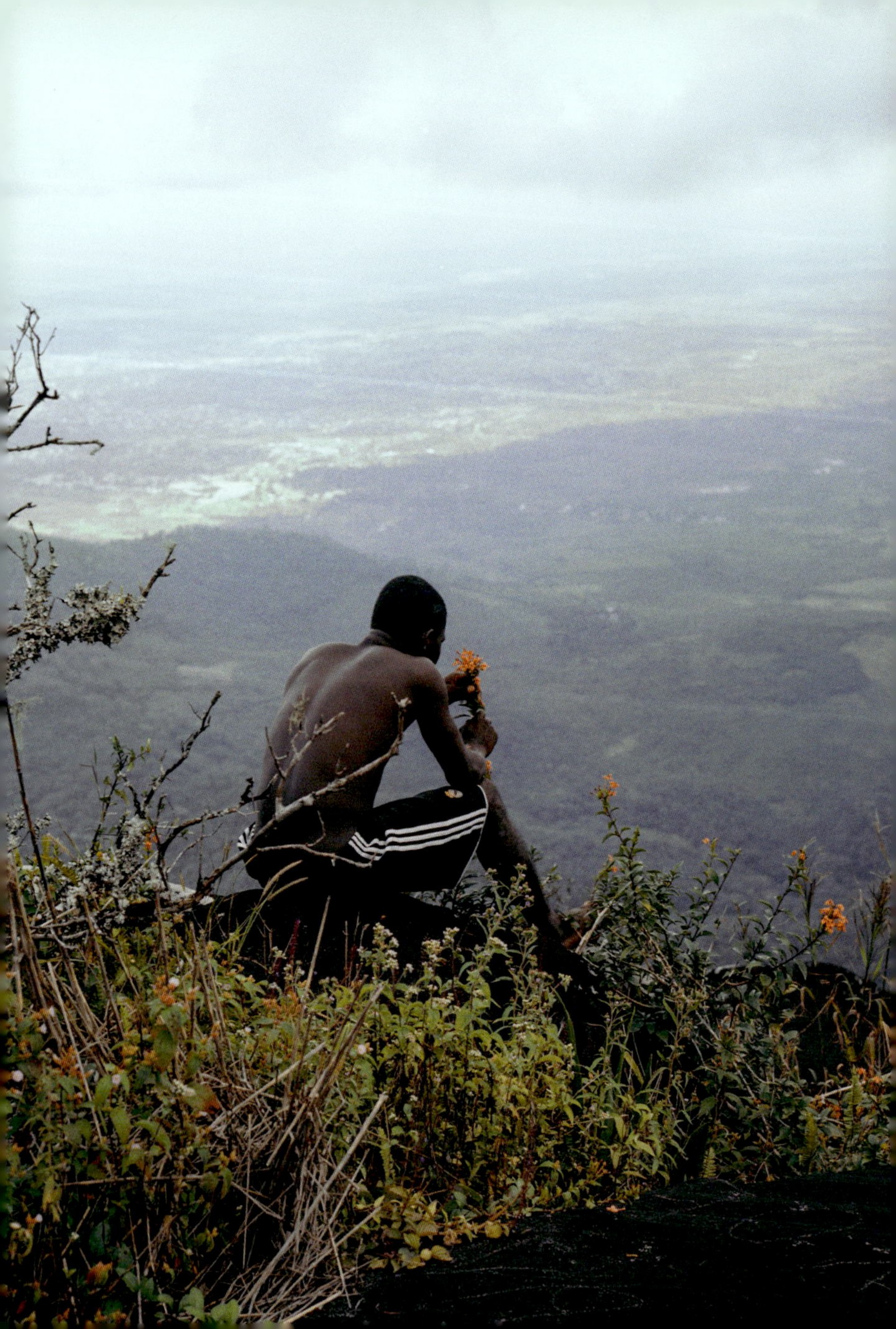

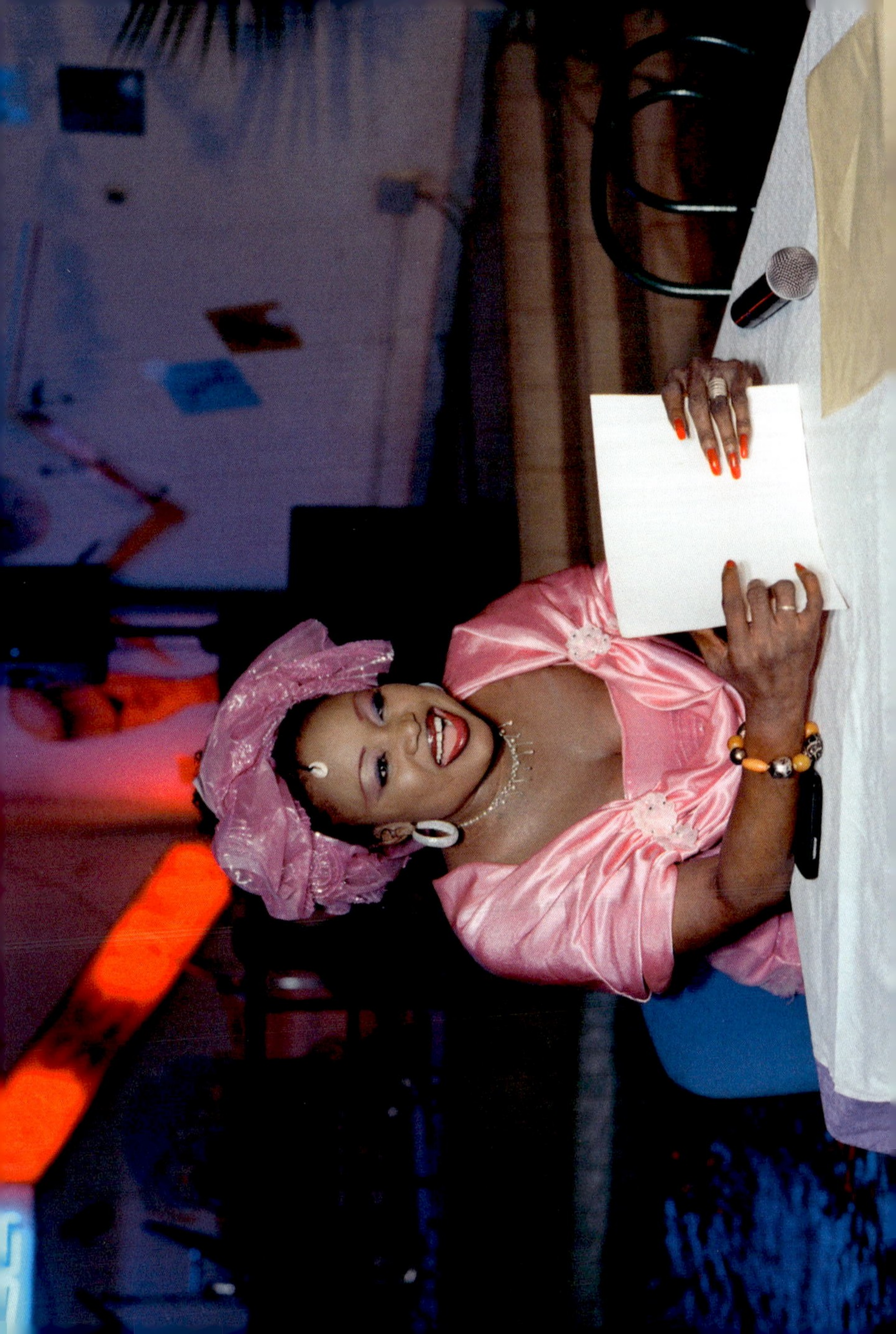

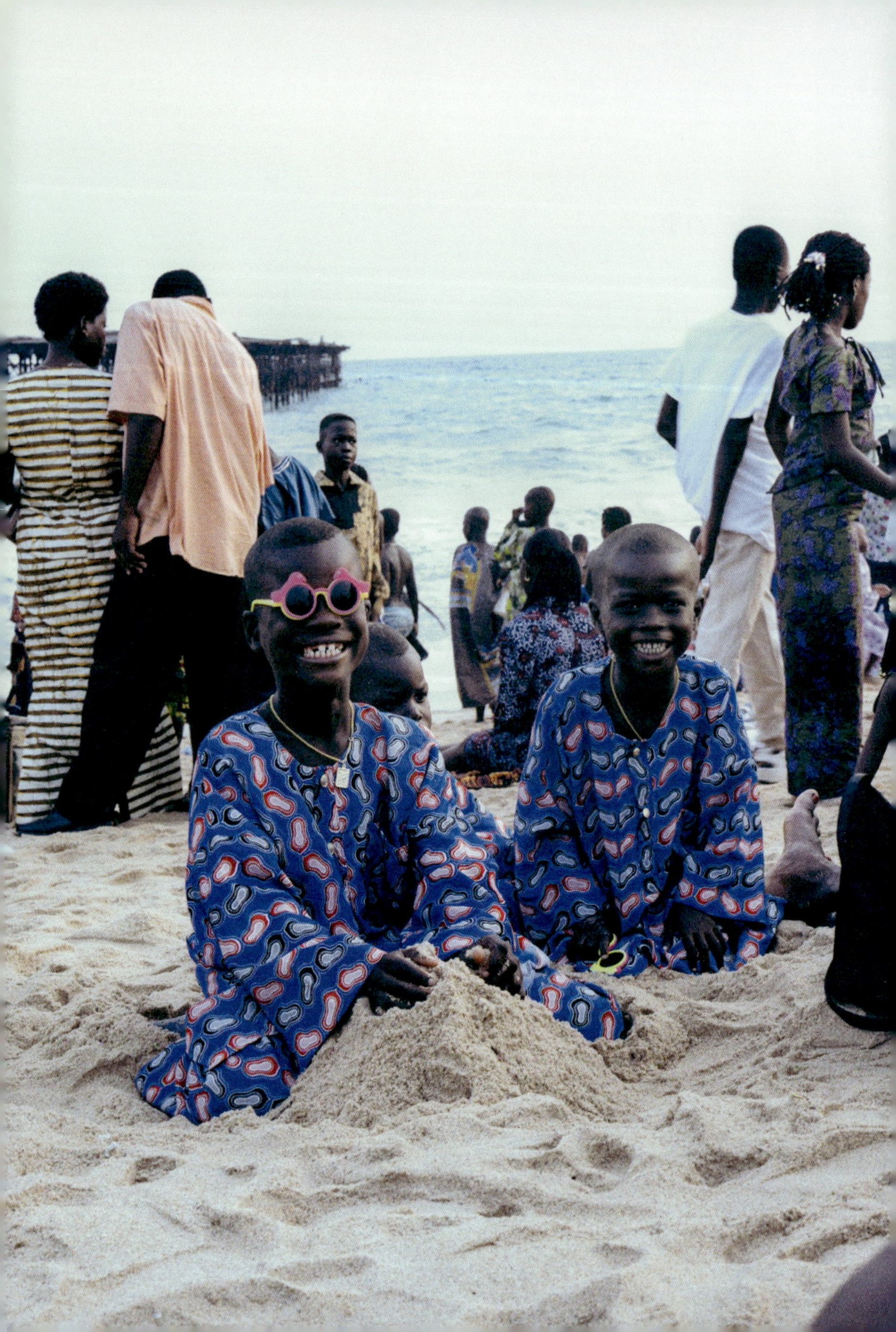

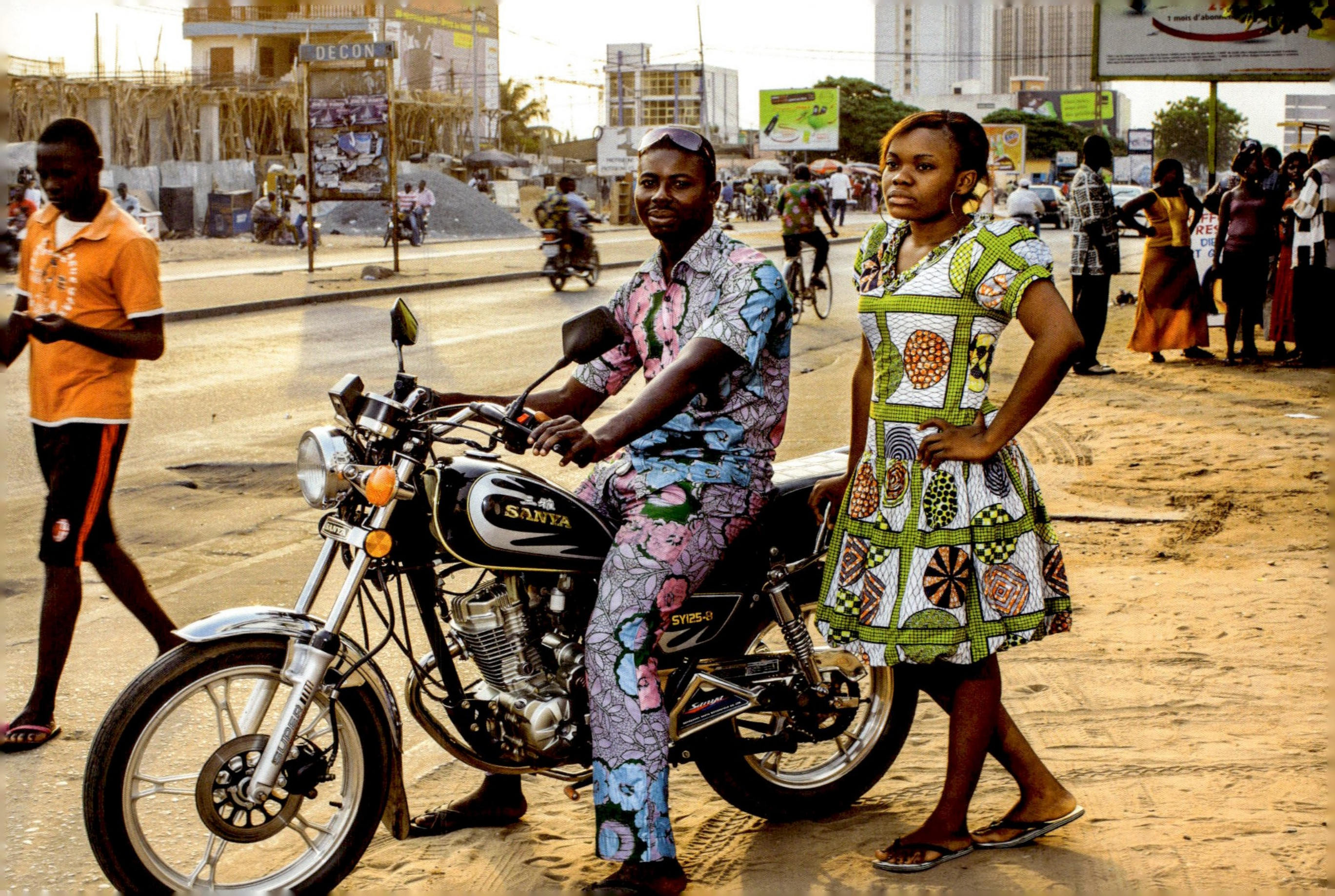
DECON
SANYA
SY125-8

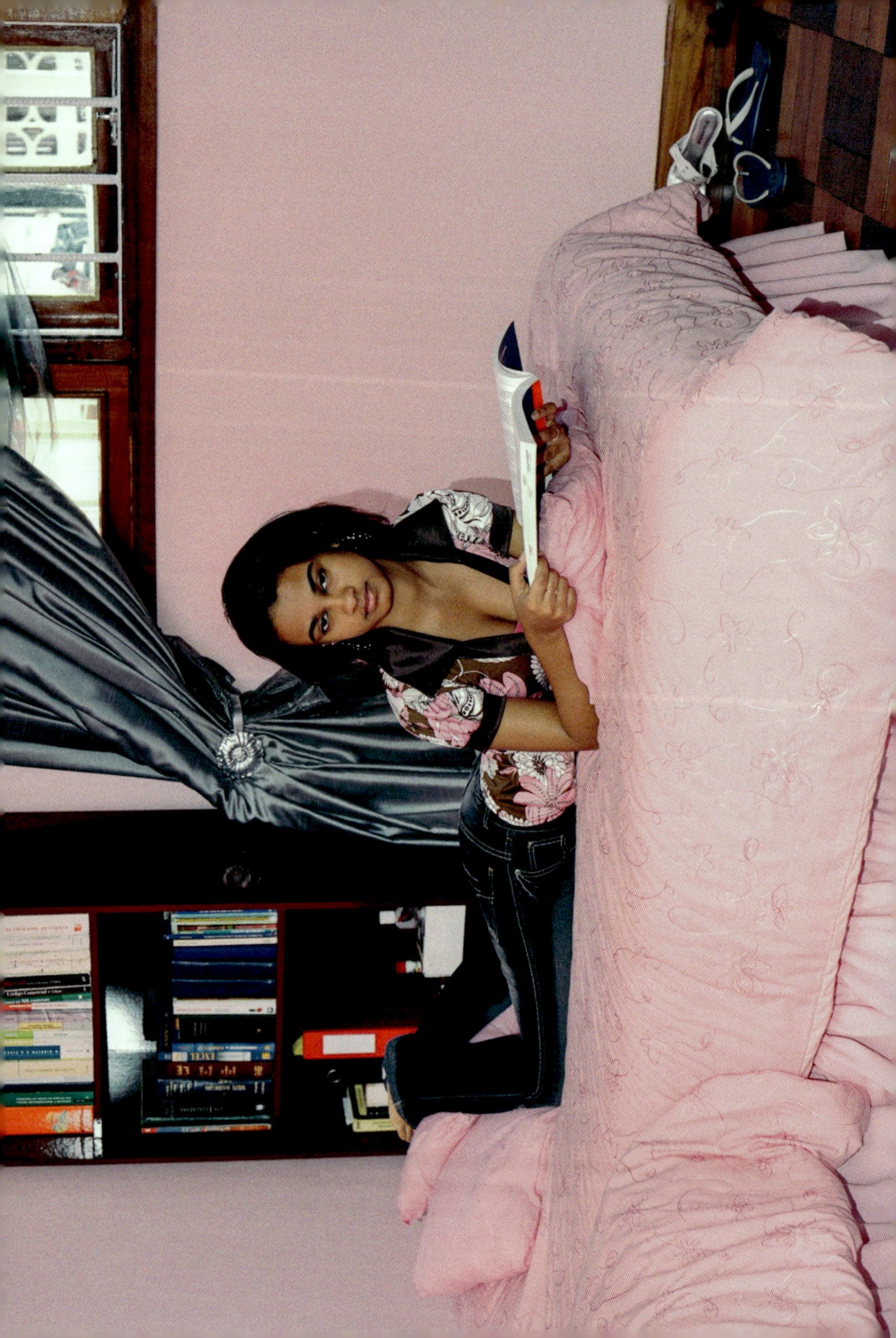

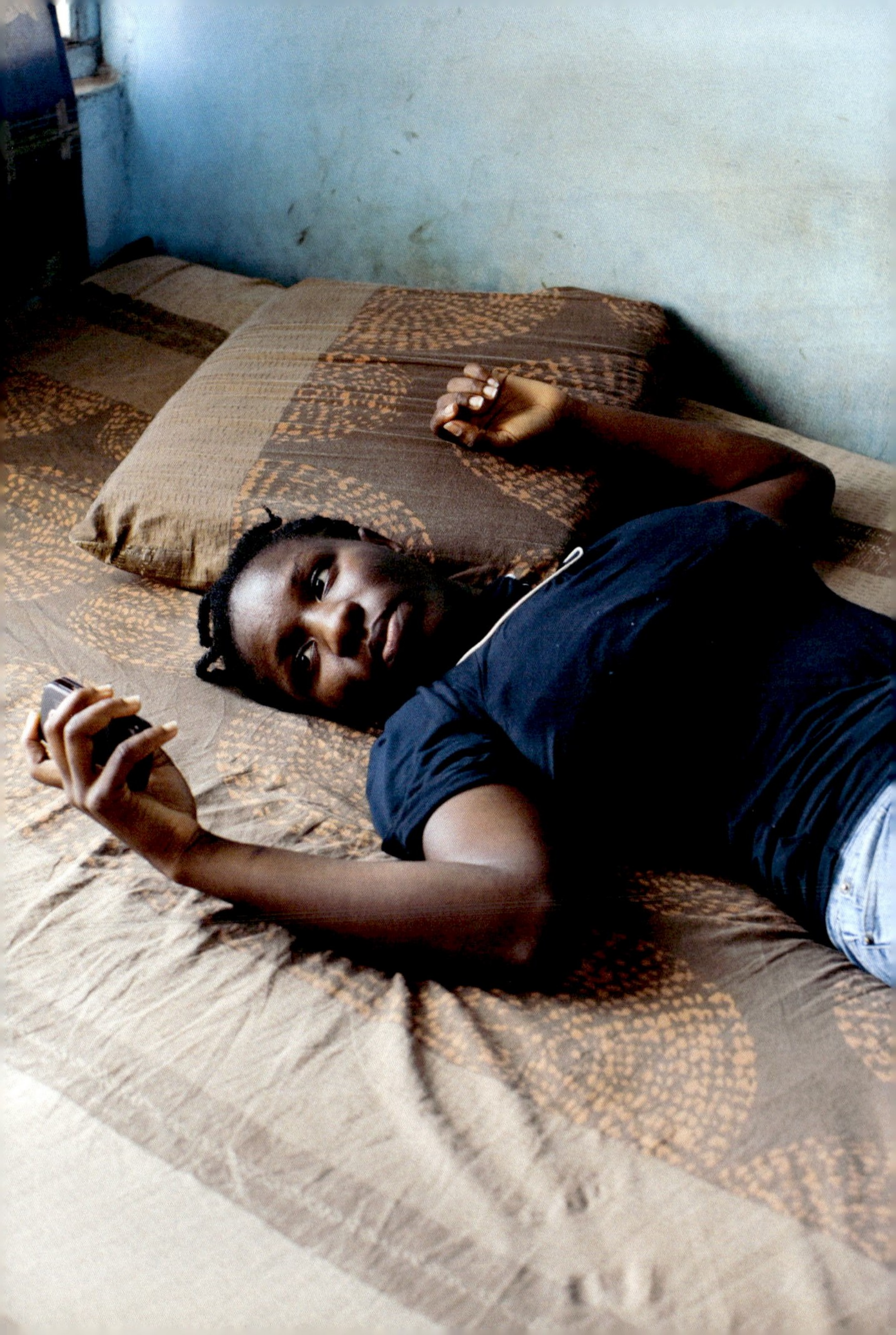

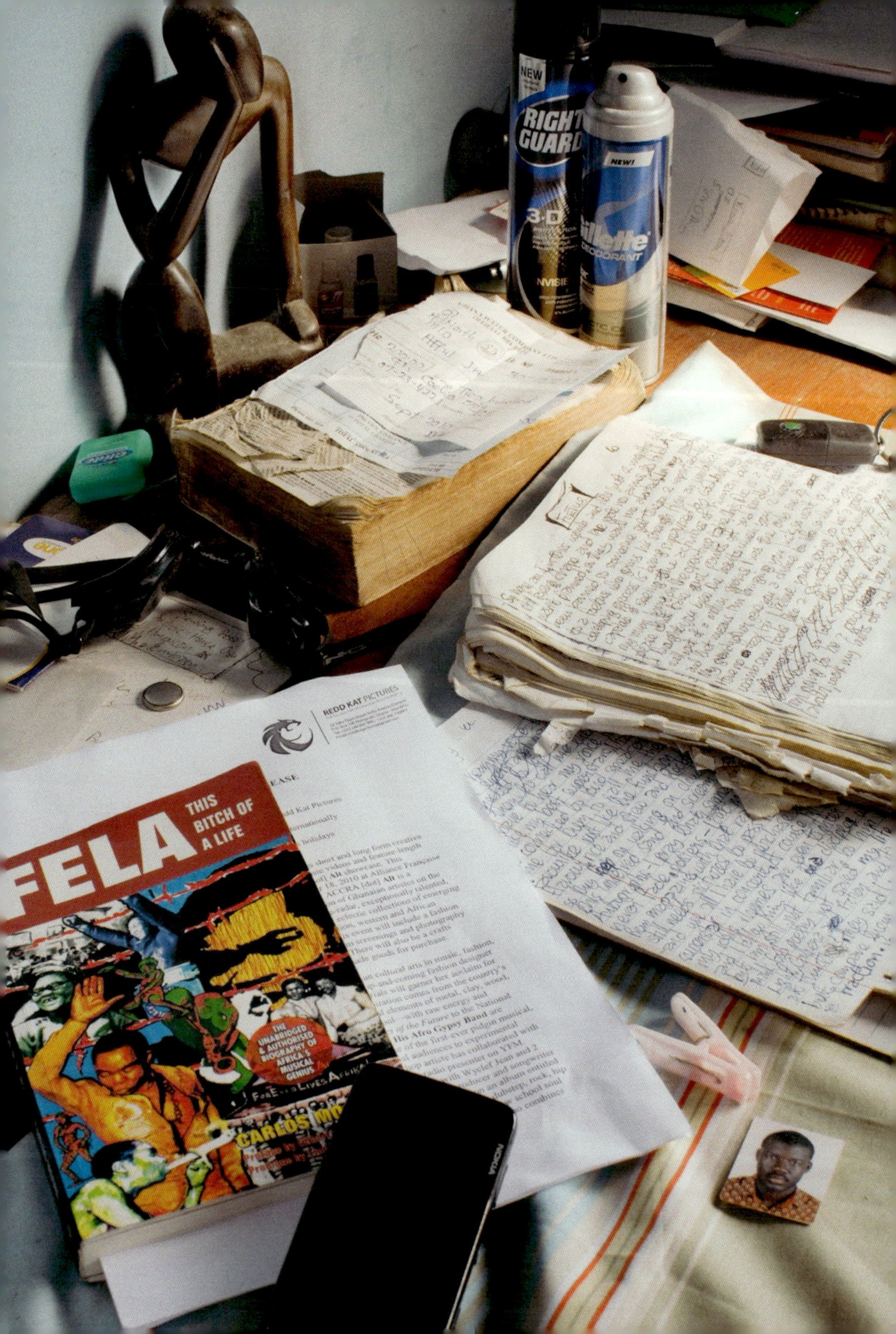

RIGHT GUARD
3-D
Gillette
DEODORANT
REDD KAT PICTURES
FELA
THIS BITCH OF A LIFE
THE UNABRIDGED & AUTHORISED BIOGRAPHY OF AFRICA'S MUSICAL GENIUS
CARLOS MO

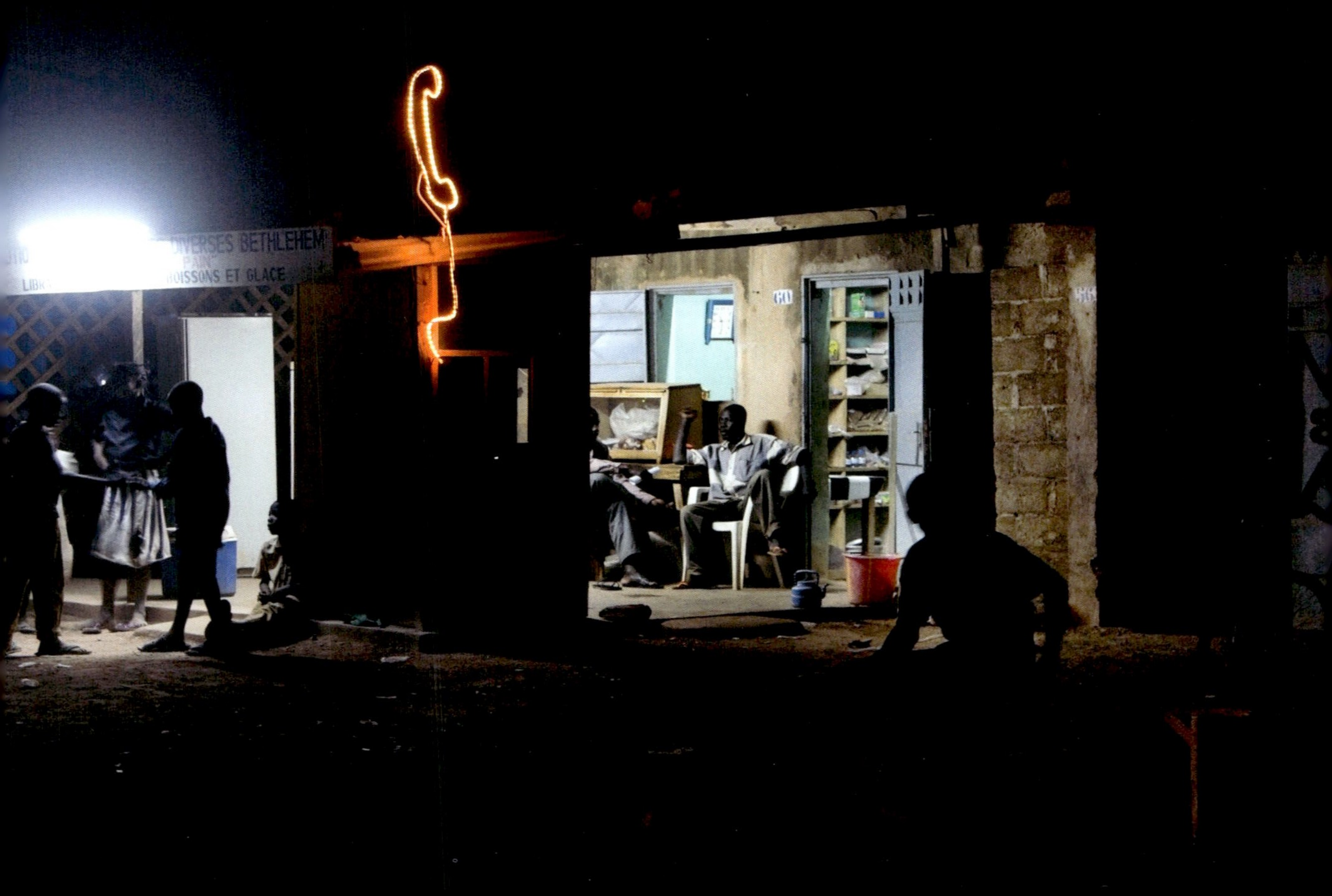
DIVERSES BETHLEHEM
PAIN
OISSONS ET GLACE

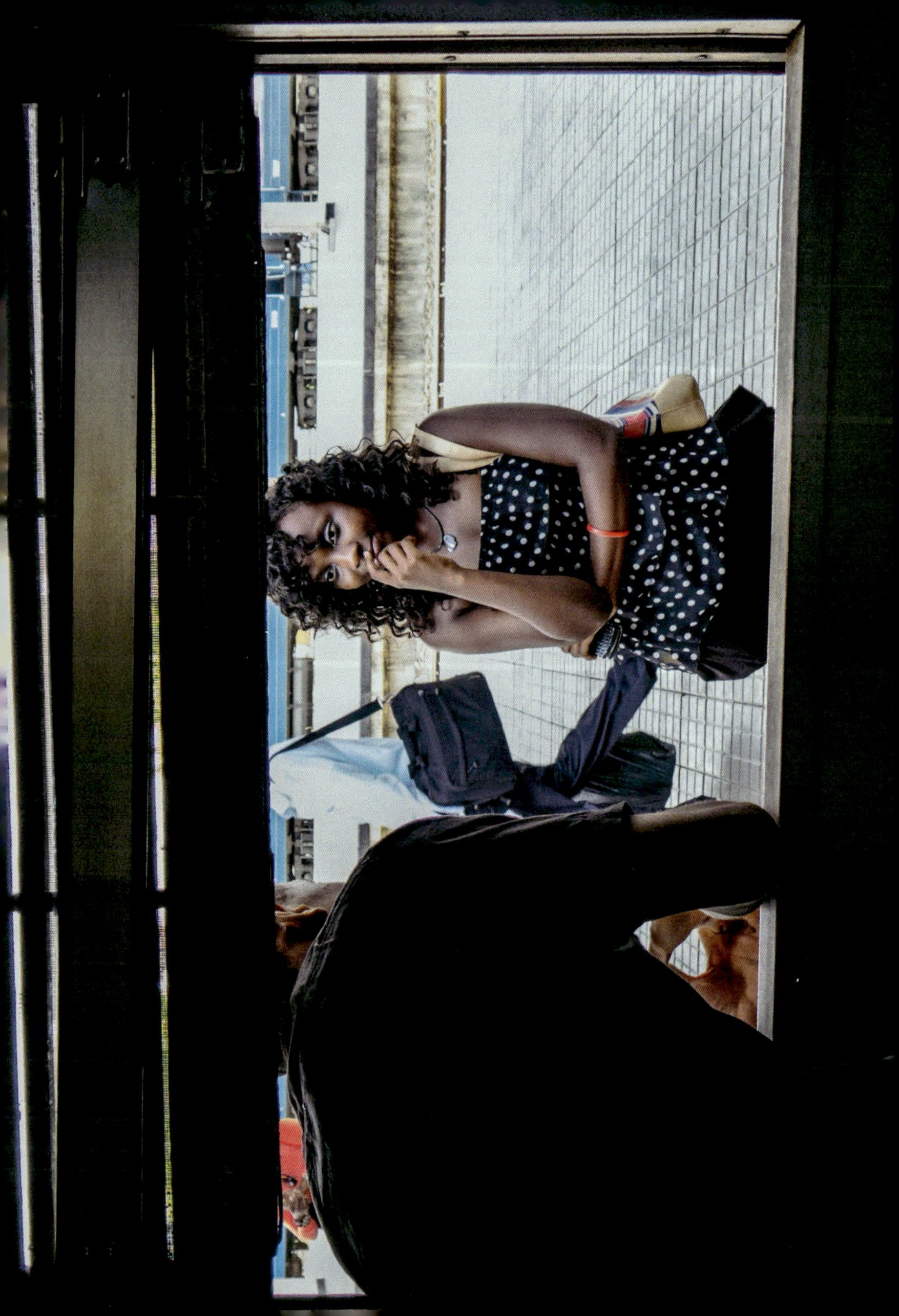

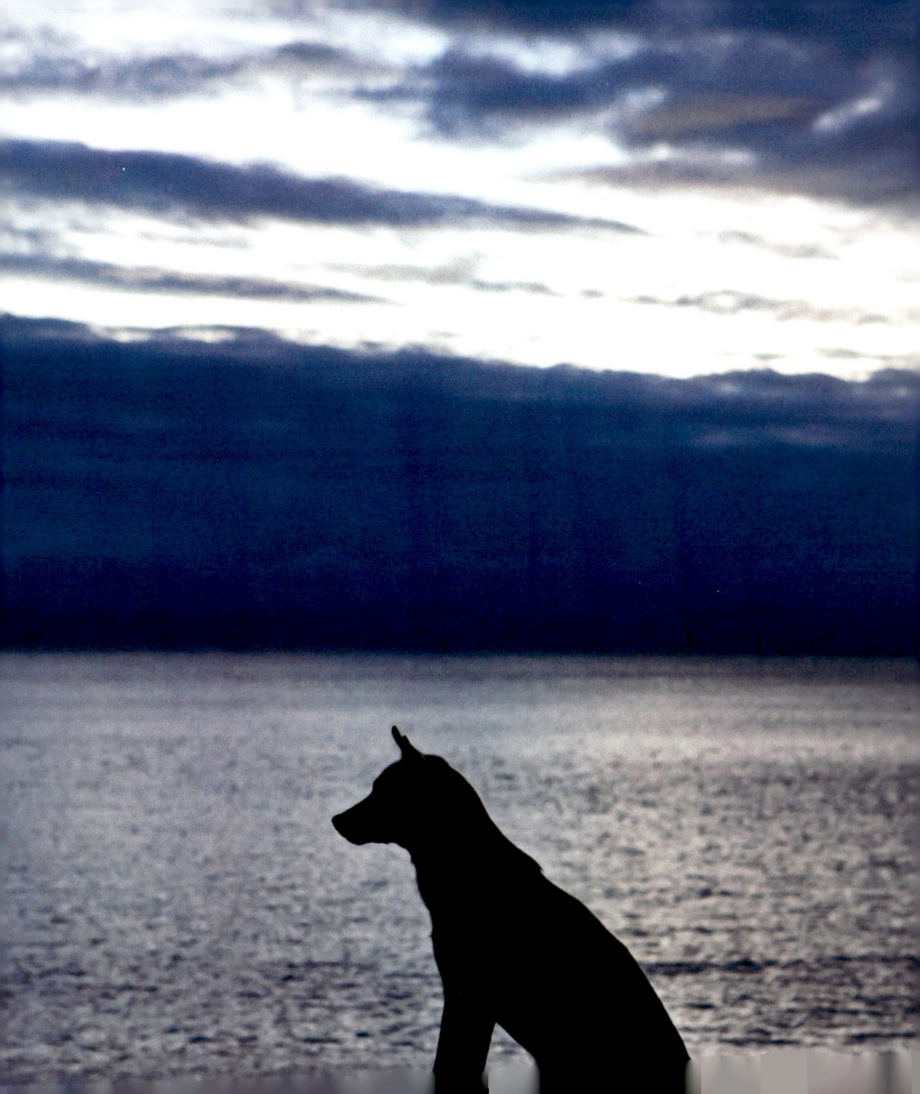

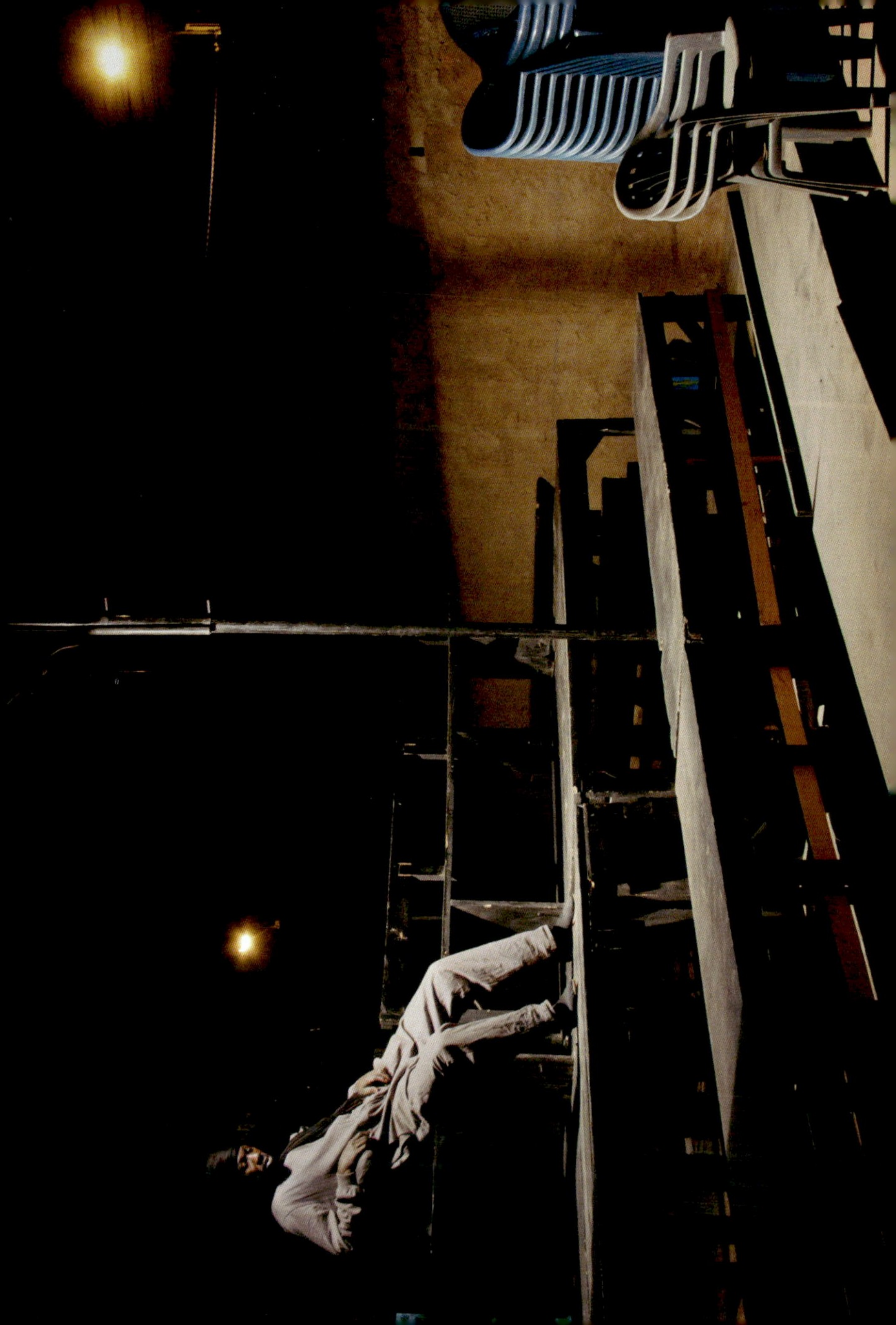

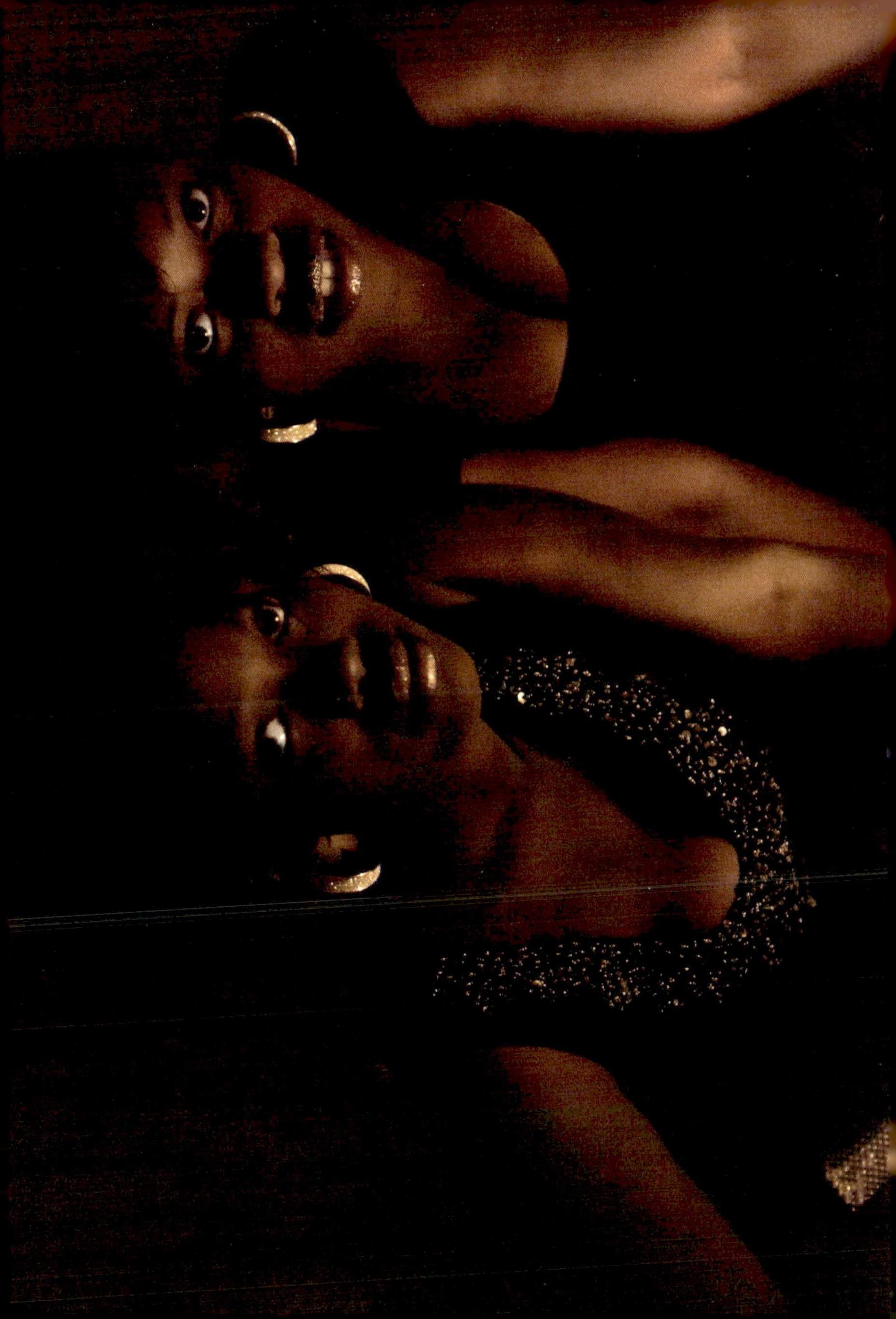

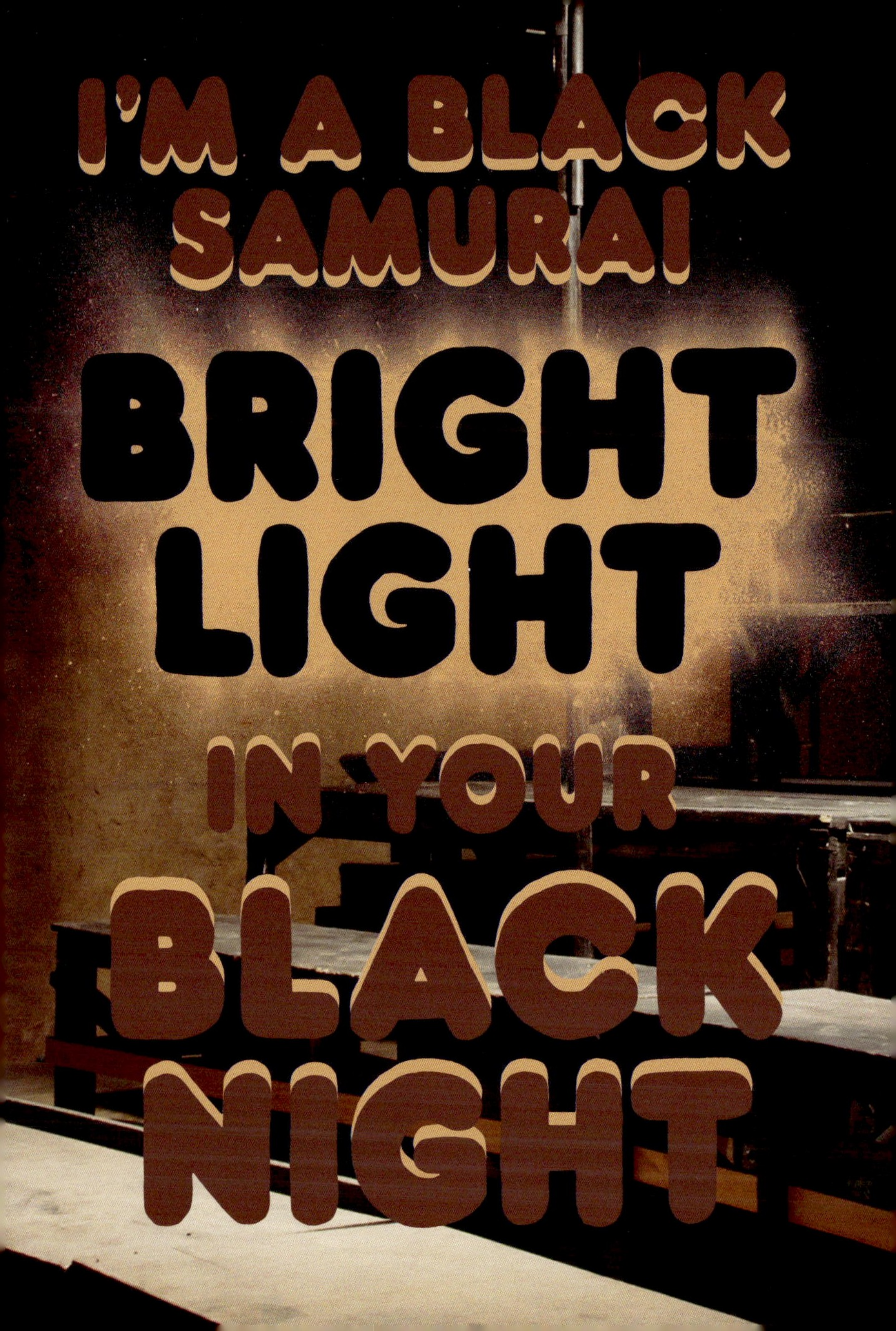
I'M A BLACK SAMURAI
BRIGHT LIGHT
IN YOUR
BLACK NIGHT

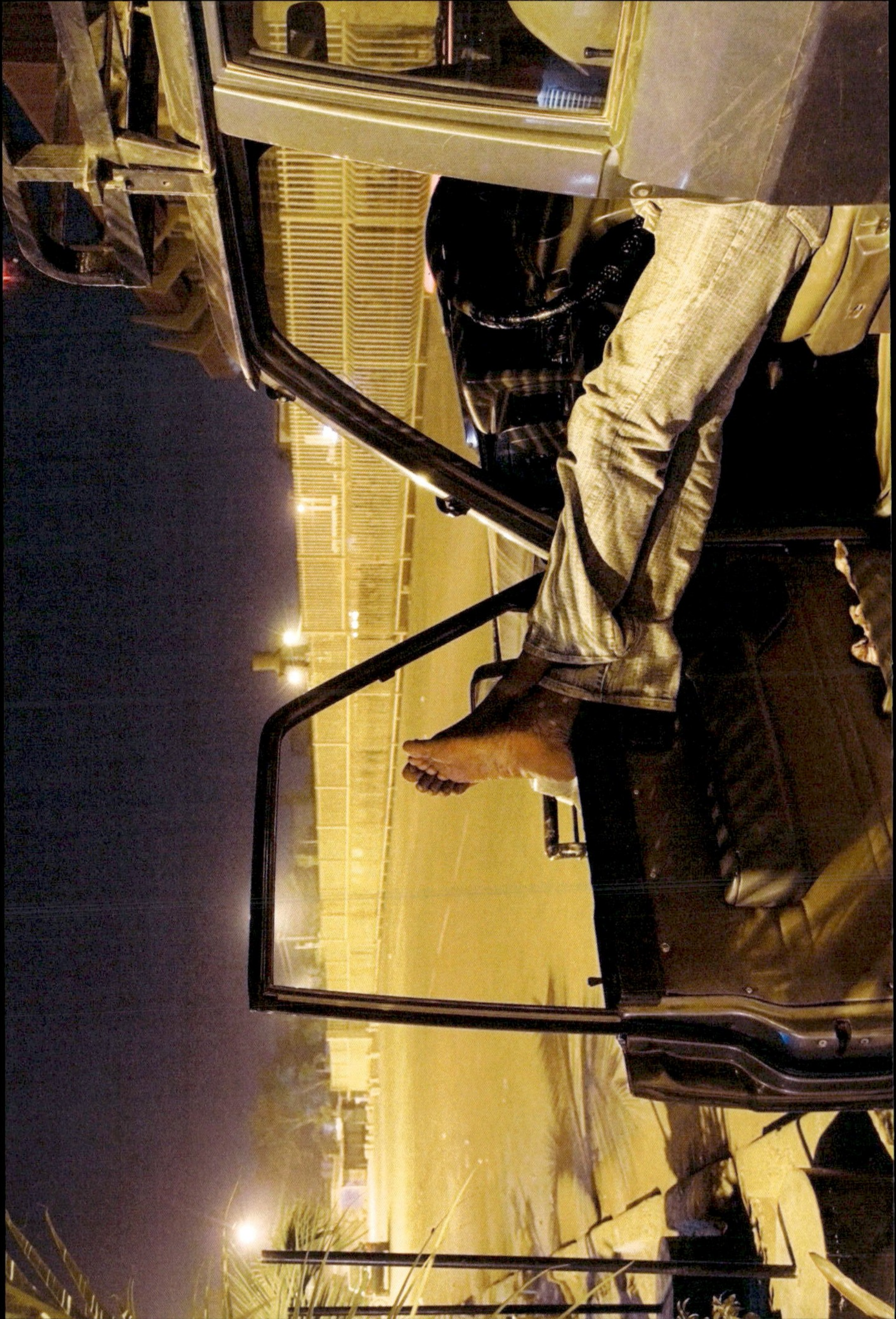

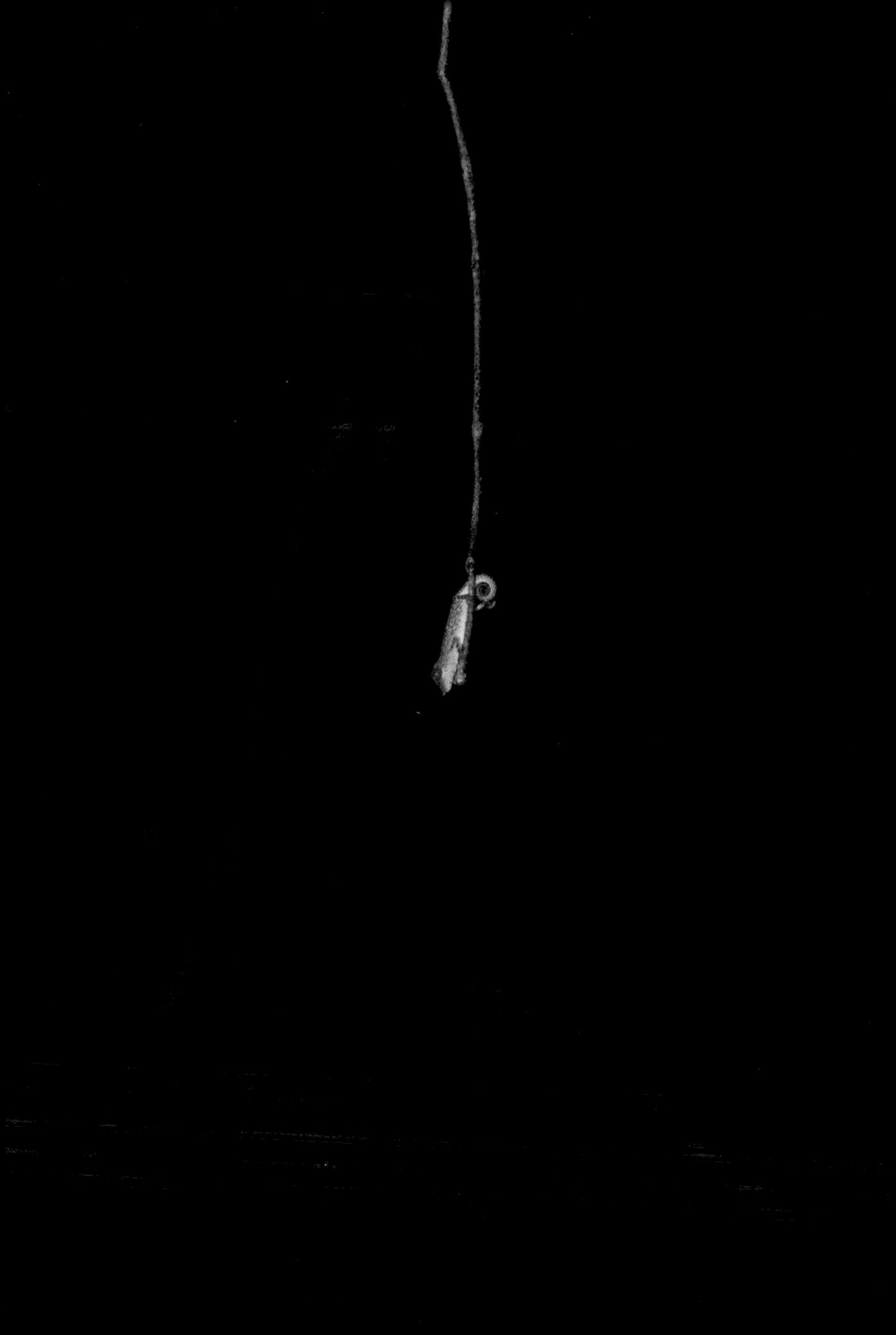

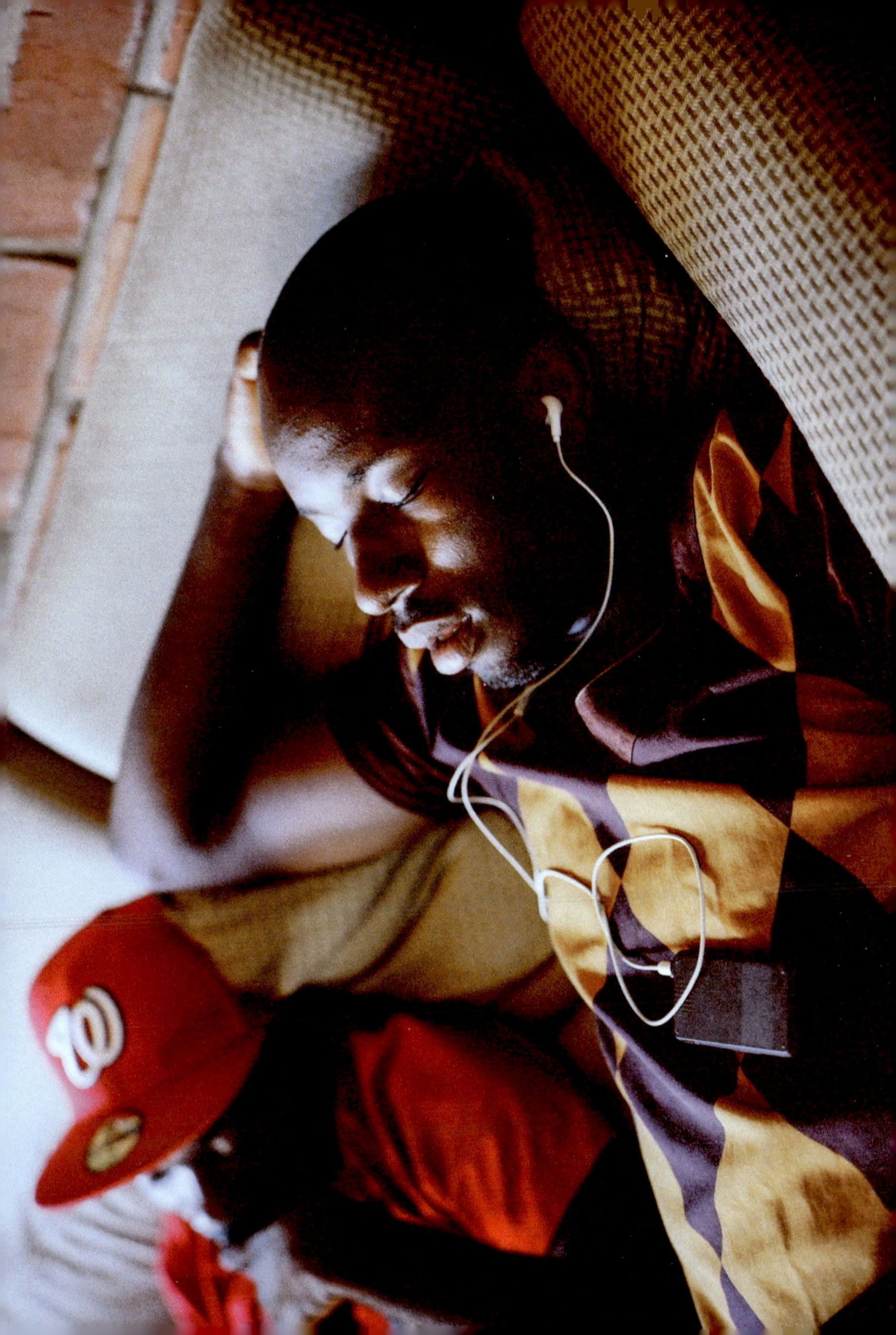

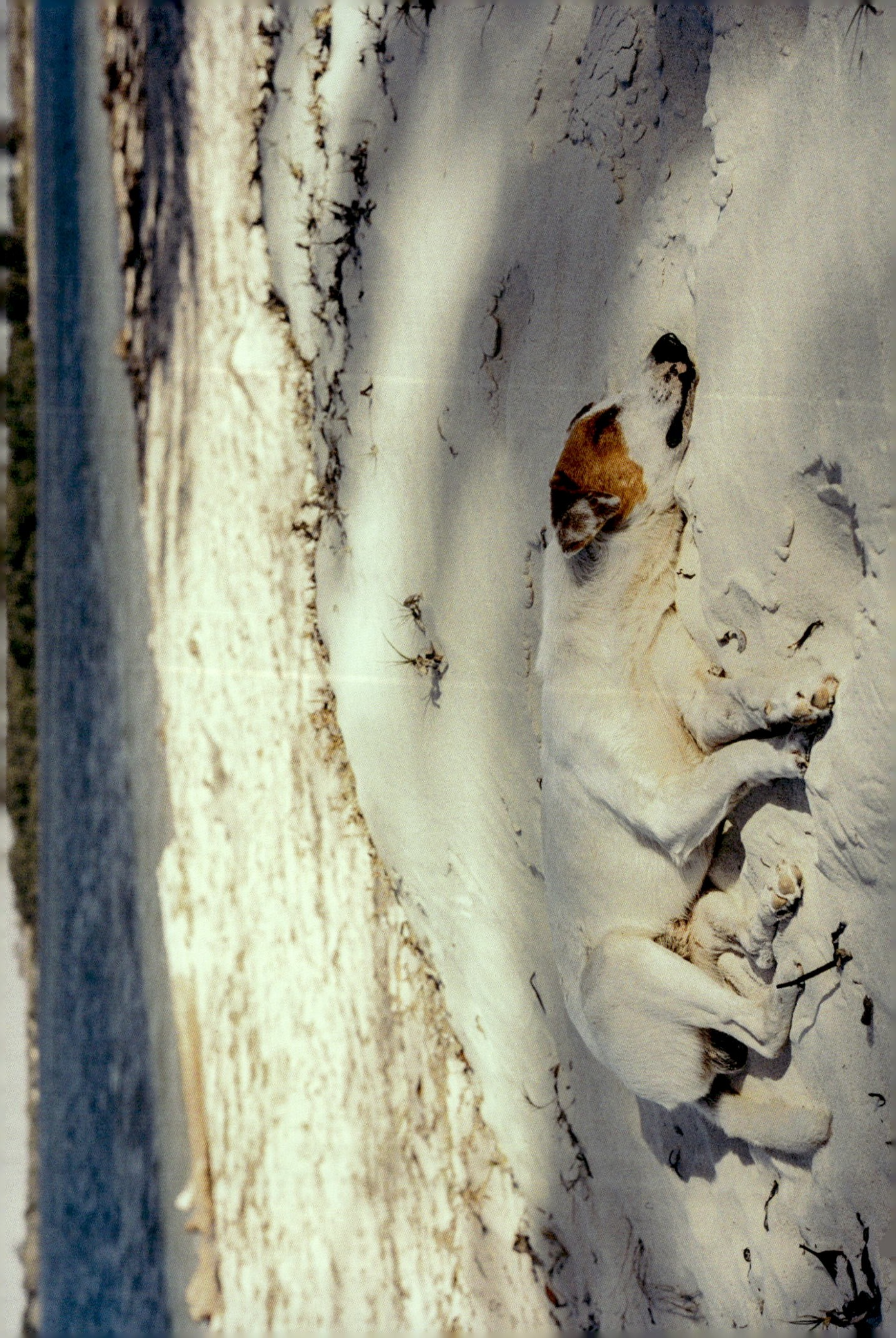

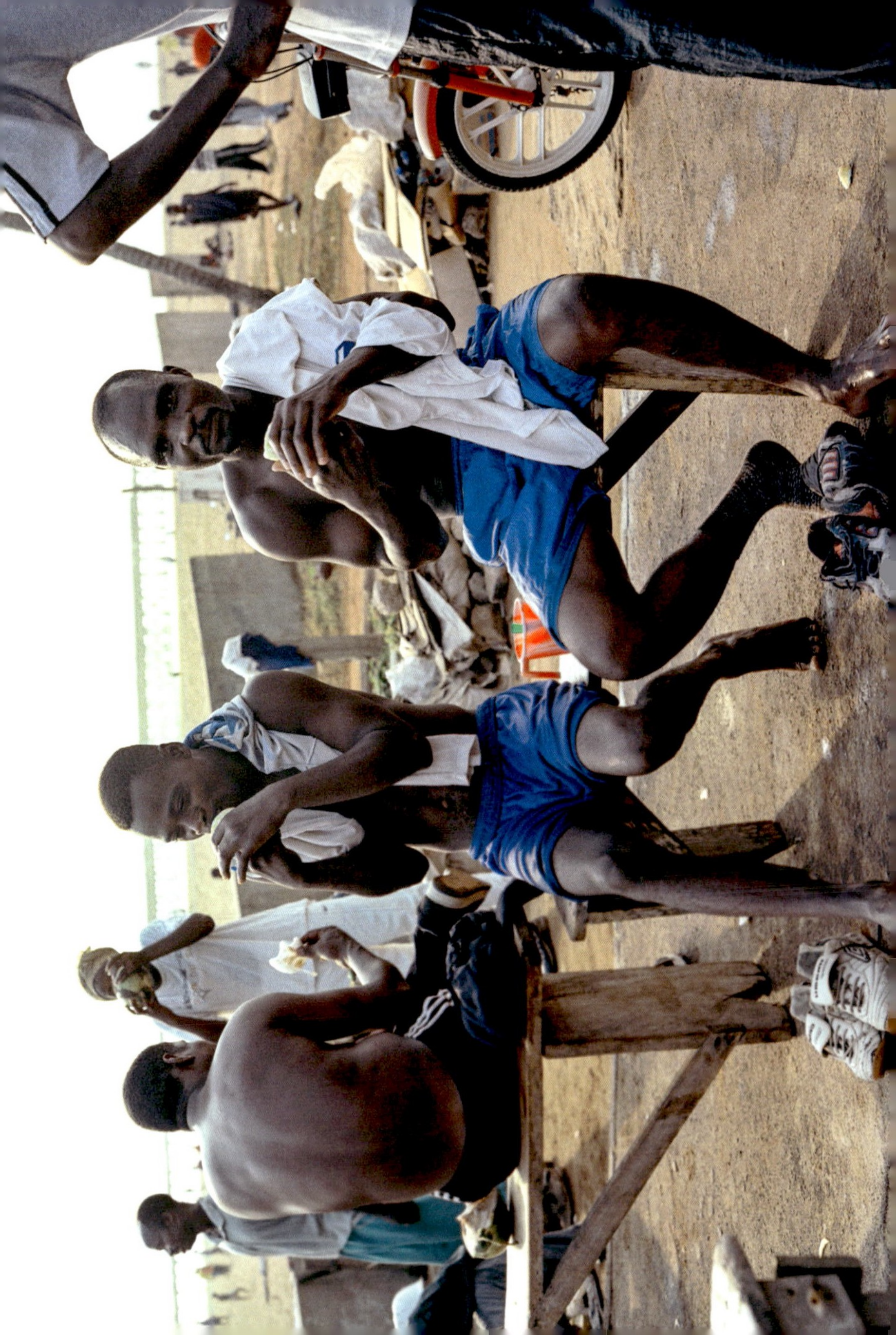

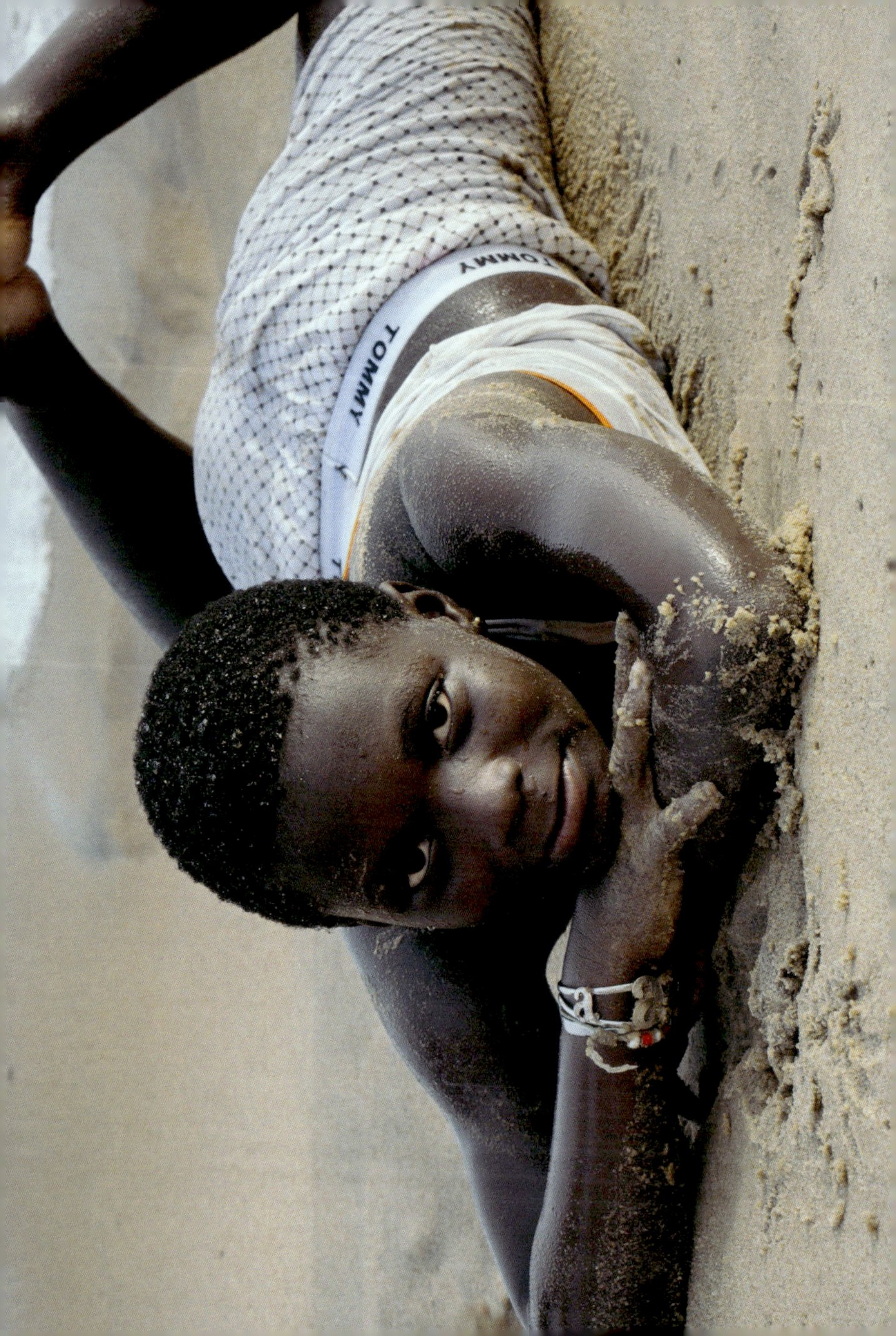
TOMMY
TOMMY

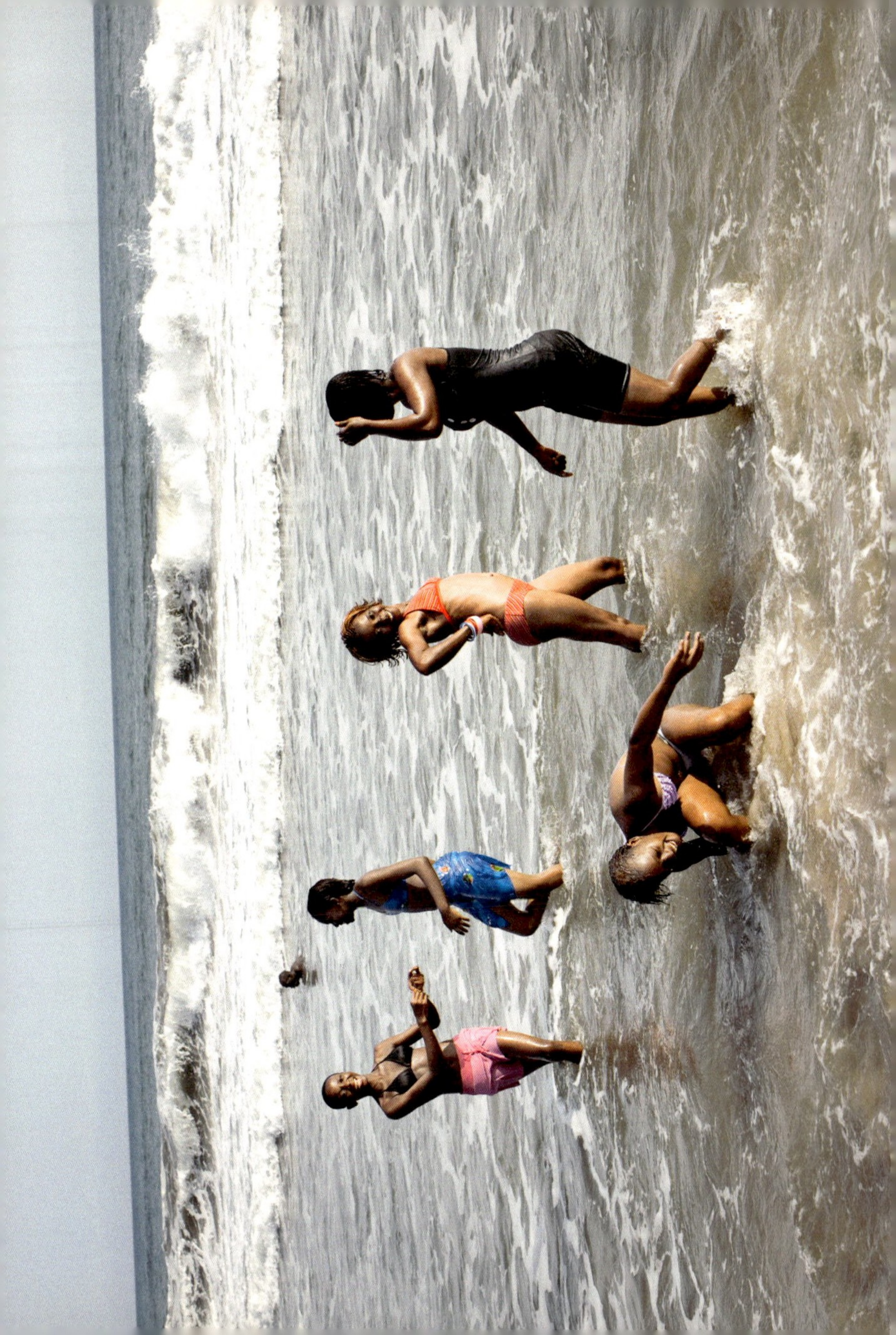

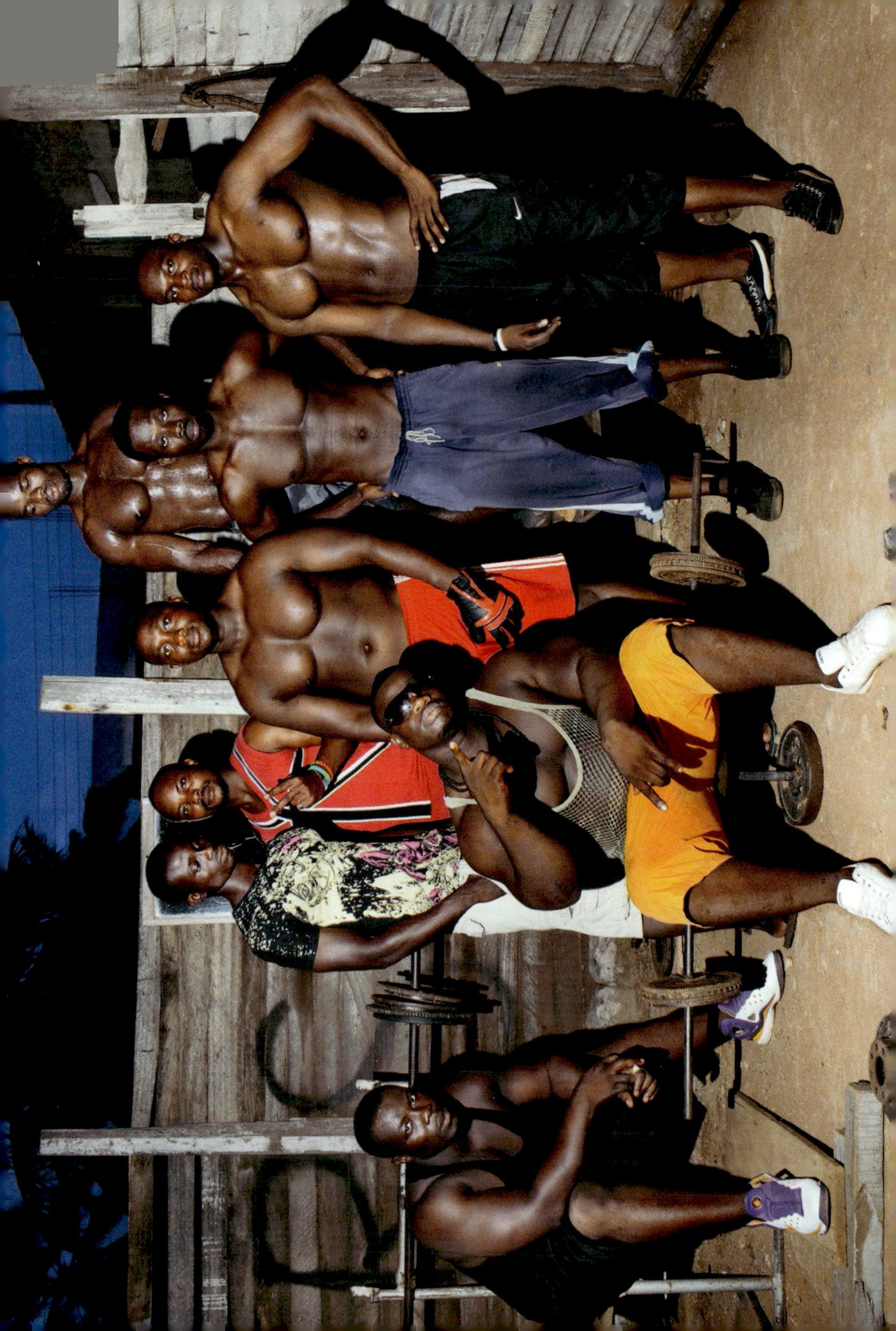

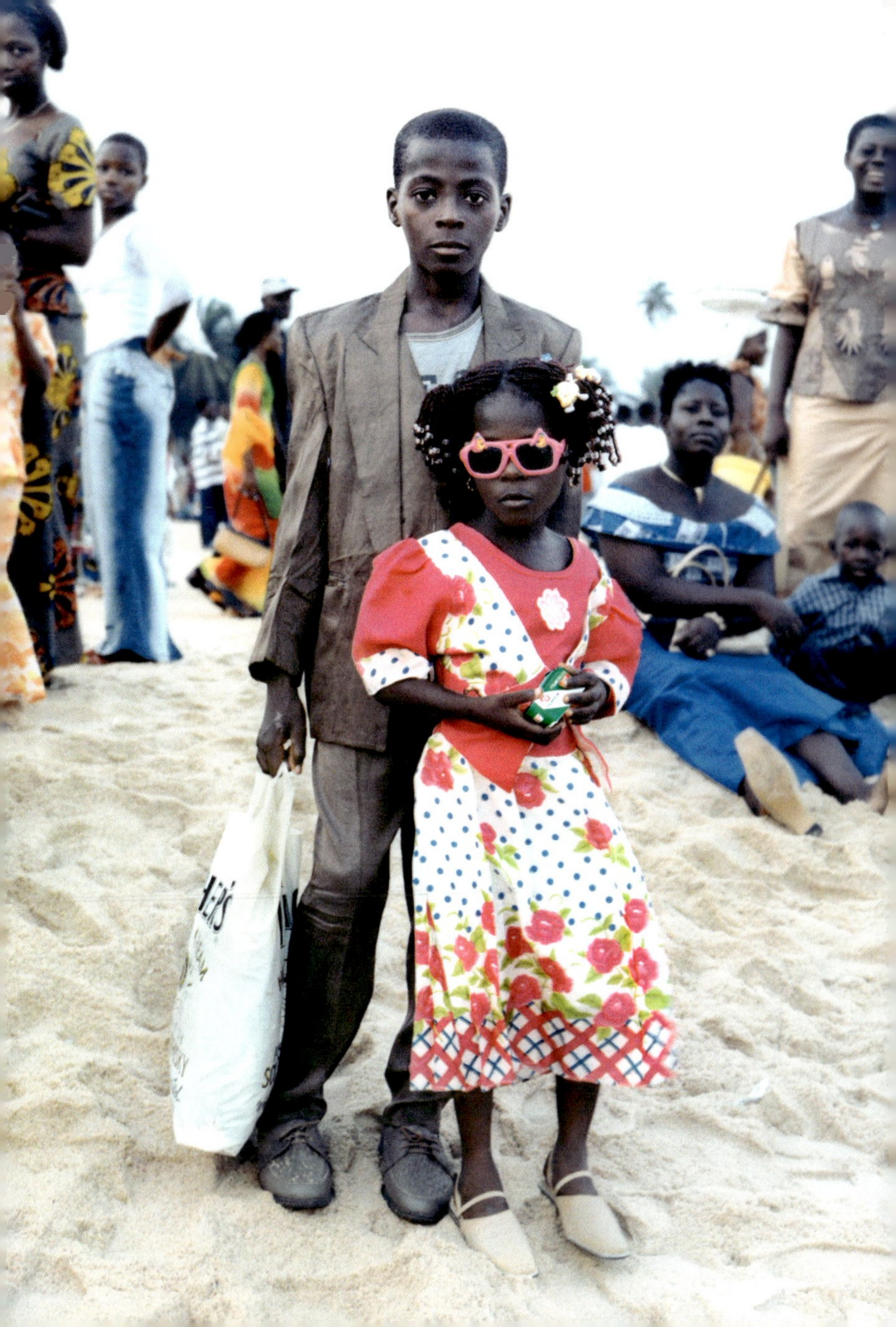

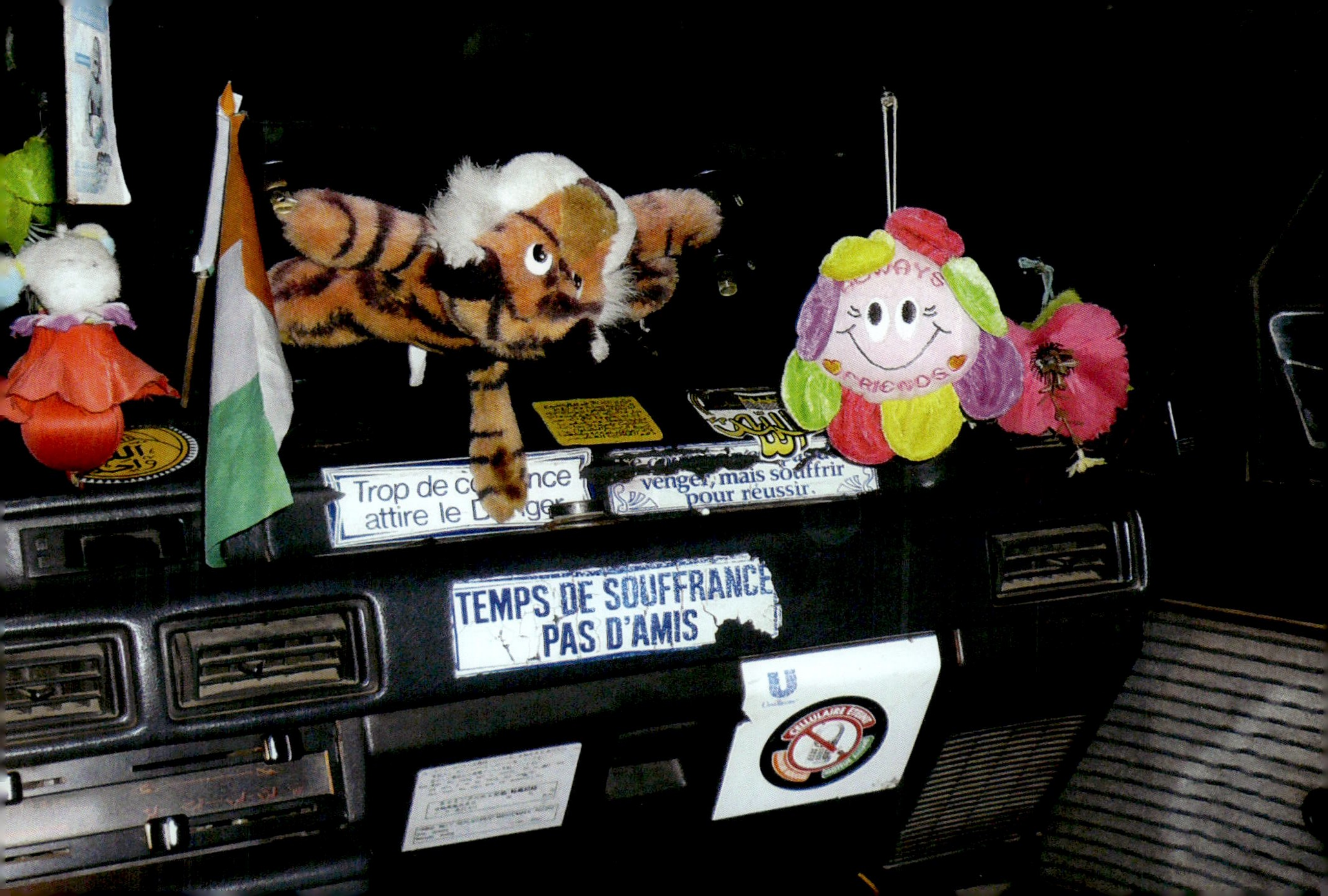
venger, mais souffrir
pour réussir.
TEMPS DE SOUFFRANCE
PAS D'AMIS
ALWAYS FRIENDS
CELLULAIRE

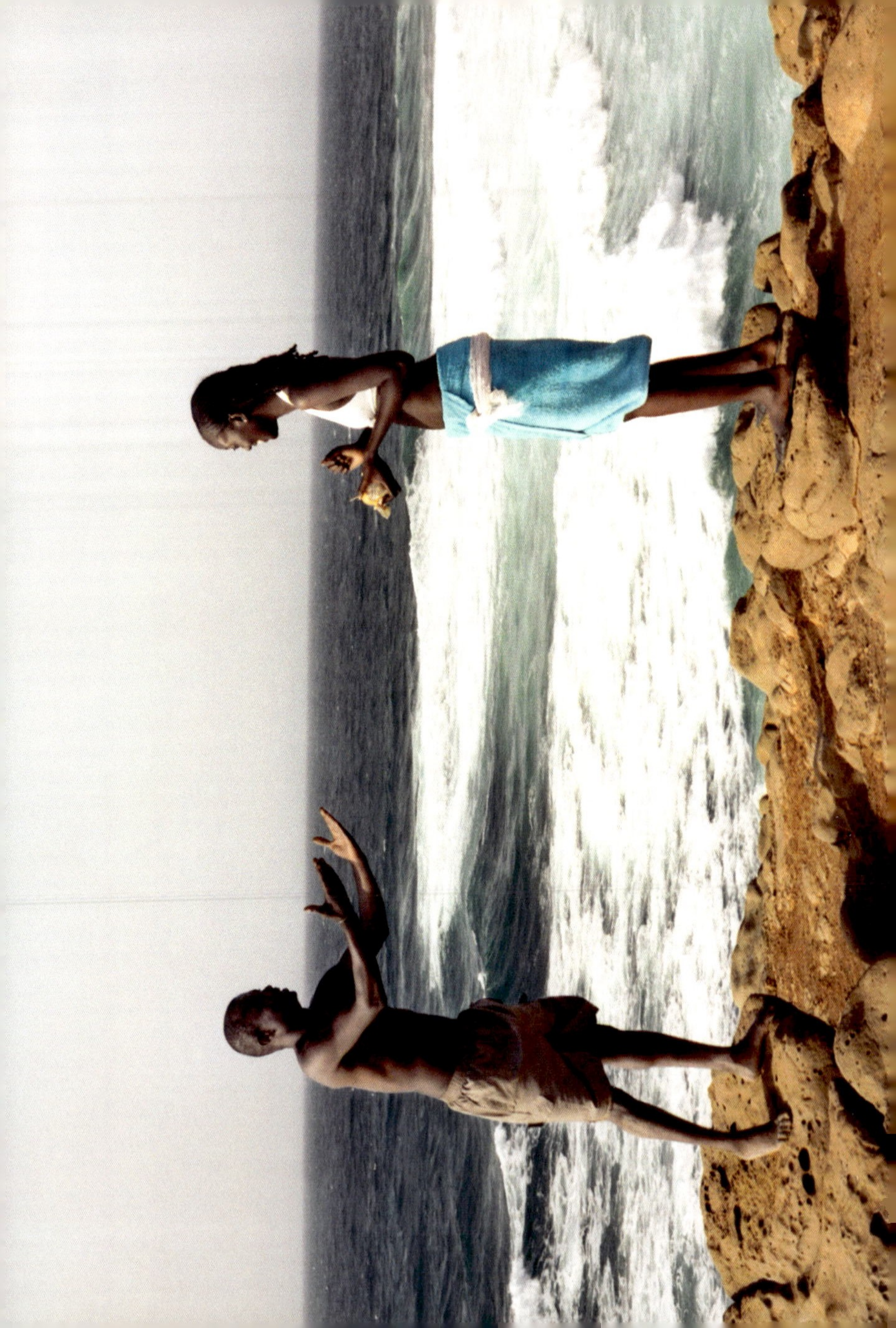

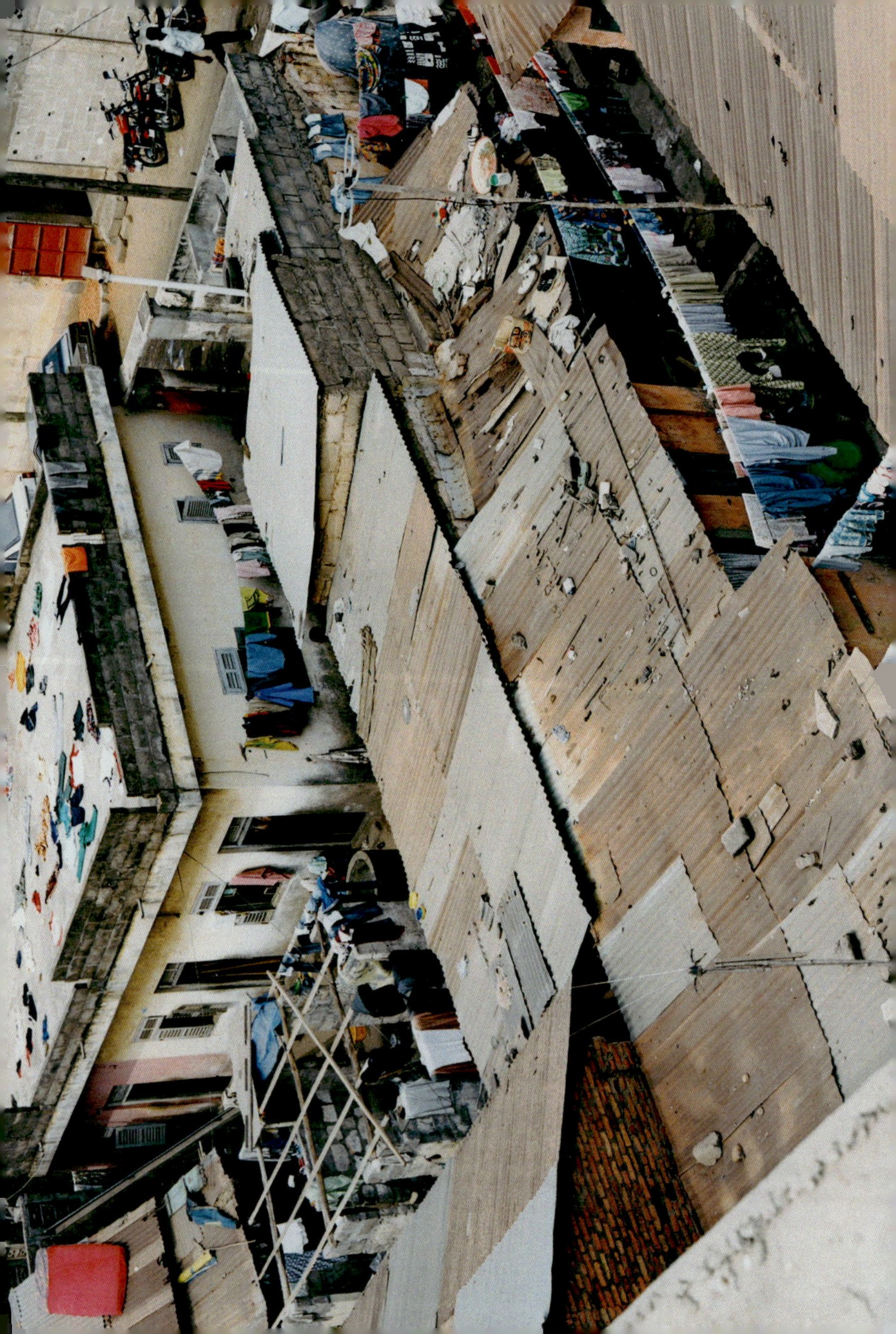

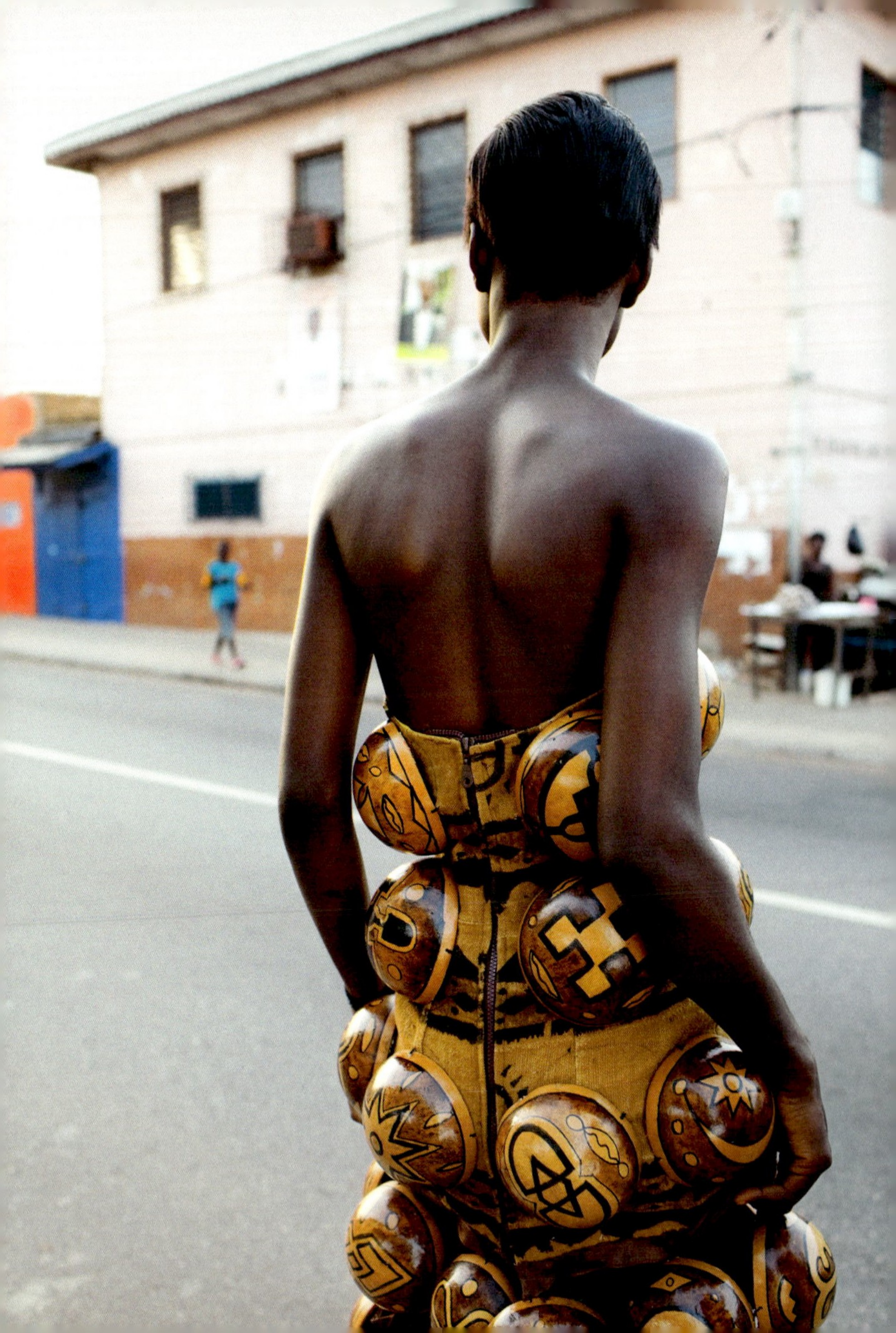

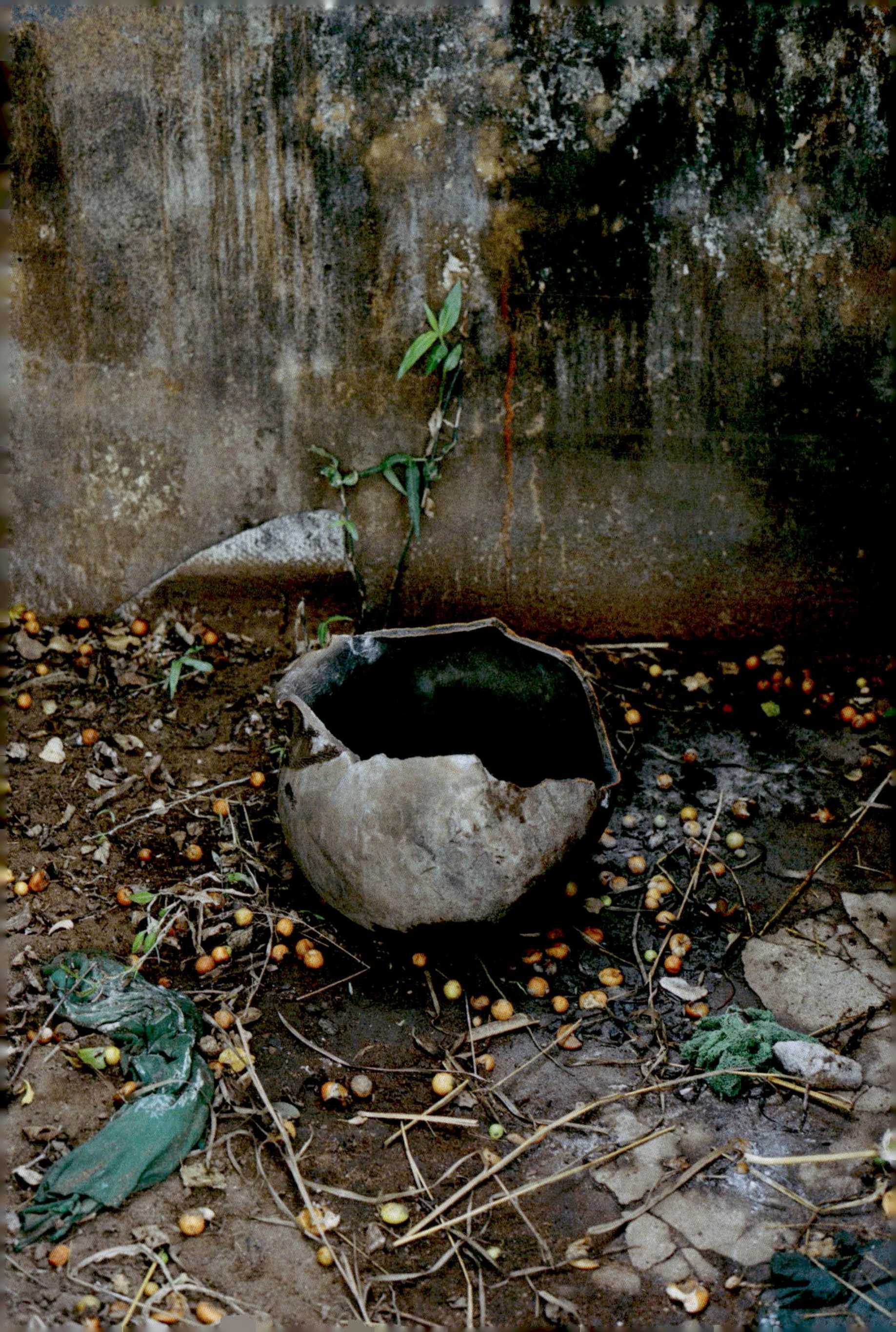

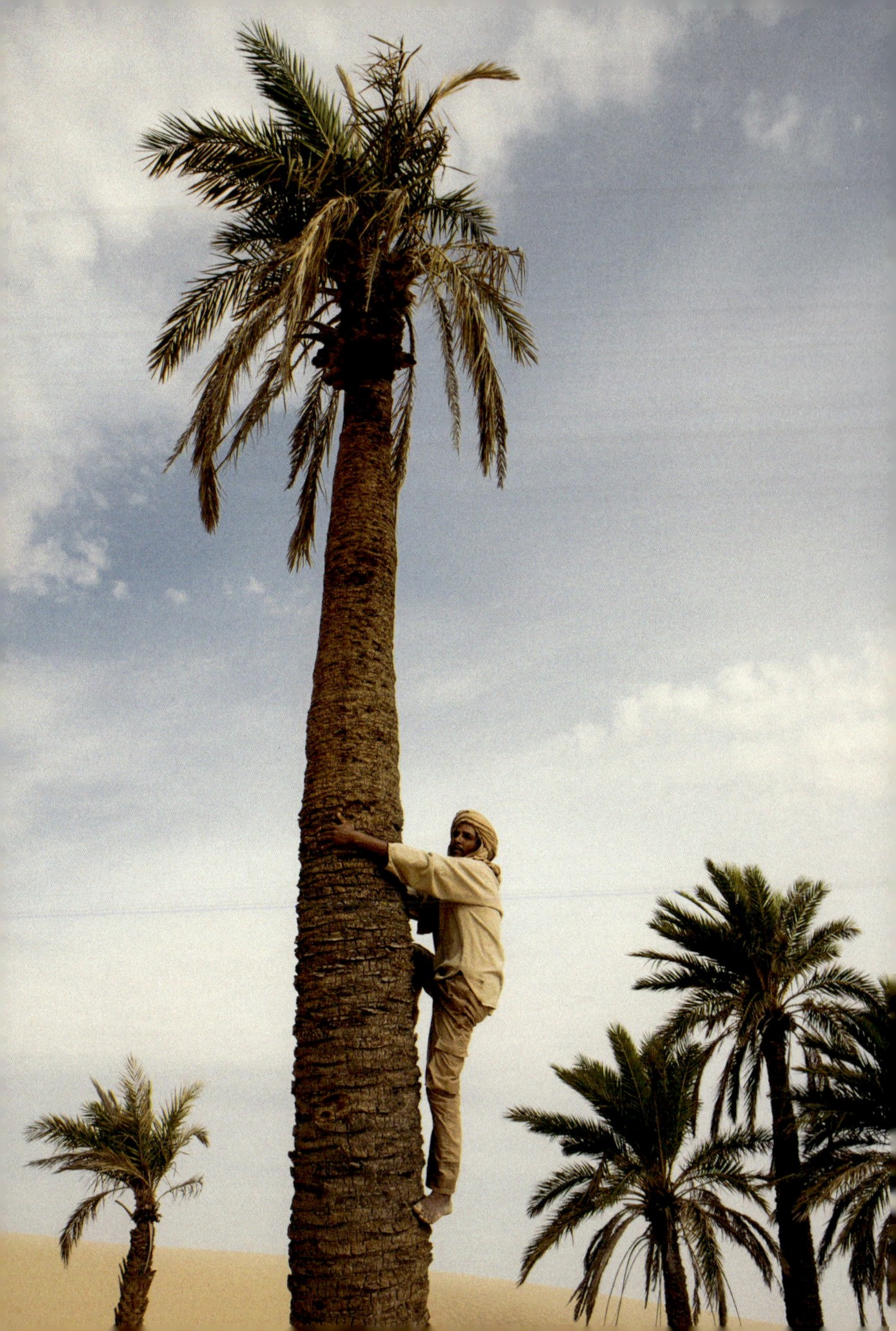

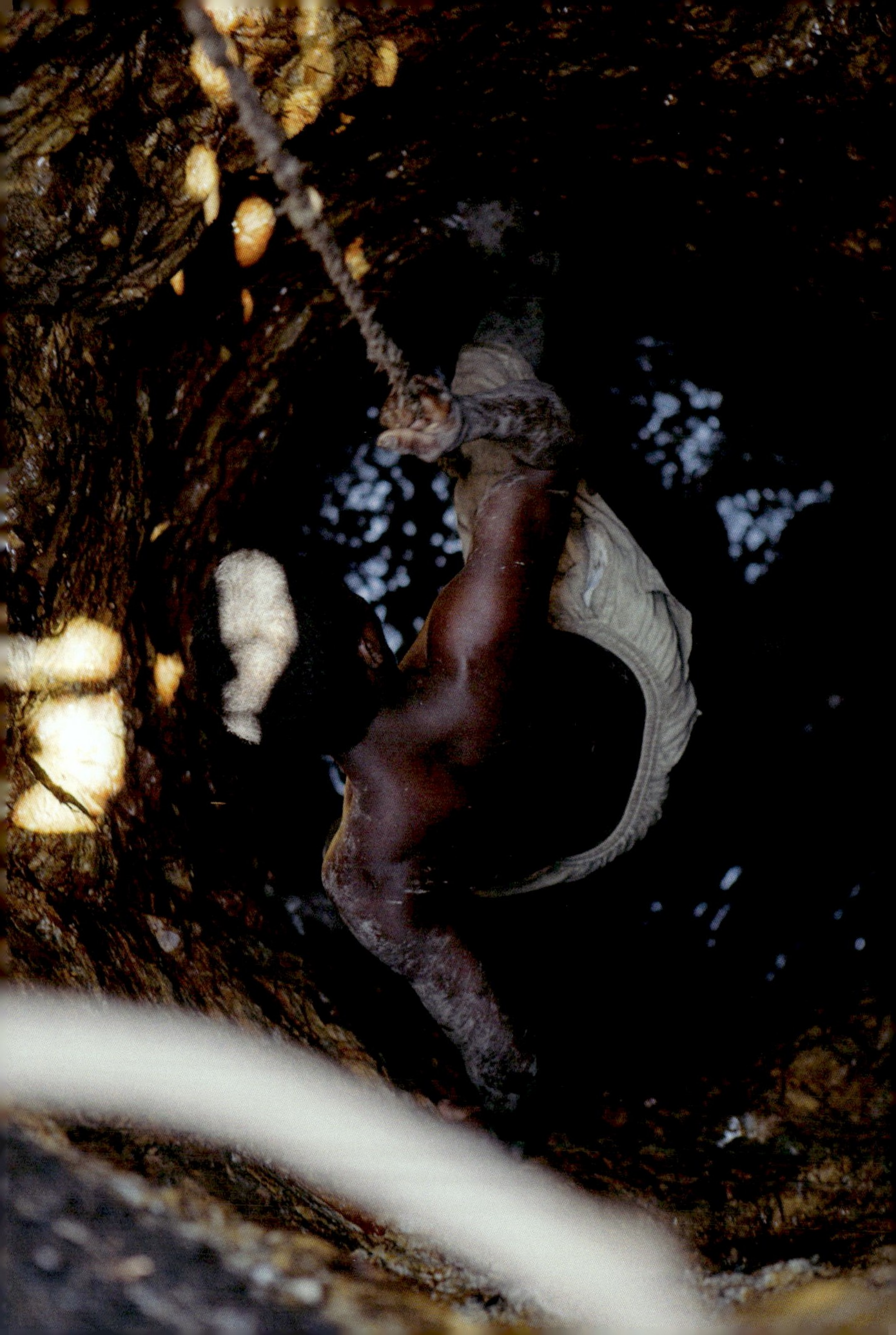

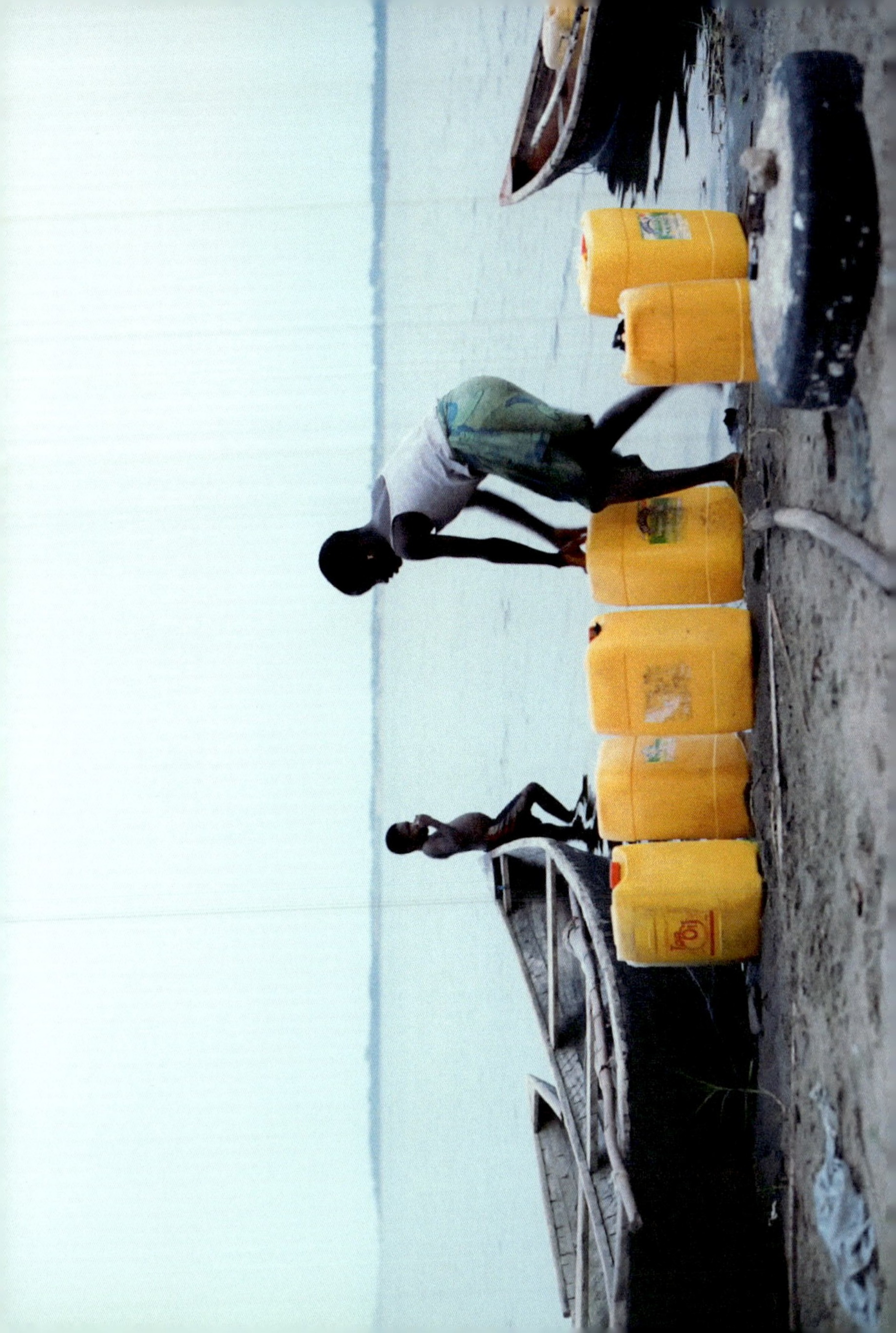

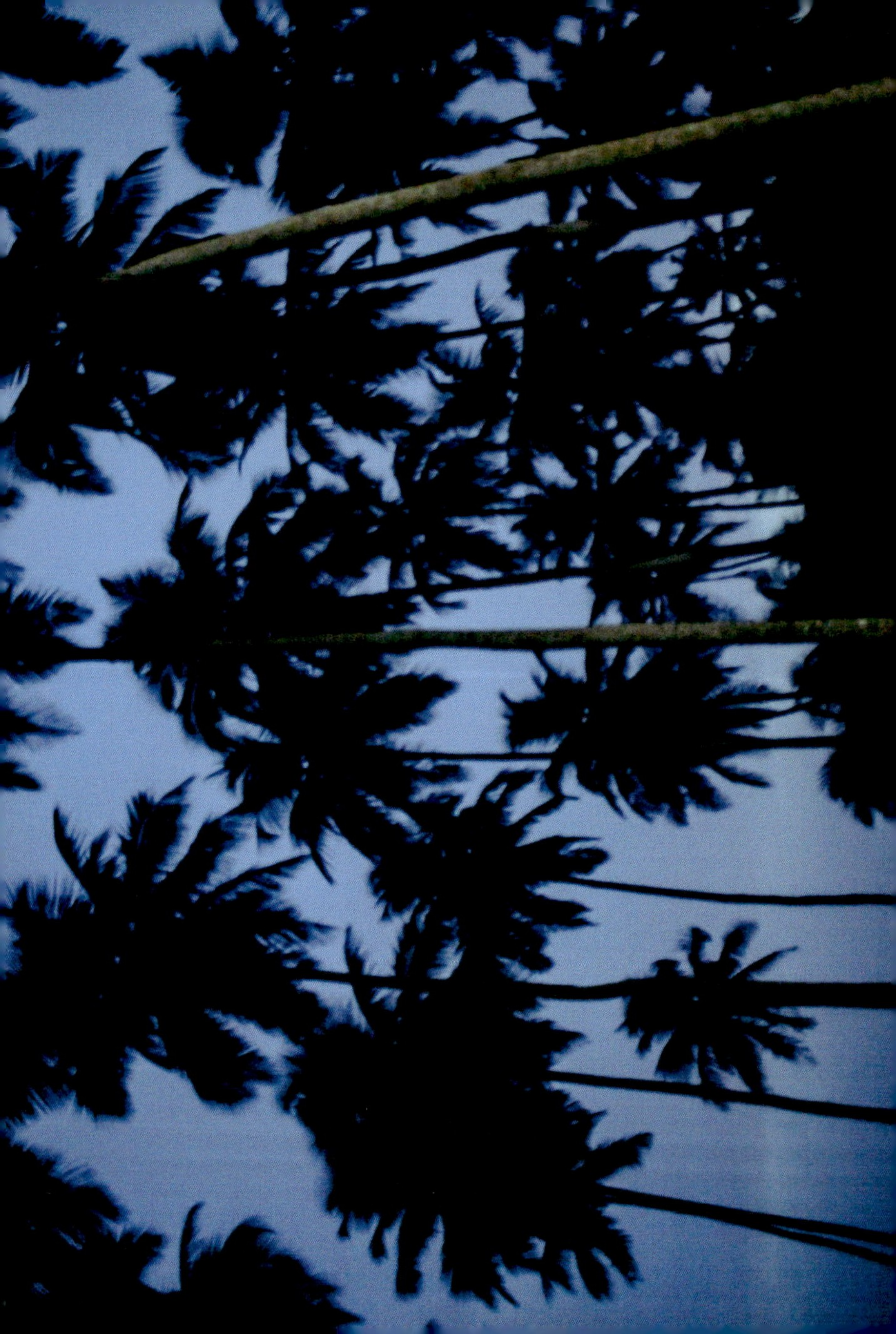

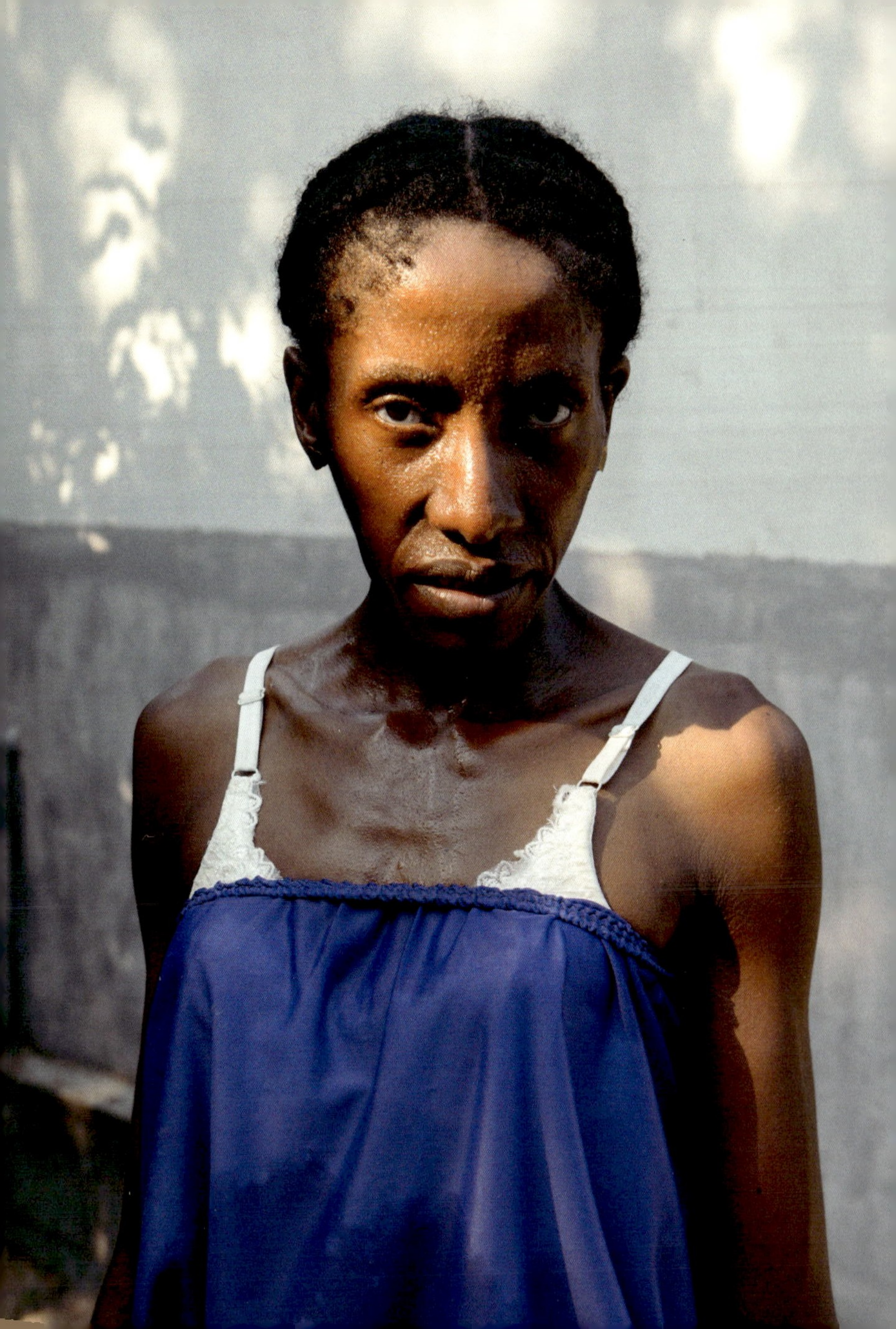

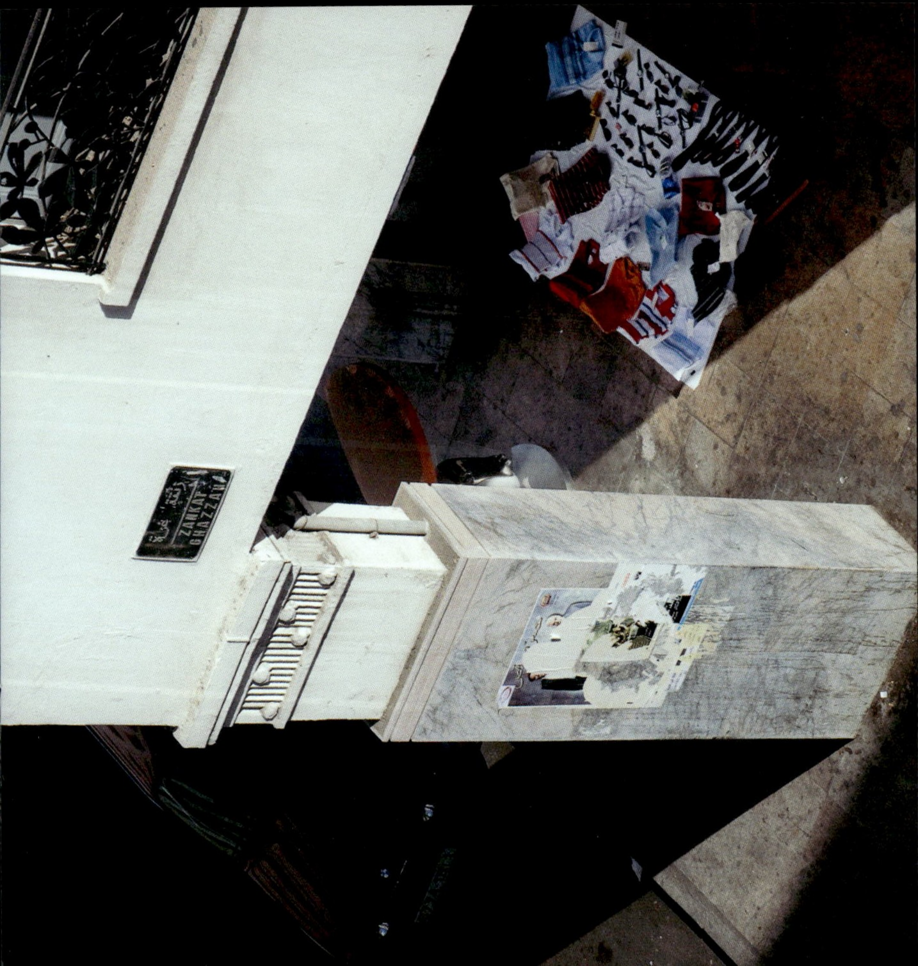
ZANKAT
GHAZZAN

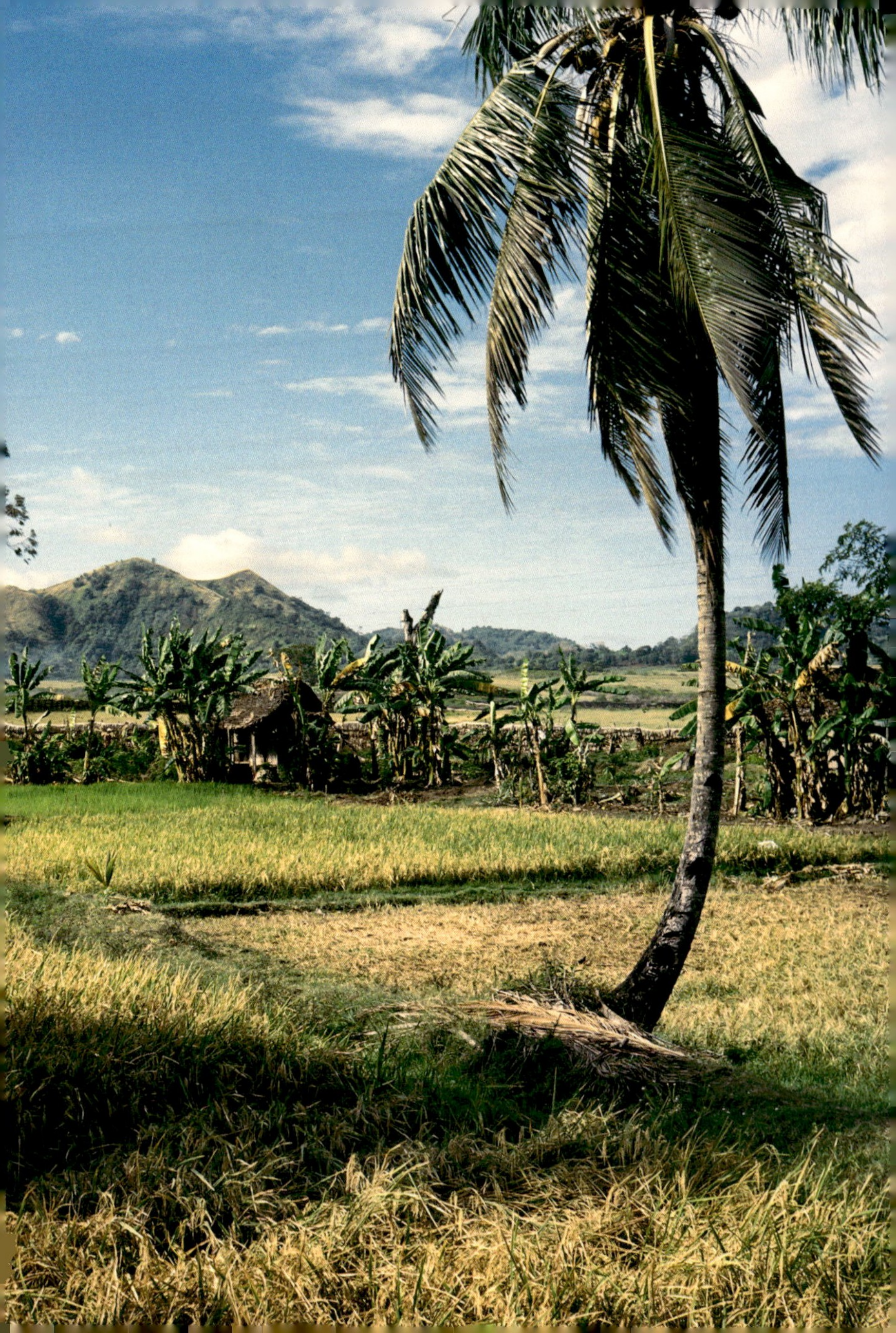

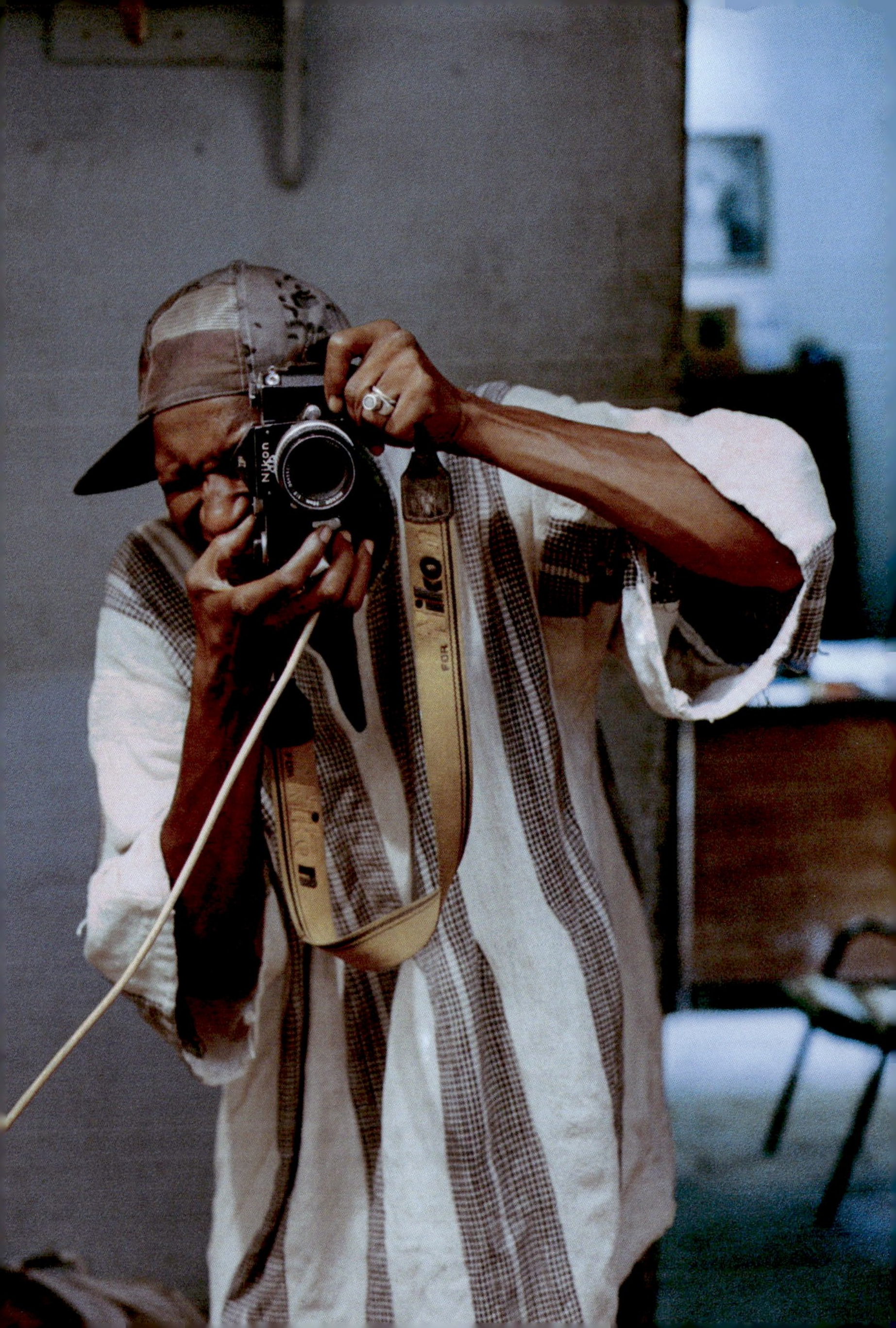
Nikon

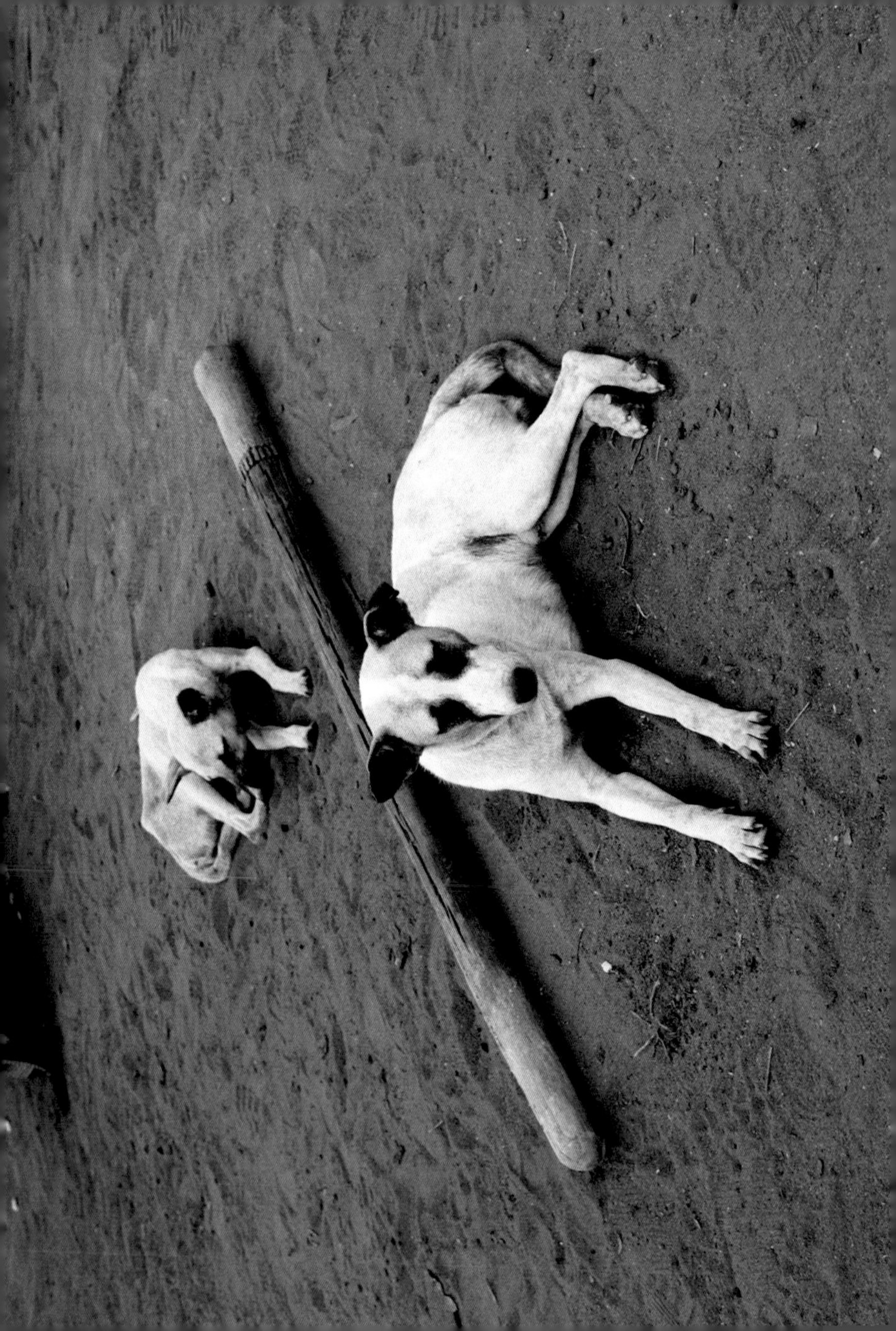

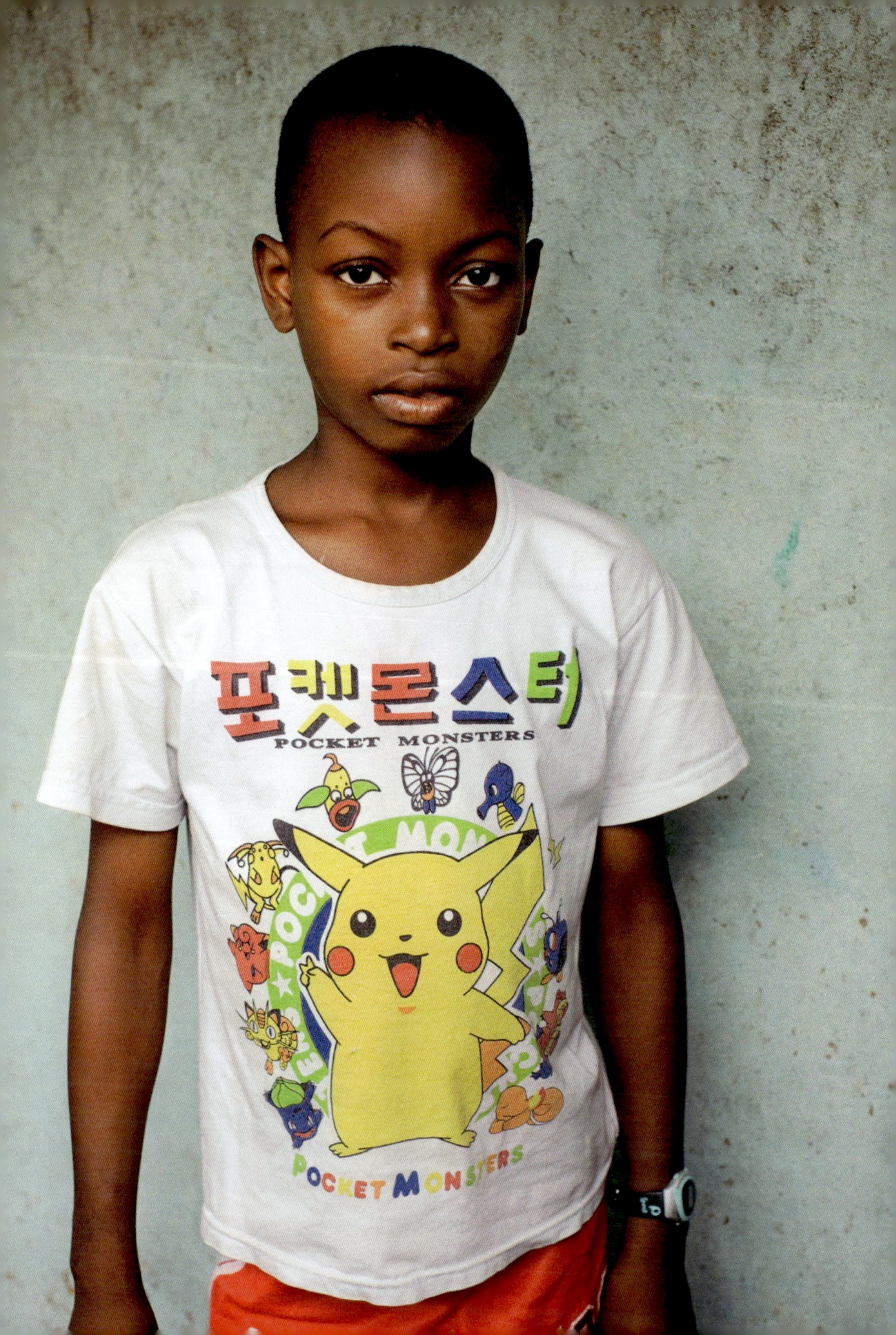
포켓몬스터
POCKET MONSTERS
POCKET MONSTERS

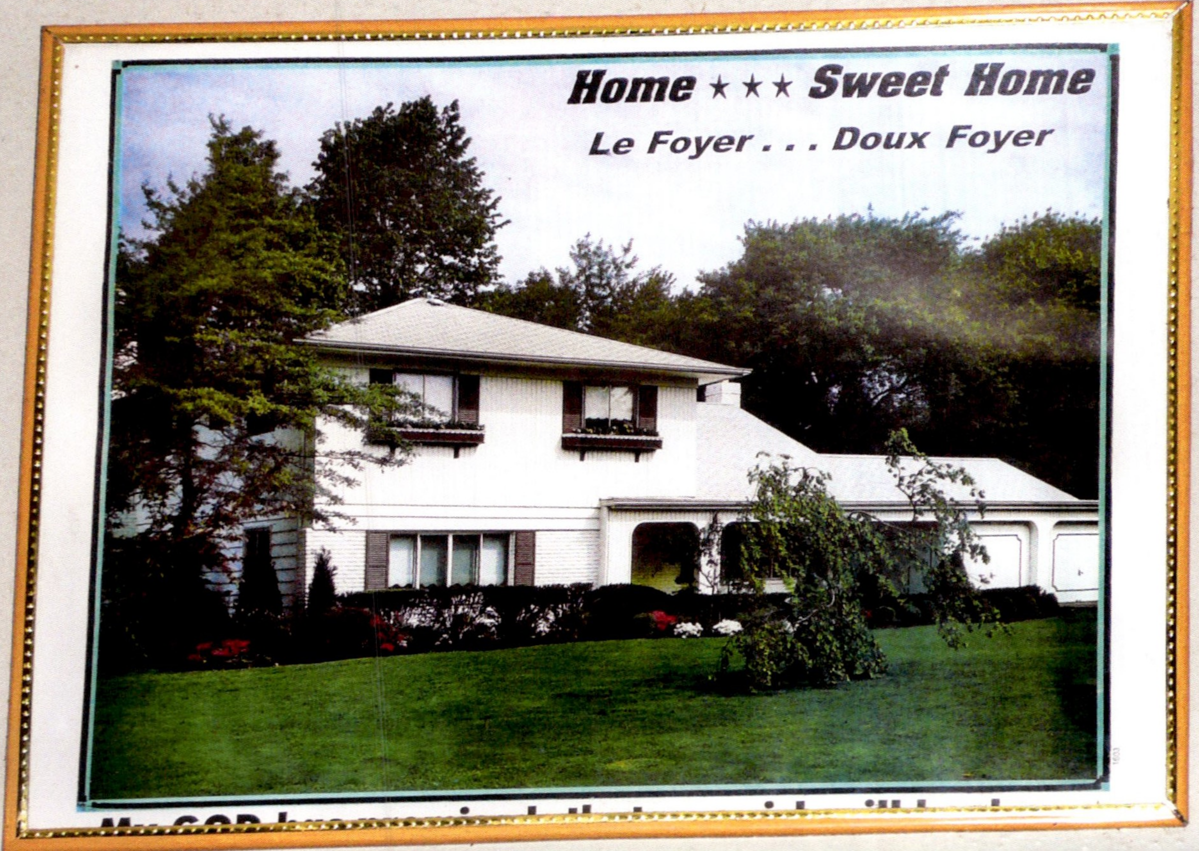
Home ★★★ Sweet Home
Le Foyer . . . Doux Foyer

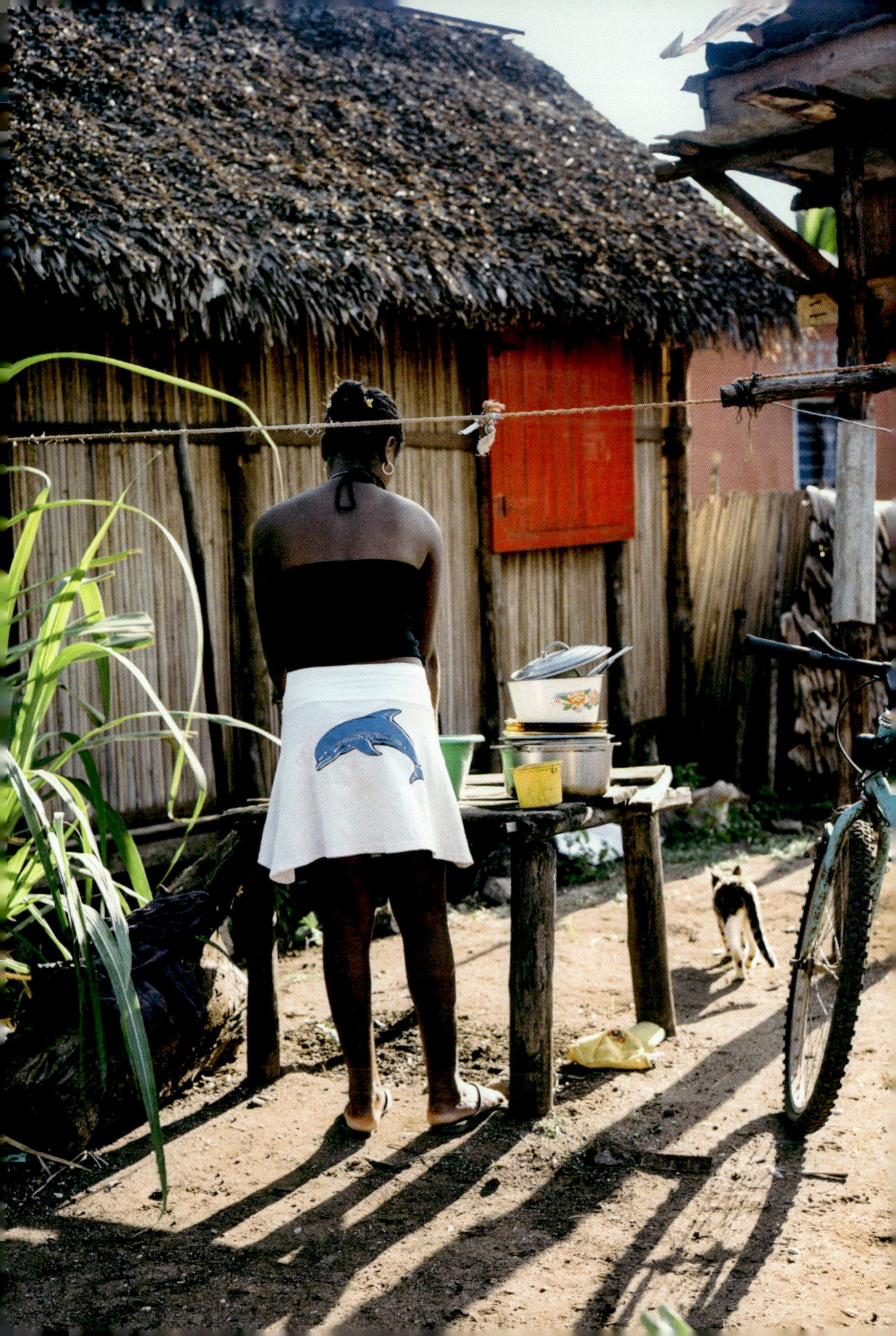

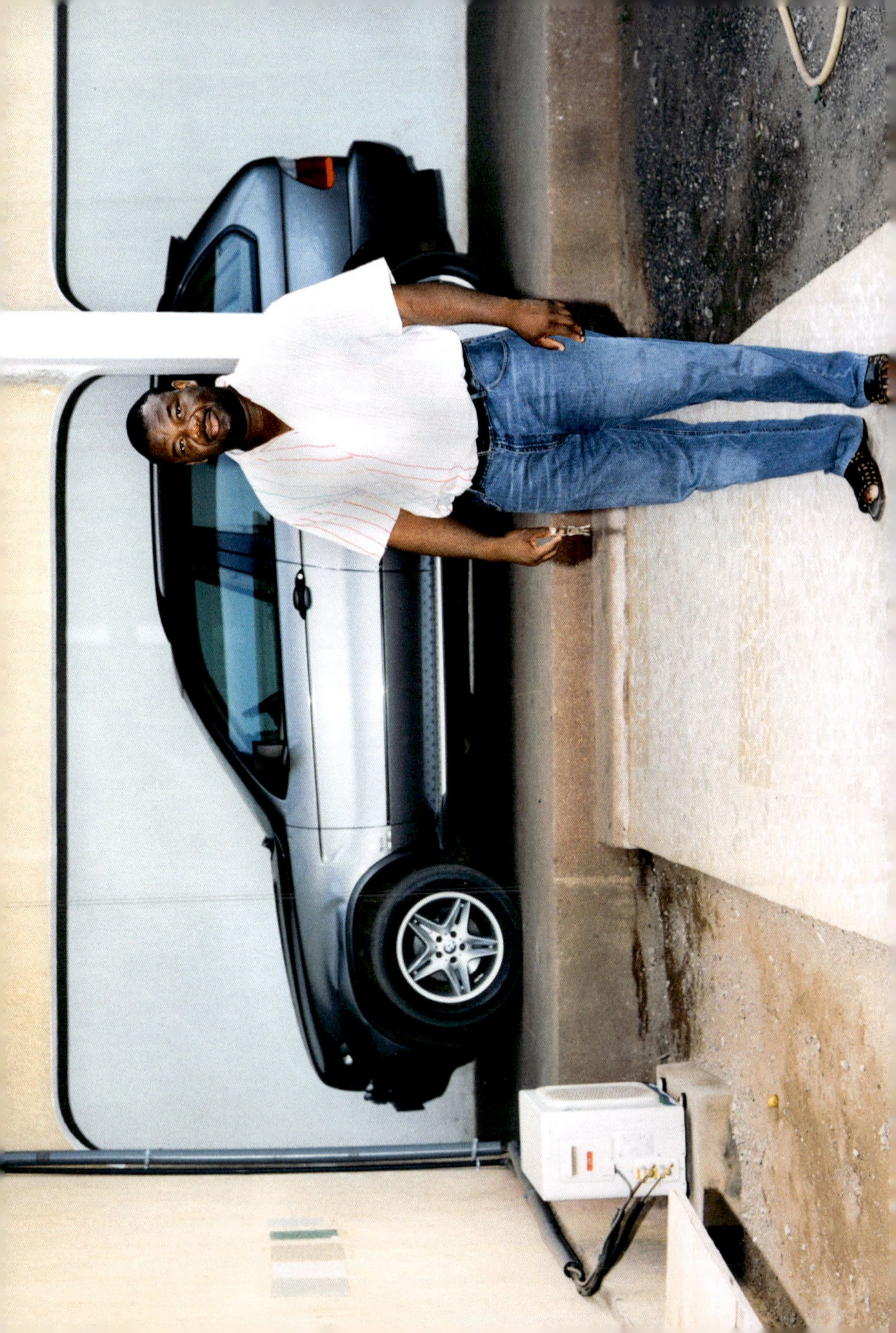

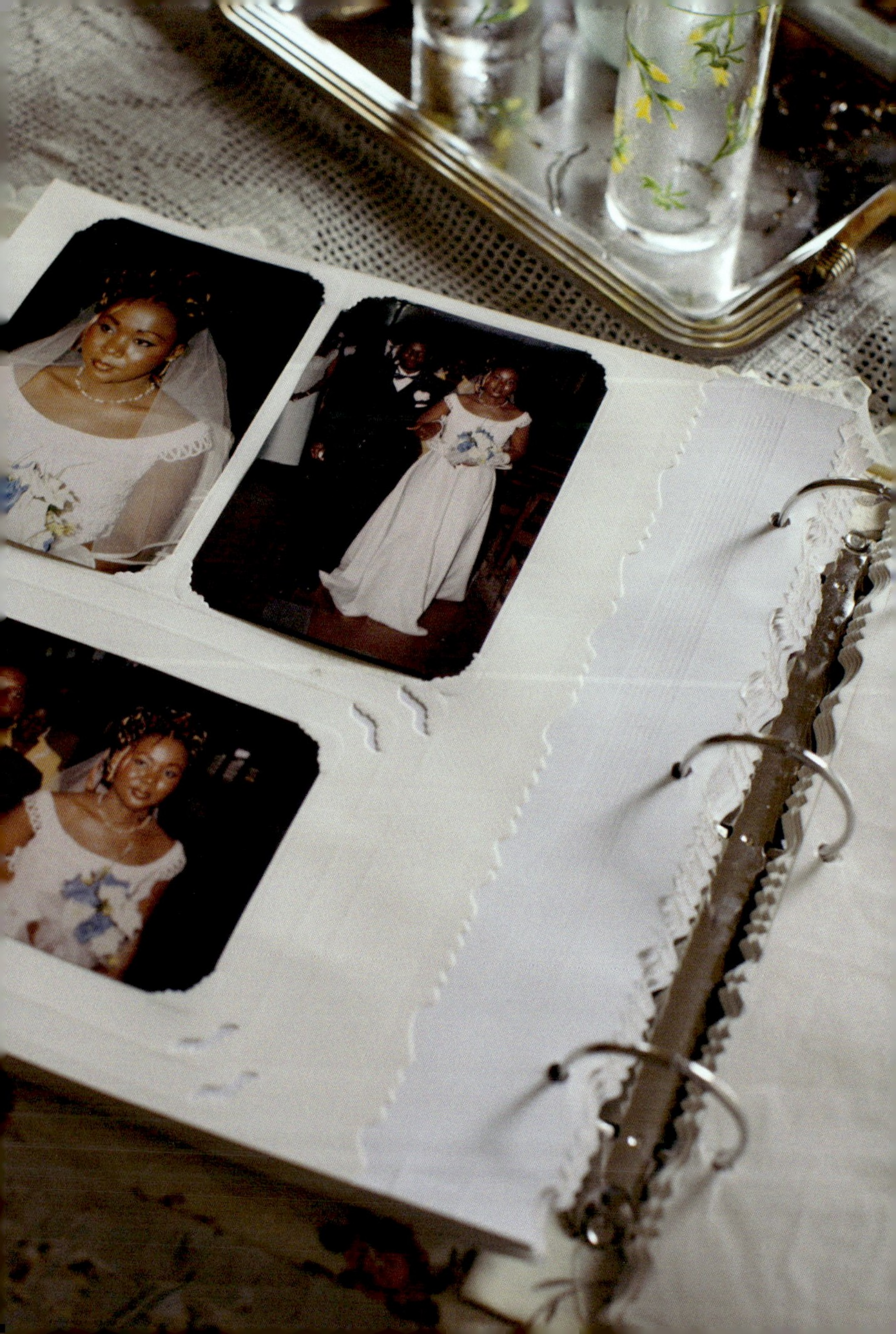

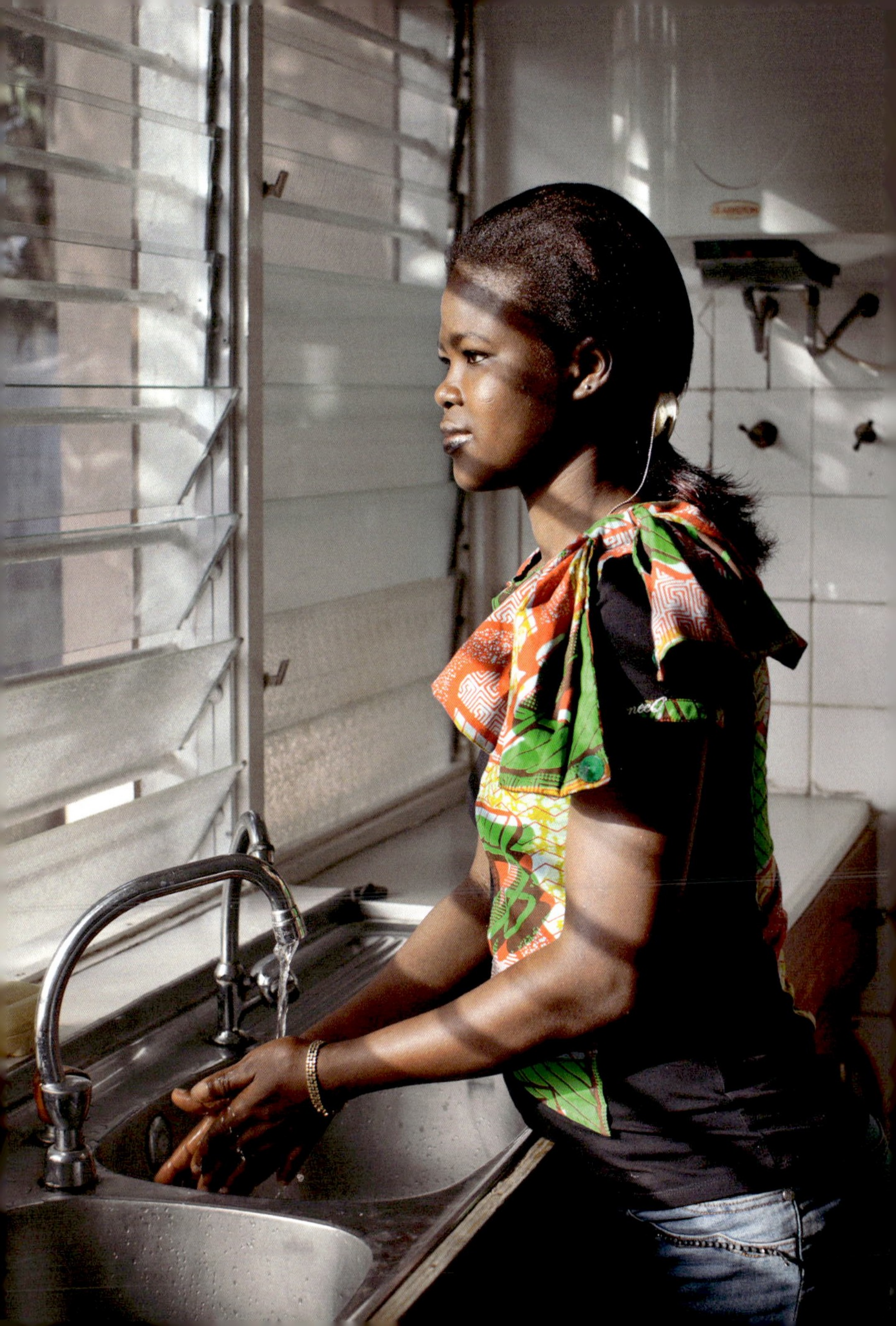

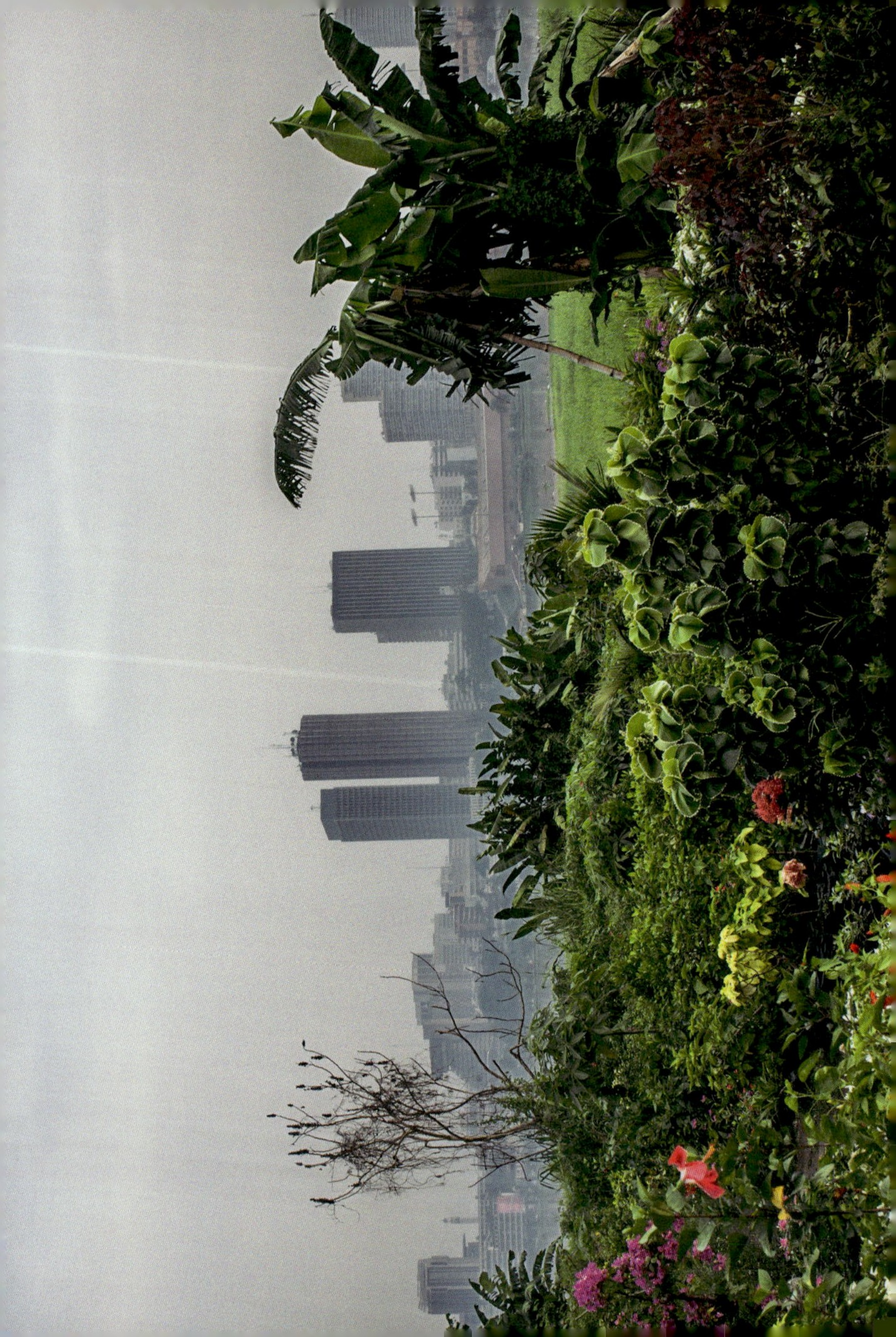

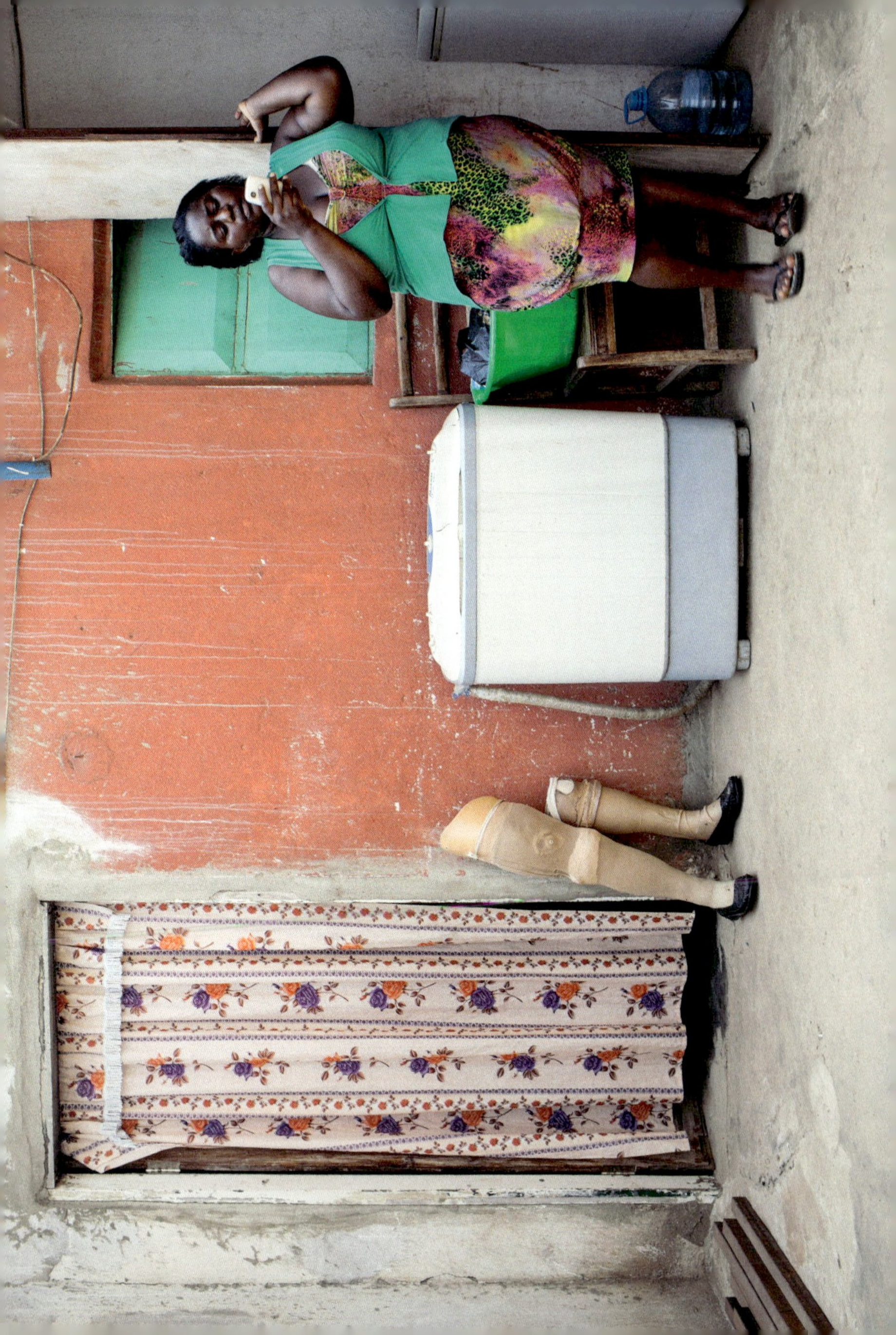

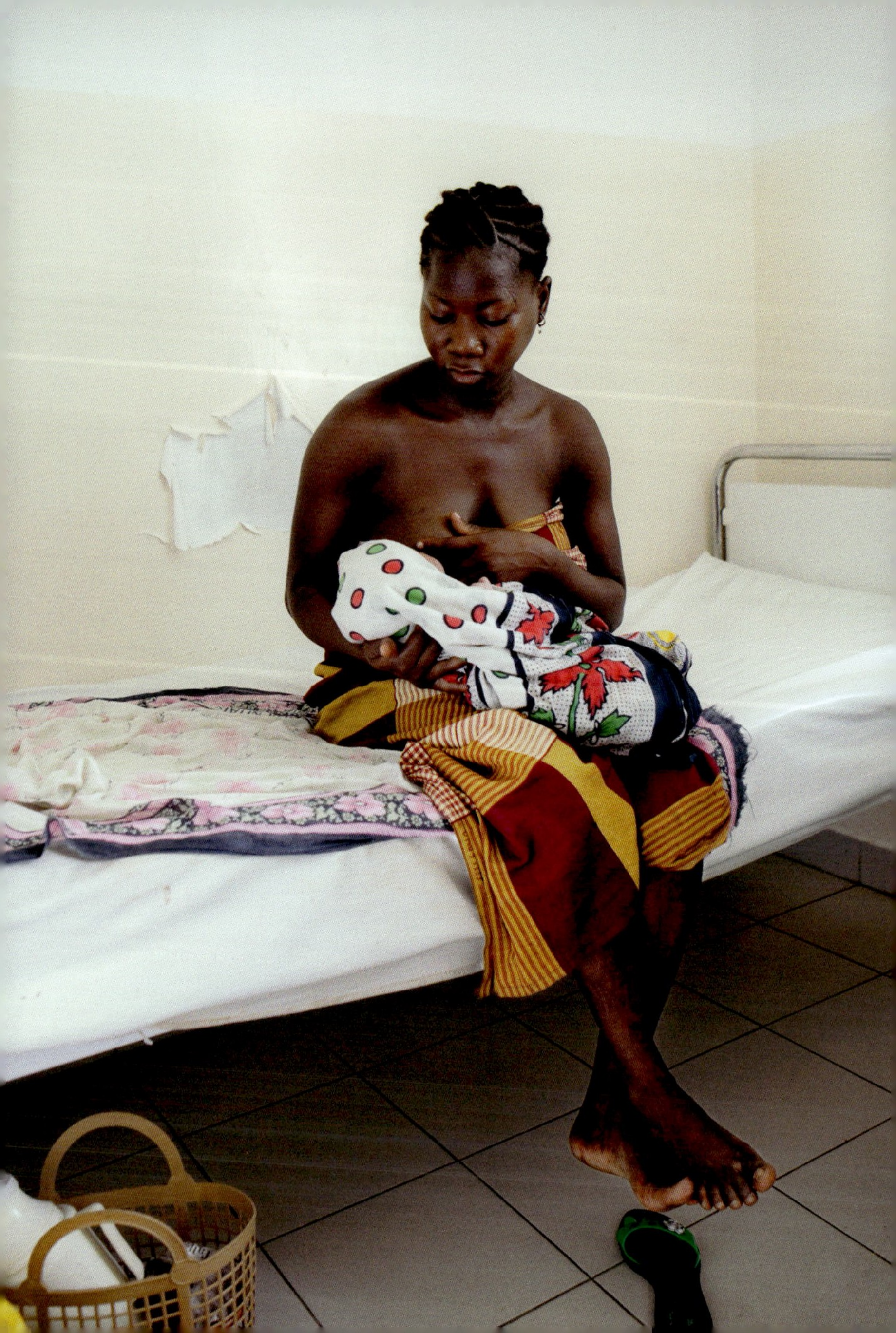

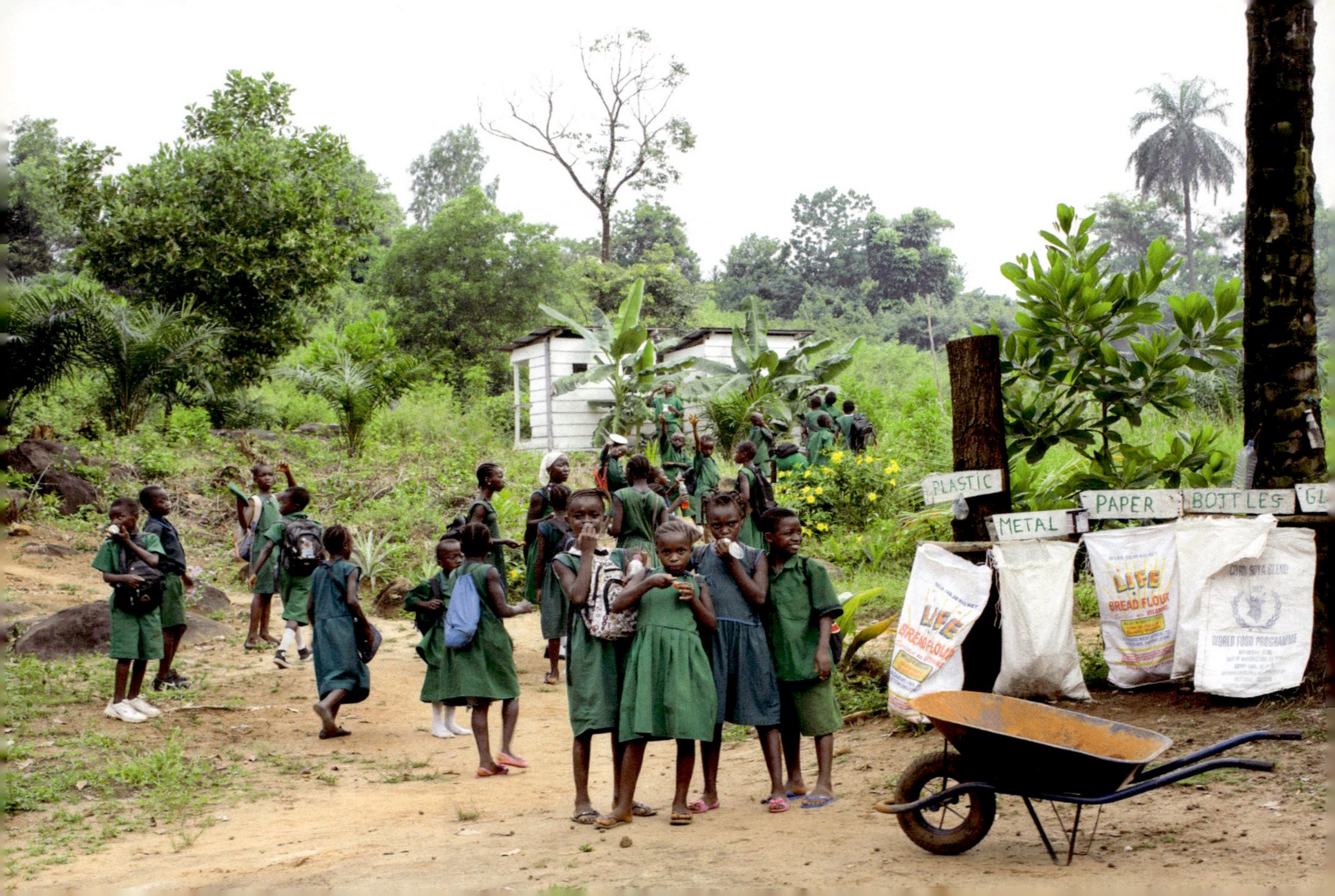
PLASTIC
METAL
PAPER
BOTTLES
LIFE
BREAD FLOUR
LIFE
BREAD FLOUR
WORLD FOOD PROGRAMME

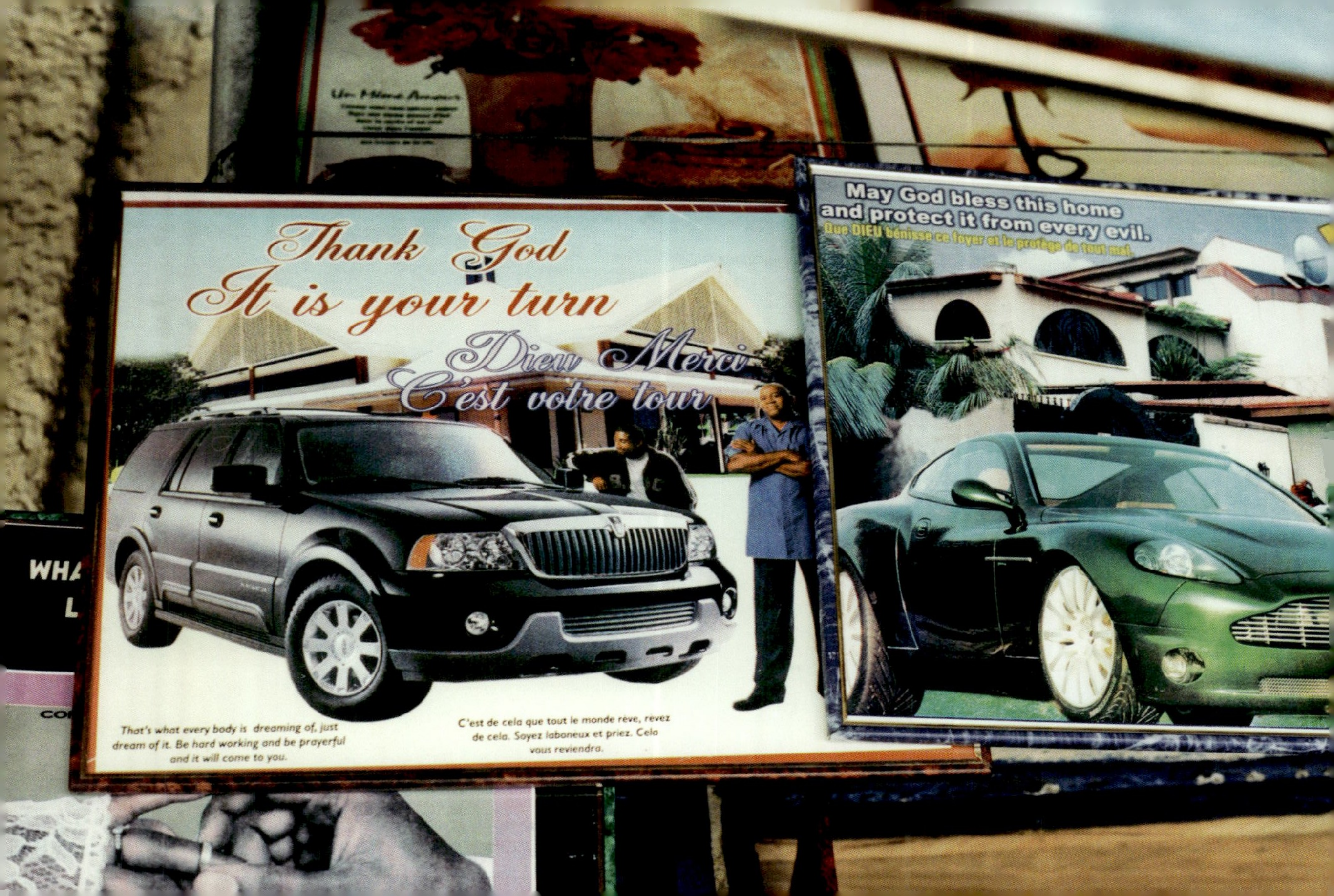
Thank God
It is your turn
Dieu Merci
C'est votre tour
That's what every body is dreaming of, just dream of it. Be hard working and be prayerful and it will come to you.
C'est de cela que tout le monde rêve, revez de cela. Soyez laboneux et priez. Cela vous reviendra.
May God bless this home and protect it from every evil.
Que DIEU bénisse ce foyer et le protège de tout mal.

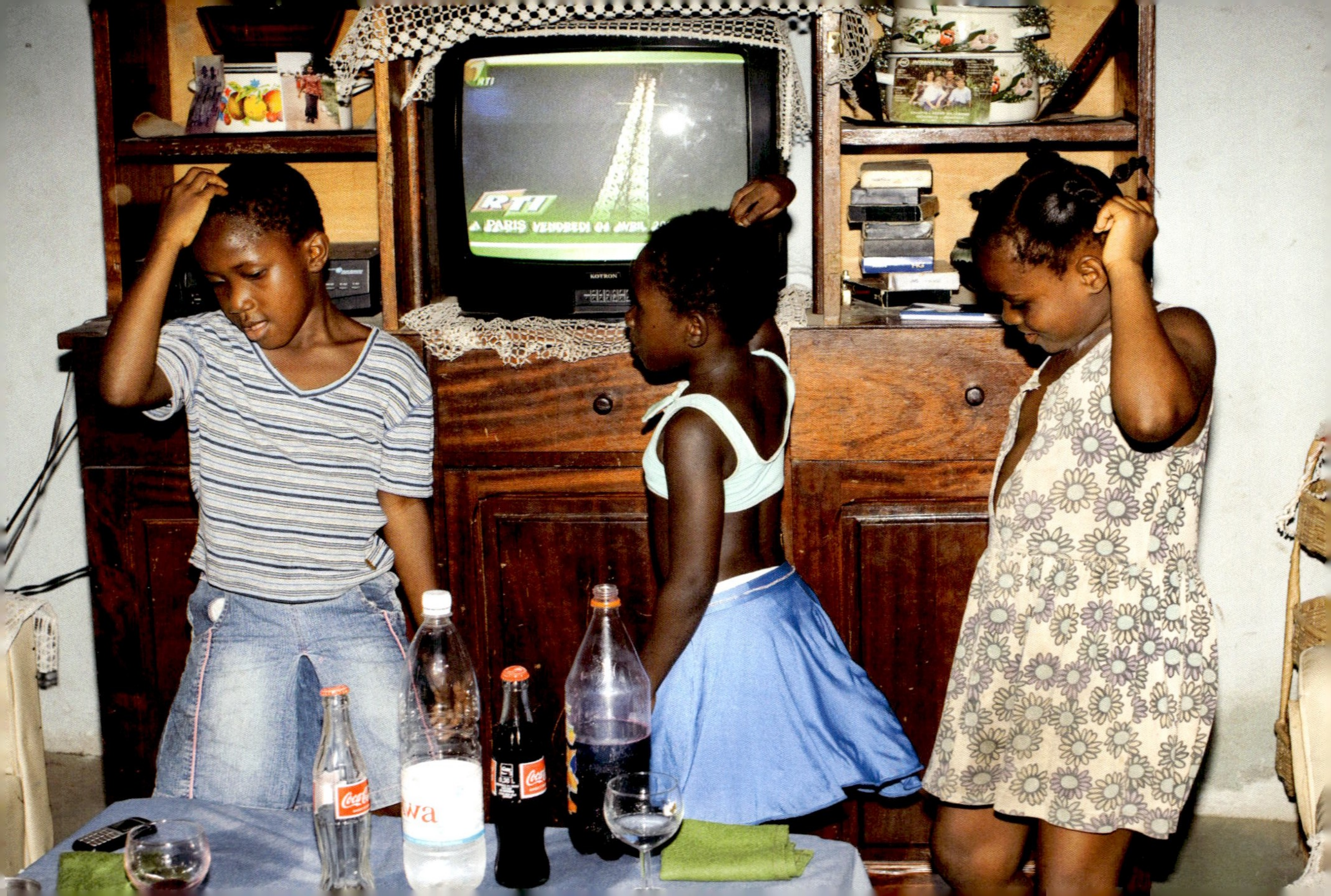
RTI
PARIS VENDREDI 04 AVRIL
KOTRON
Coca-Cola
Coca-Cola

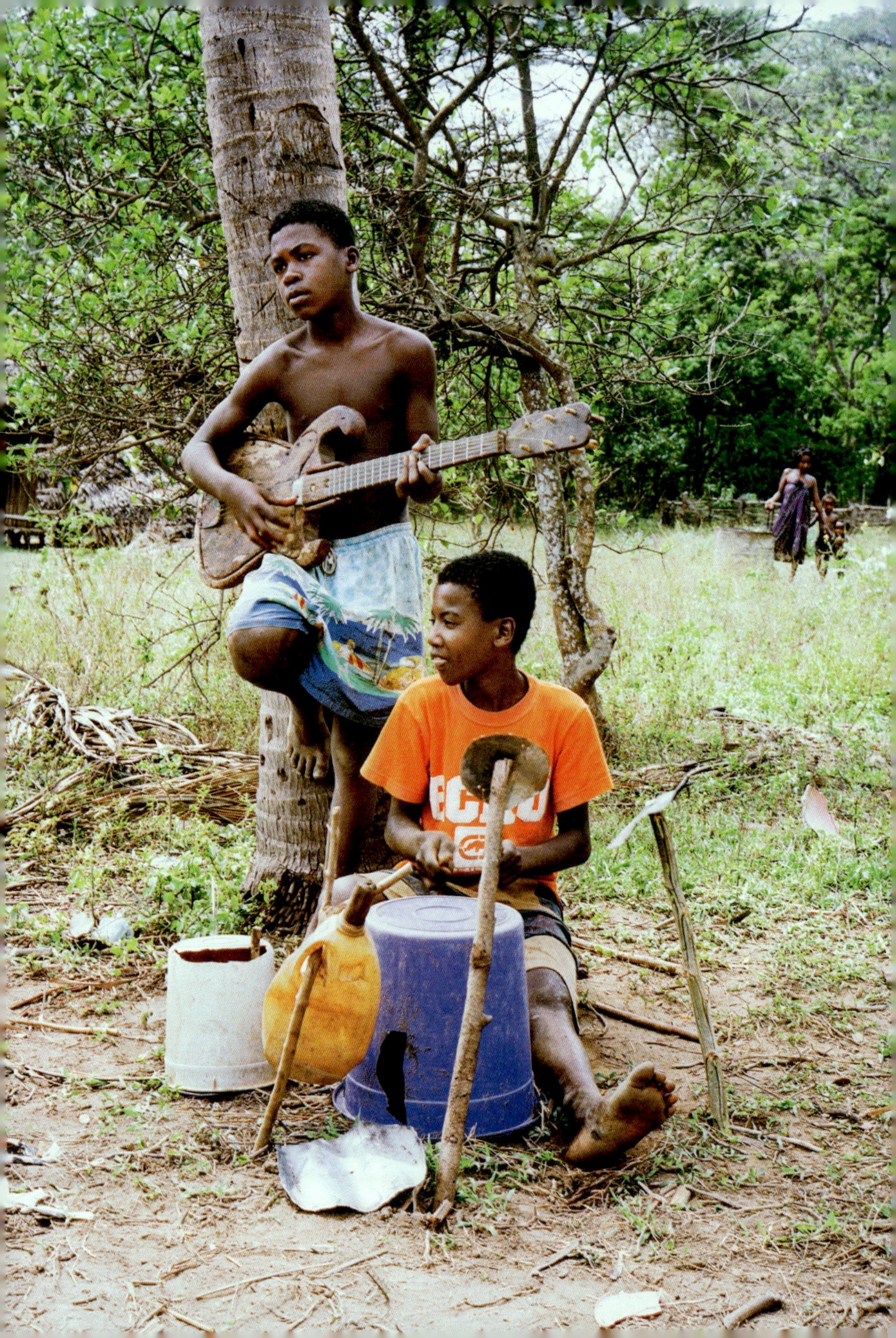

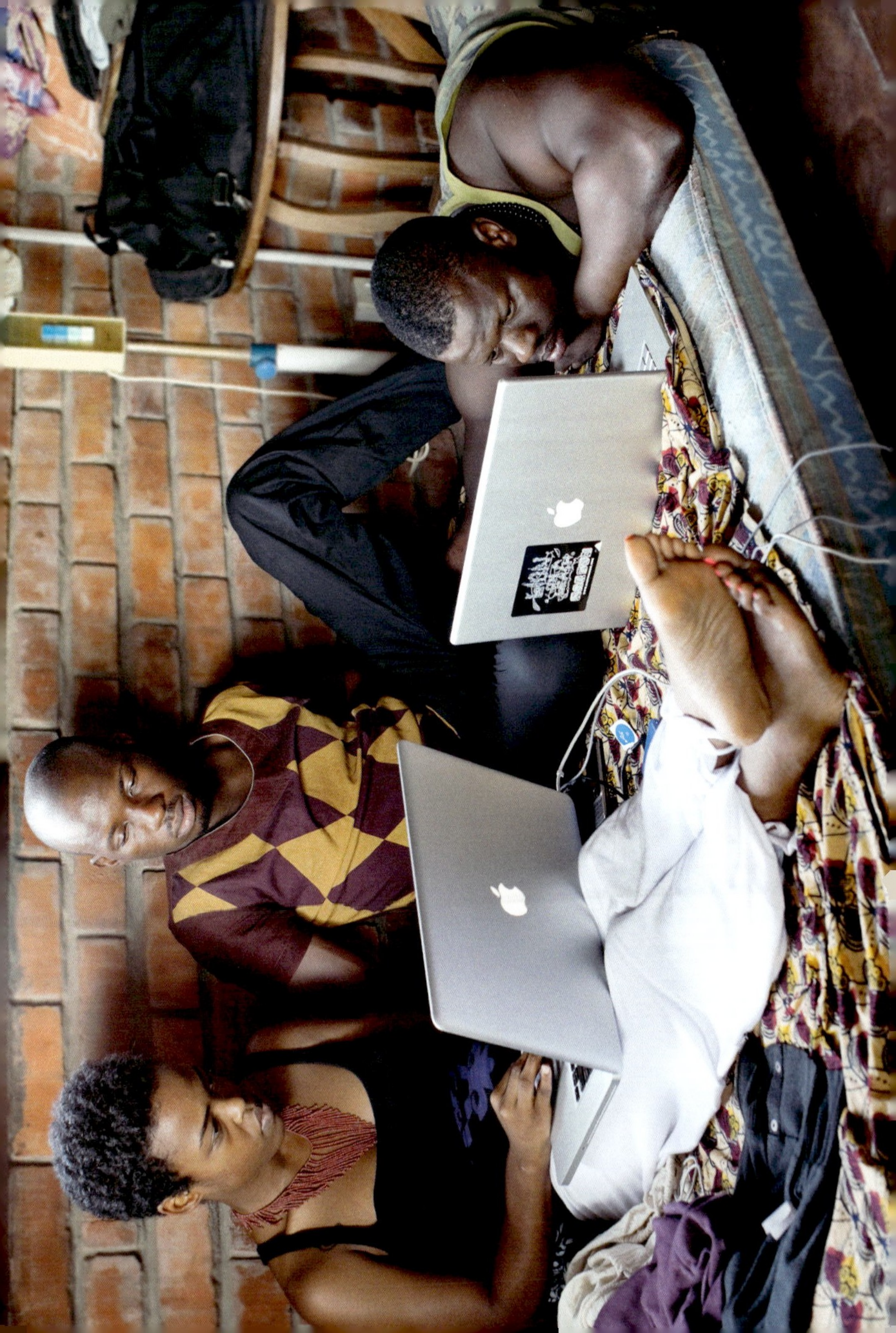

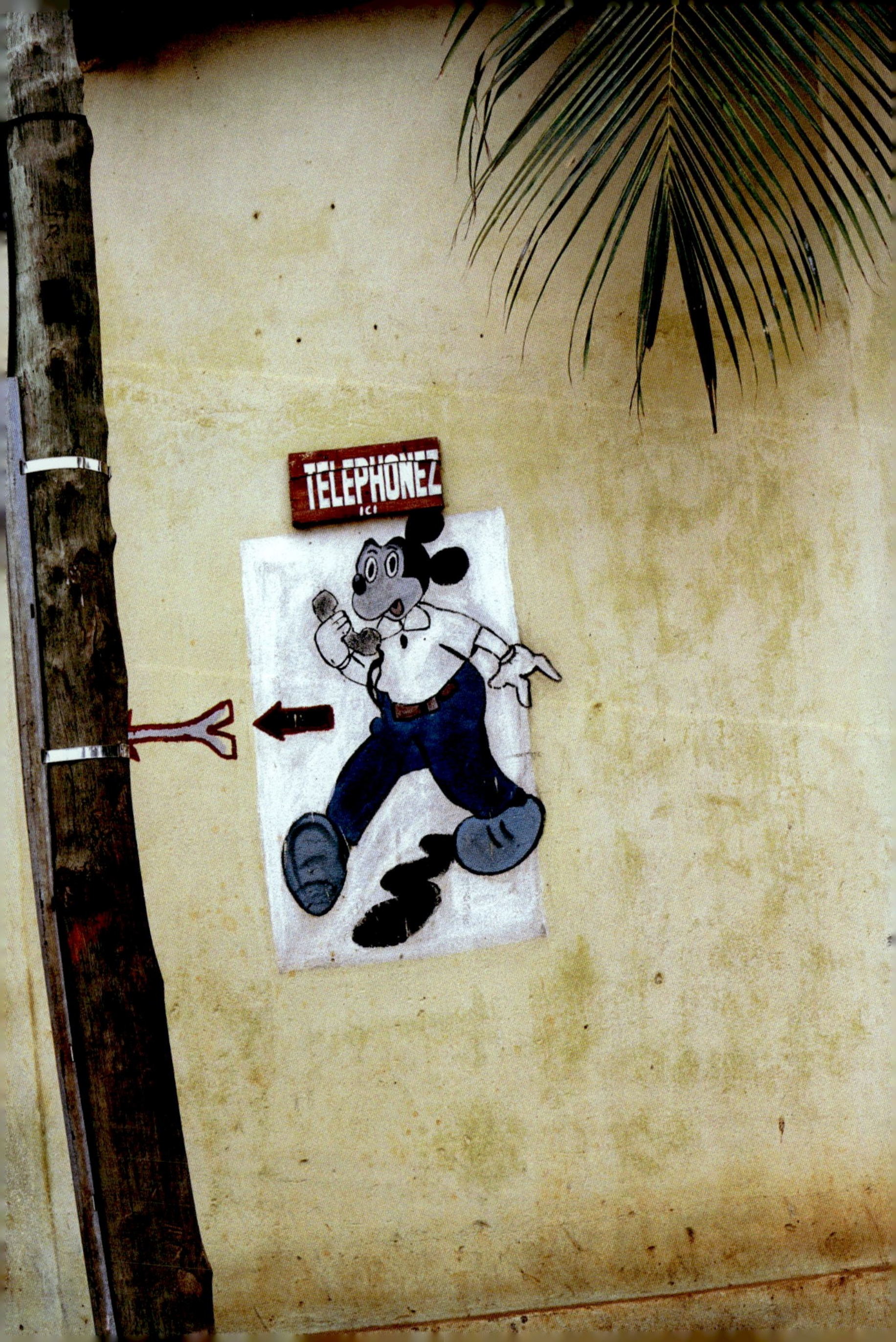
TELEPHONEZ
ICI

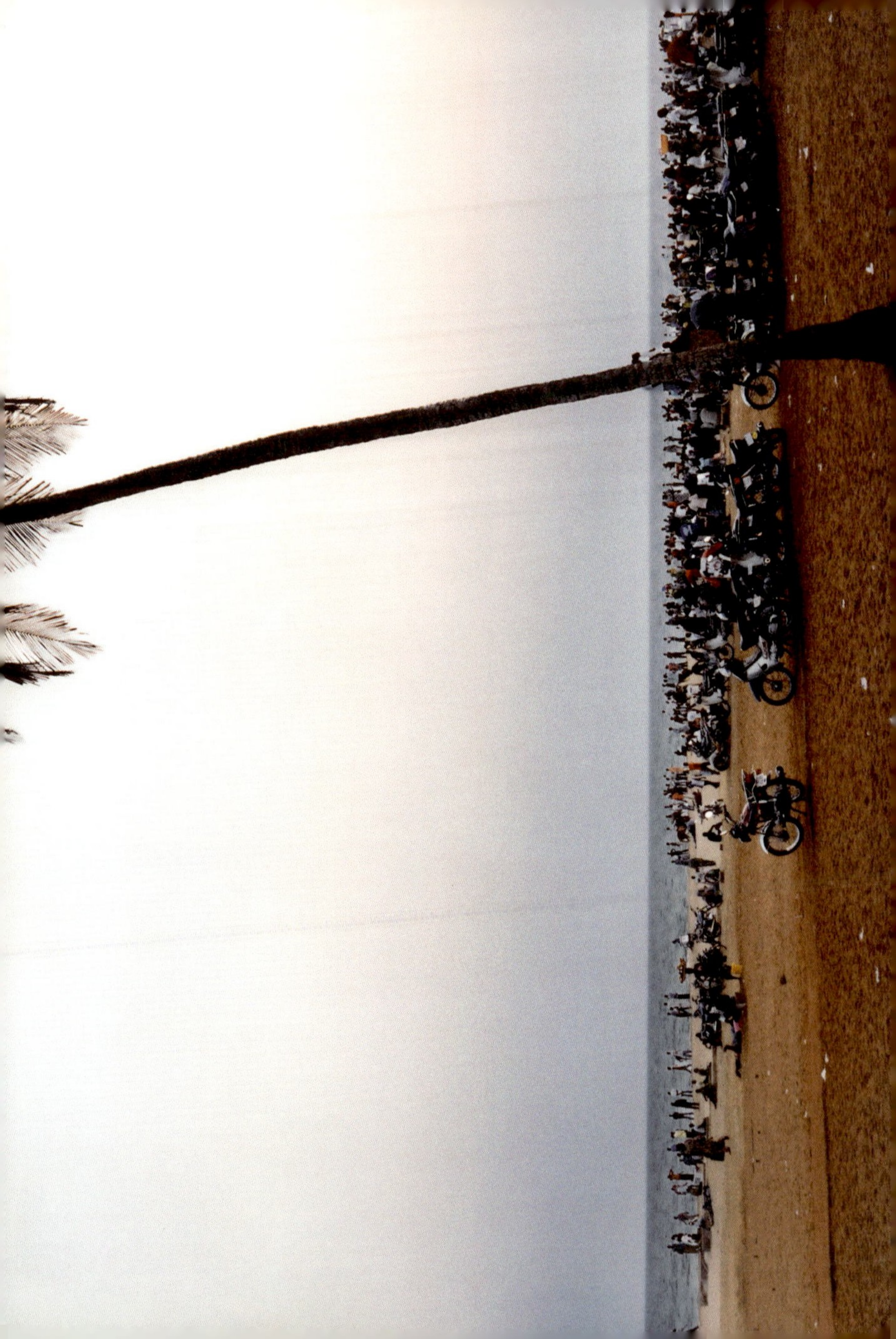

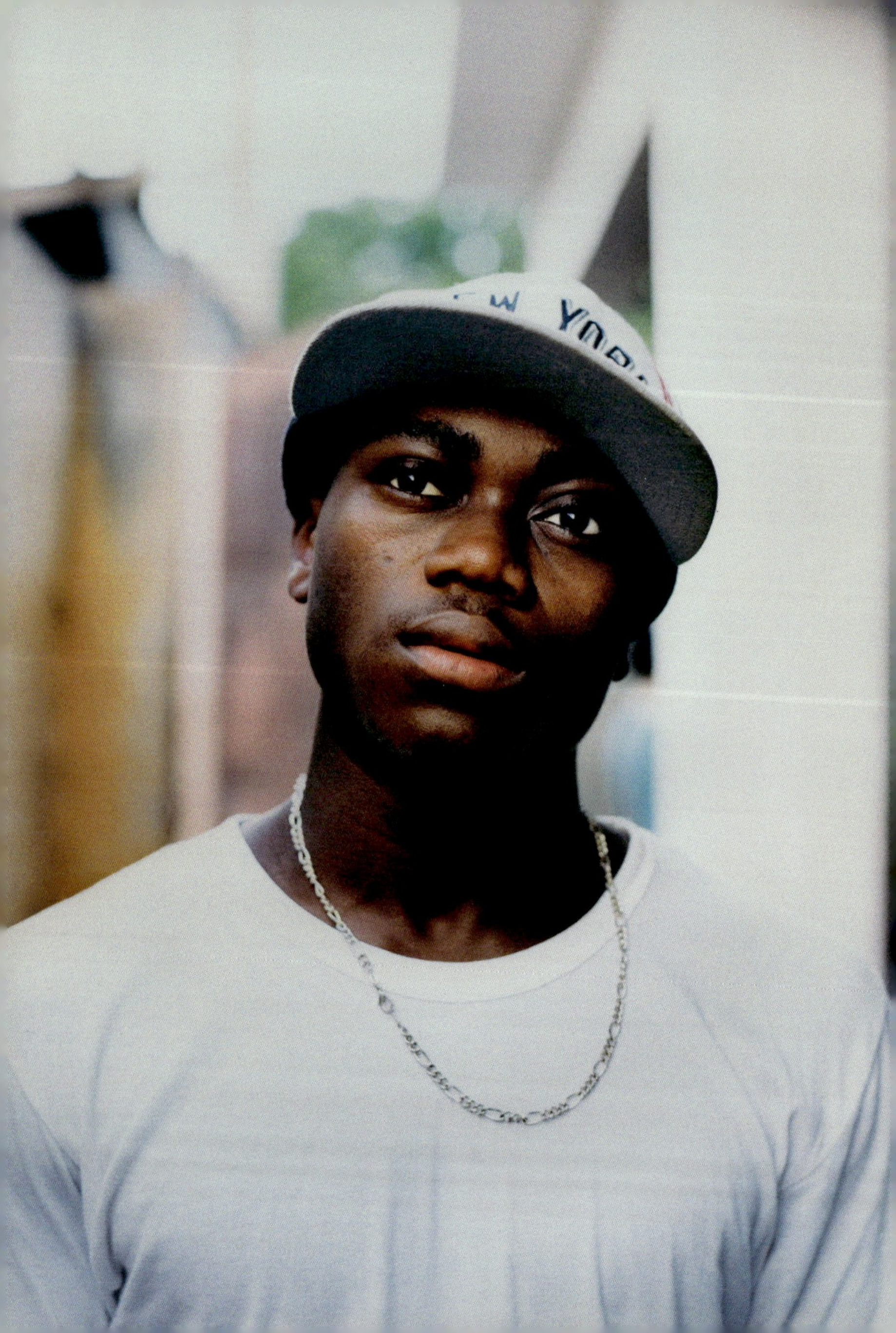

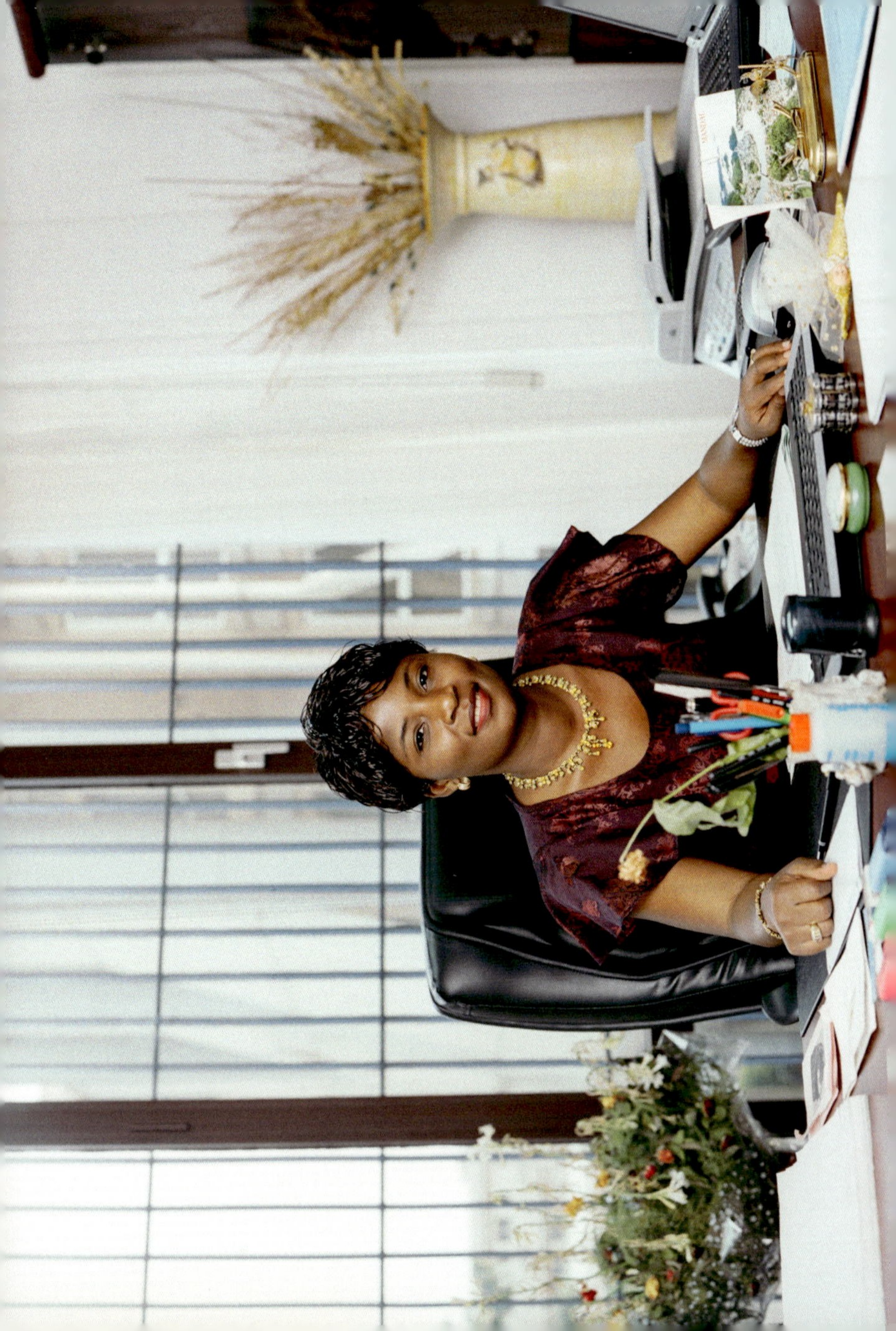

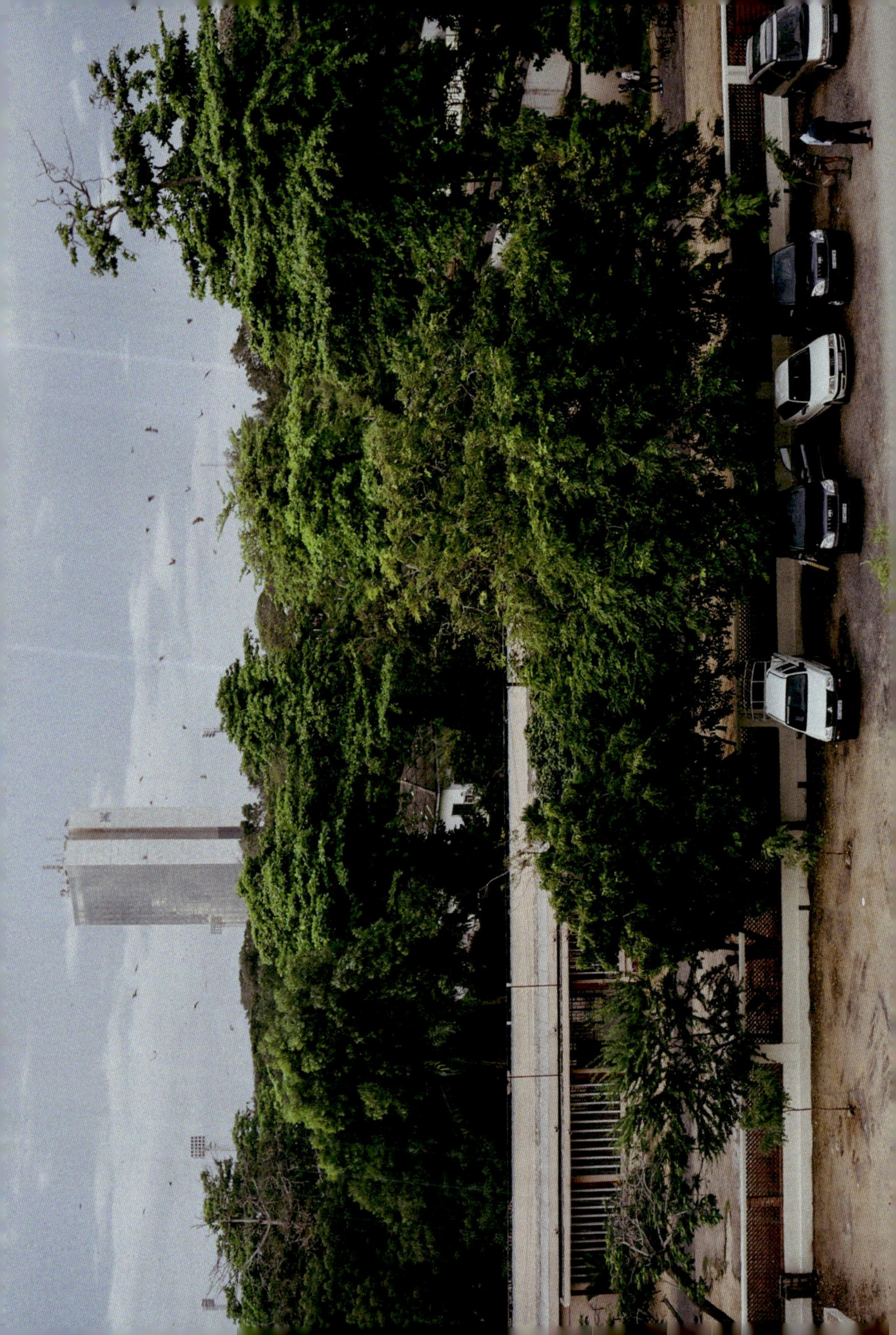

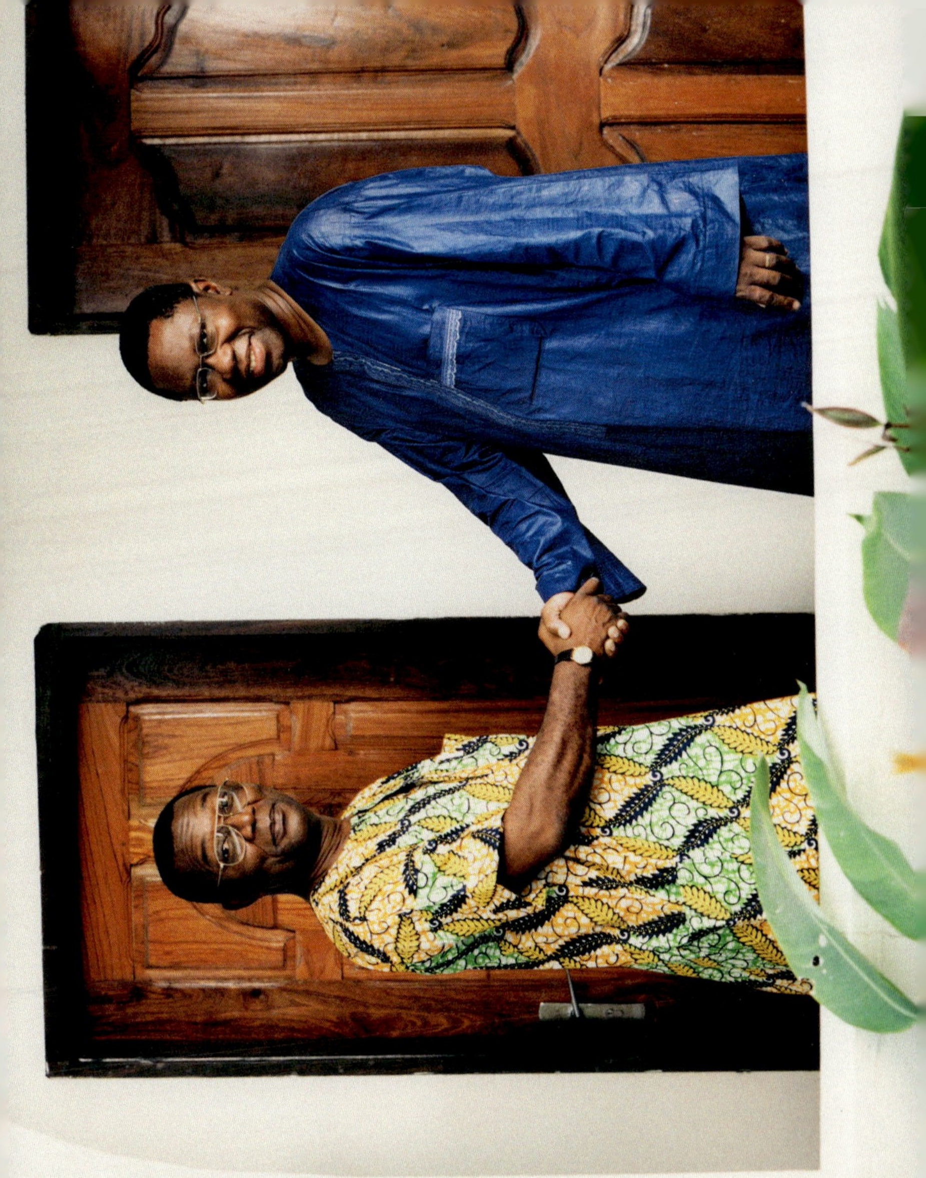

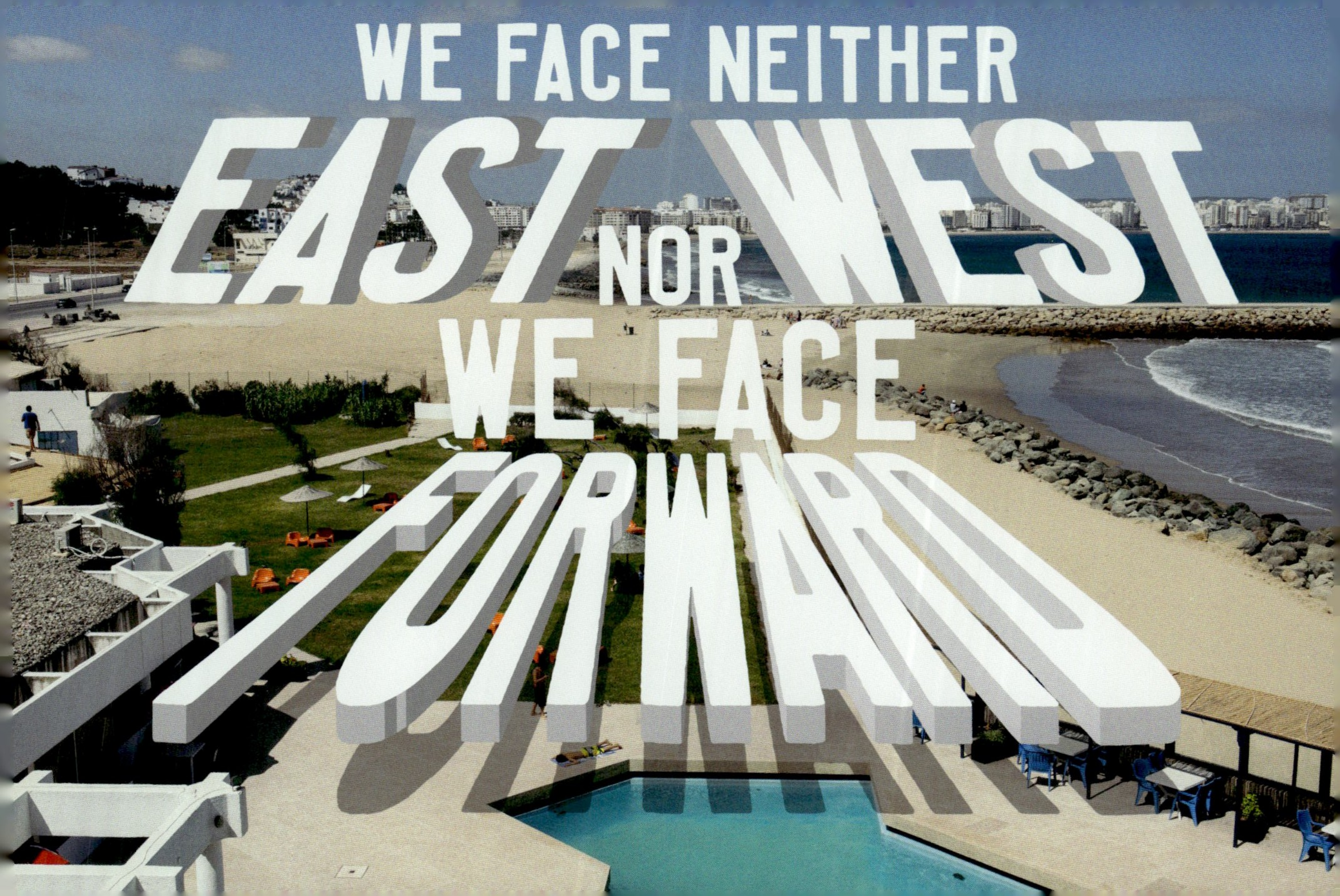
WE FACE NEITHER
EAST NOR WEST
WE FACE
FORWARD

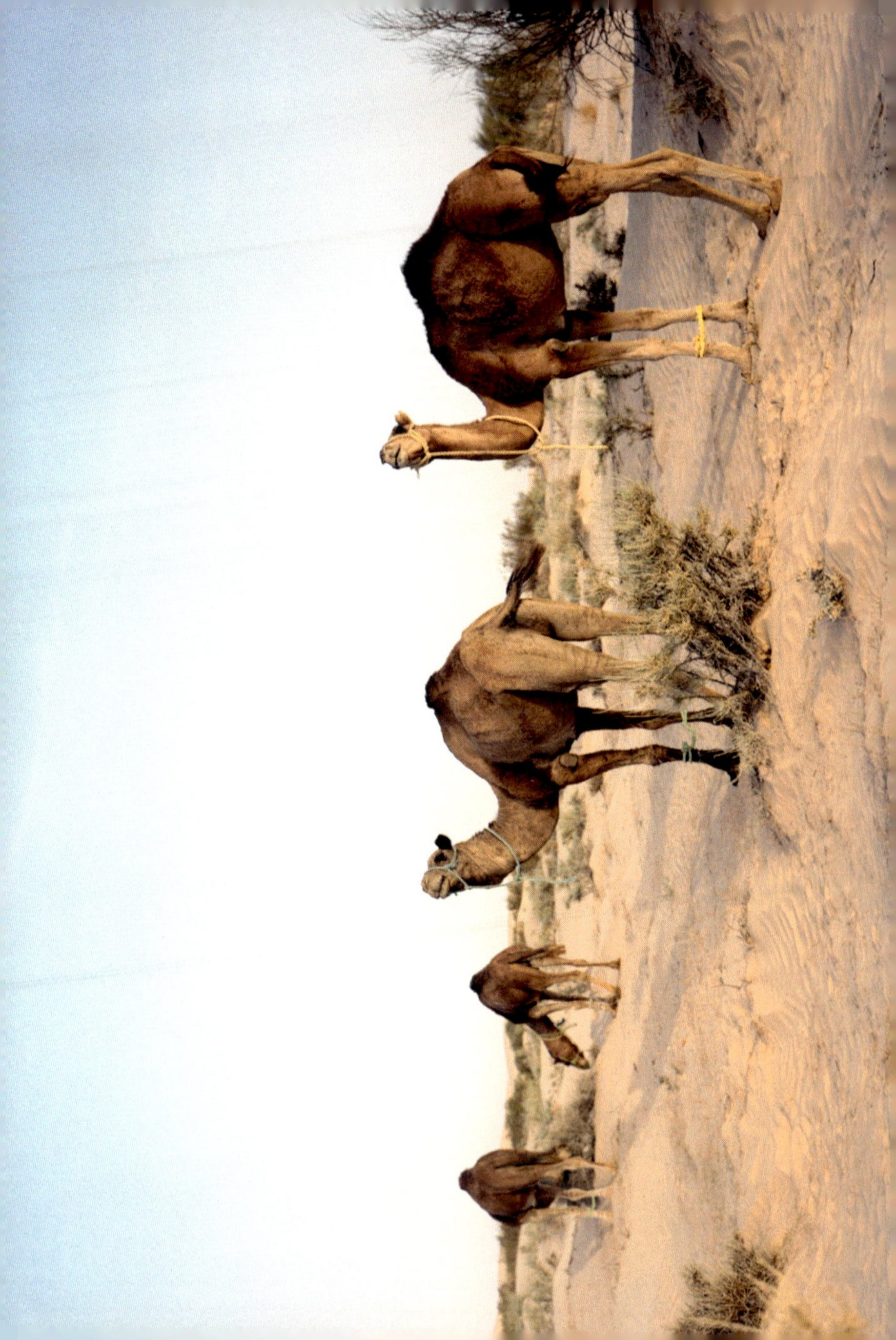

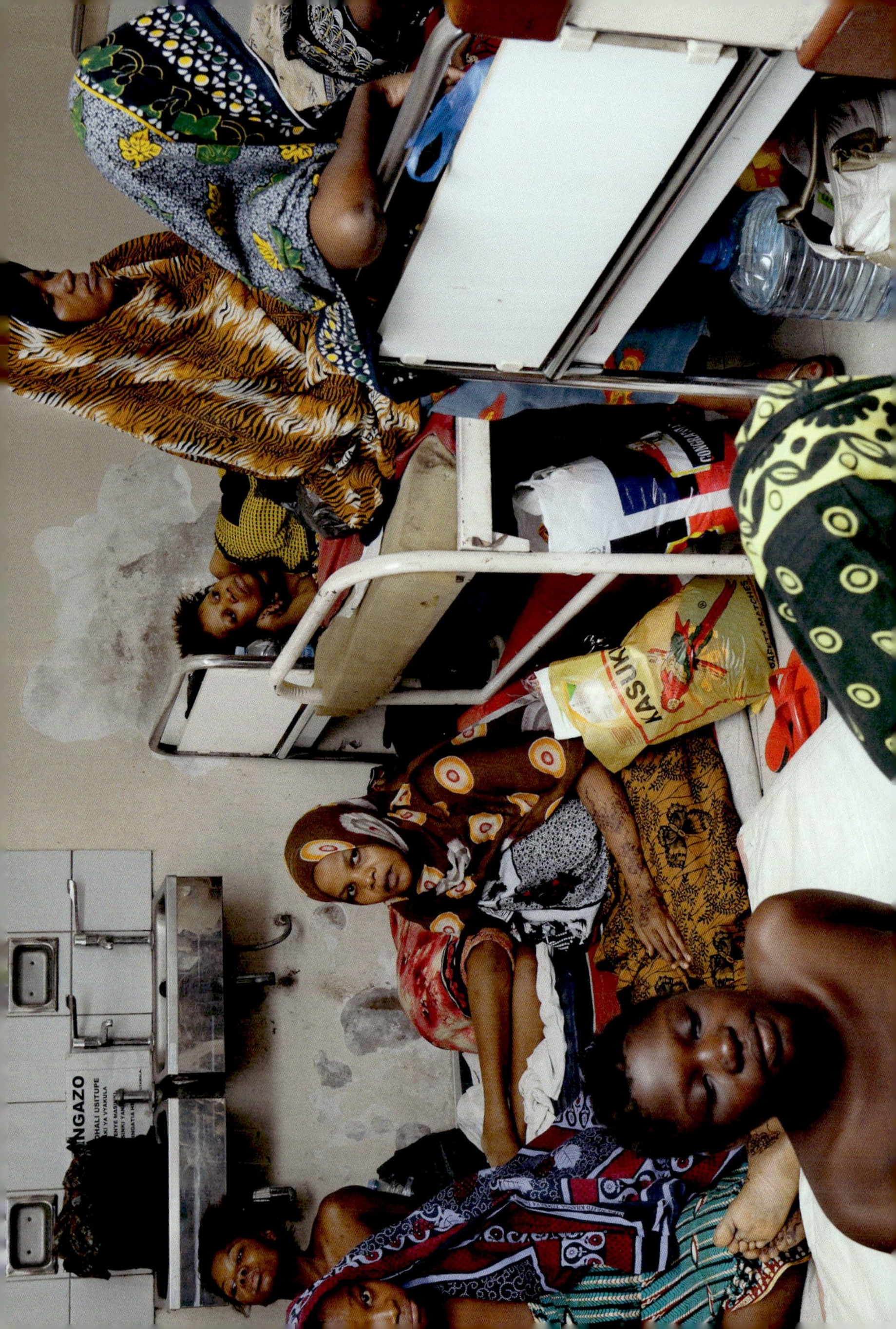
KASUKU

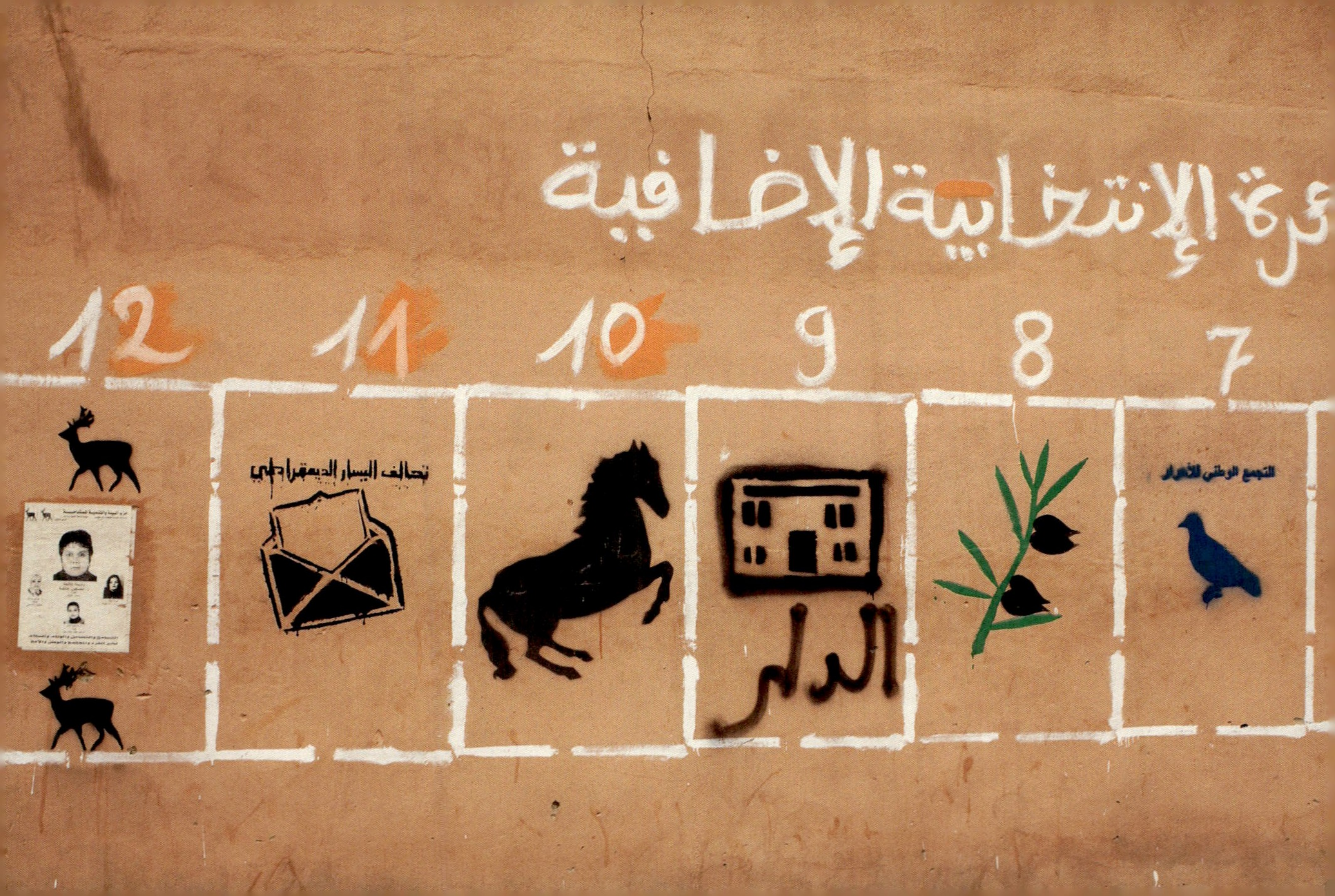

…ئرة الإنتخابية الإضافية
7
8
9
10
11
12
التجمع الوطني للأحرار
الدلو
تحالف اليسار الديمقراطي

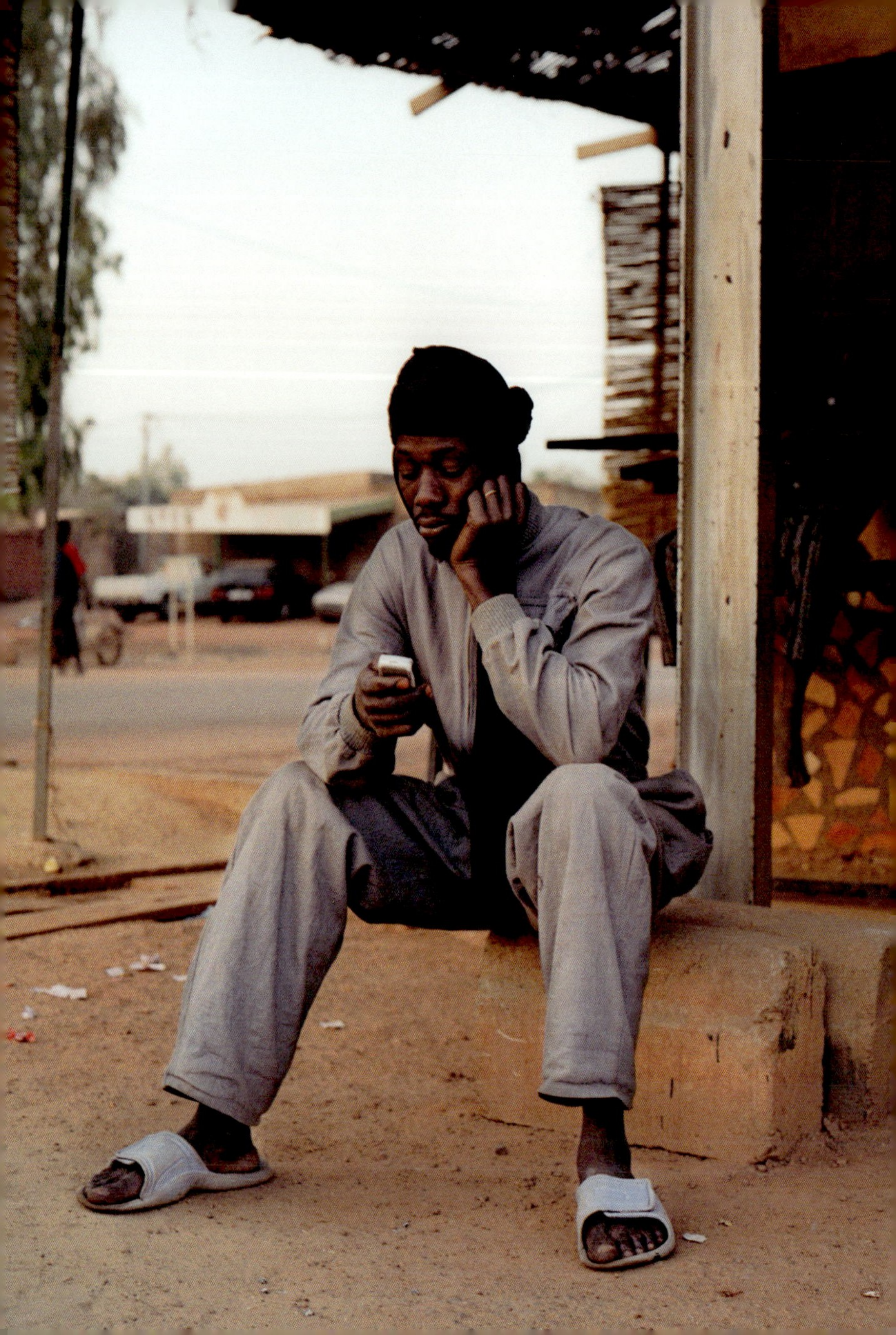

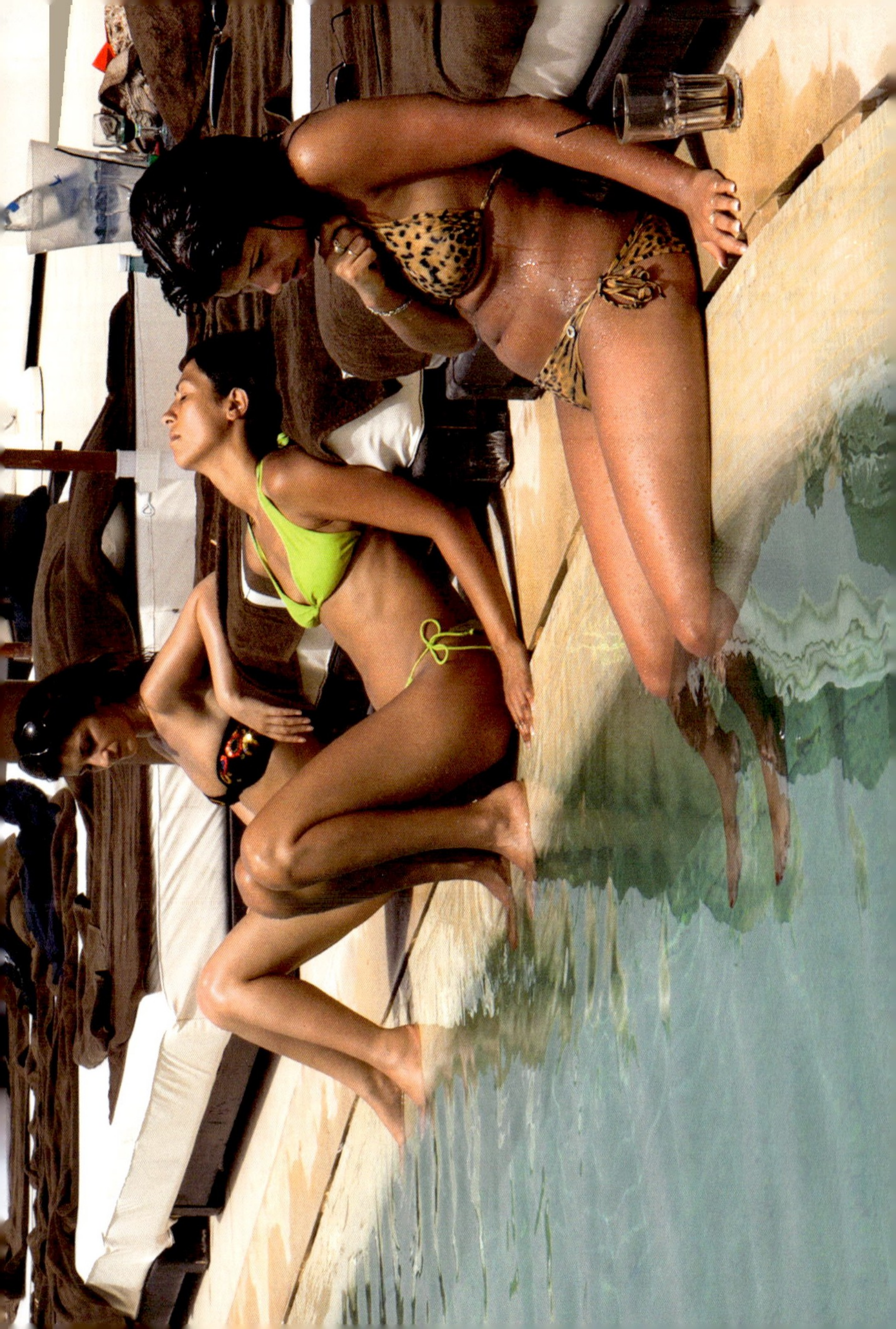

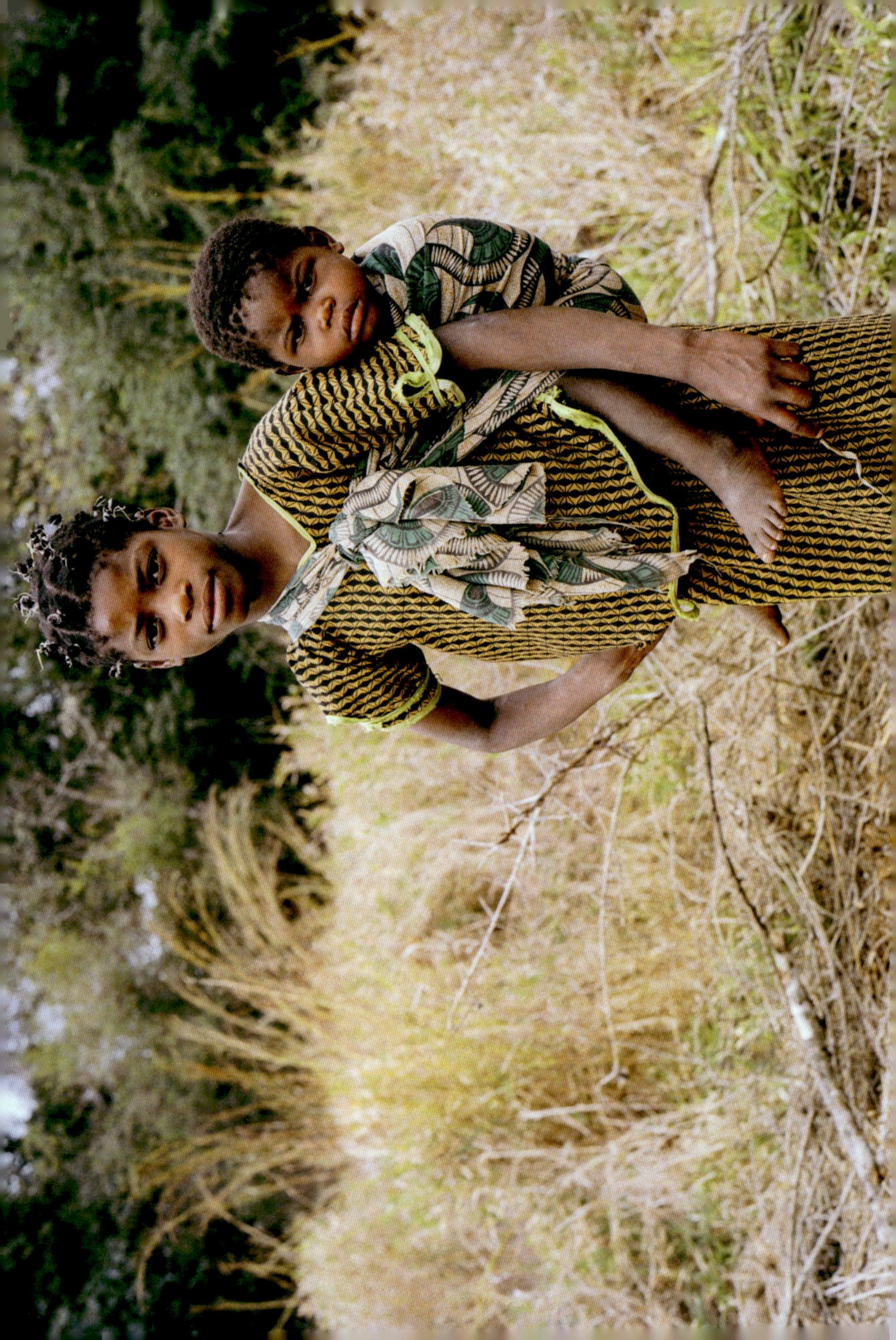

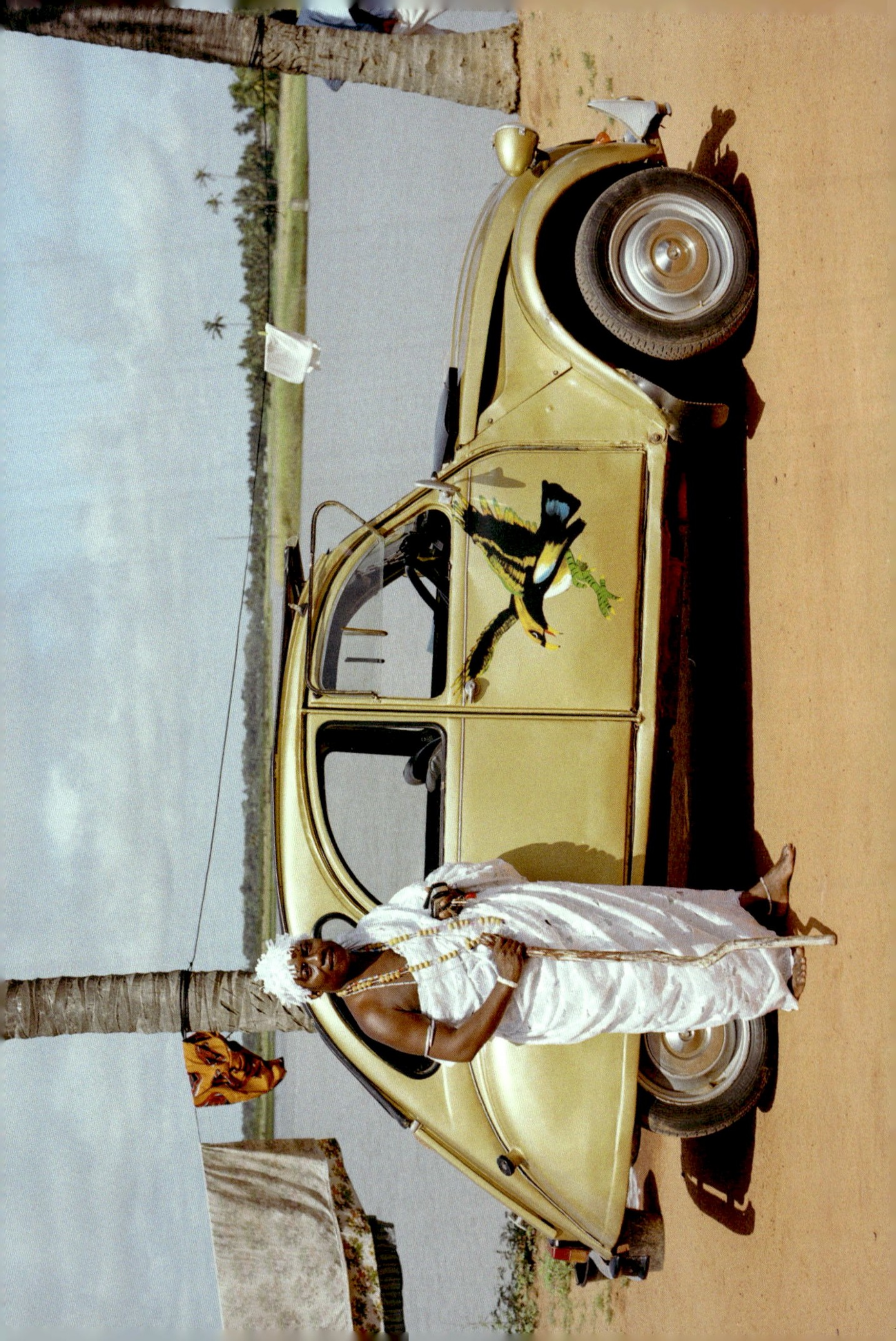

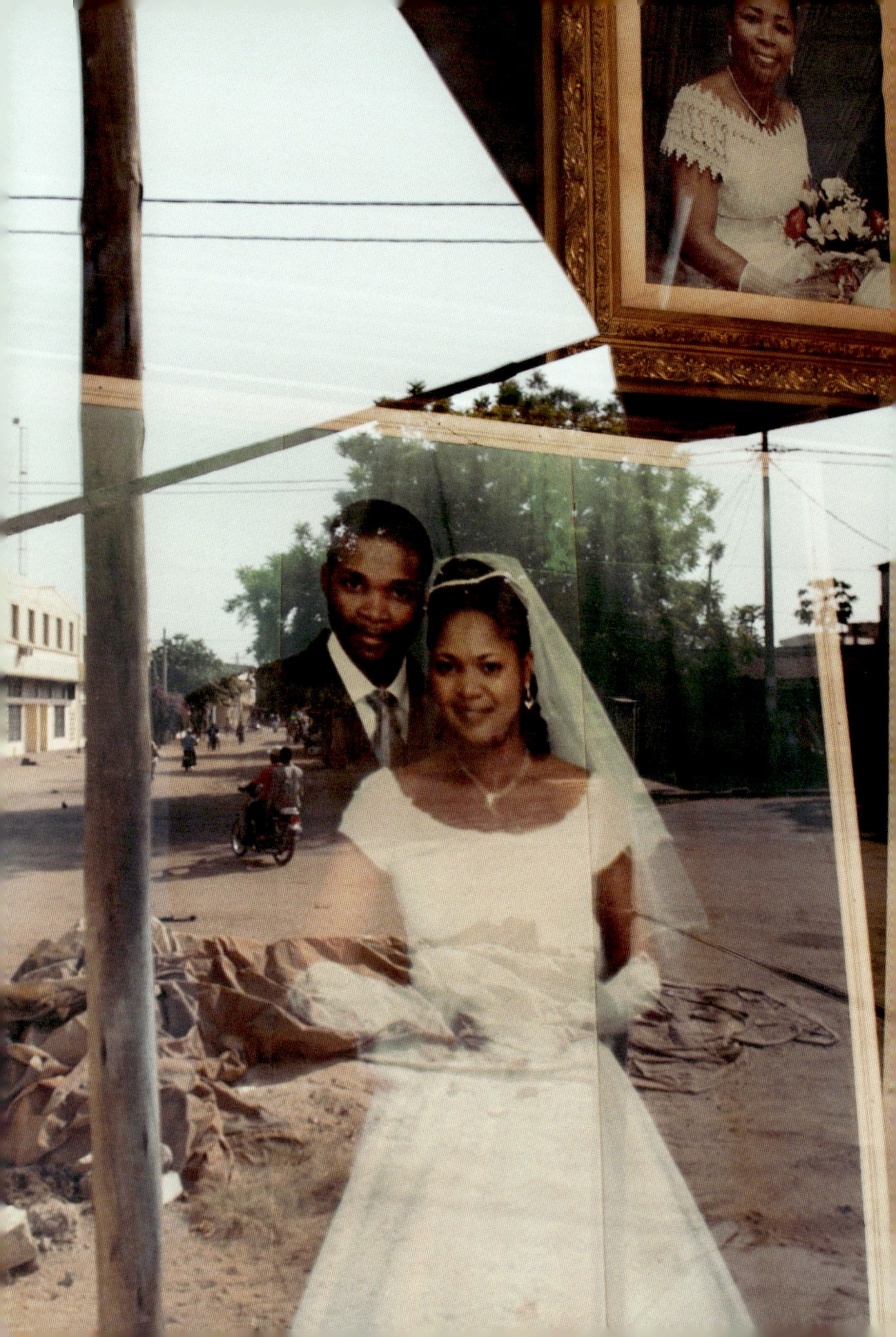

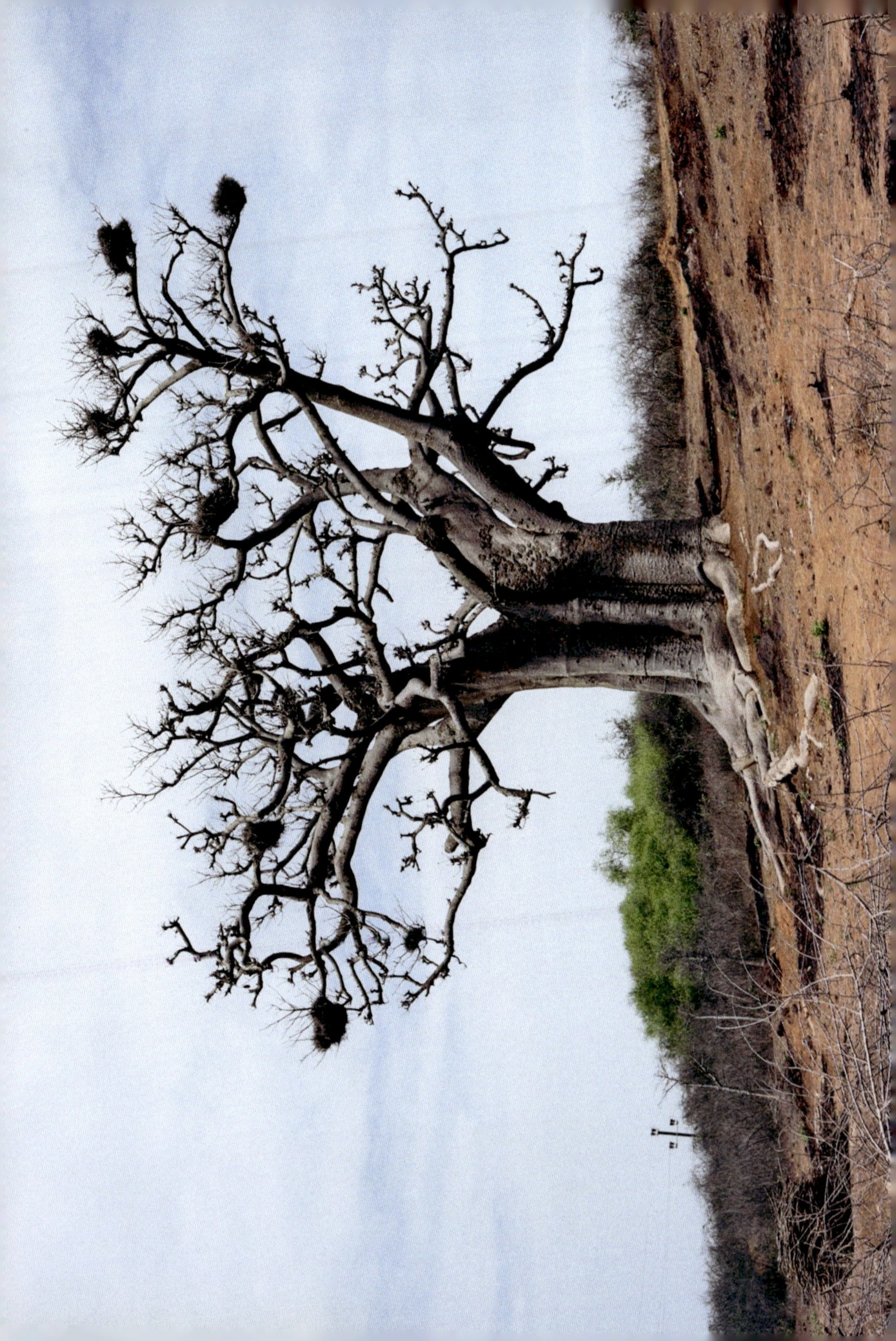

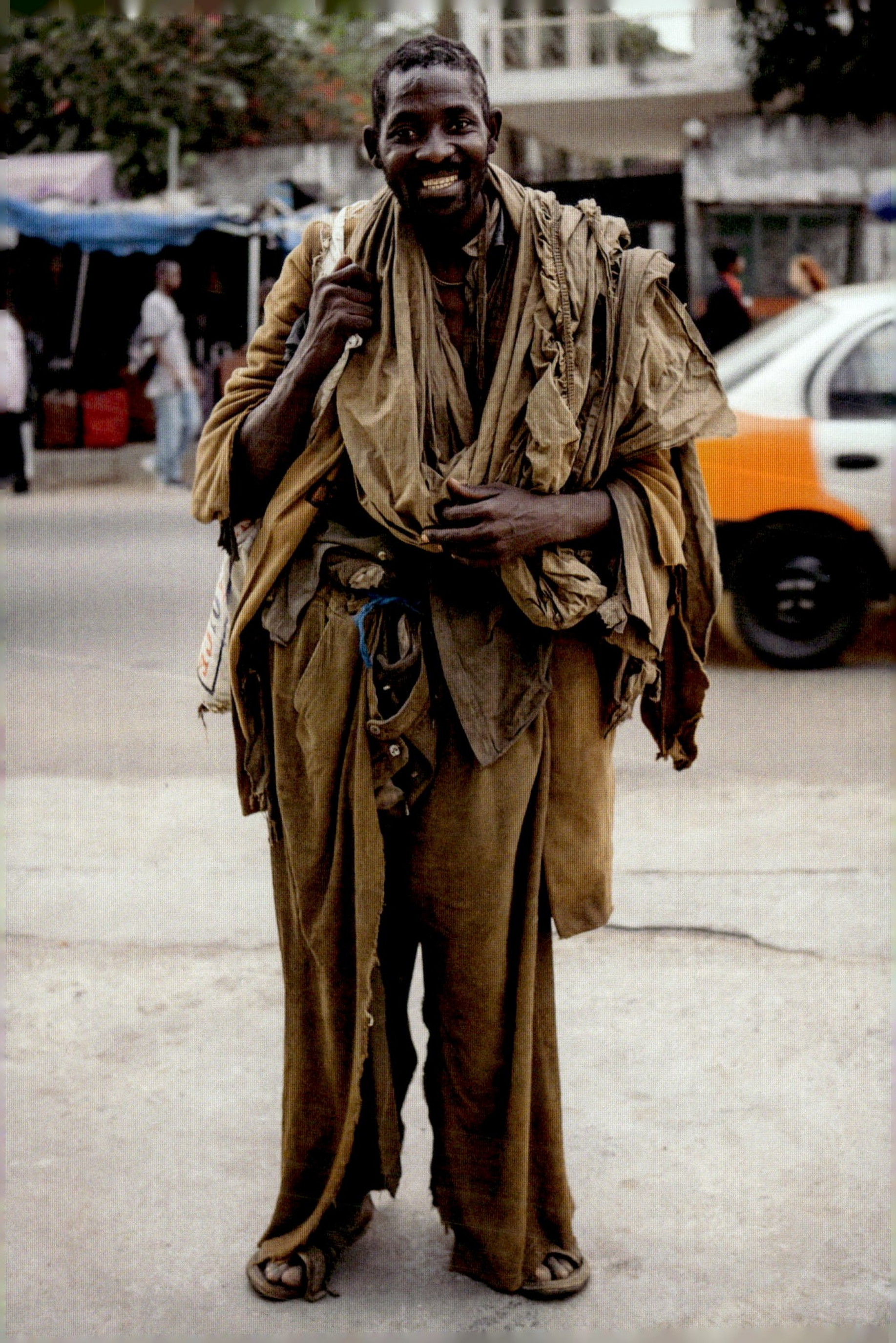

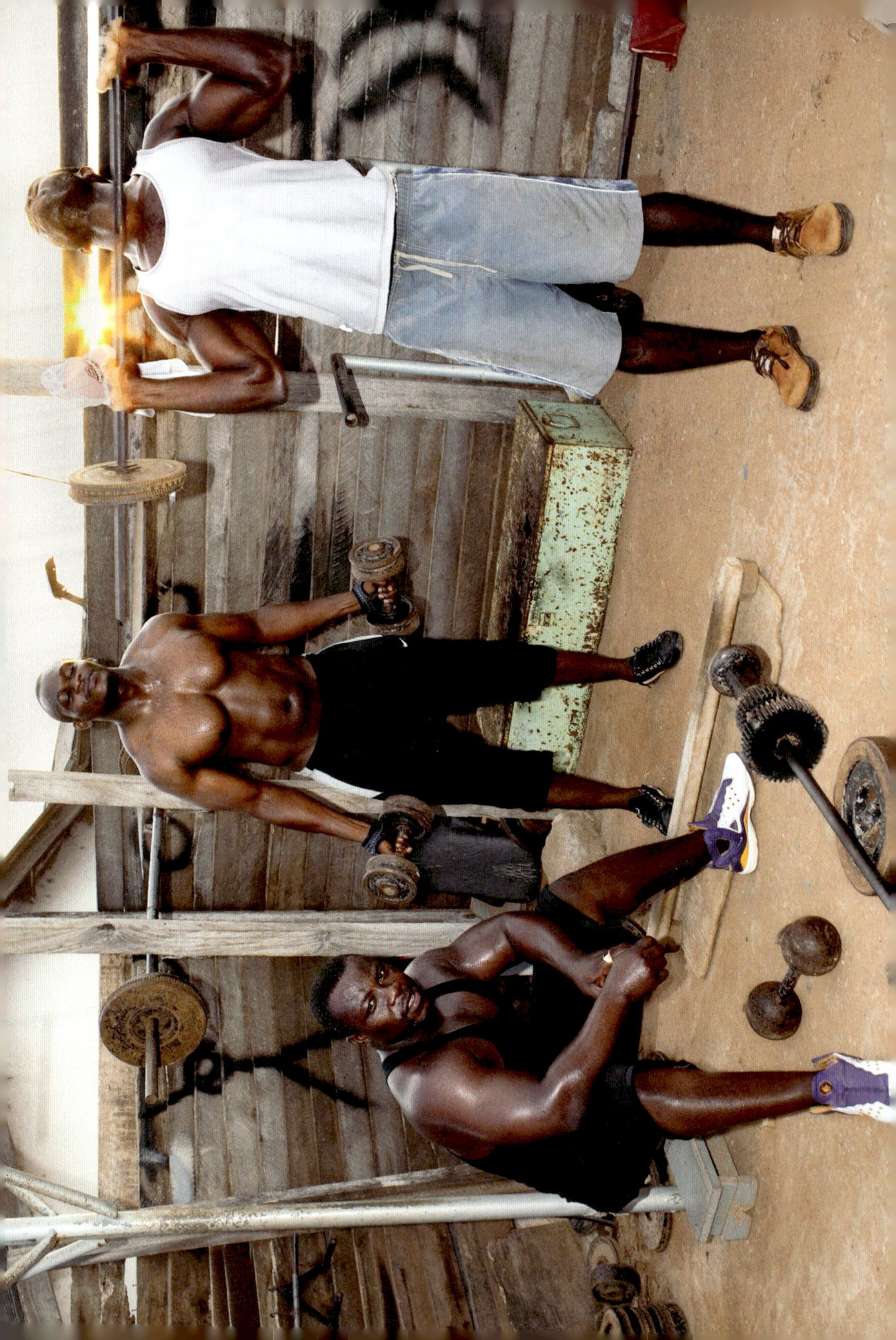

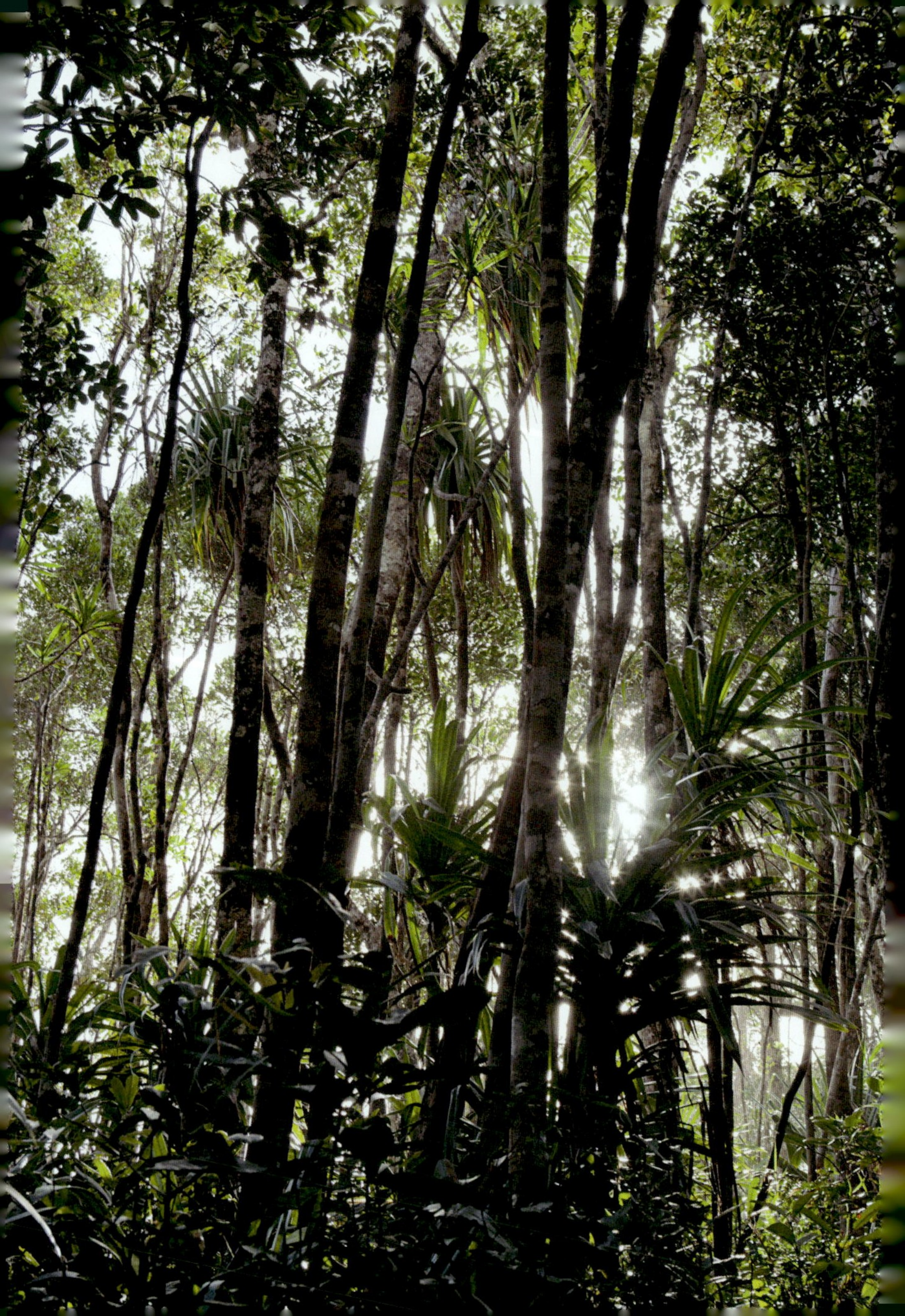

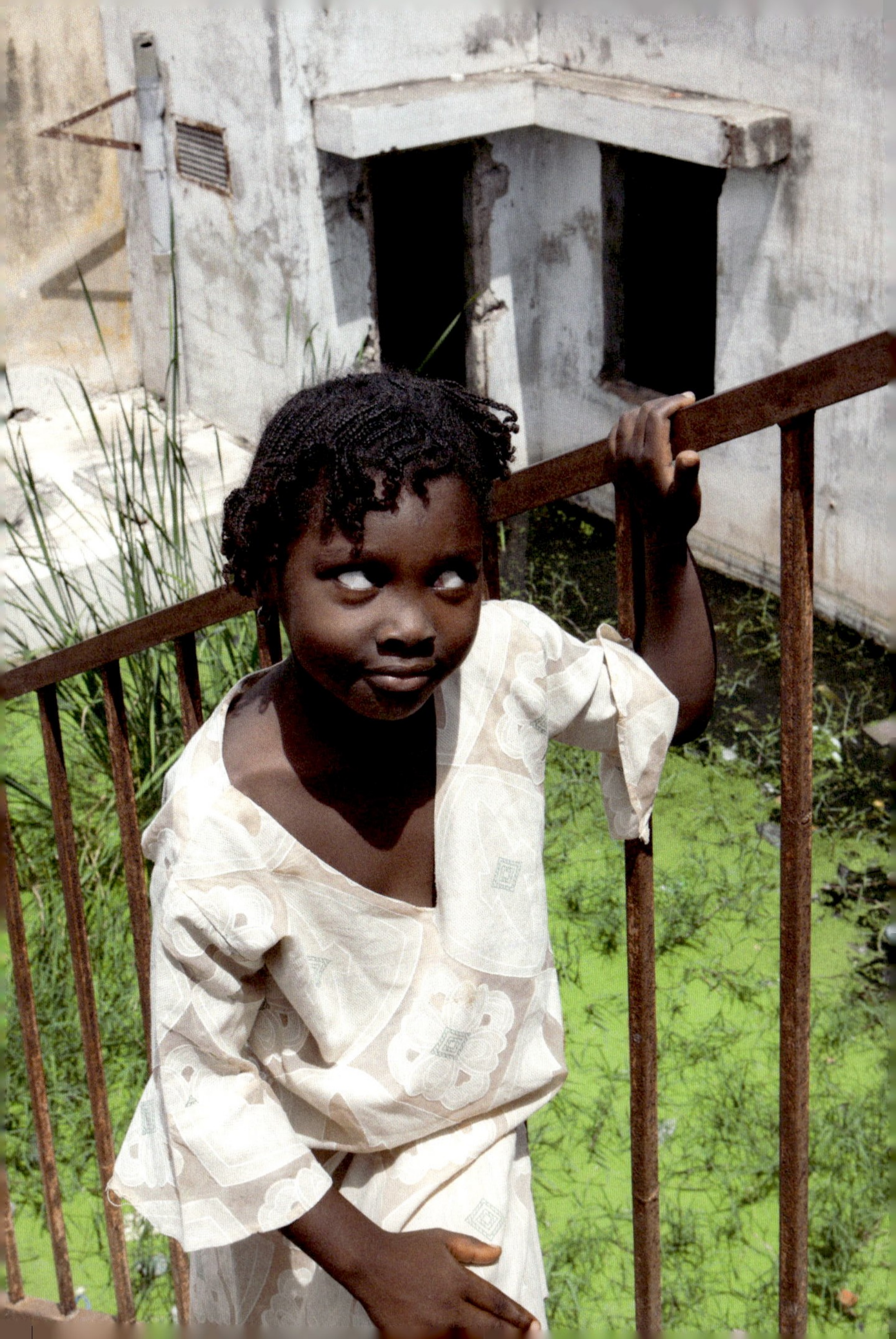

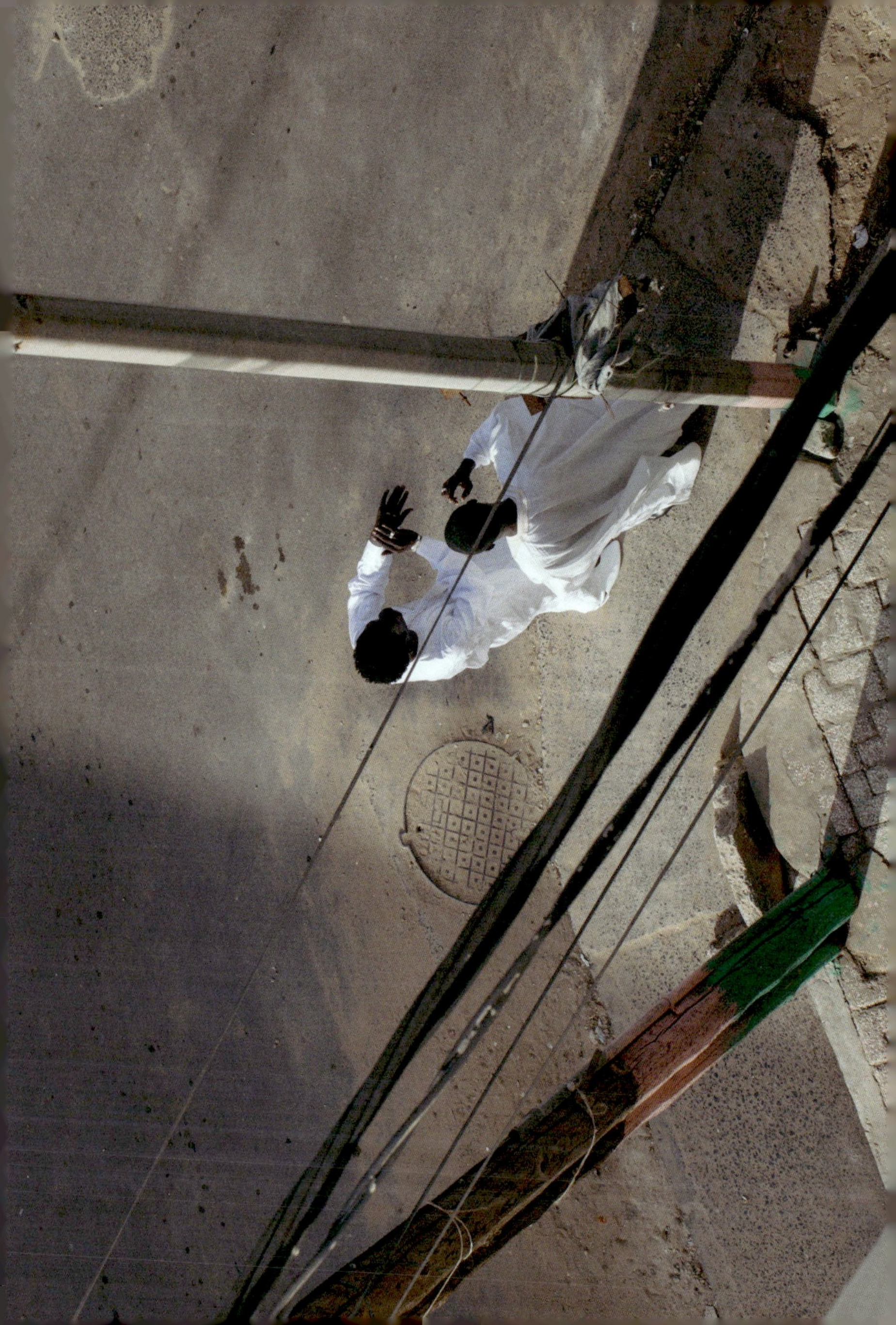

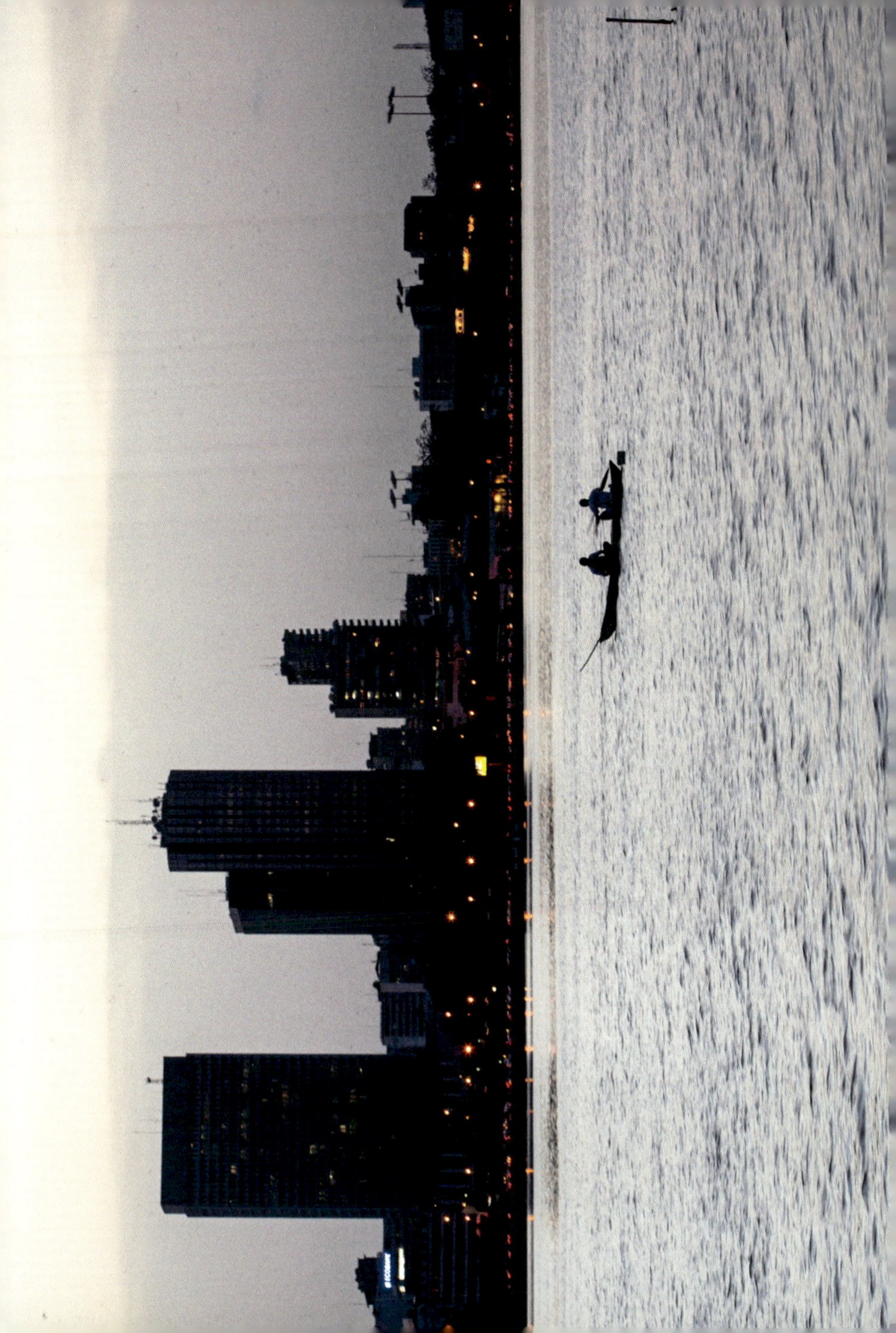

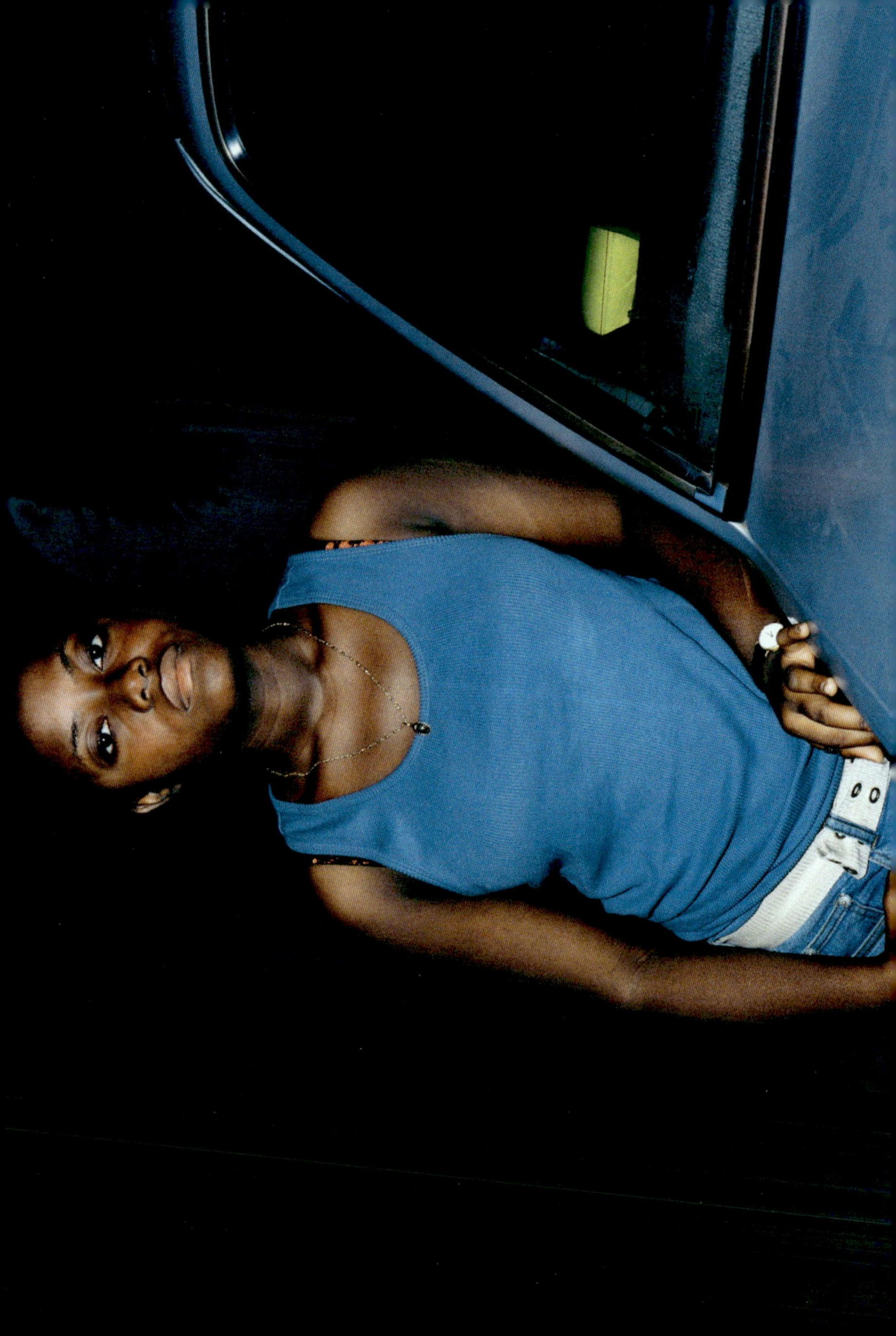

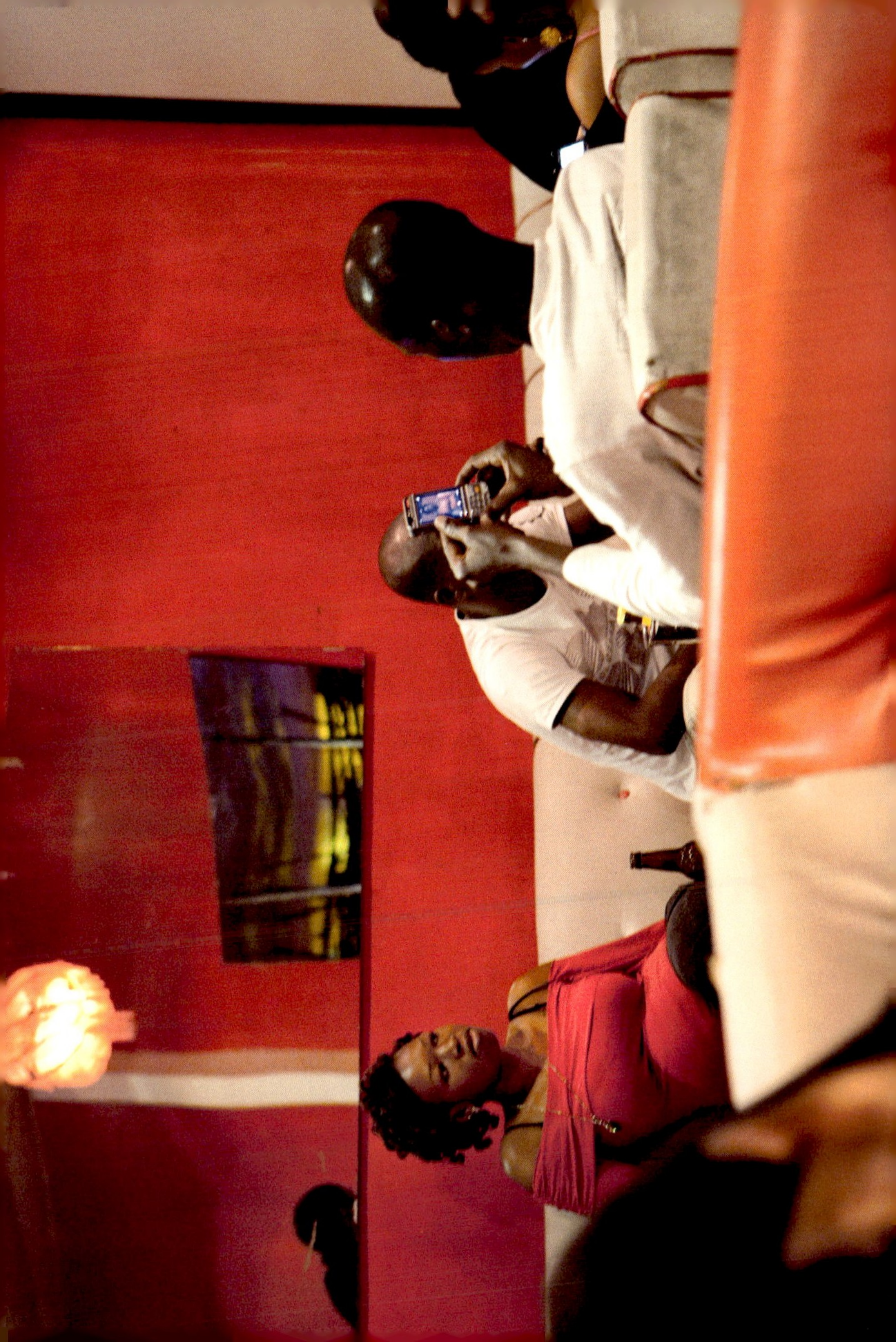

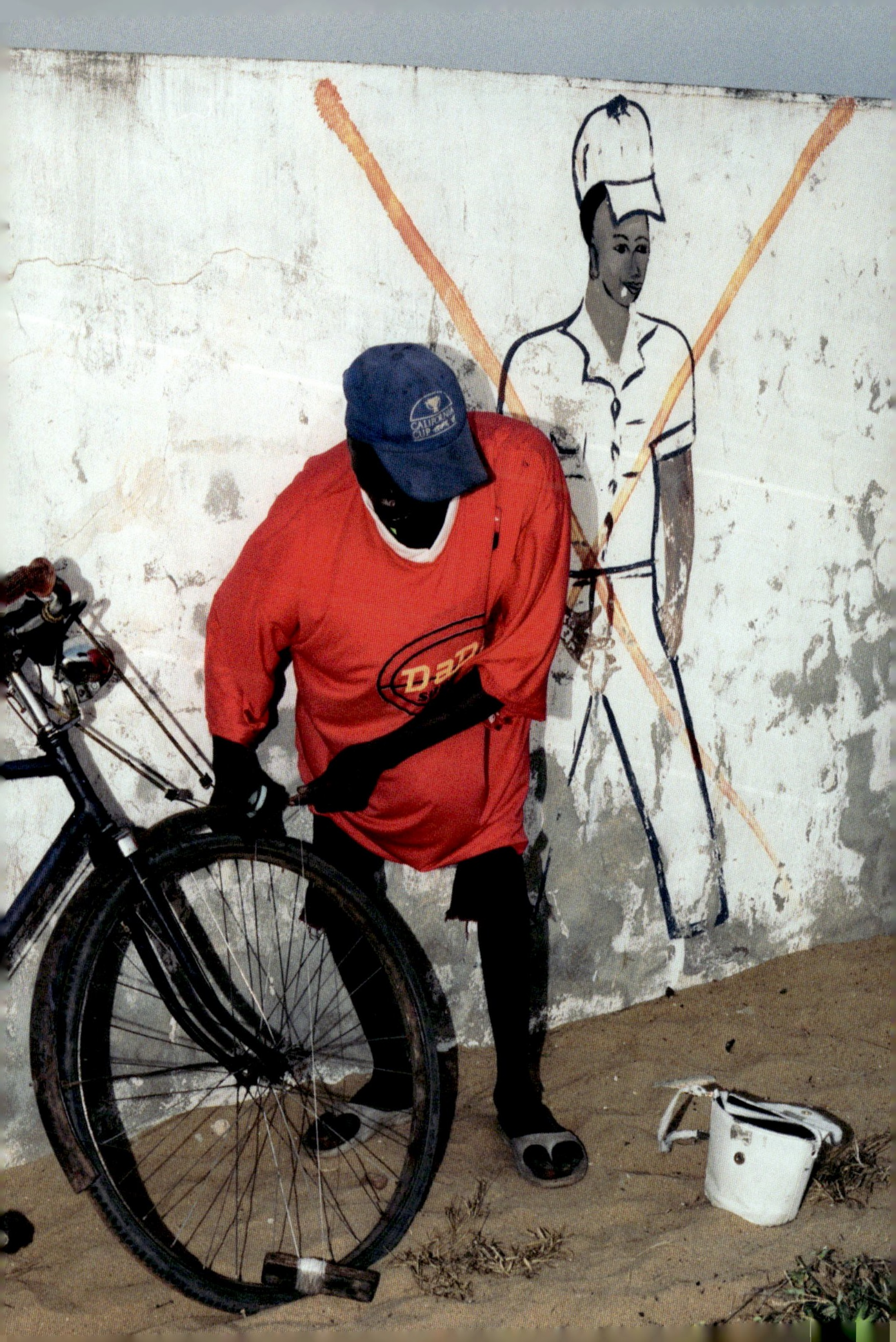

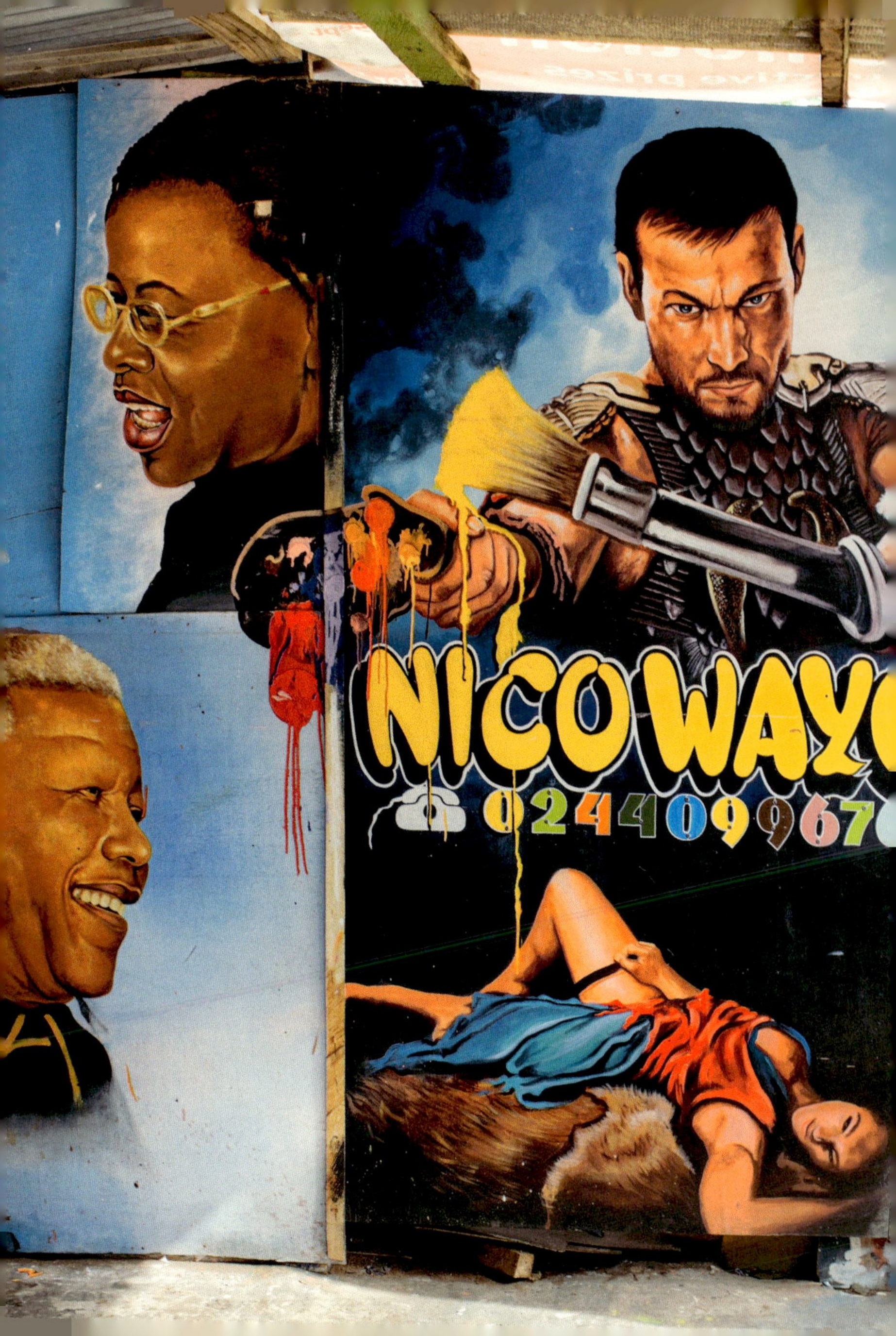
NICOWAY
024409967

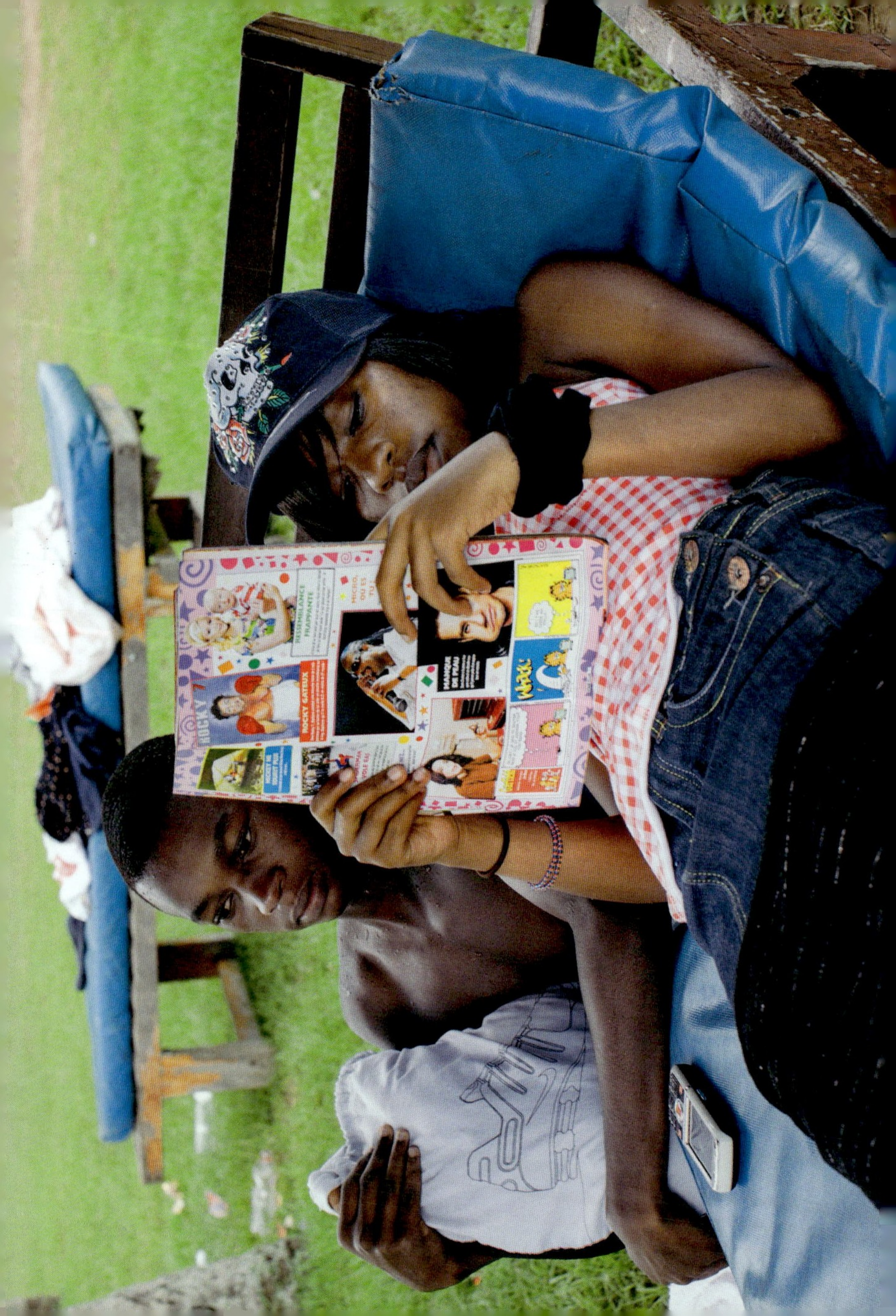

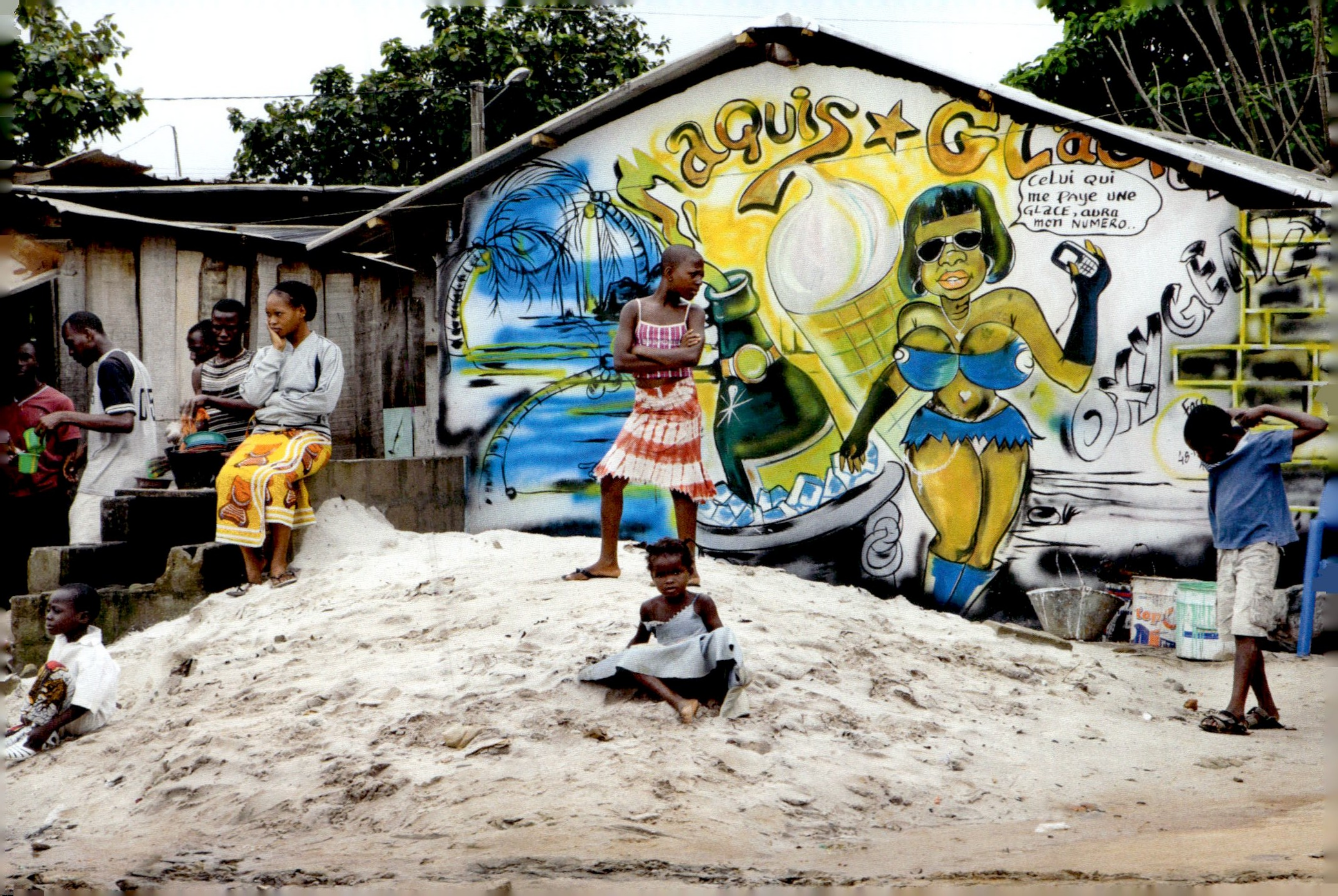
Celui qui
me Paye une
GLACE, aura
mon NUMERO..

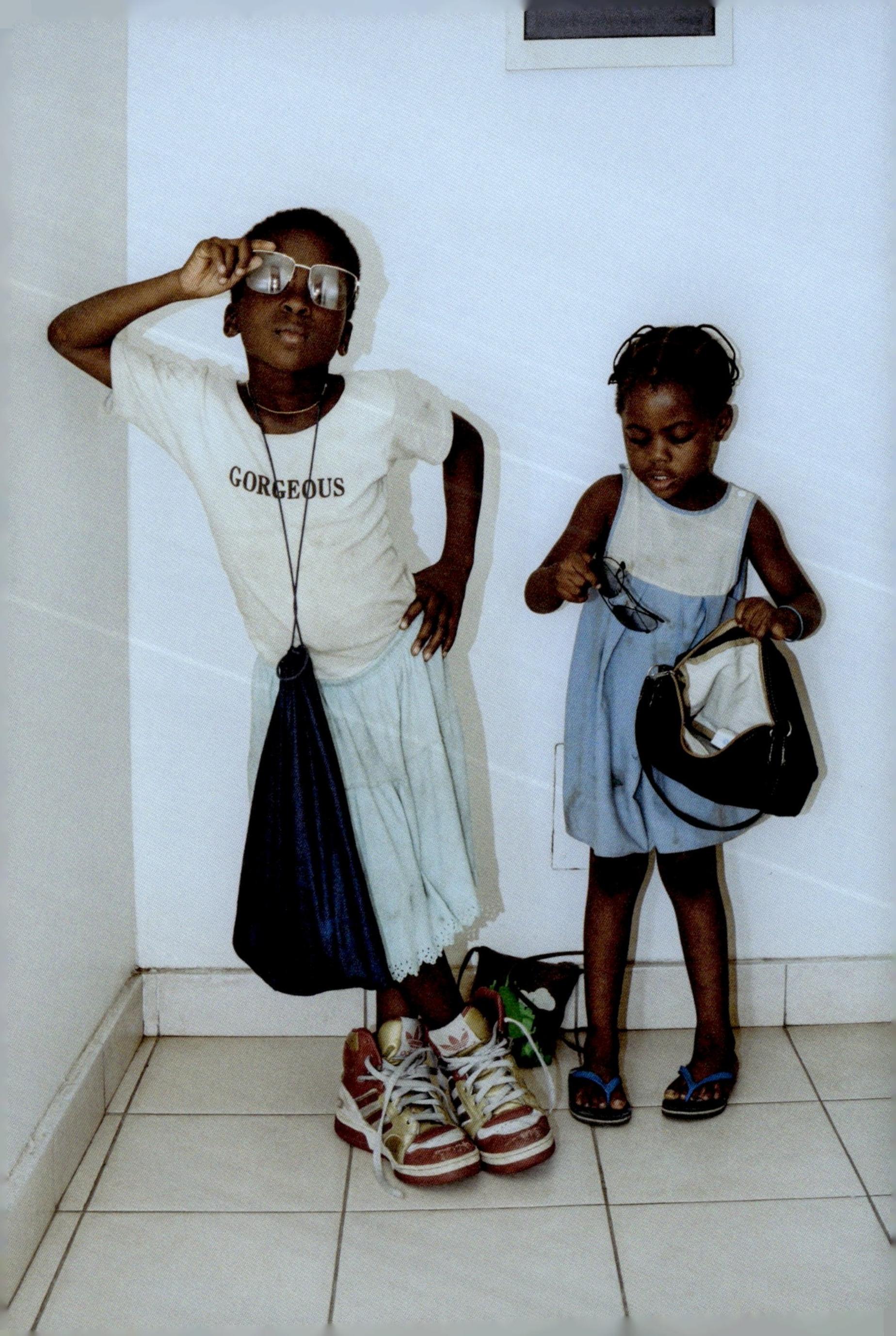
GORGEOUS

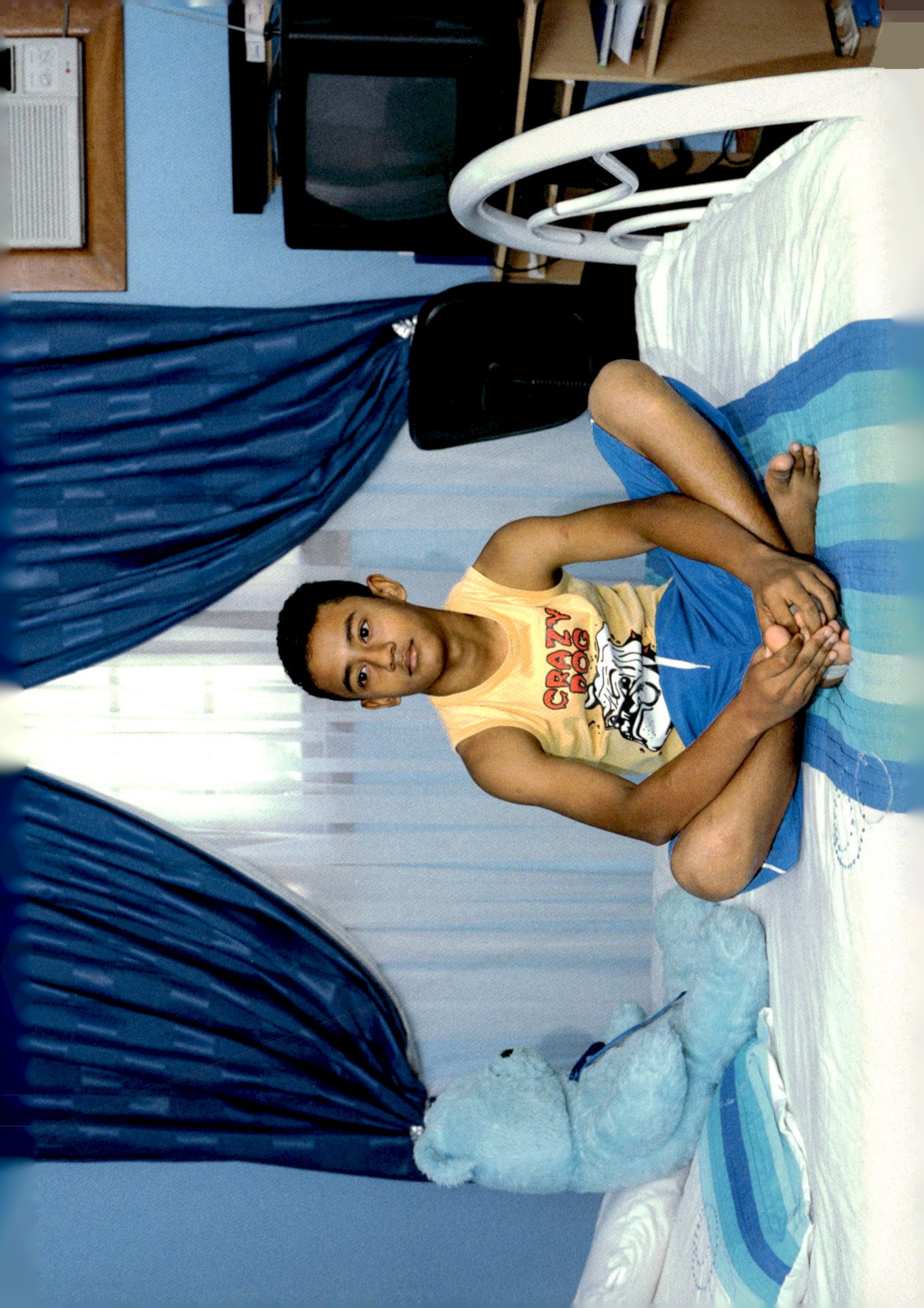
CRAZY DOG

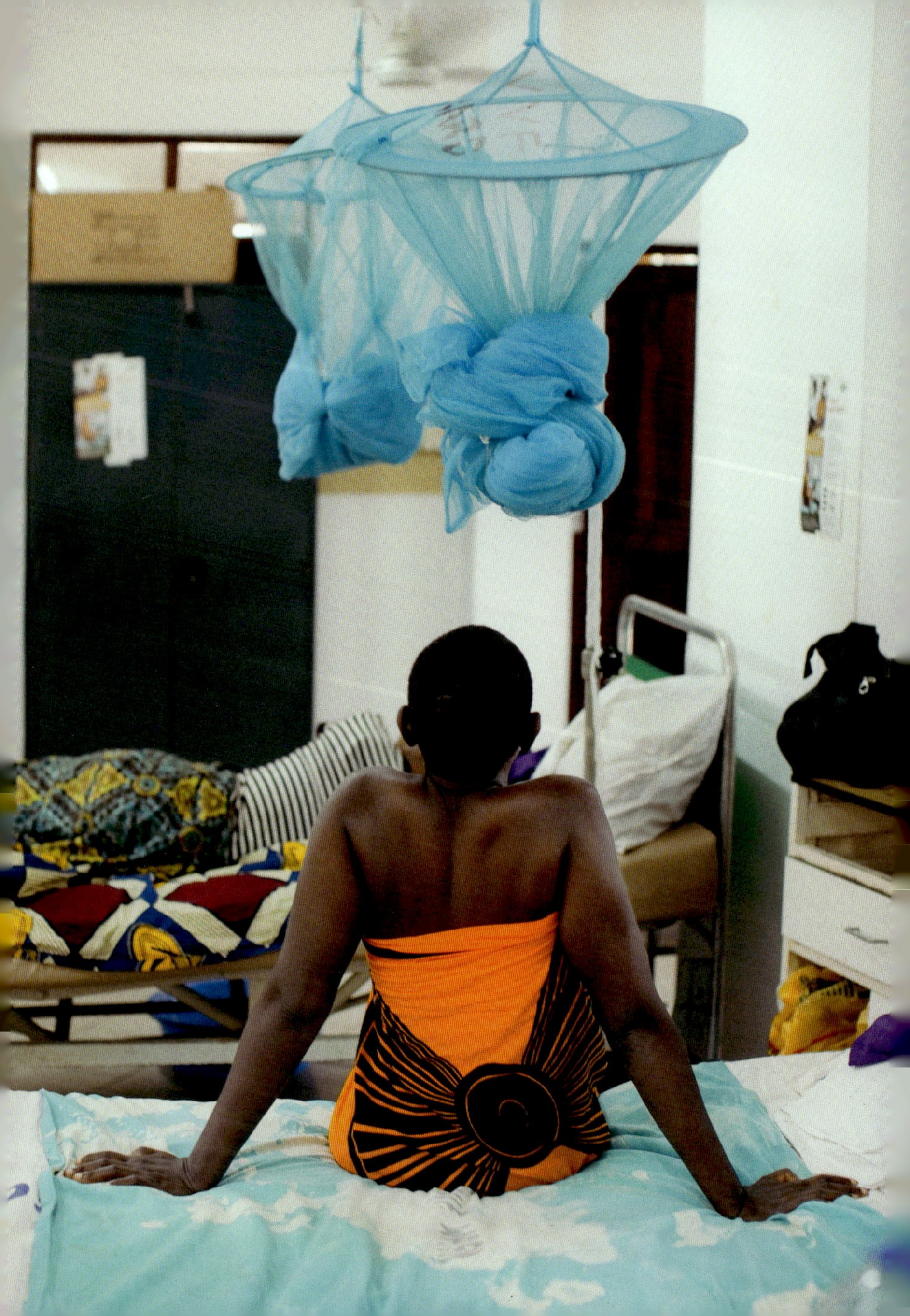

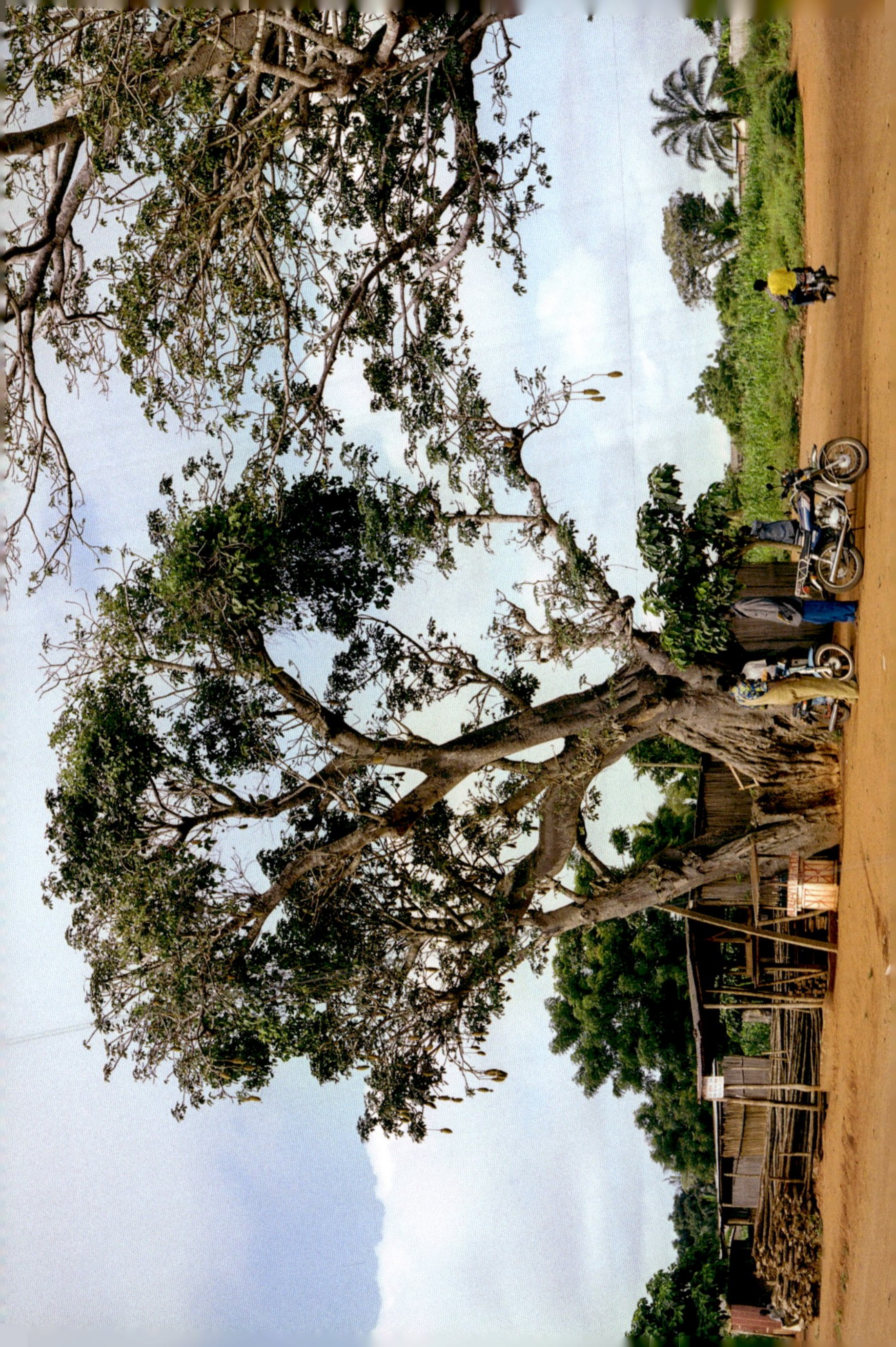

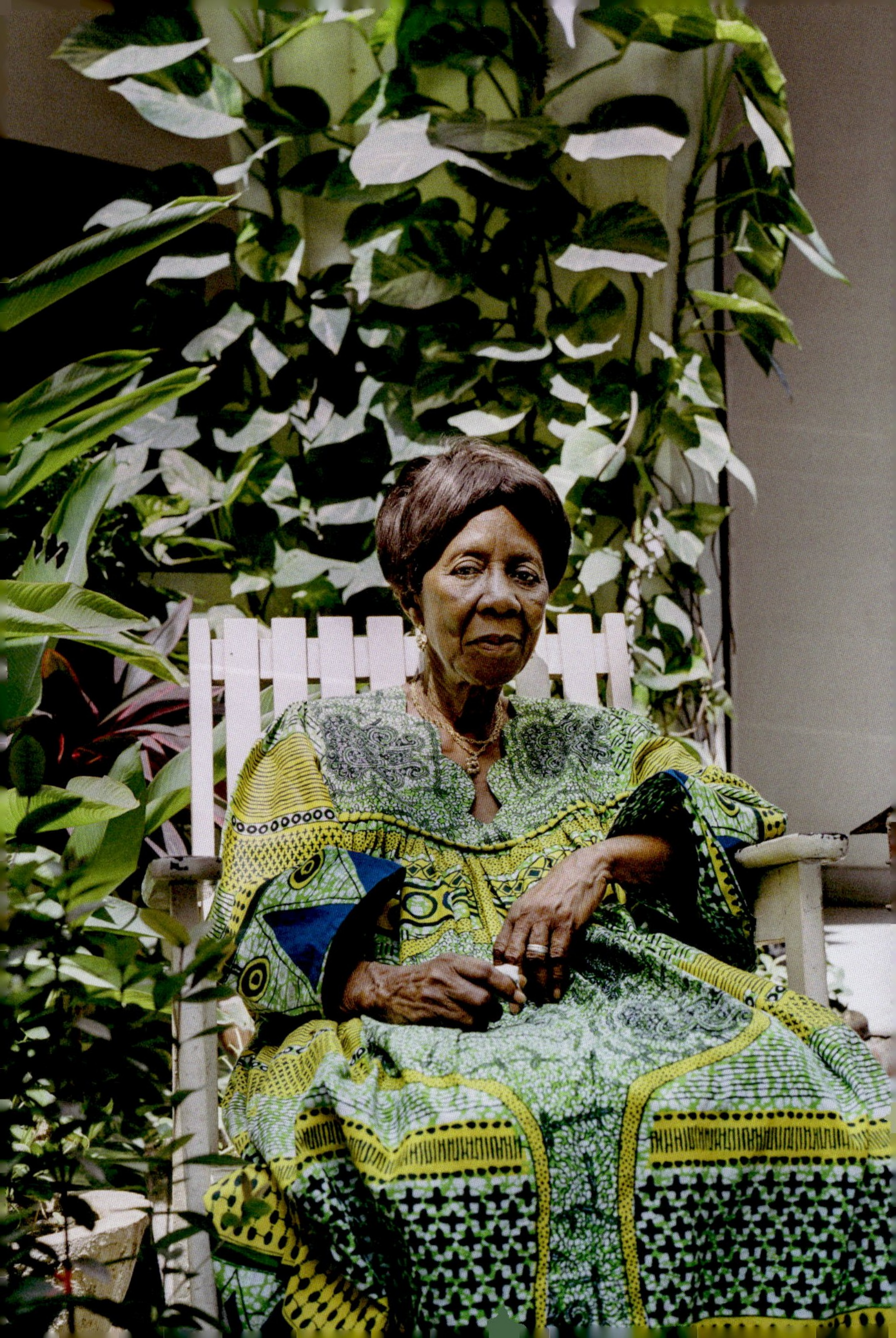

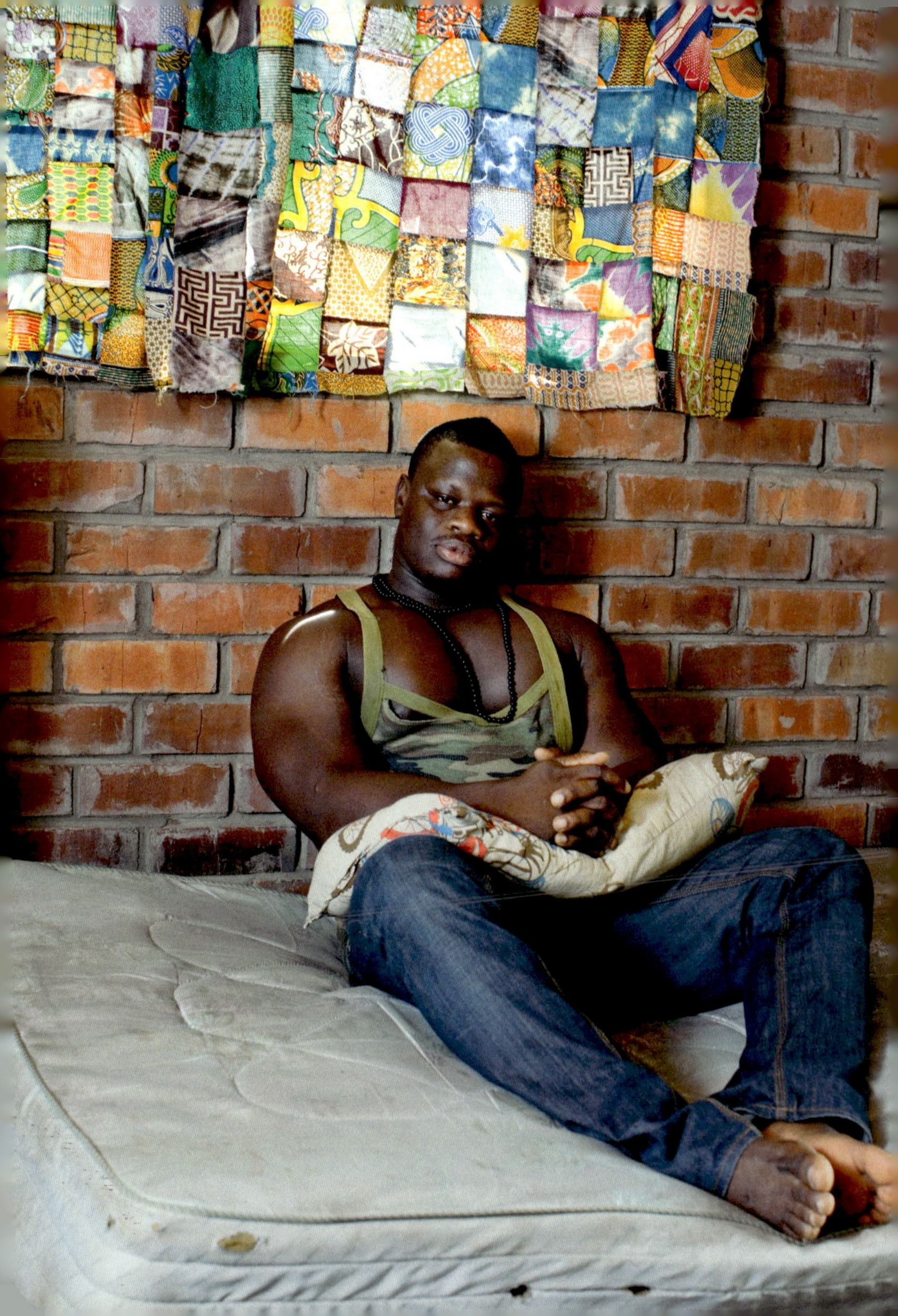

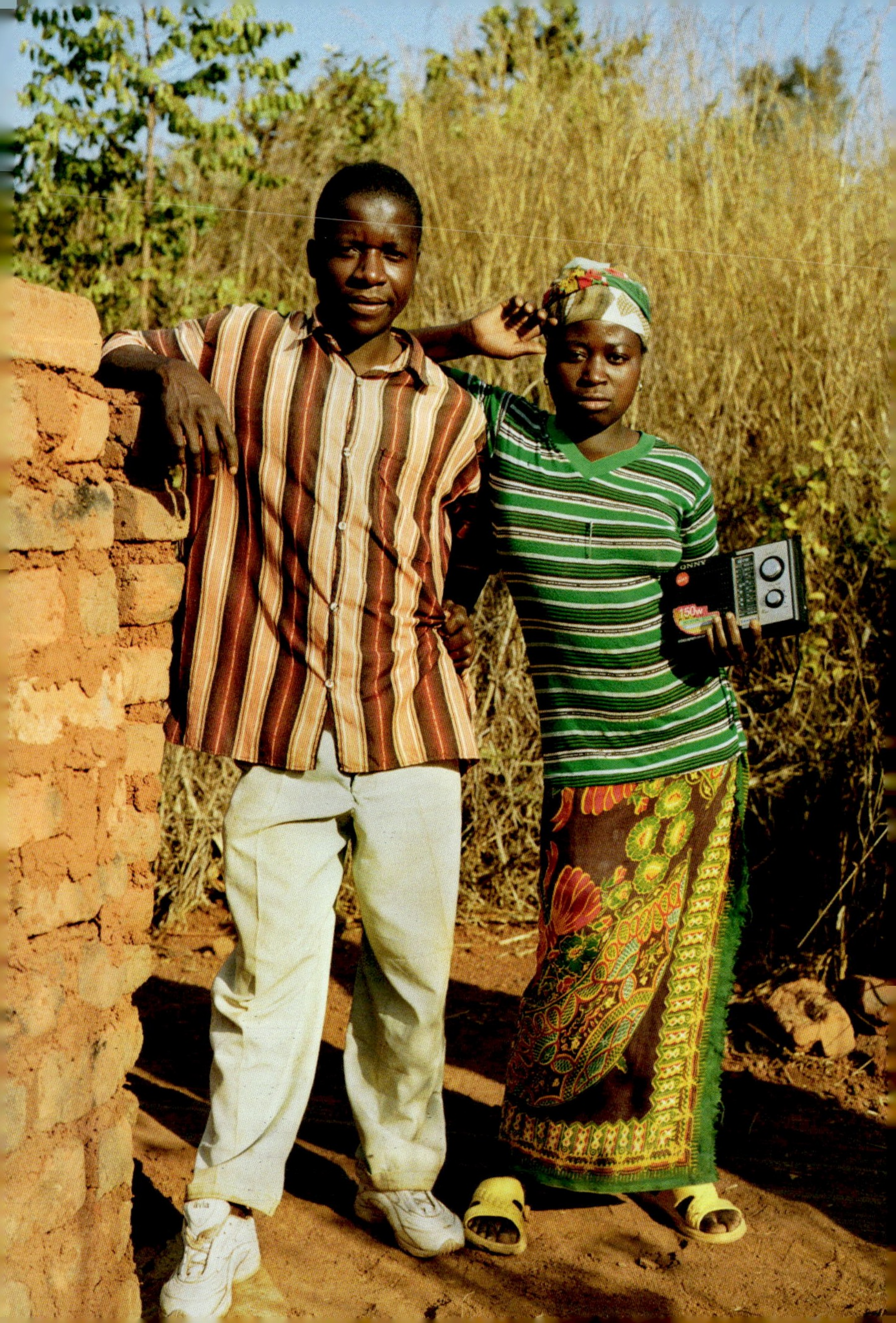
150w

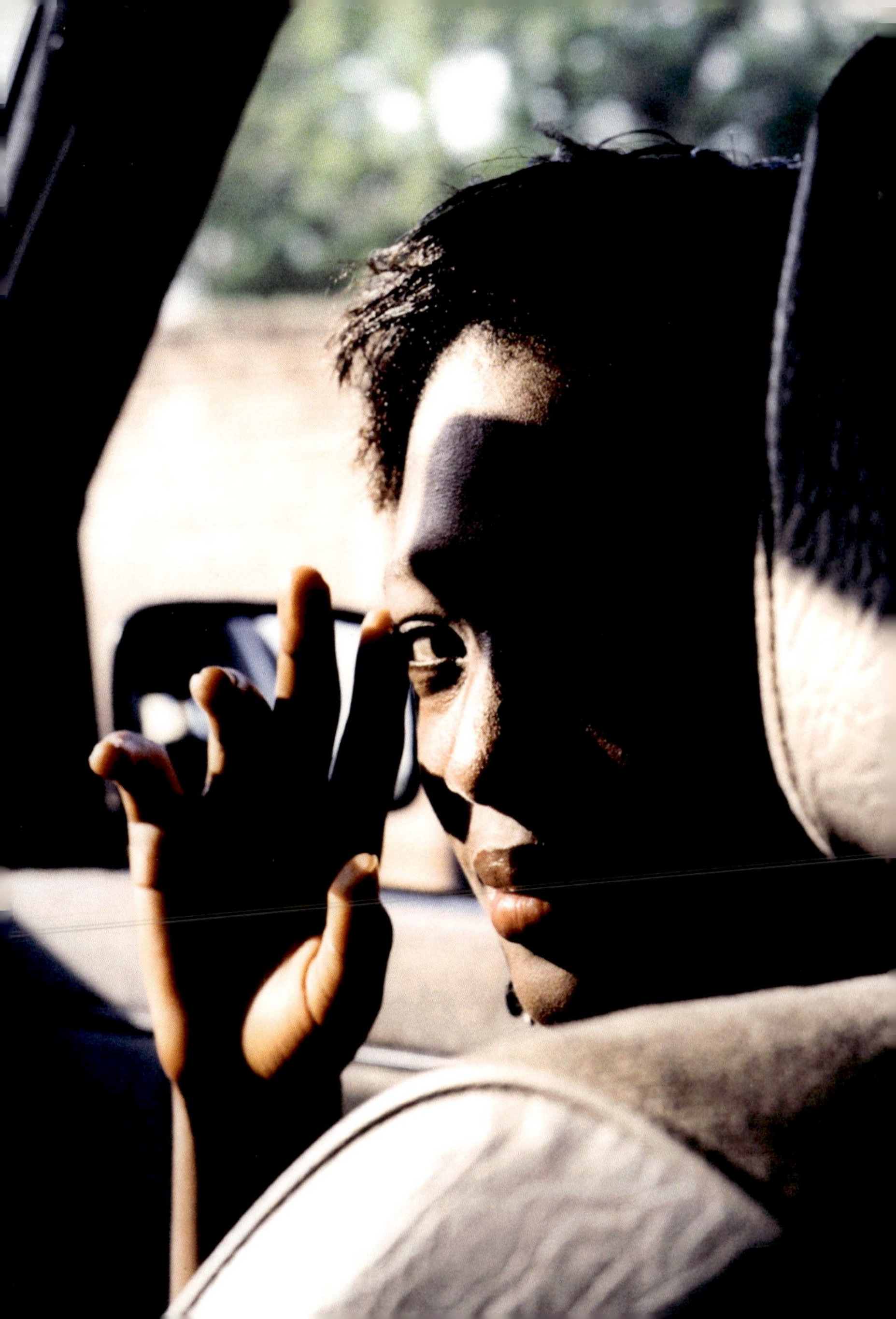

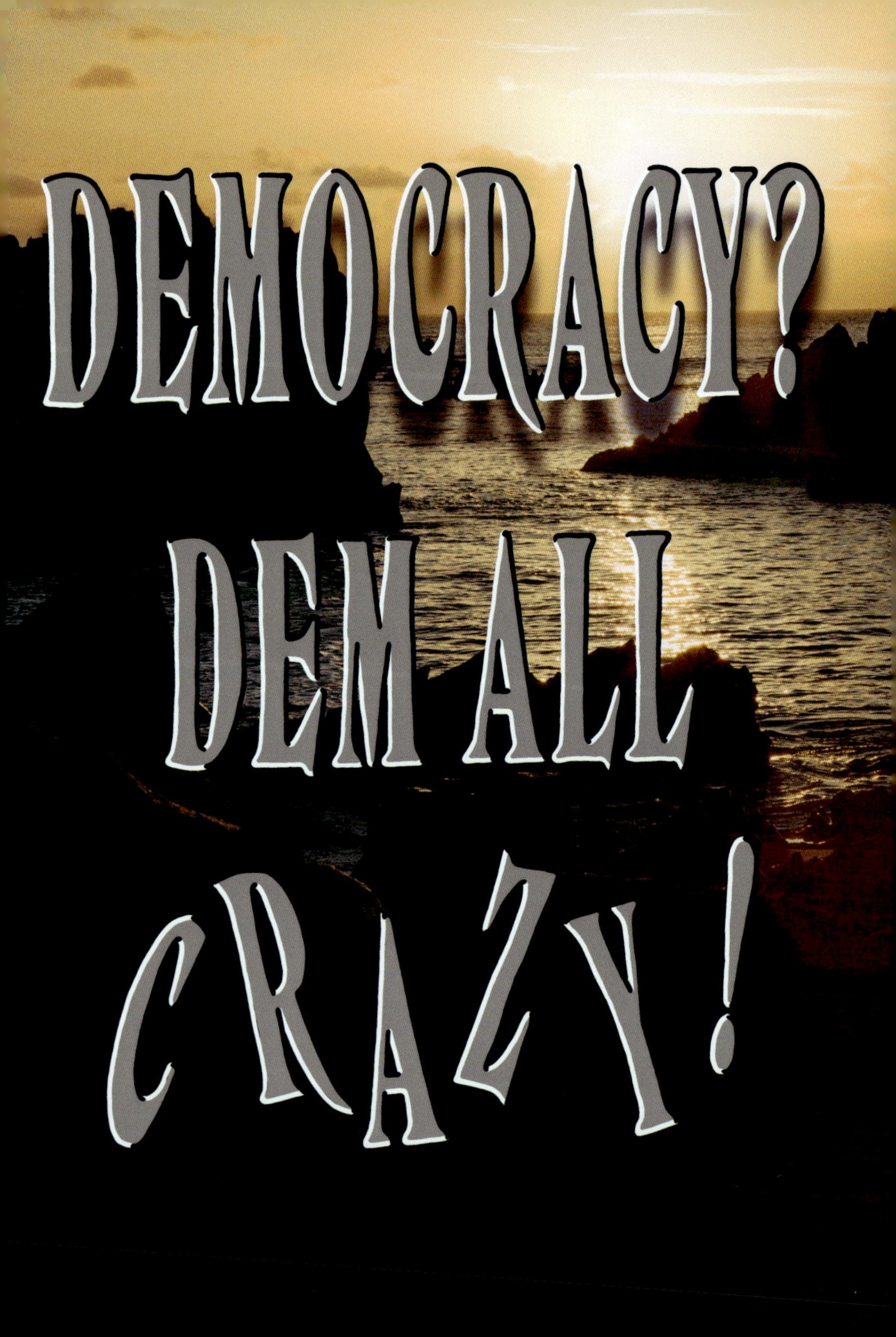
DEMOCRACY?
DEM ALL
CRAZY!

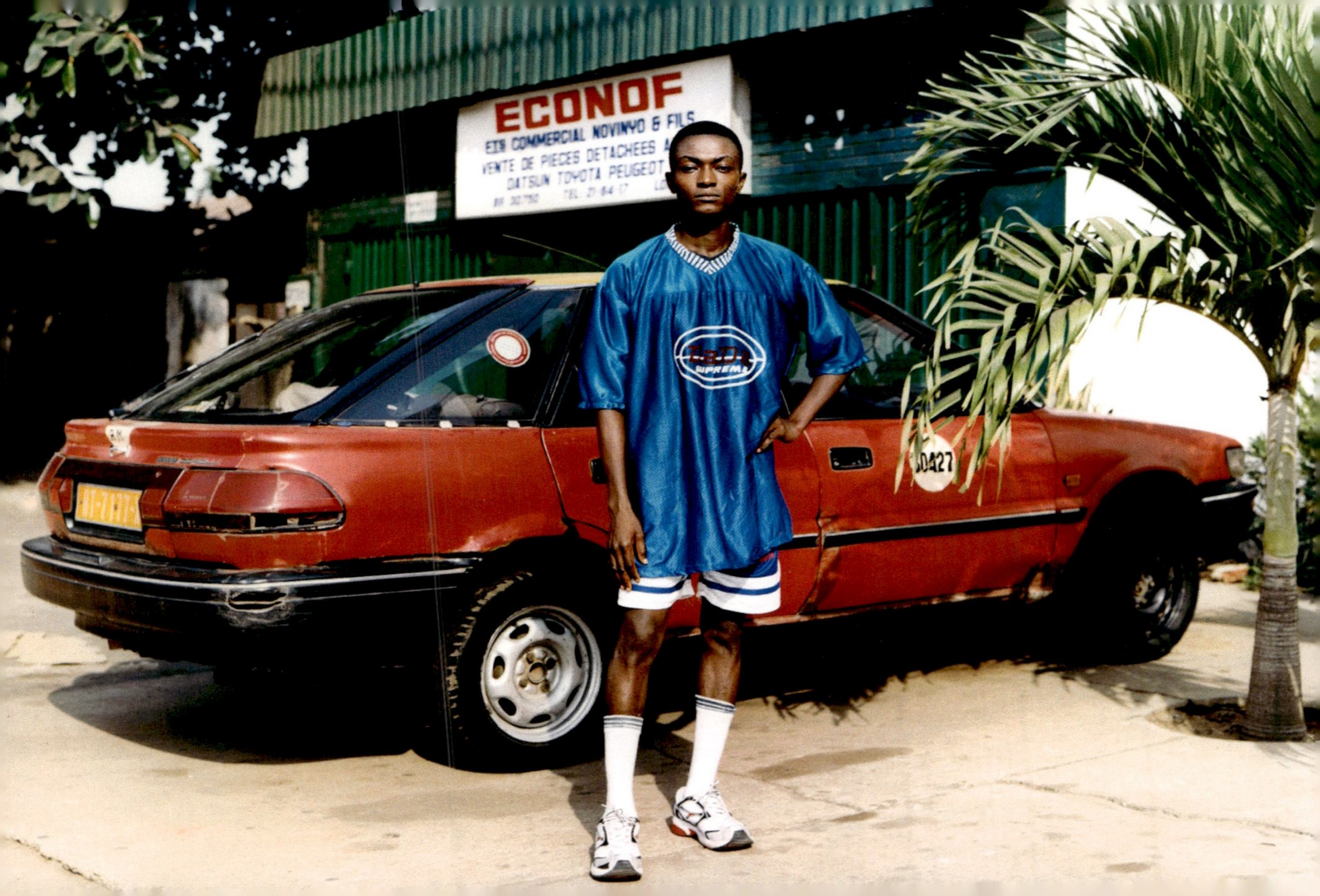
ECONOF
VENTE DE PIECES DETACHEES
DATSUN TOYOTA PEUGEOT
SD427

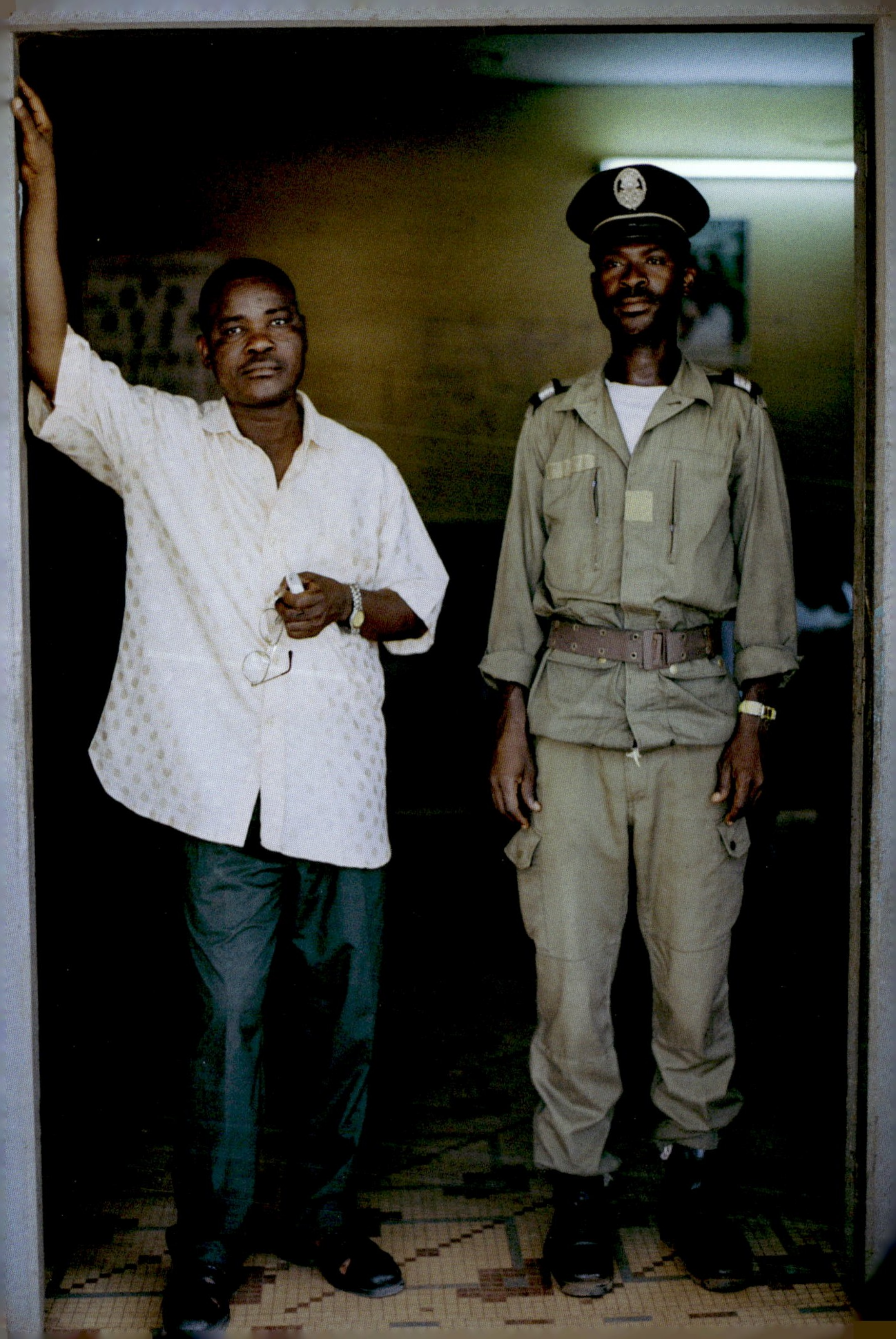

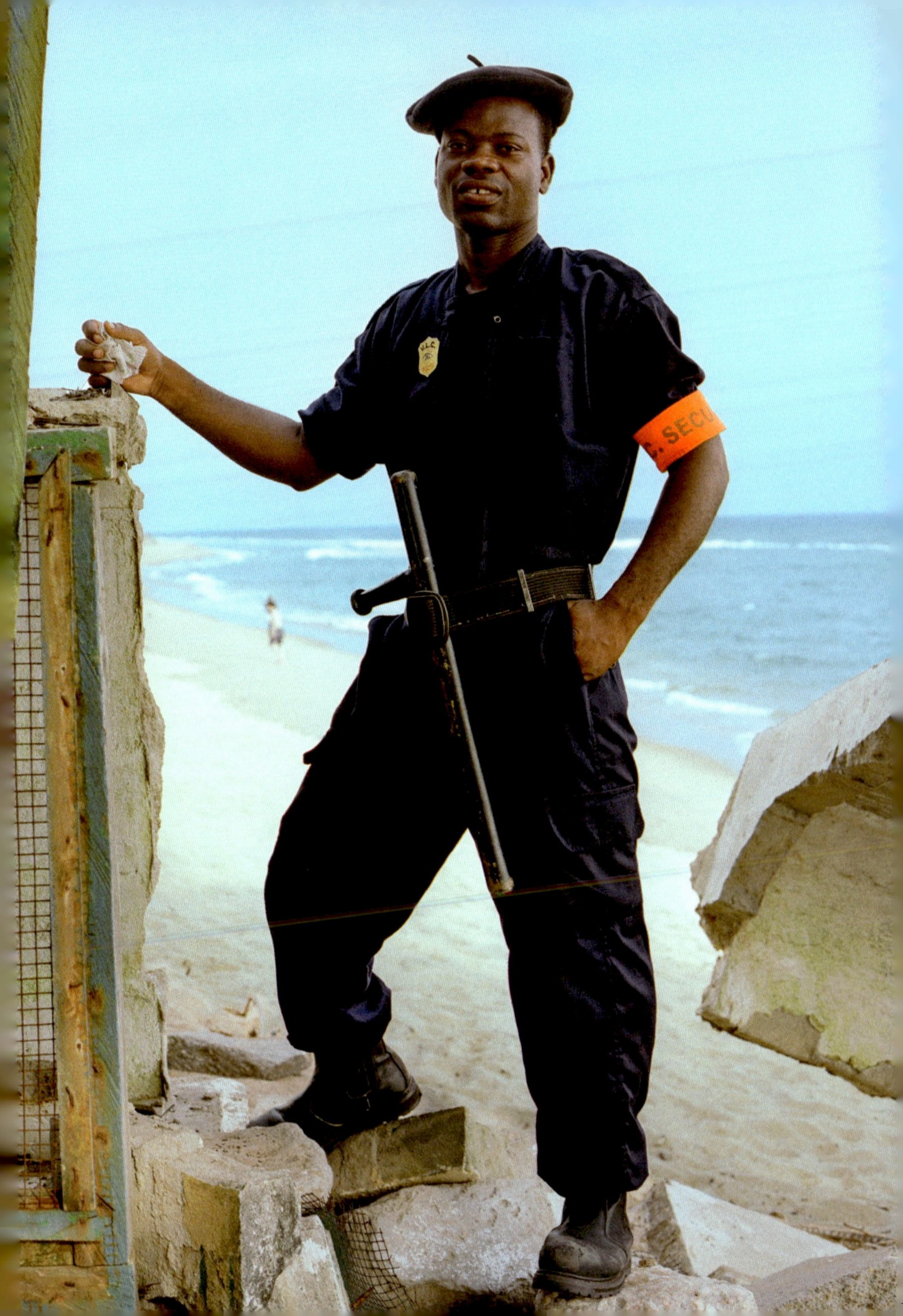
C. SECU

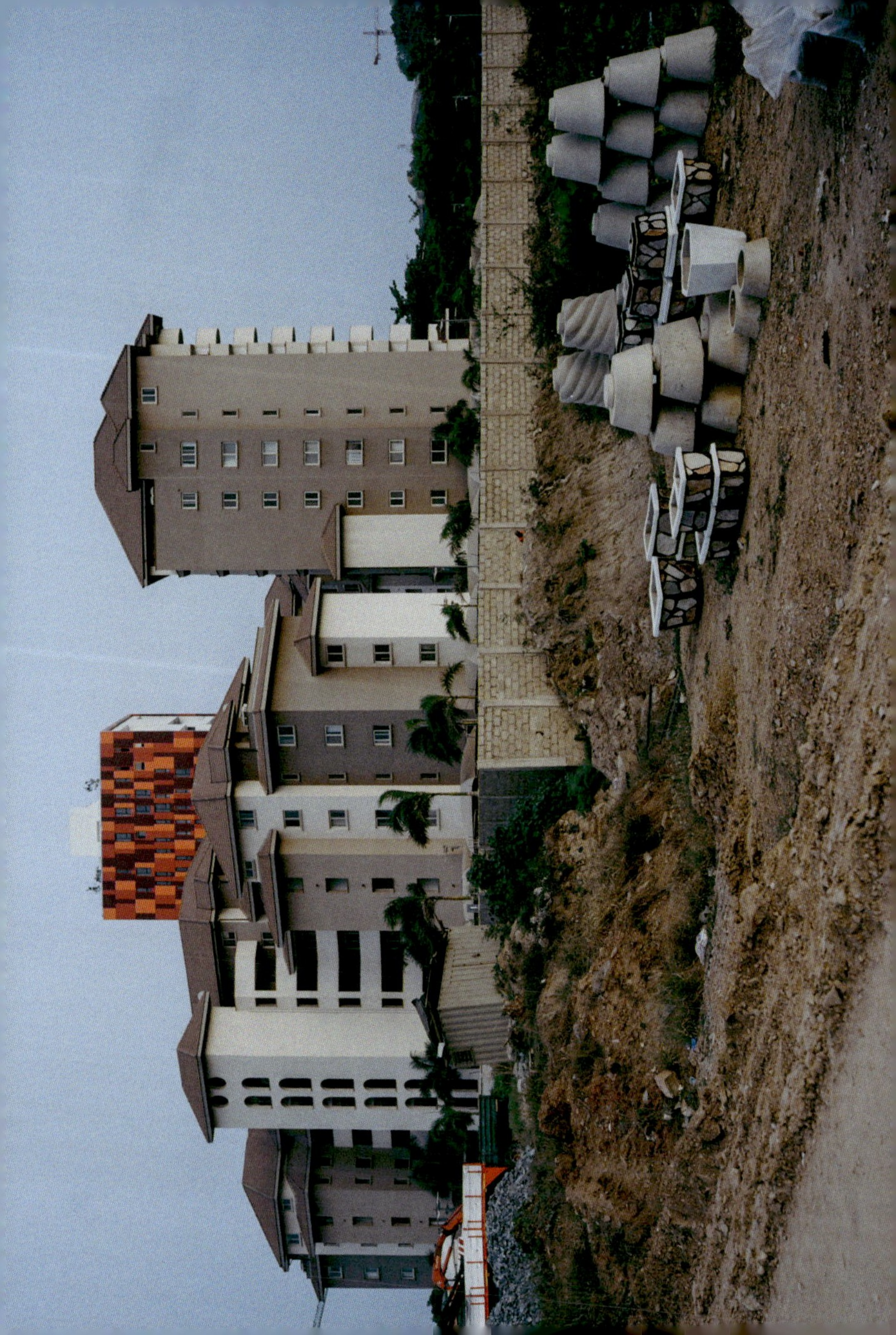

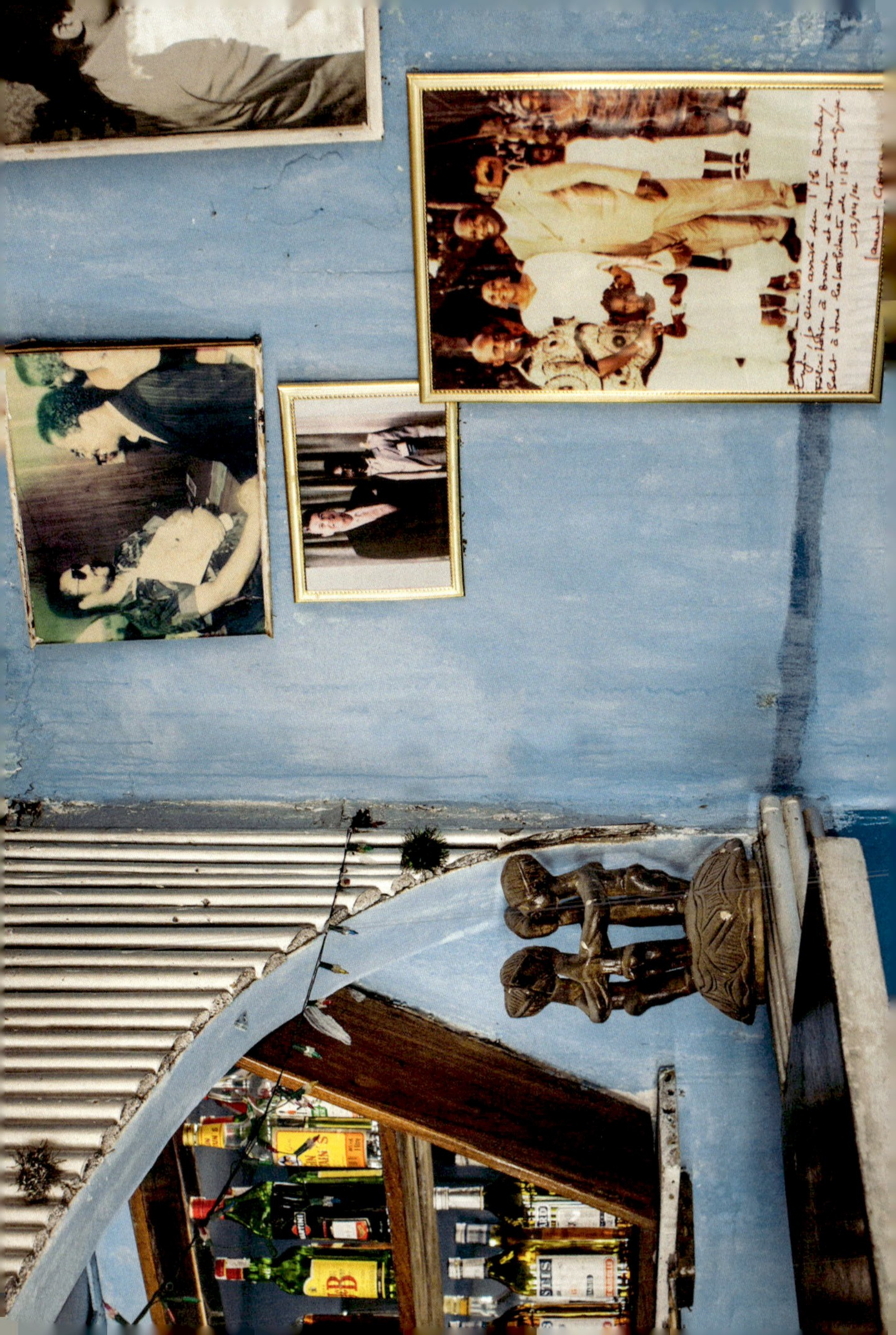

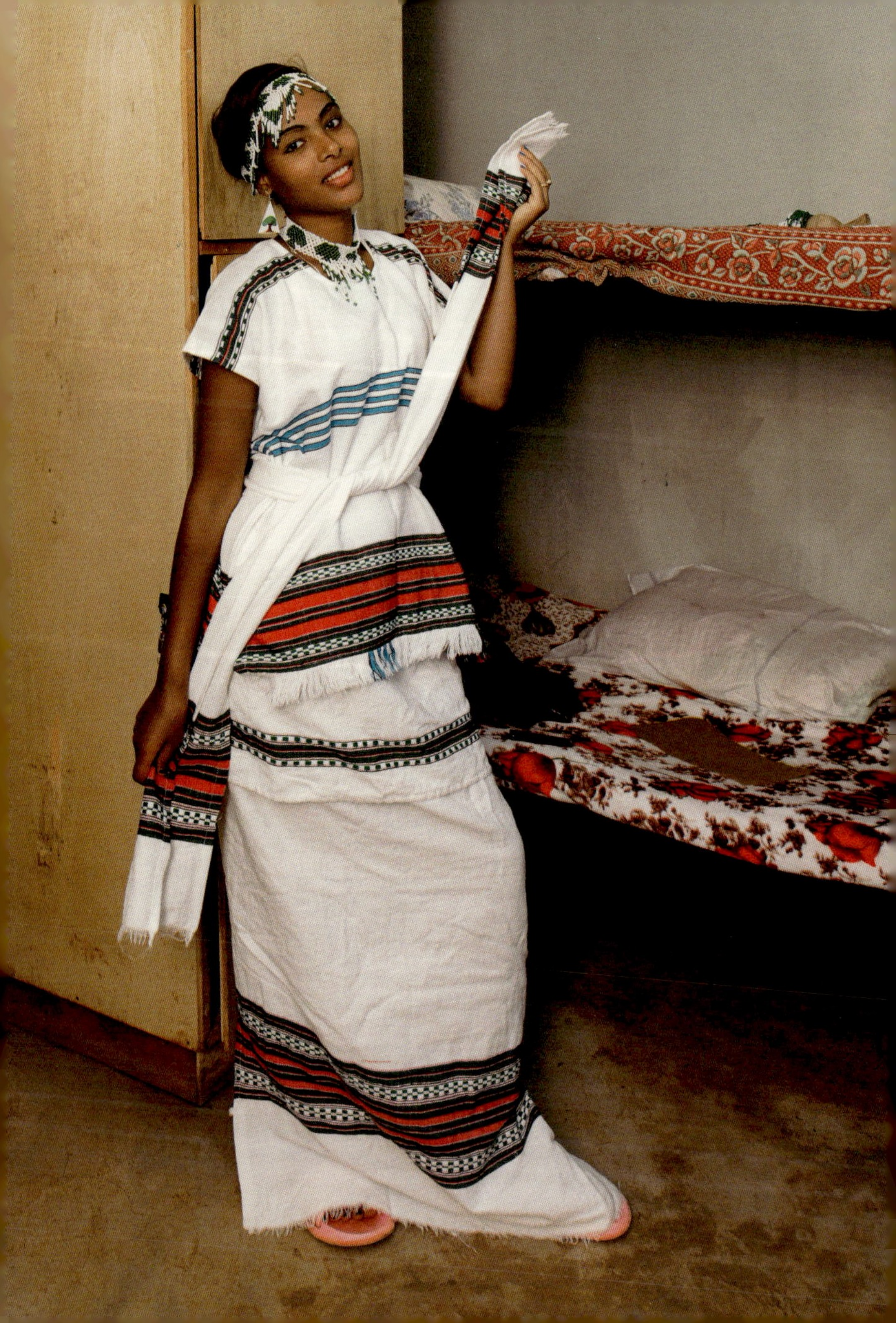

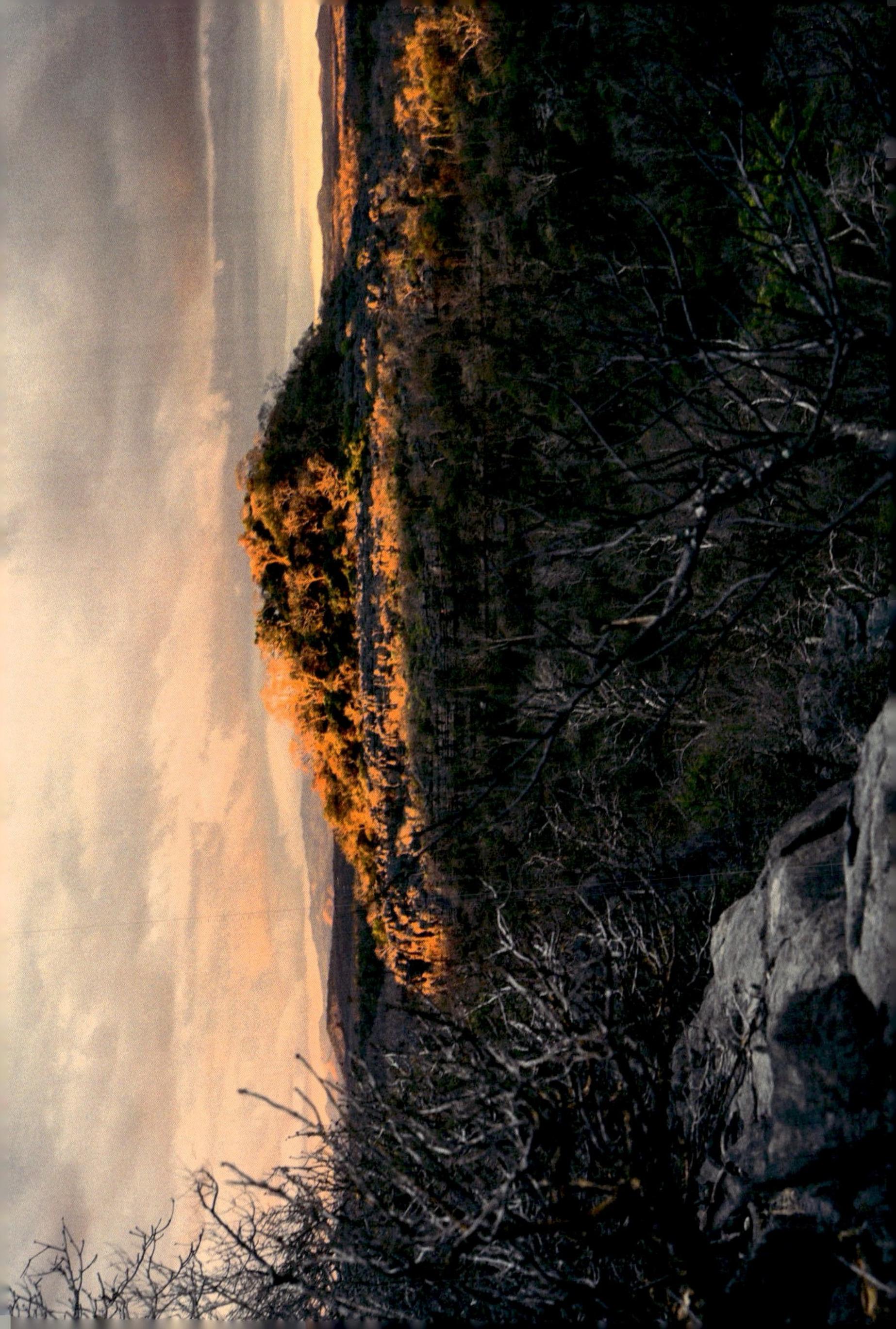

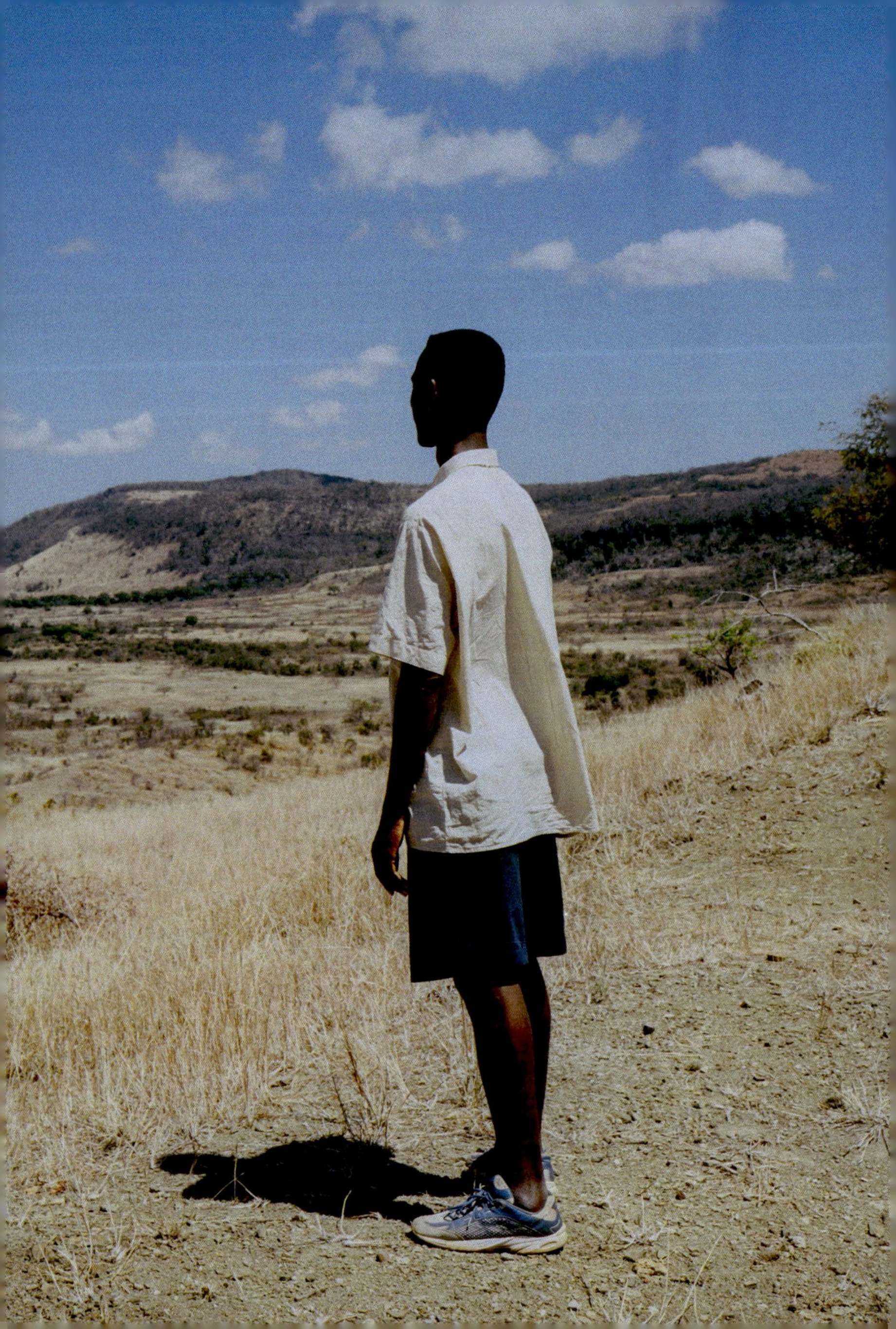

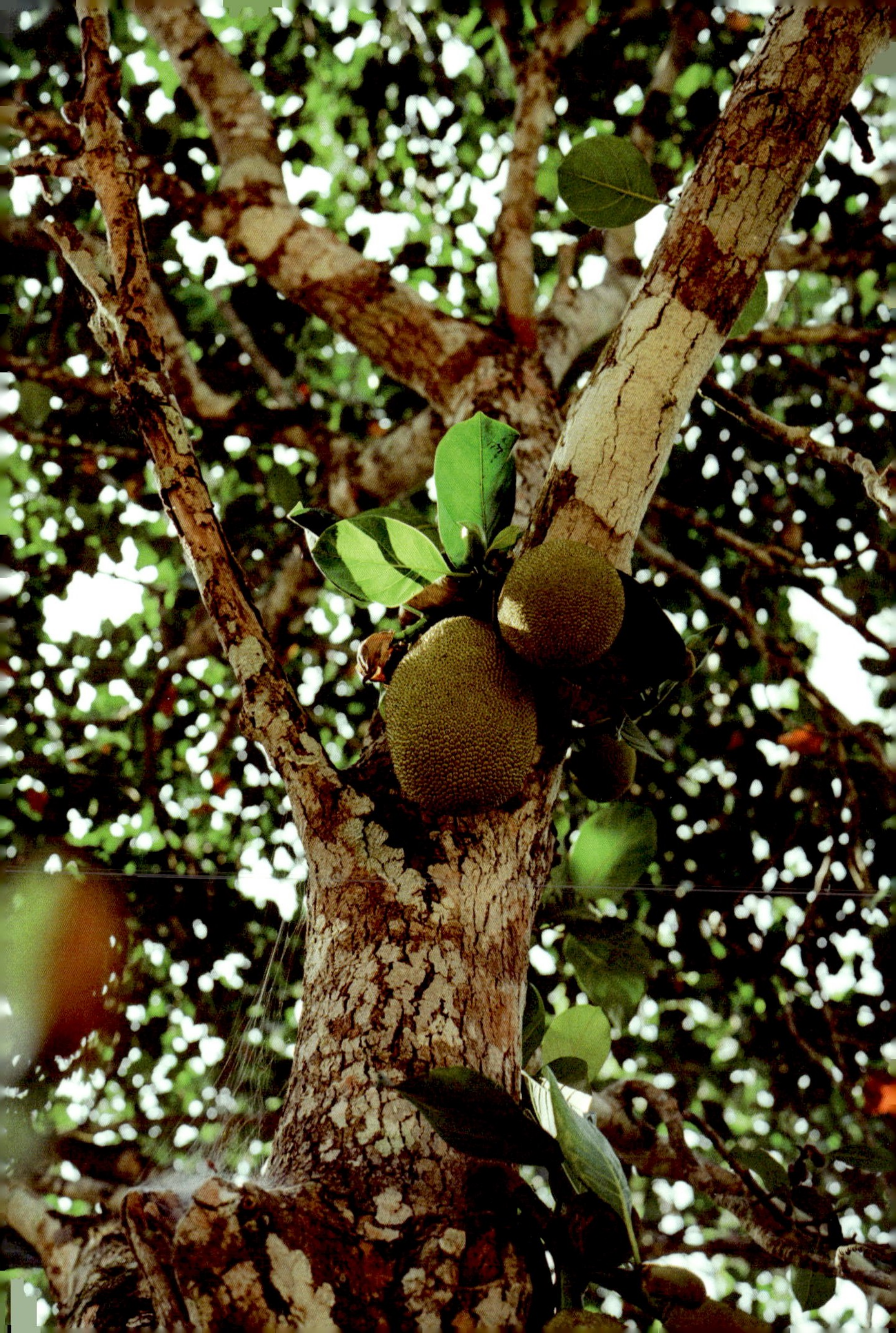

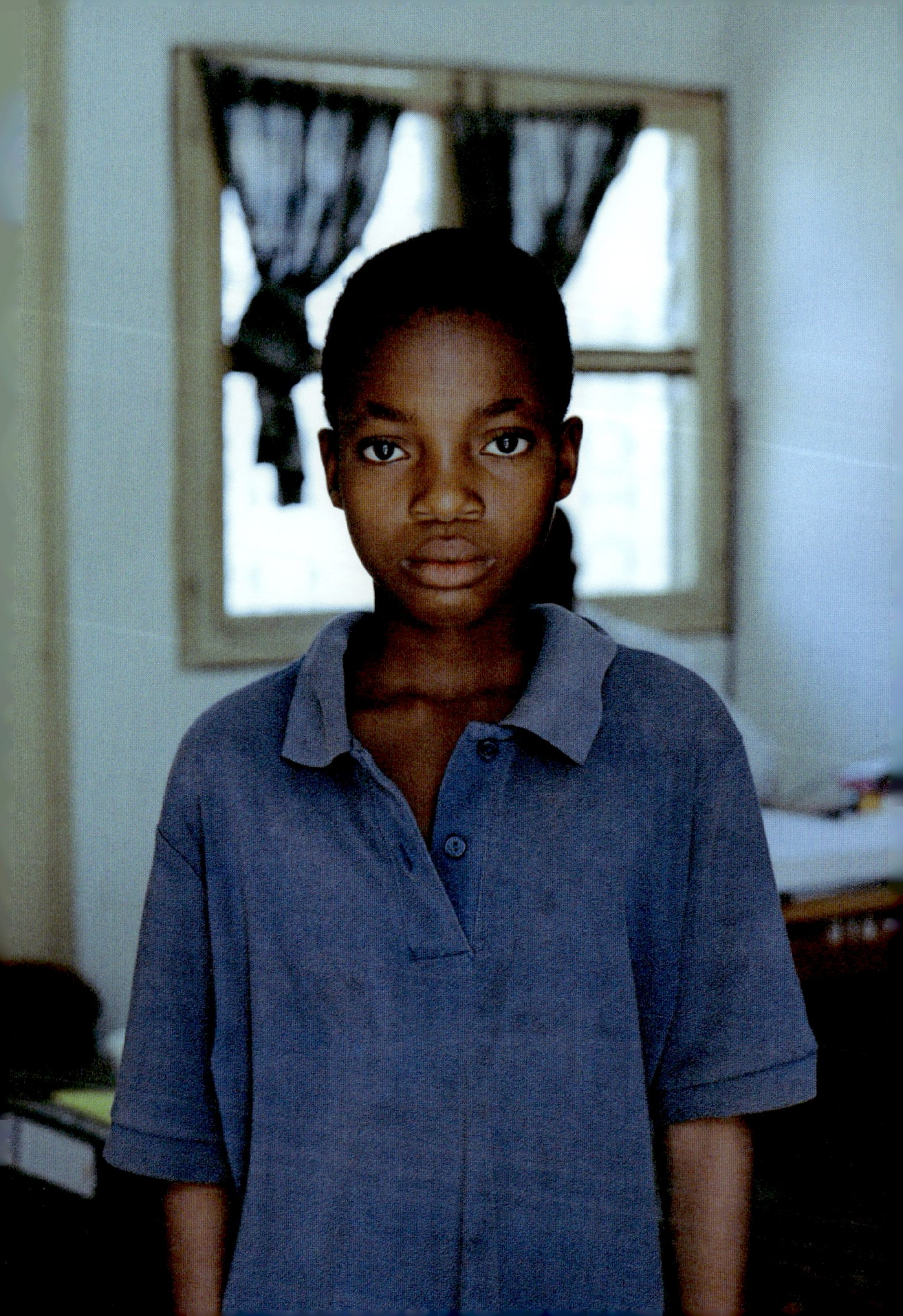

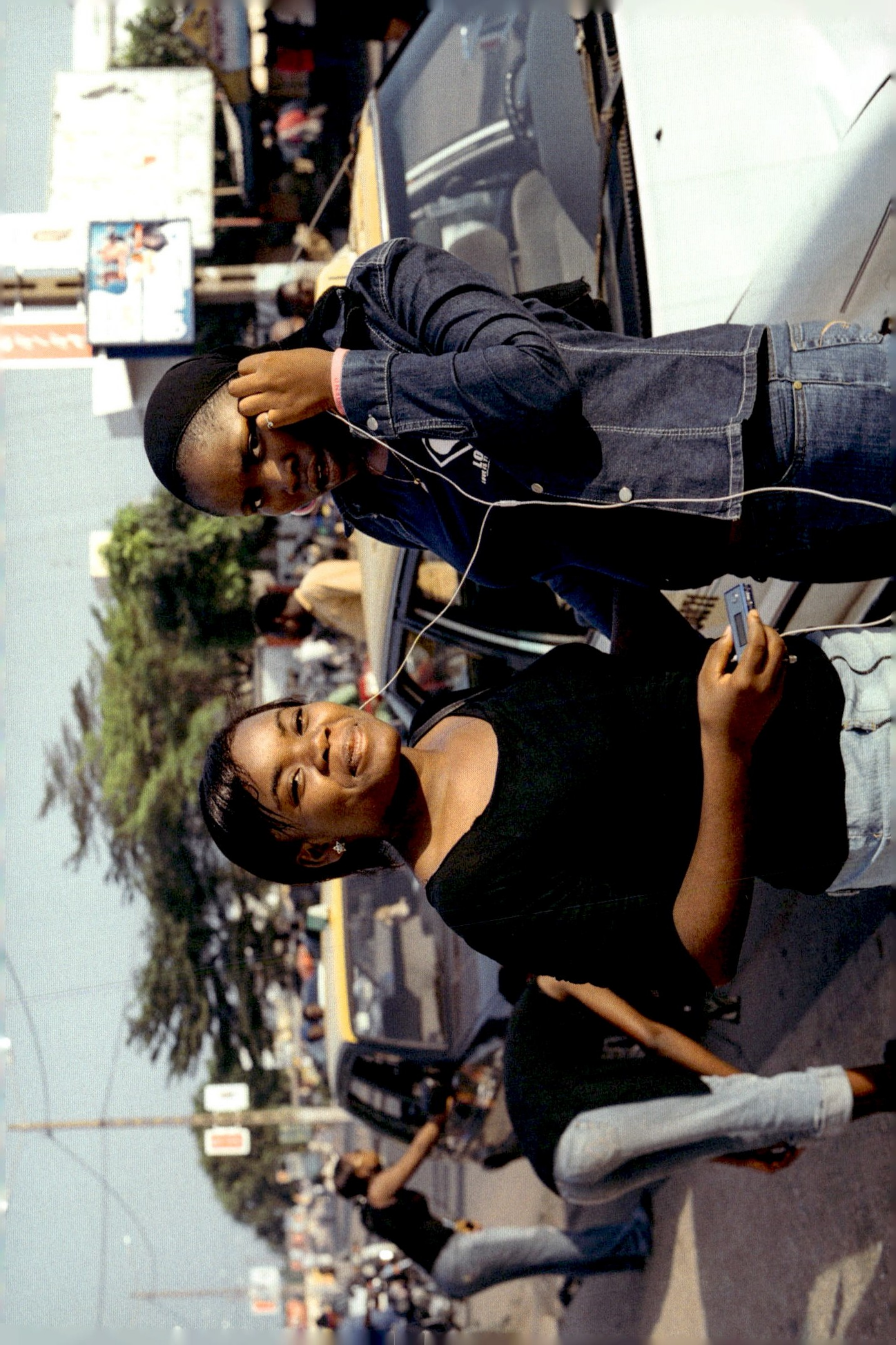

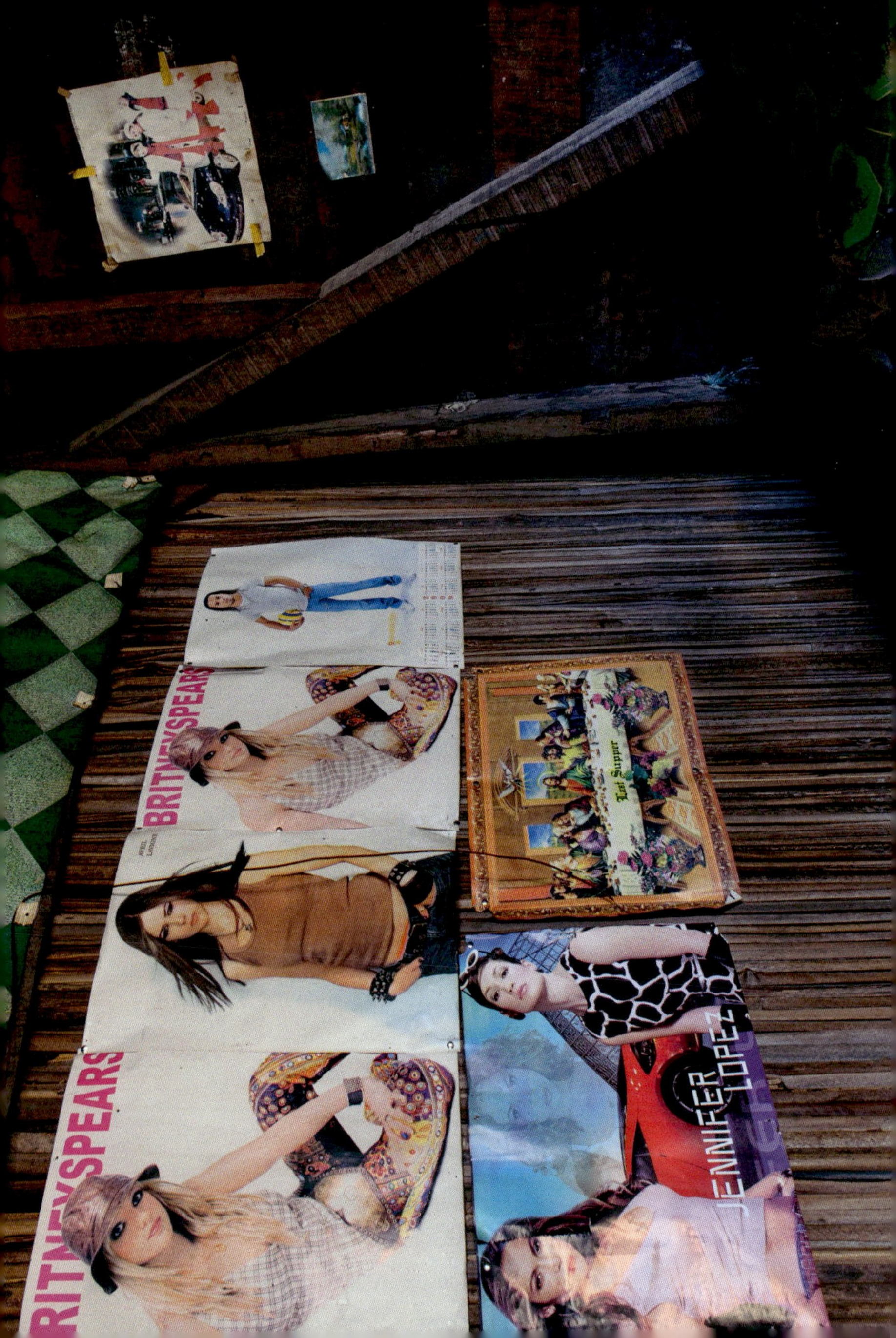

BRITNEYSPEARS
Last Supper
JENNIFER LOPEZ

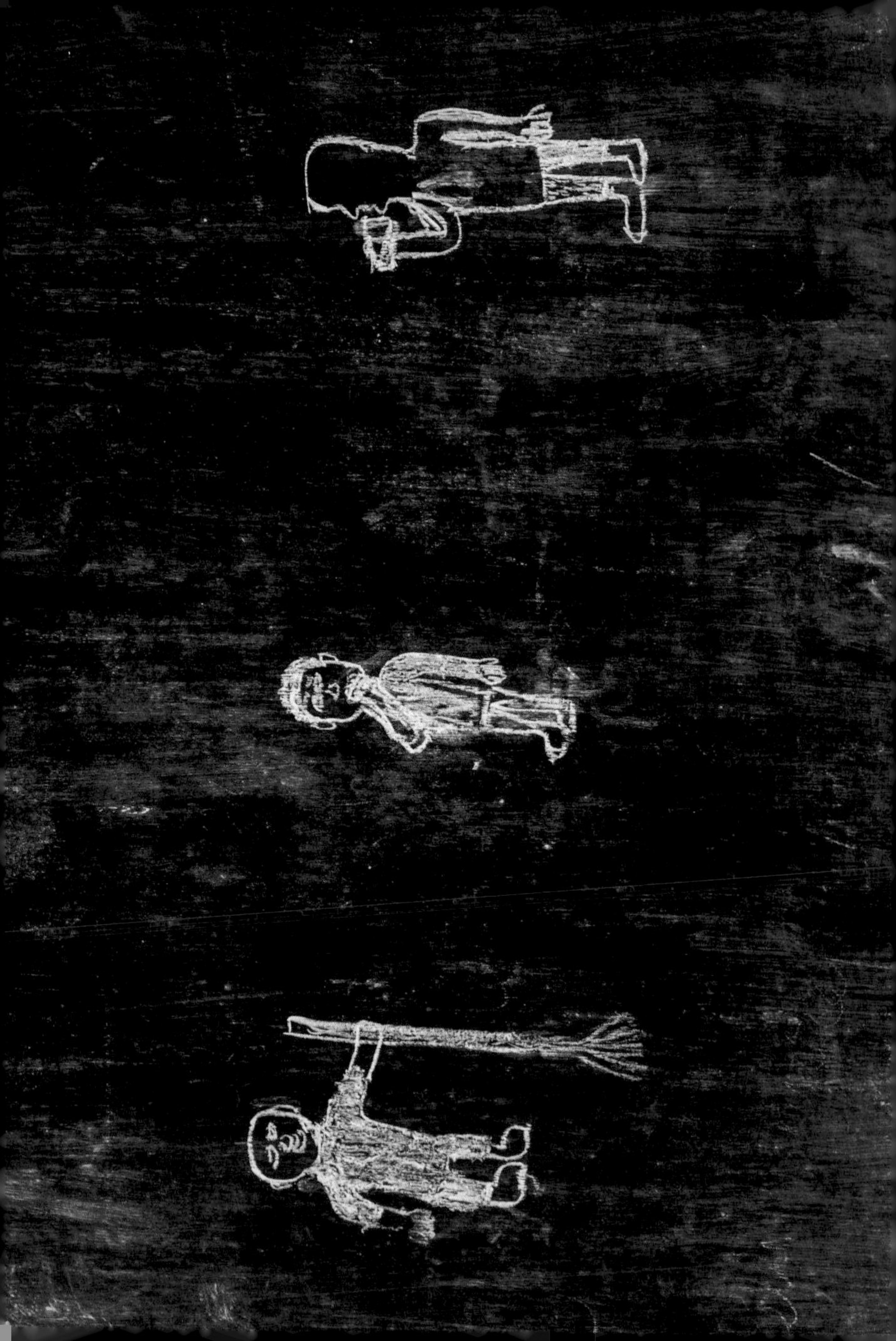

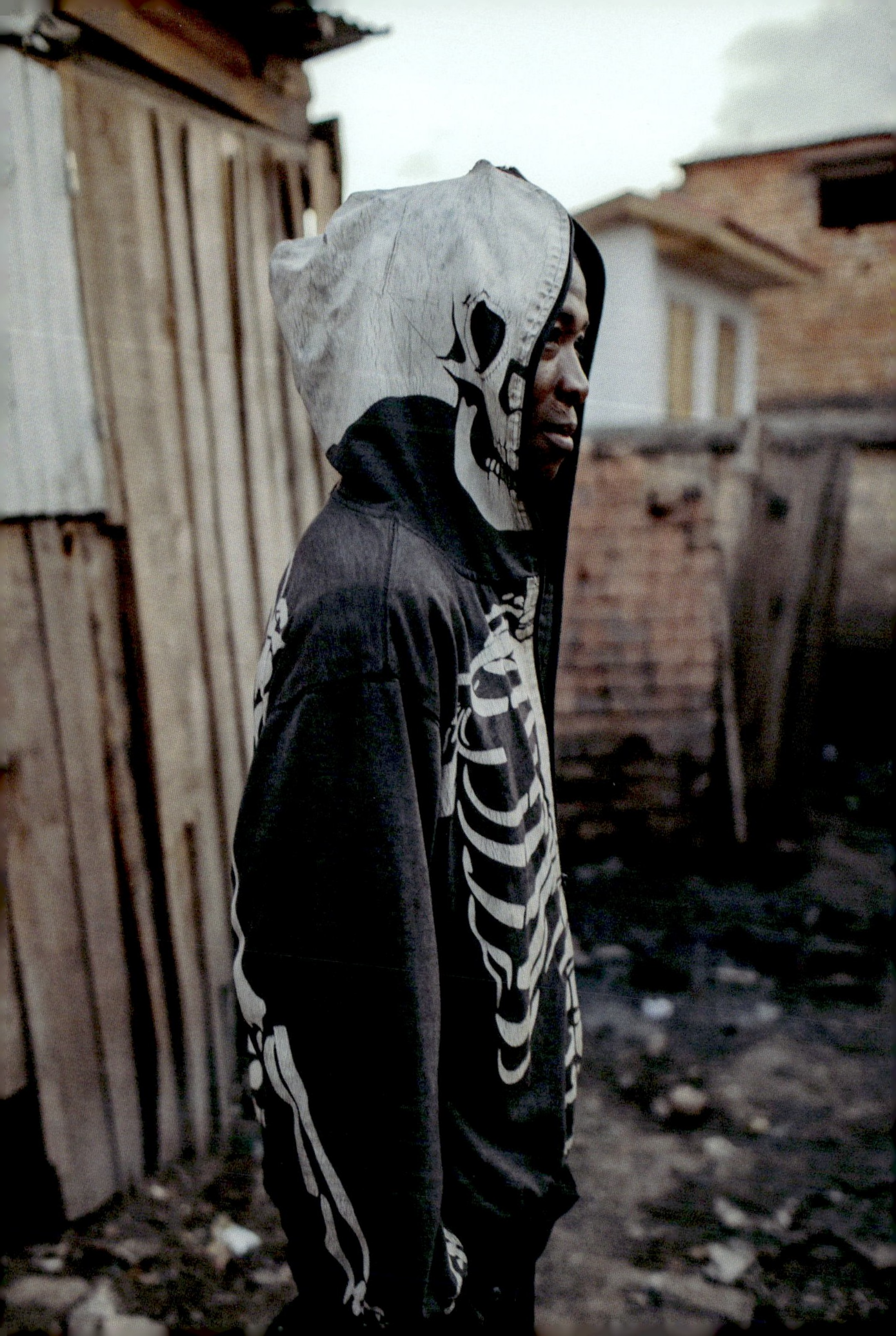

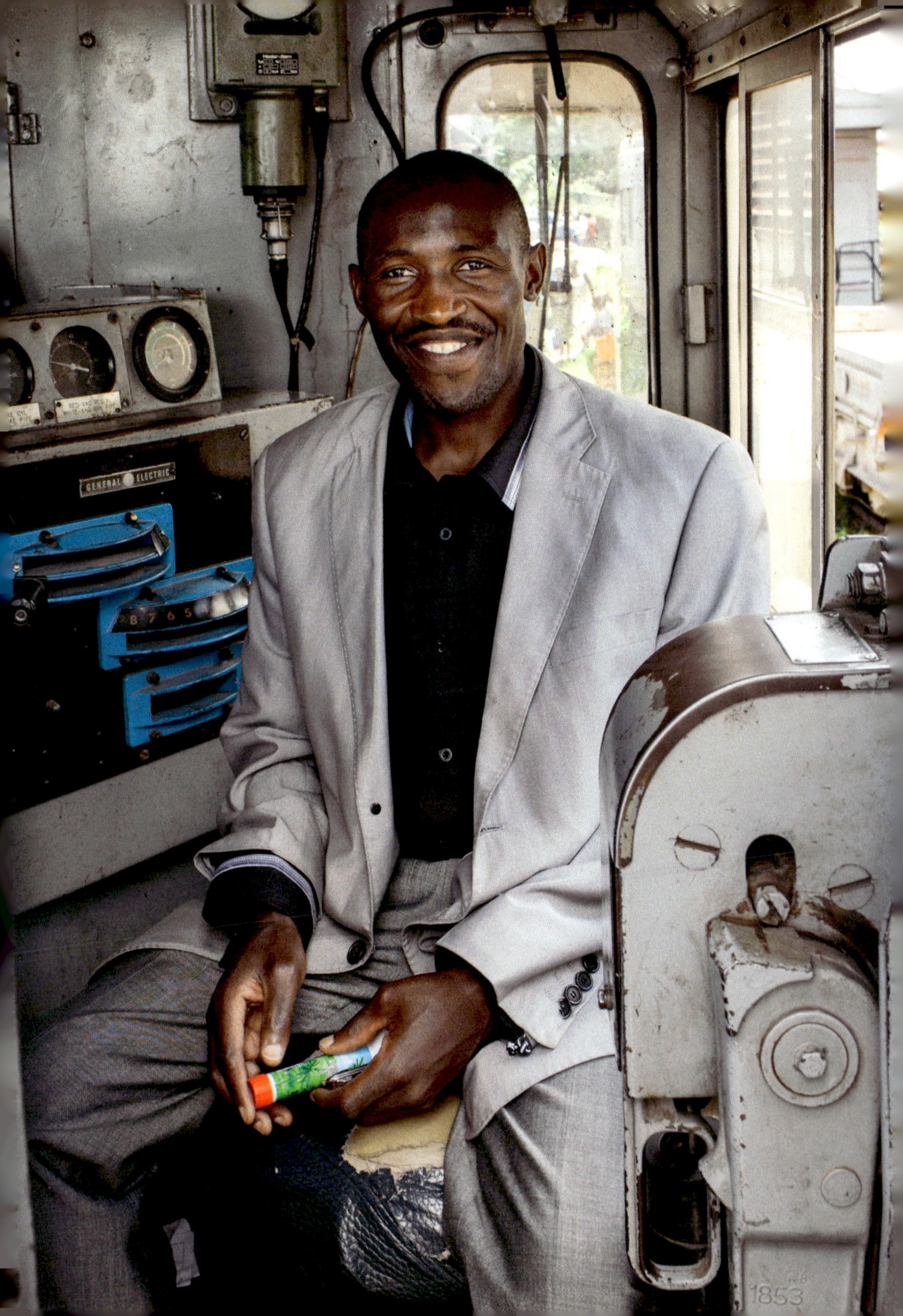
GENERAL ELECTRIC
1853

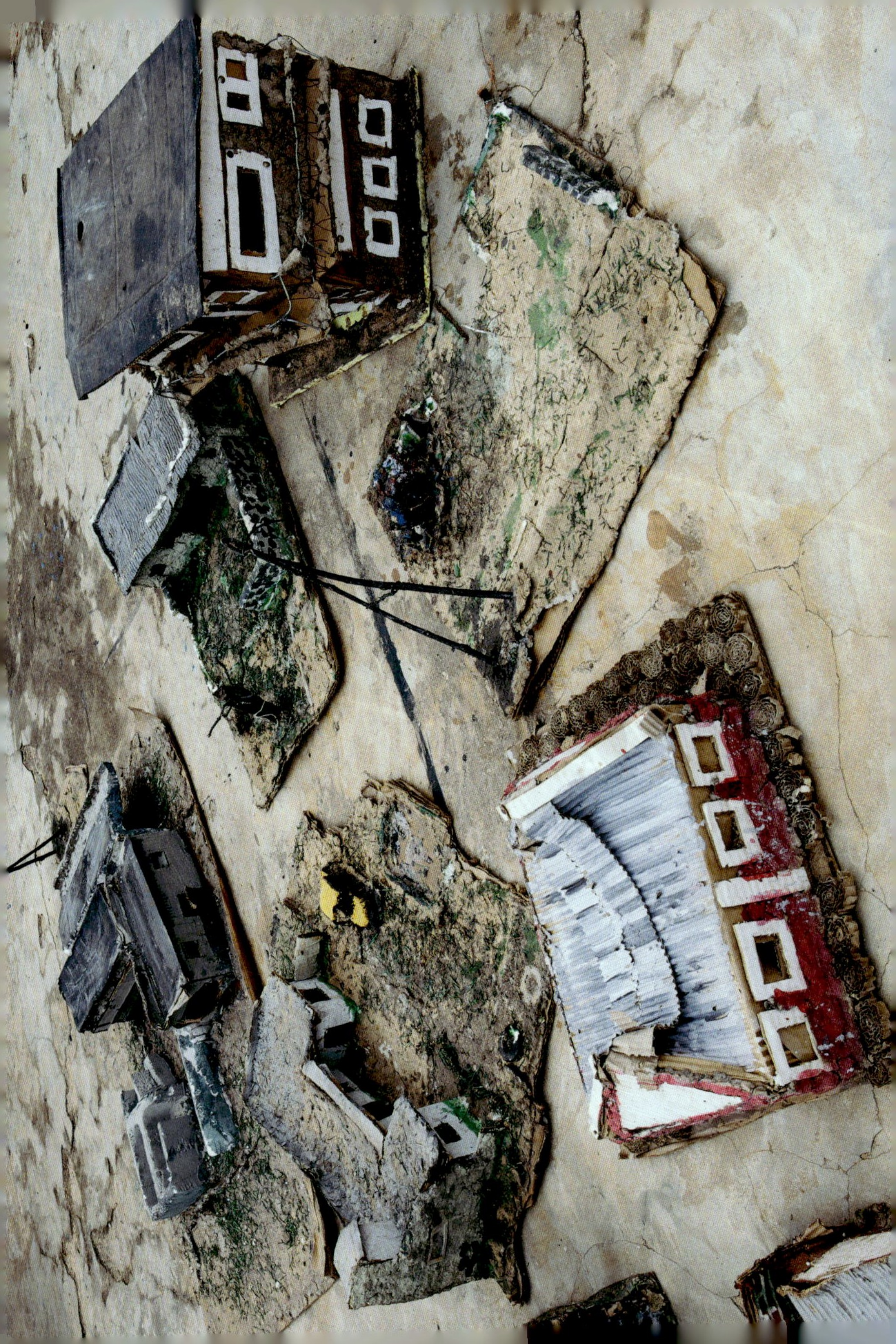

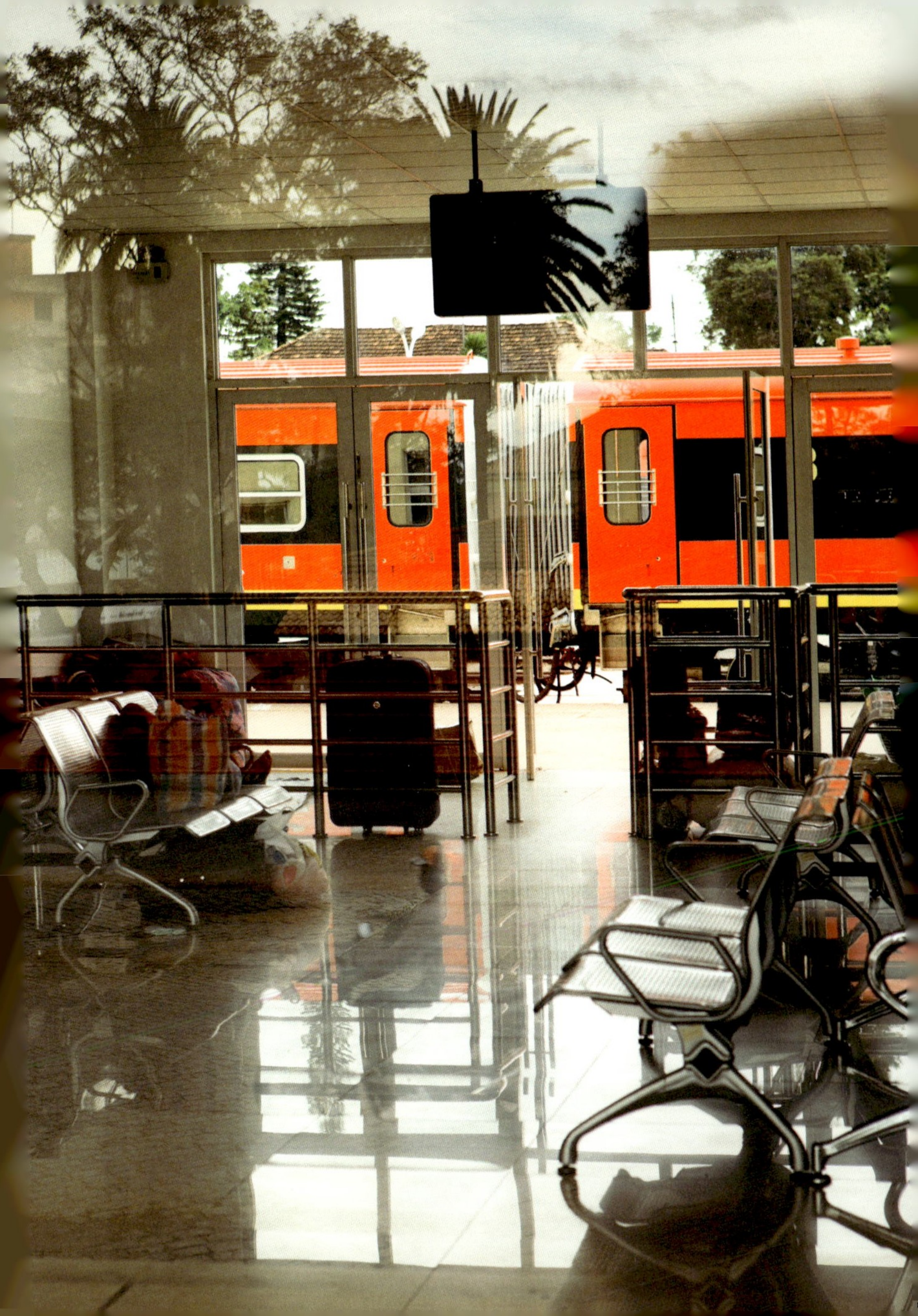

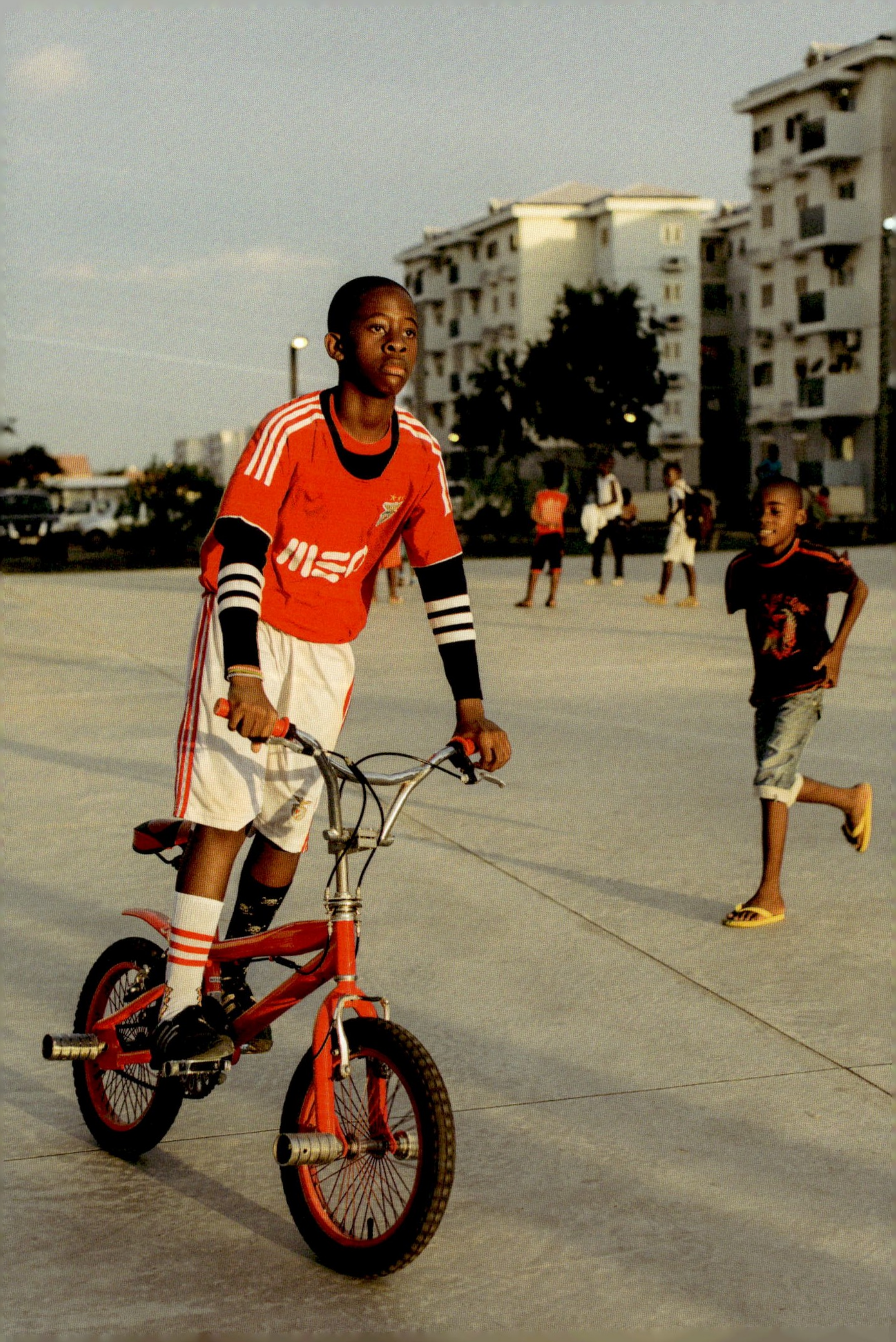

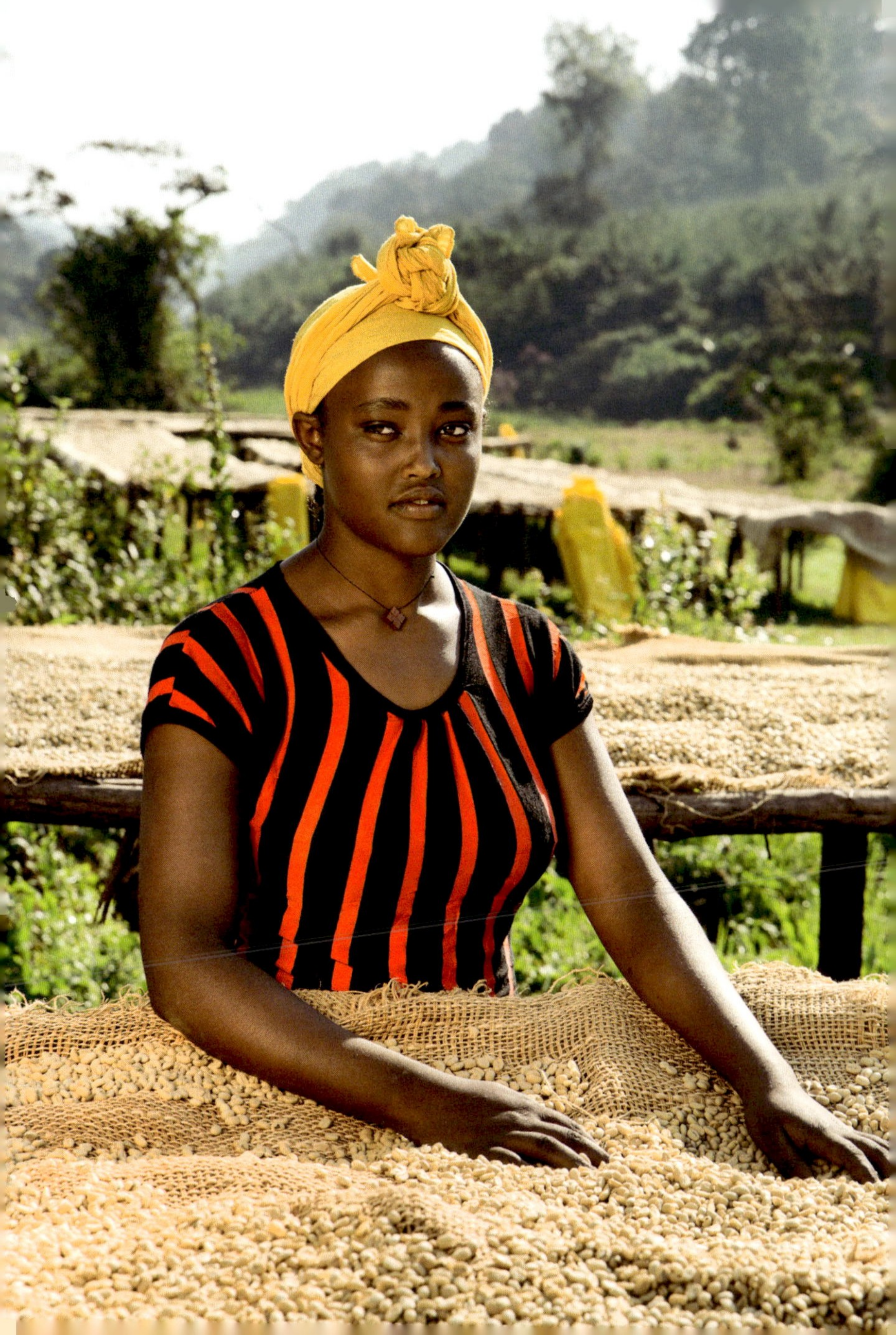

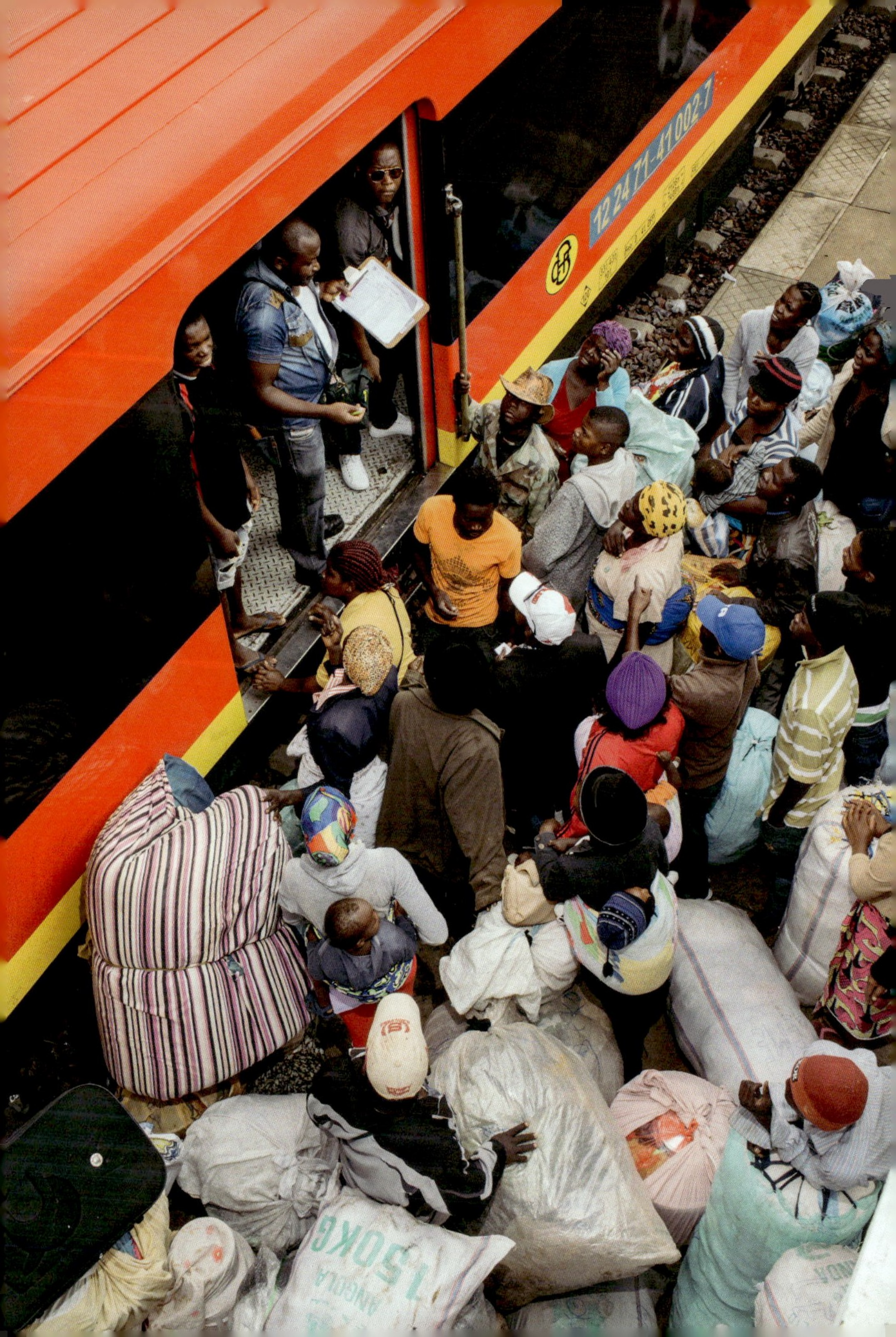
12 24 71-41 002-7
150KG
ANGOLA

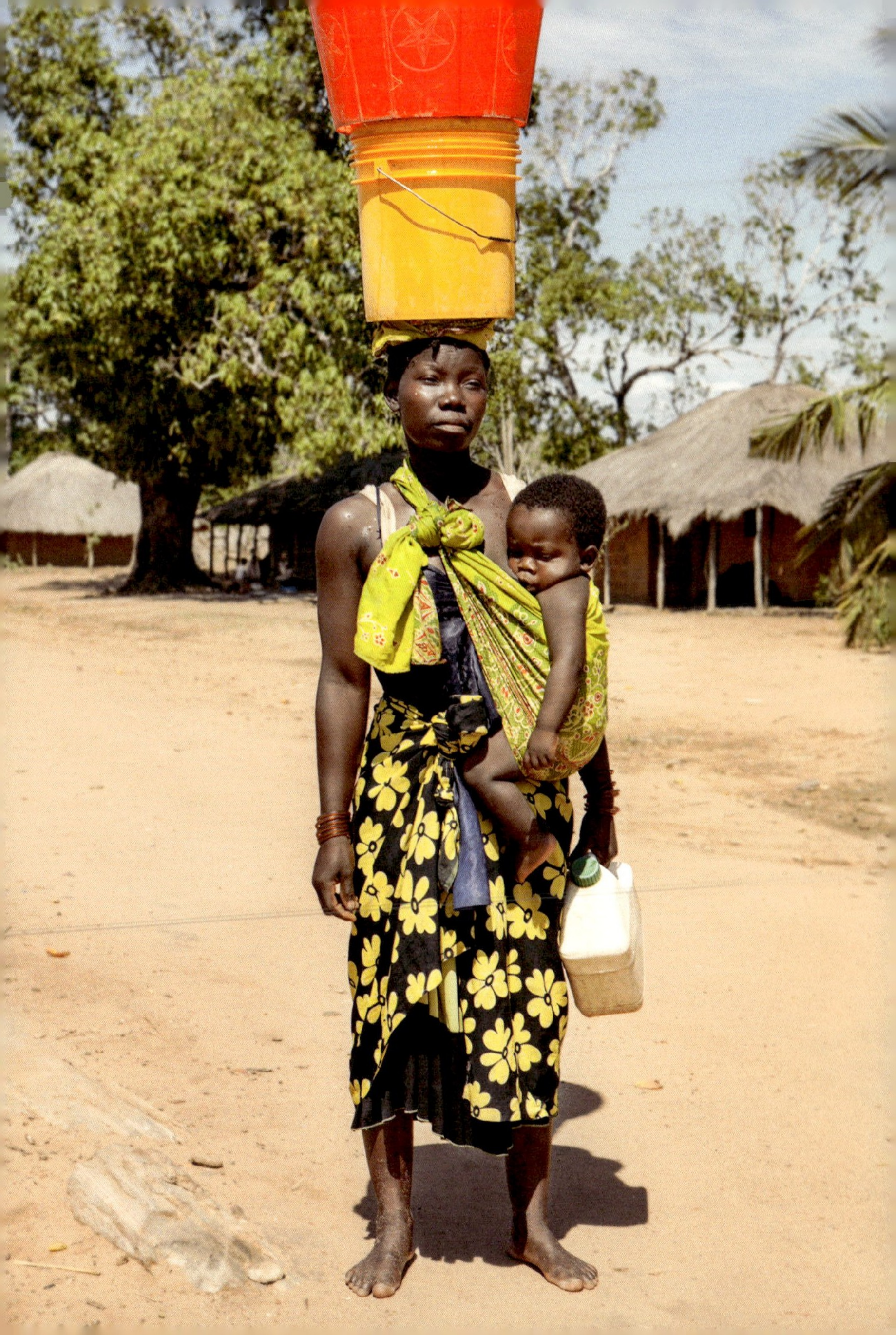

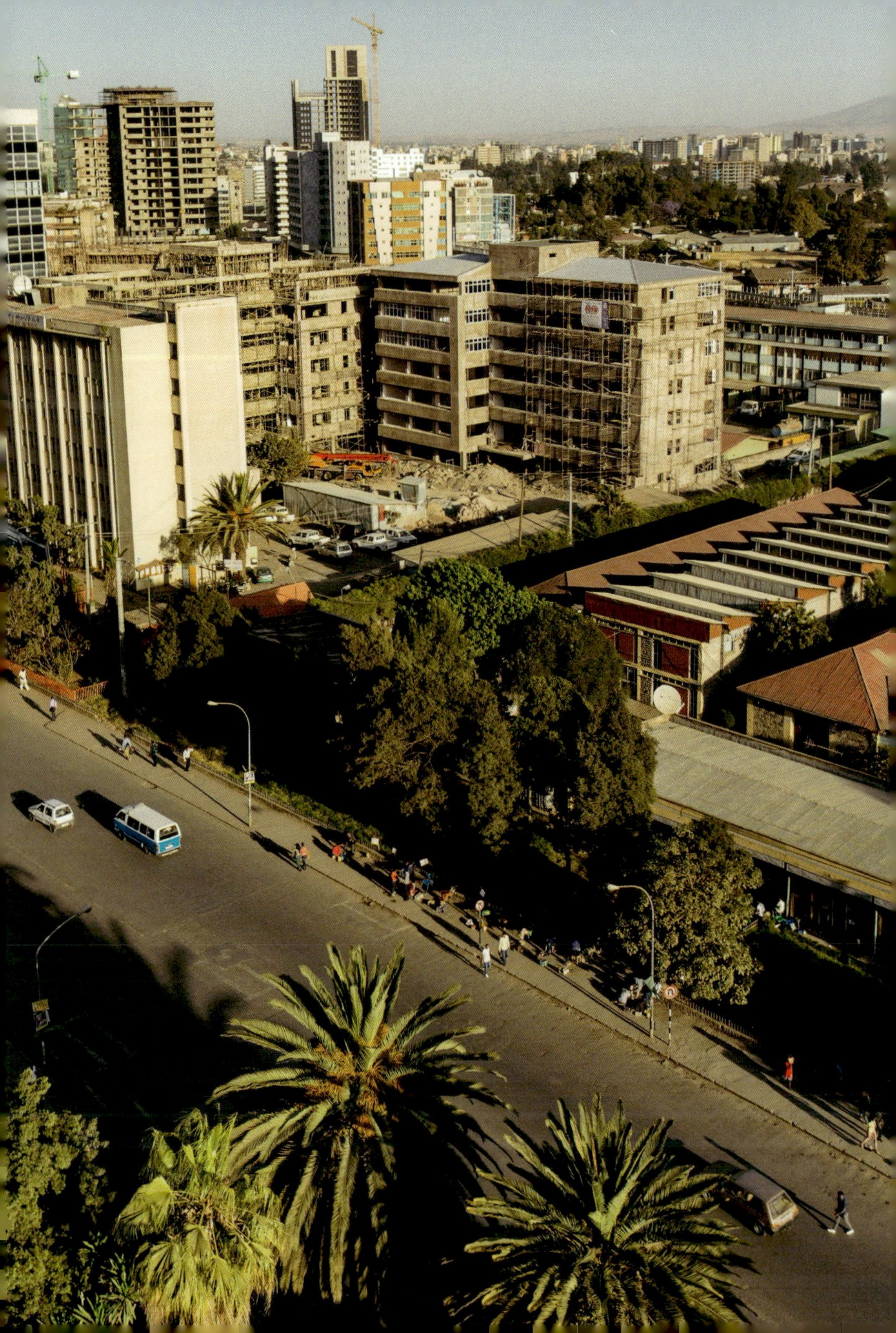

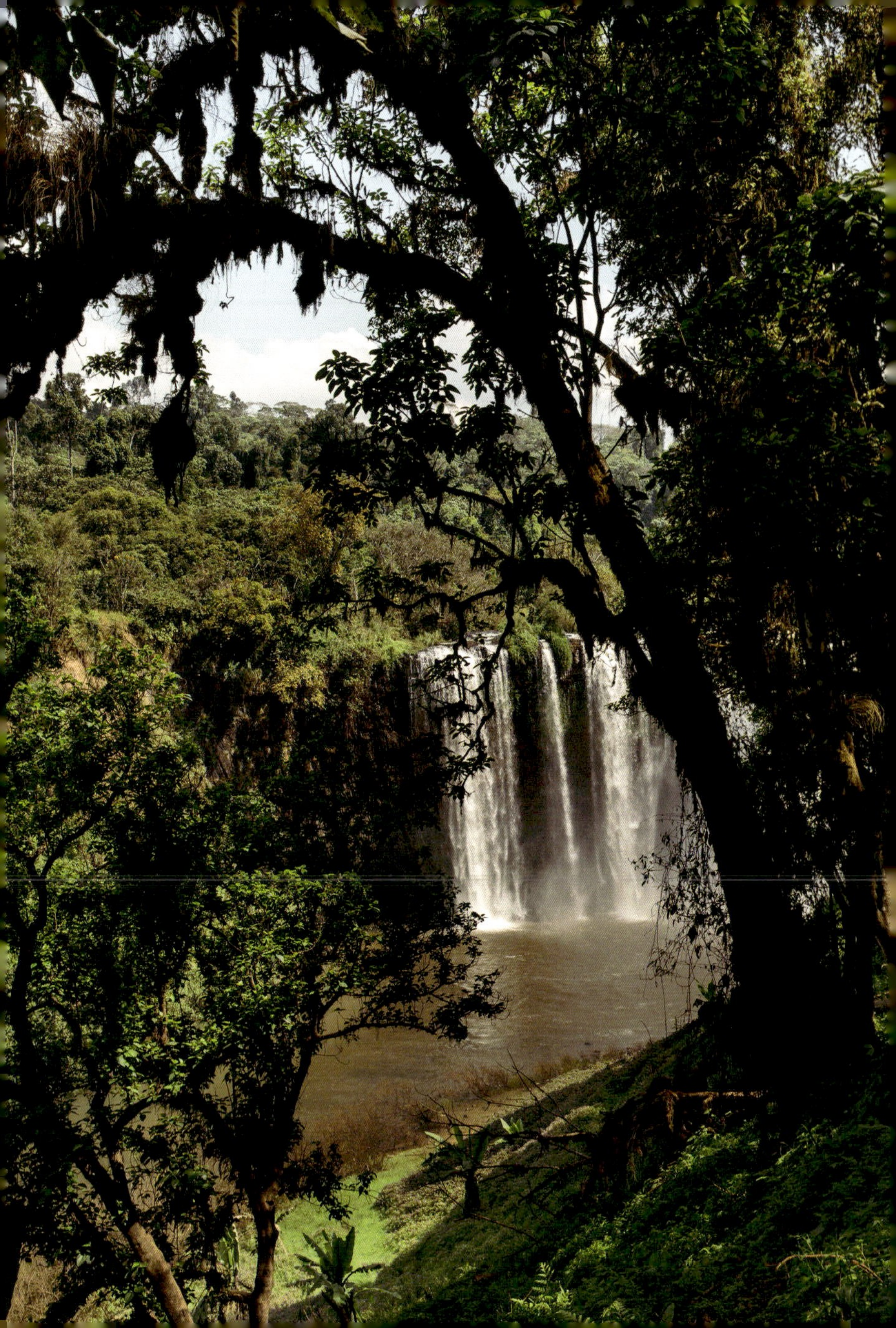

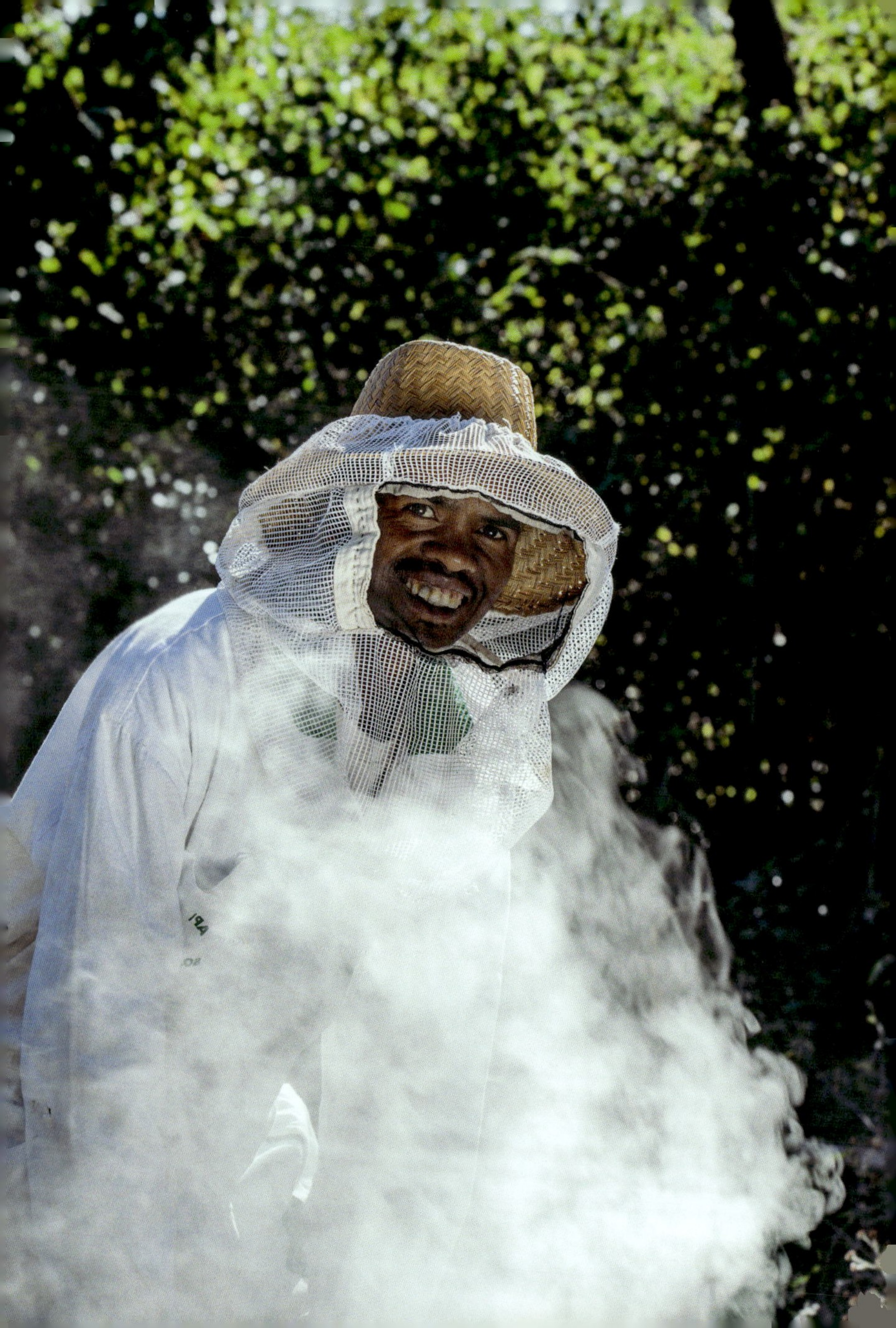

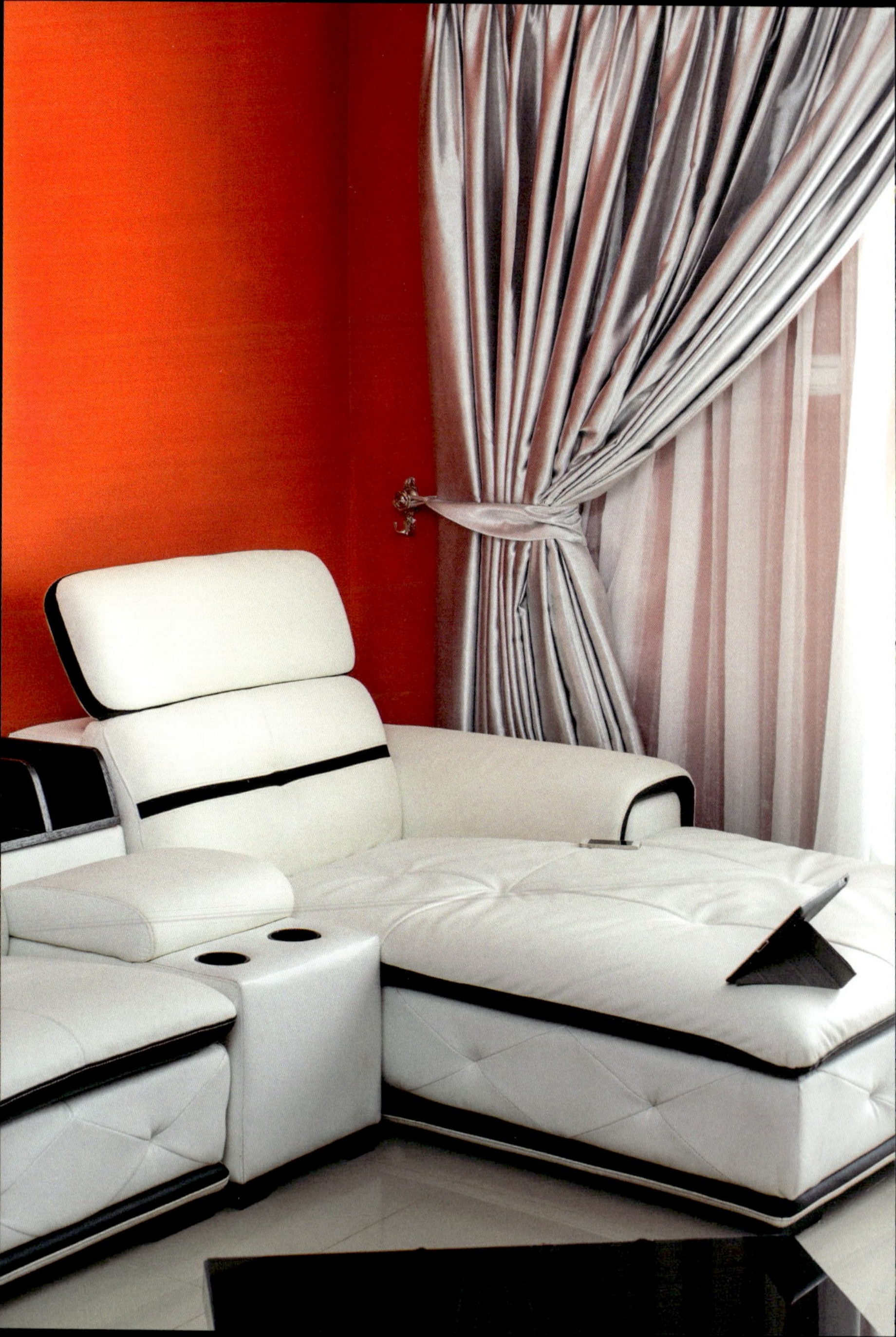

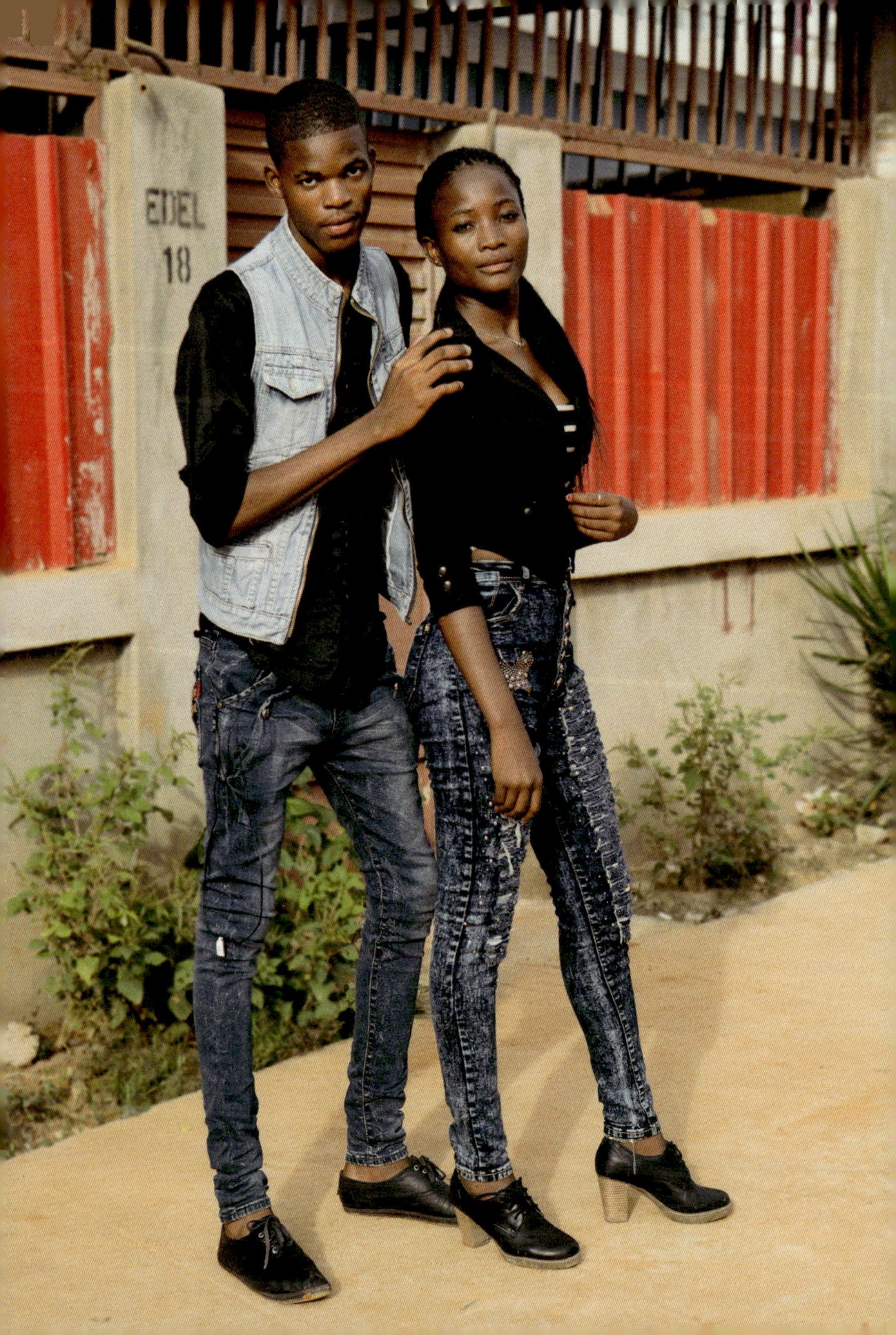
EDEL
18

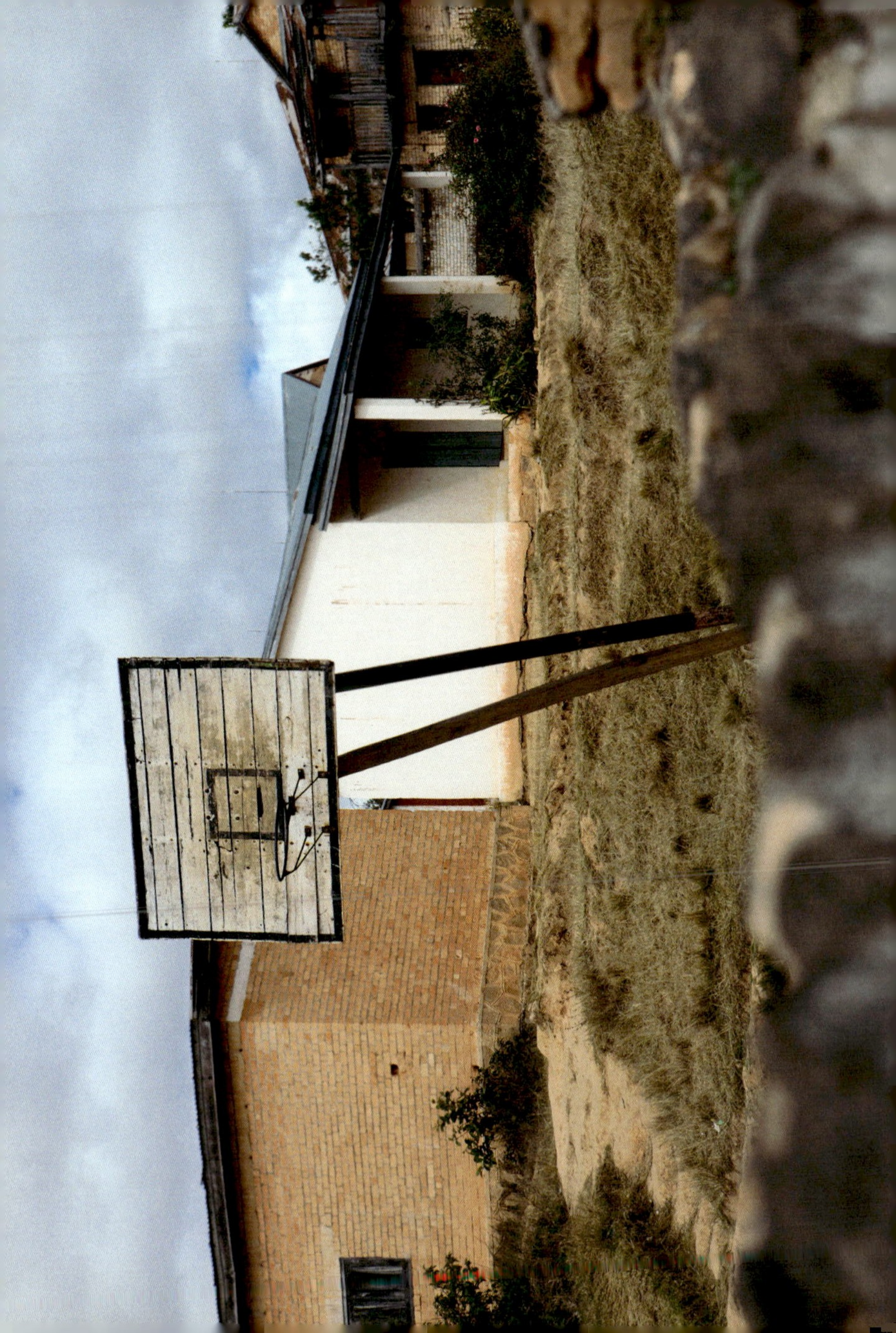

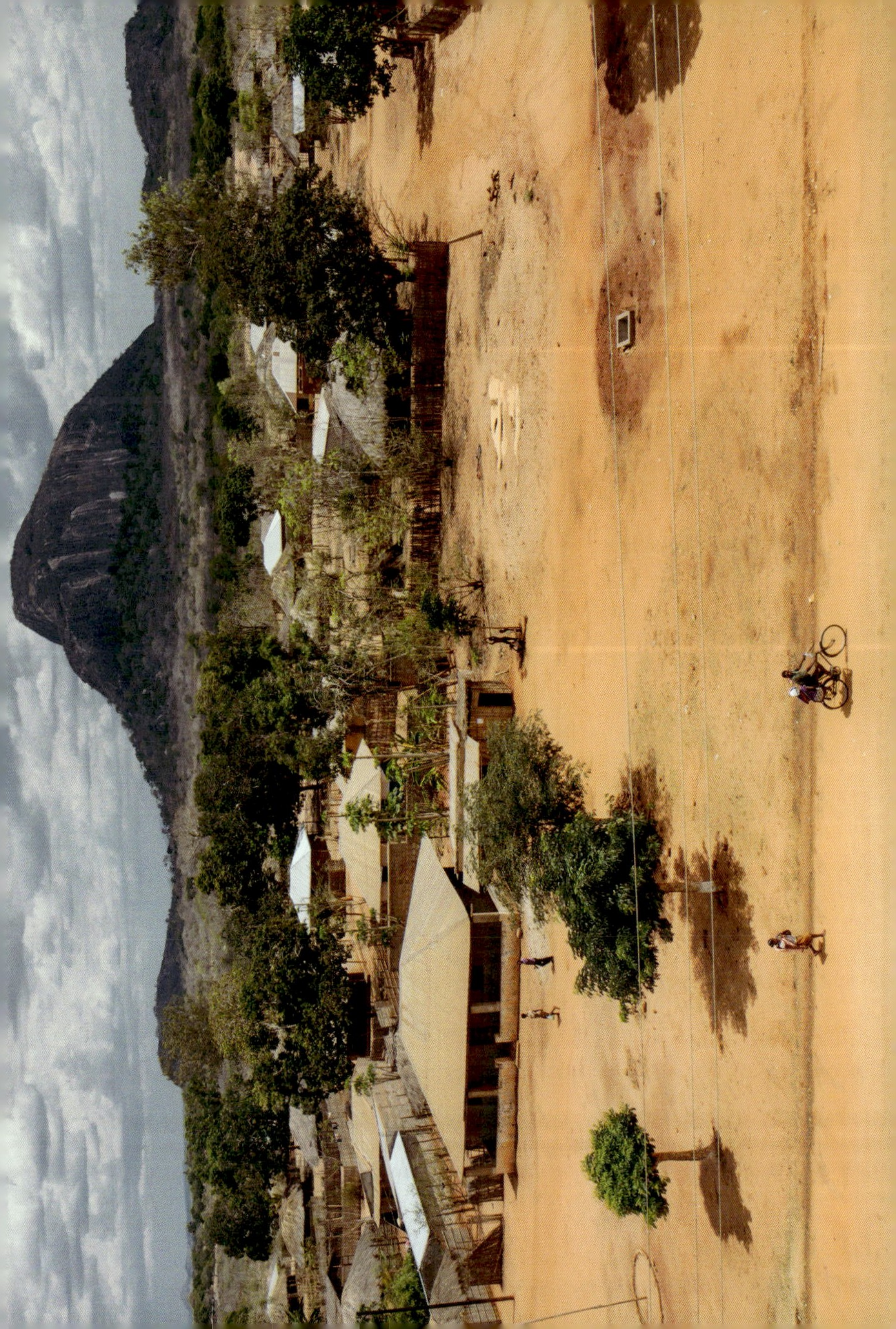

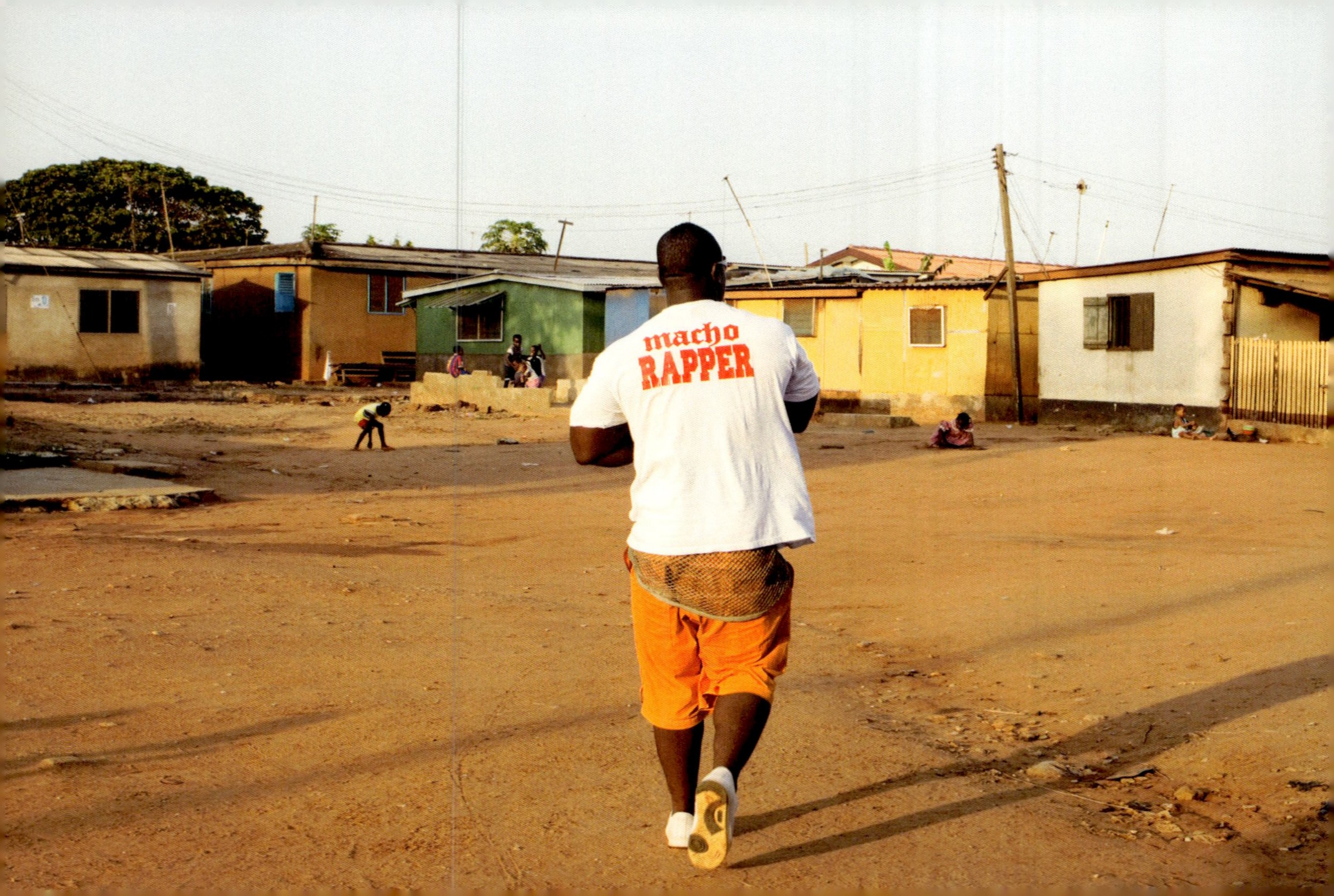
macho
RAPPER

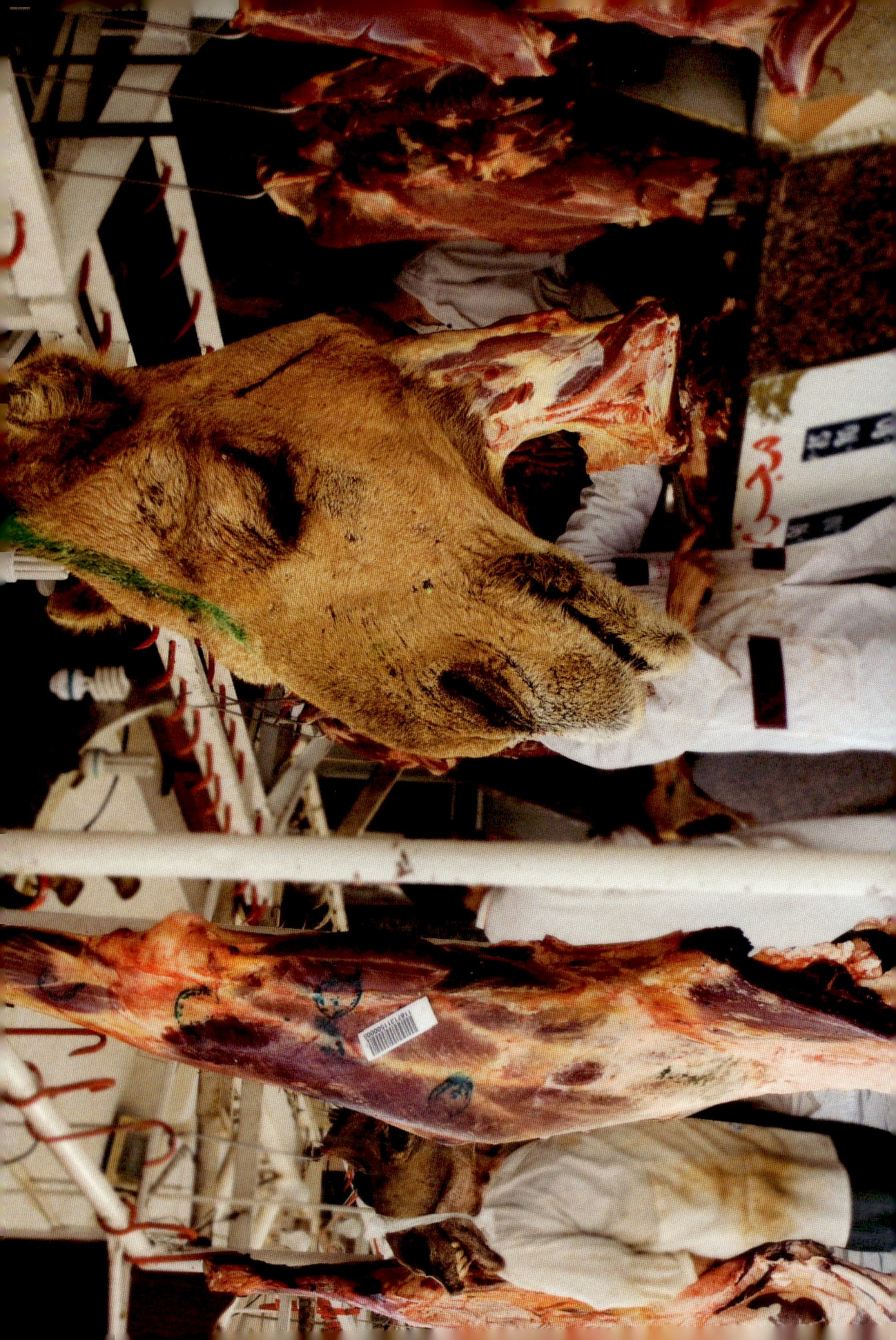

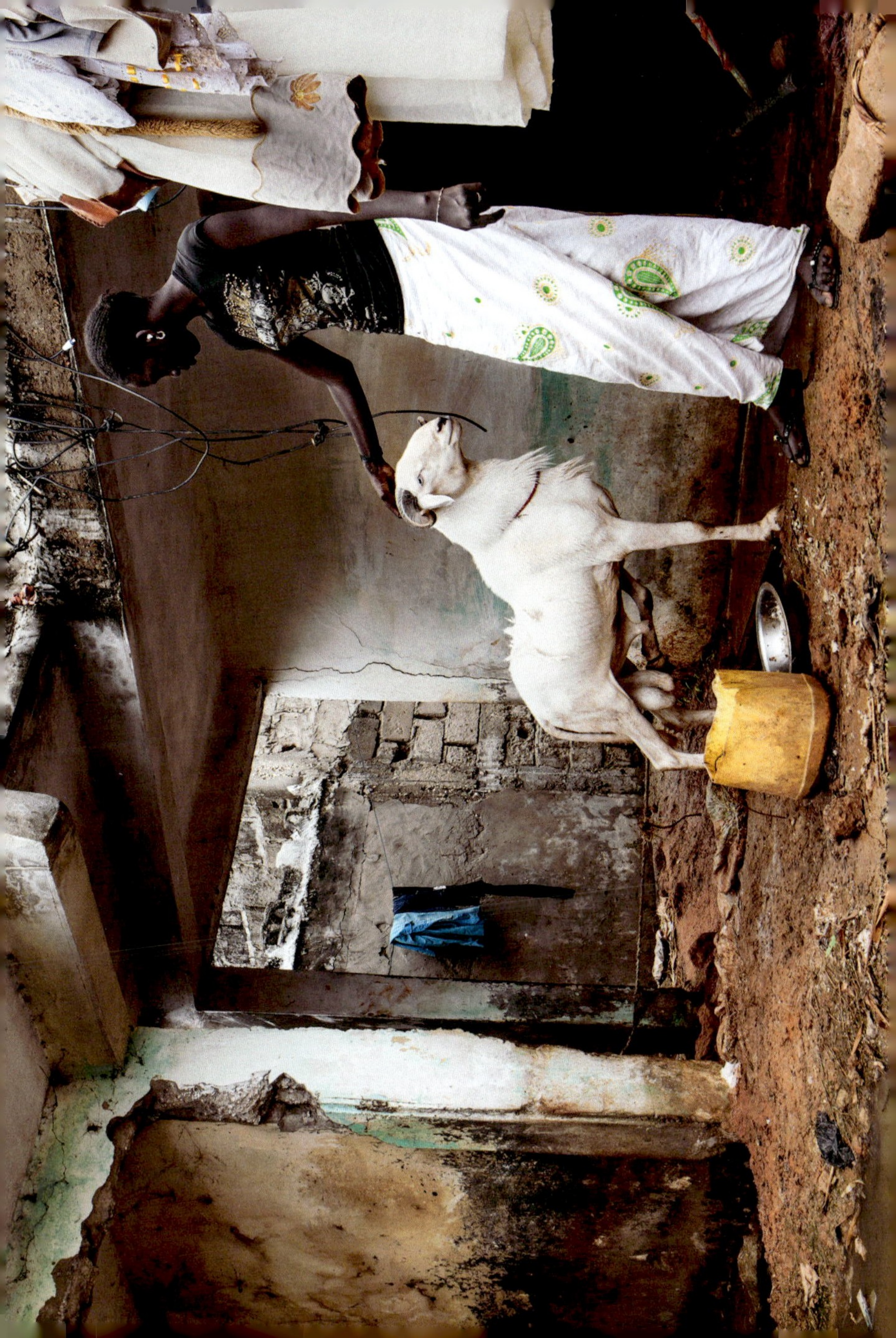

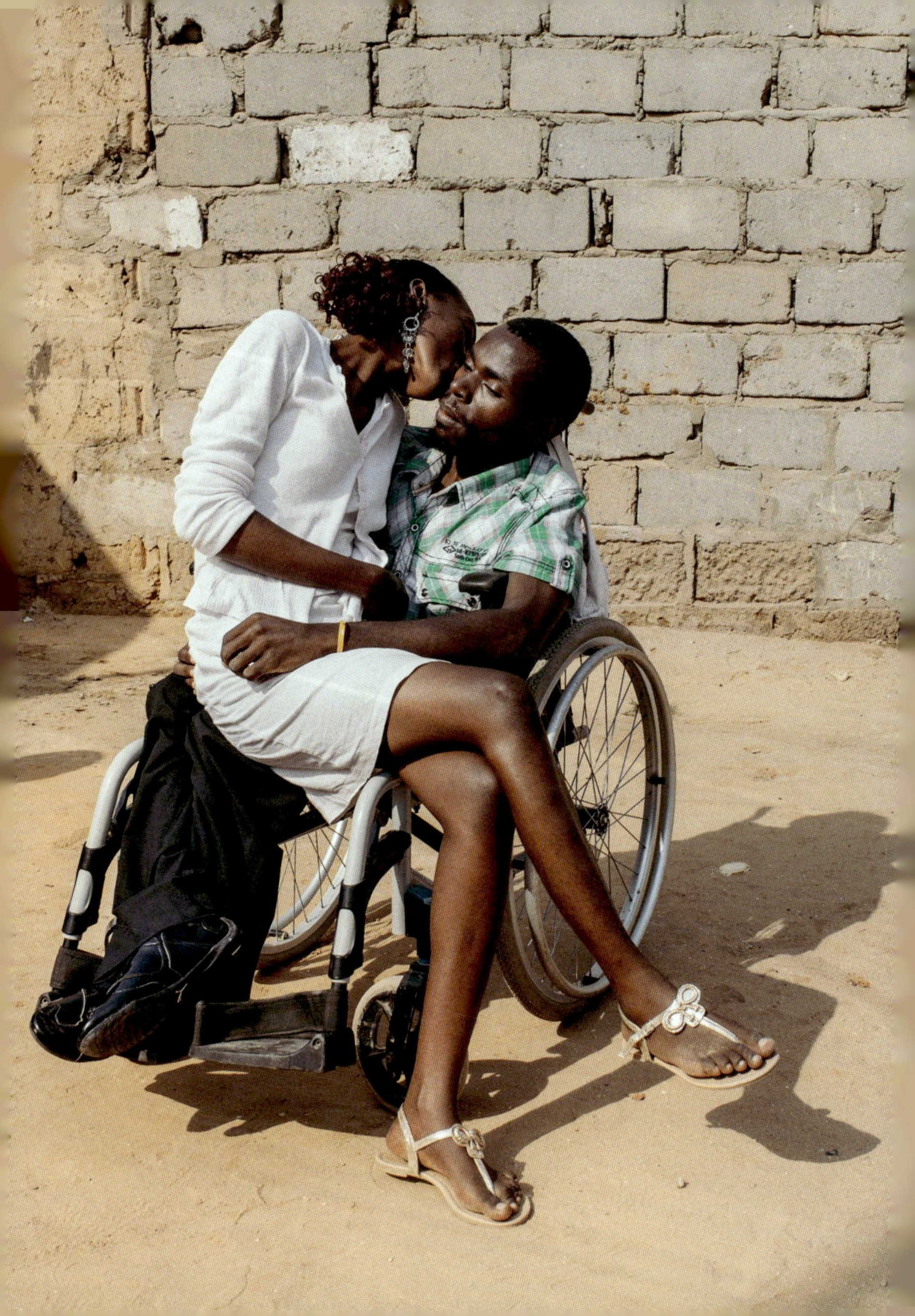

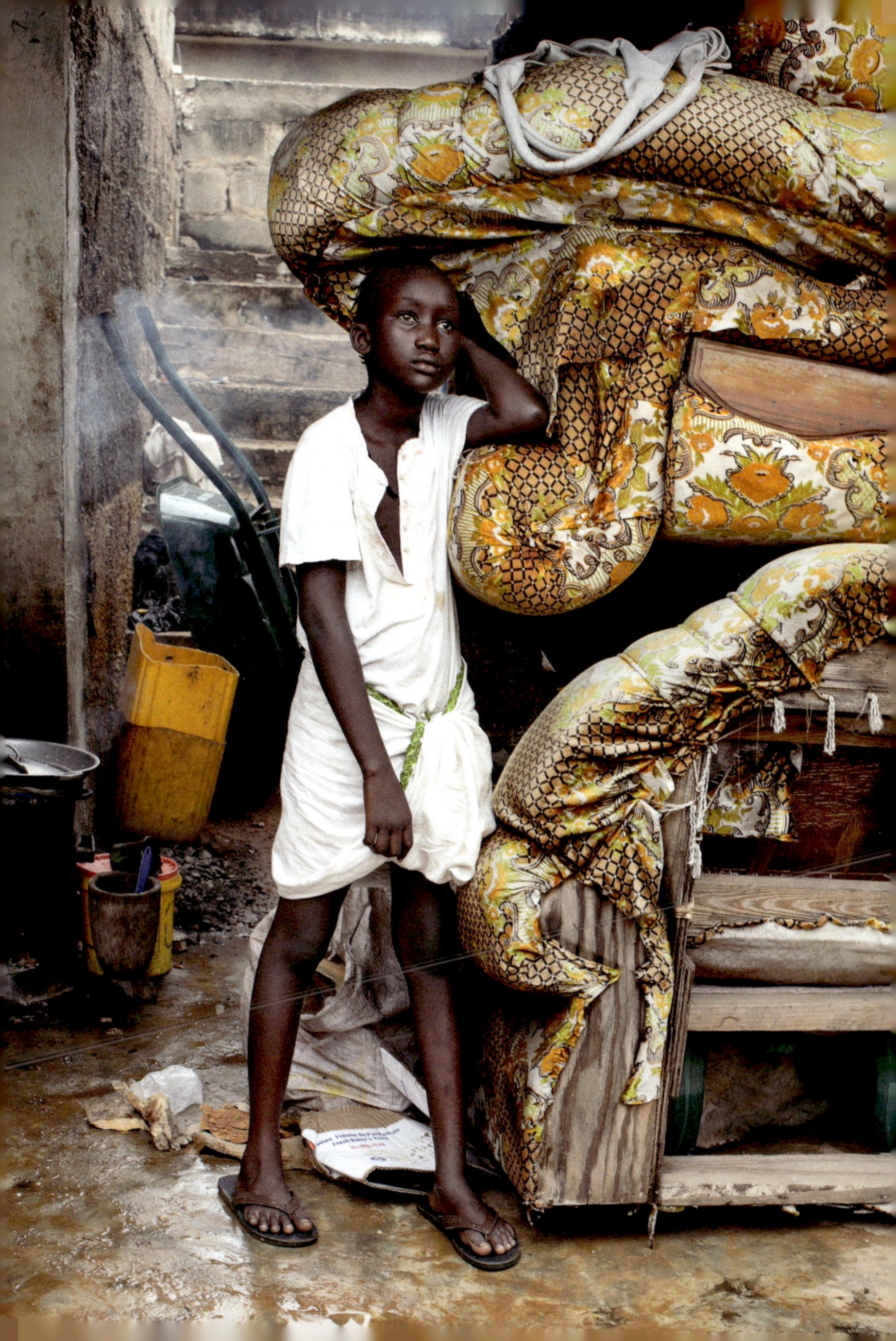

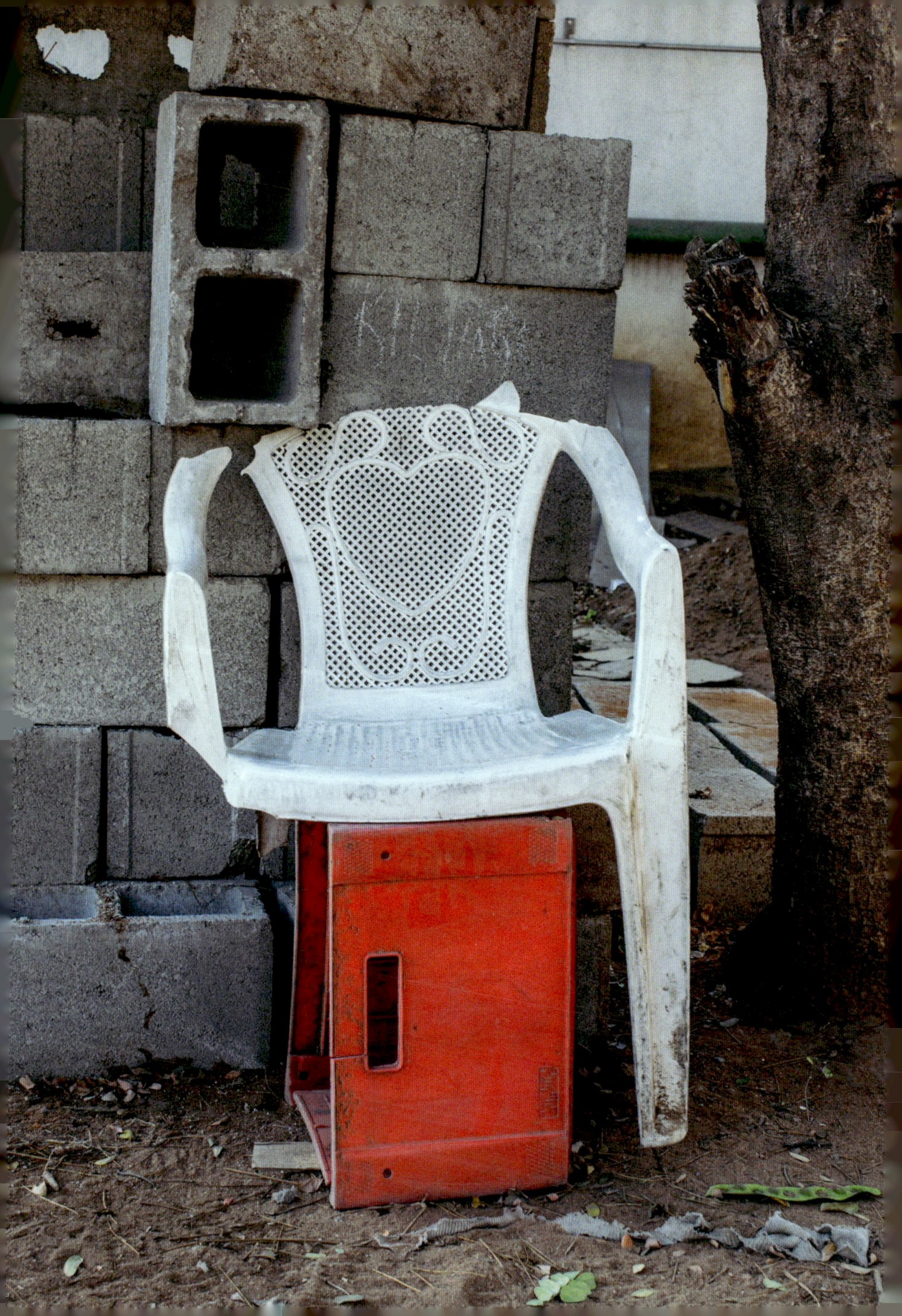

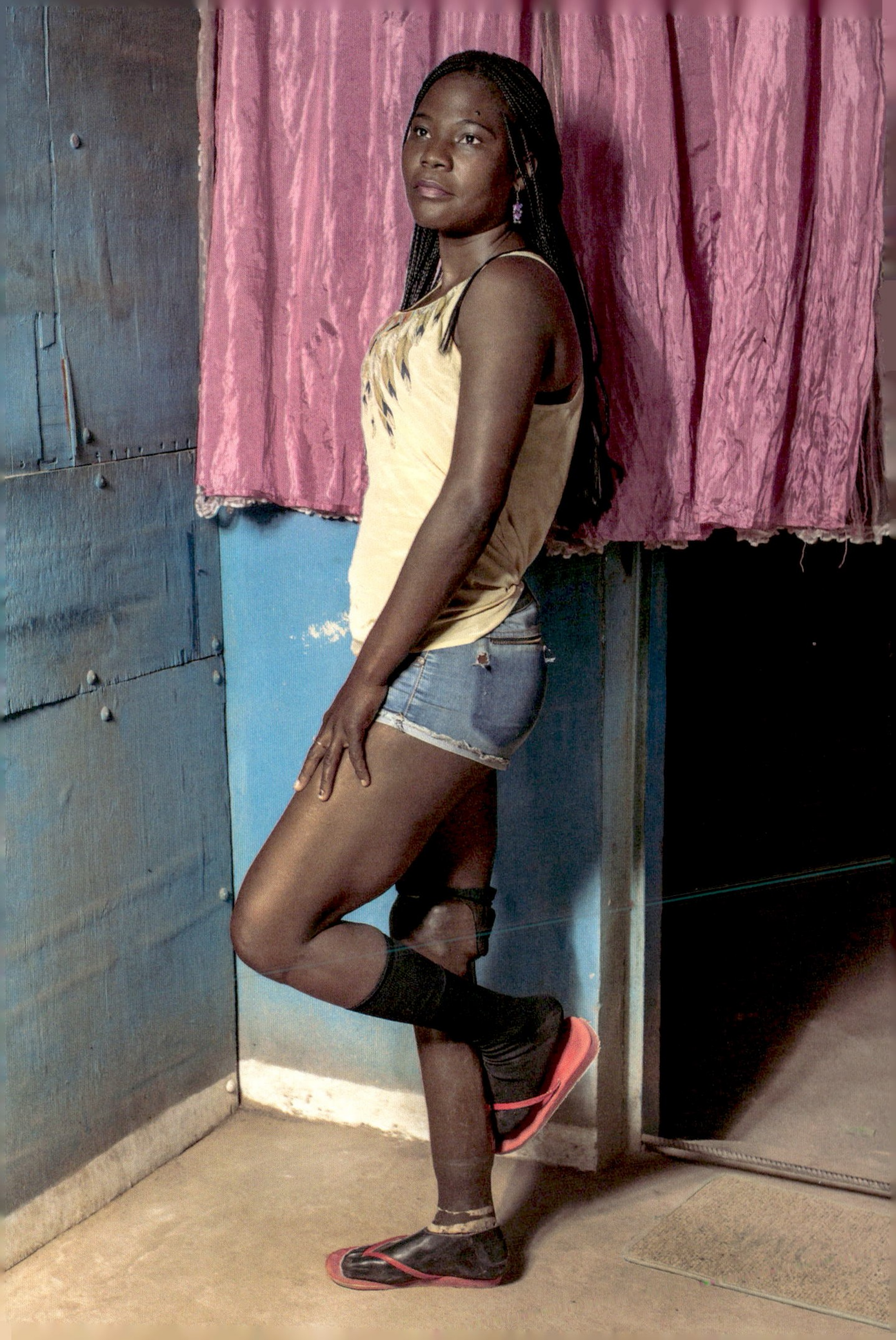

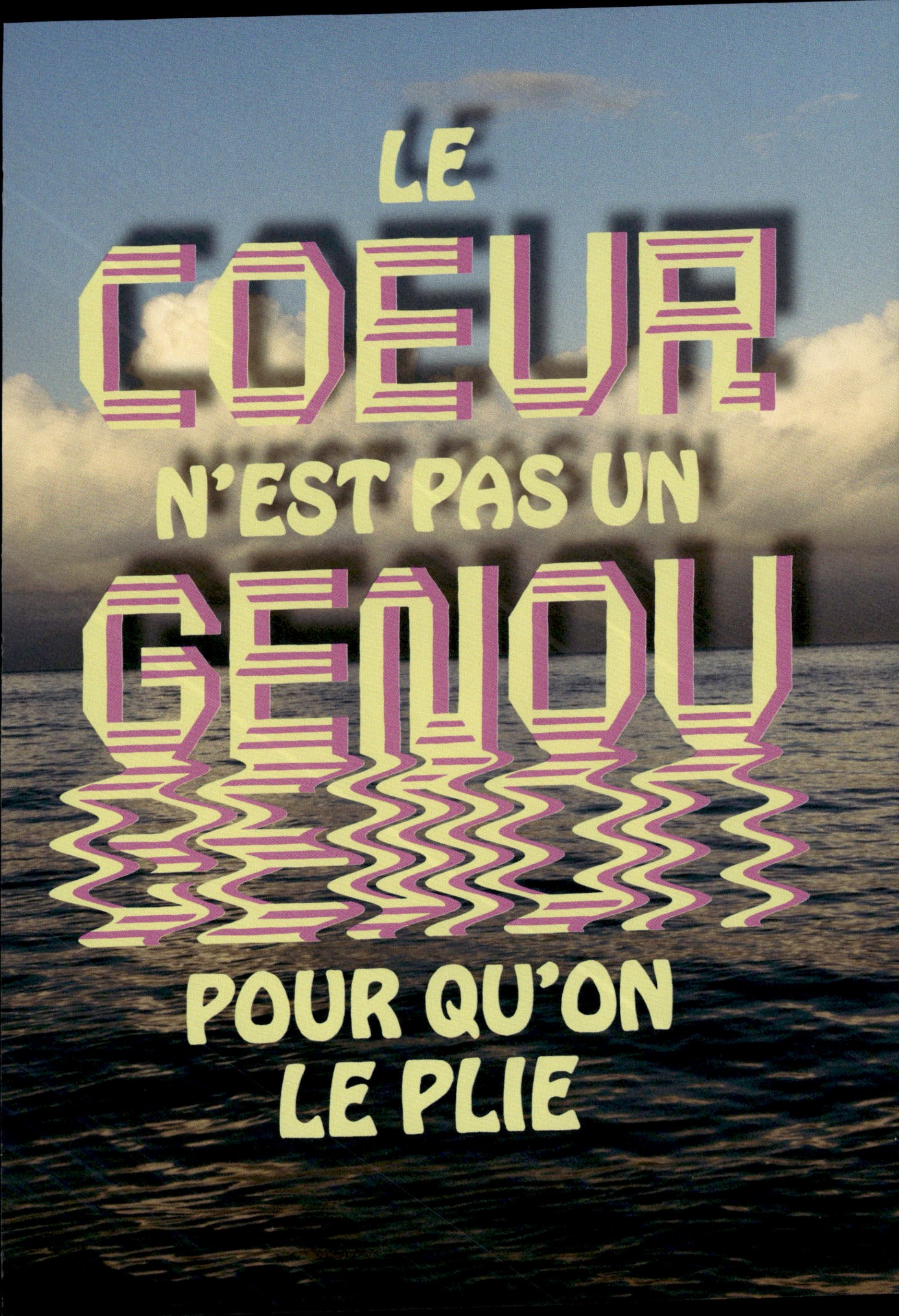
LE
COEUR
N'EST PAS UN
GENOU
POUR QU'ON
LE PLIE

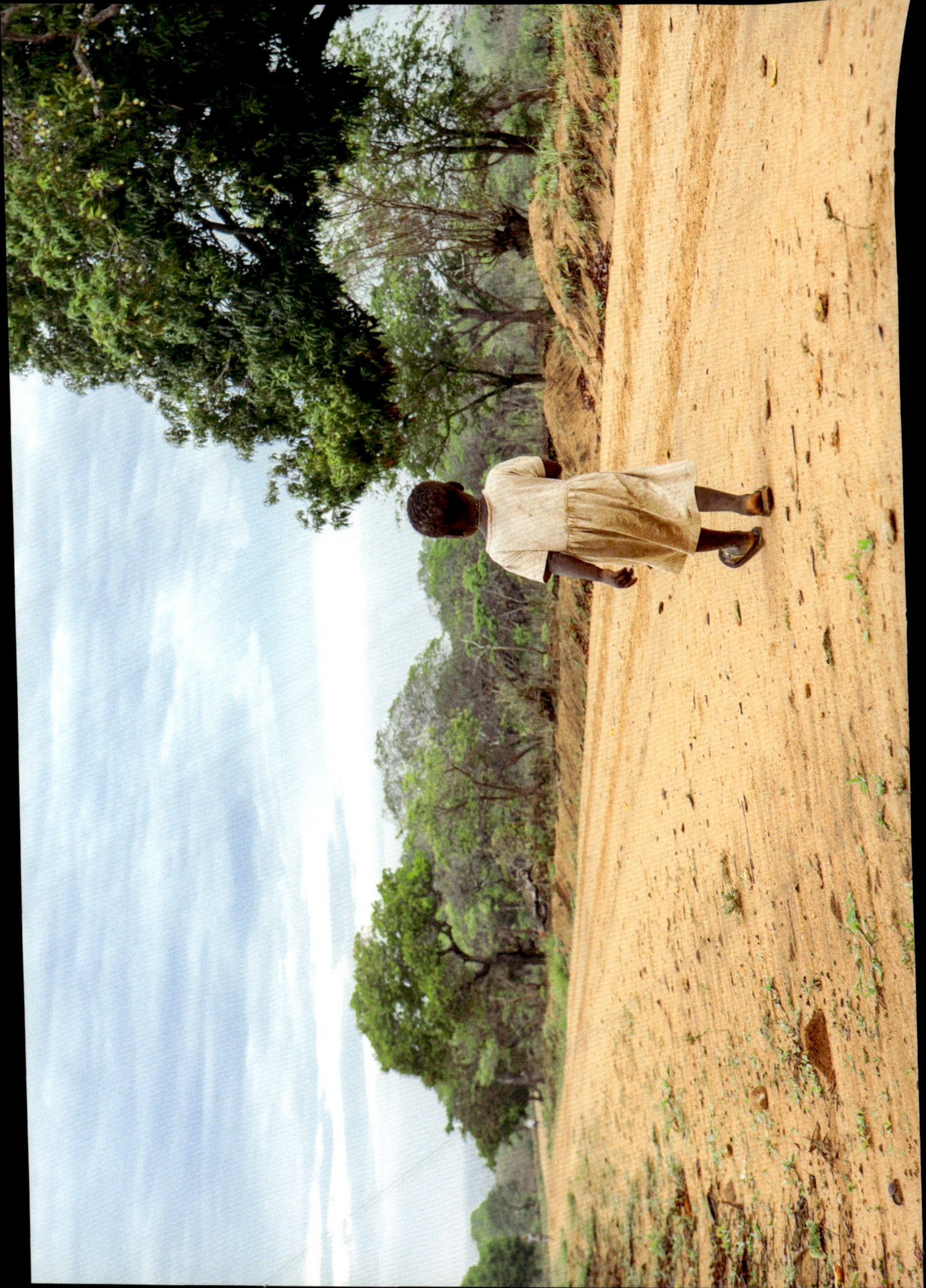

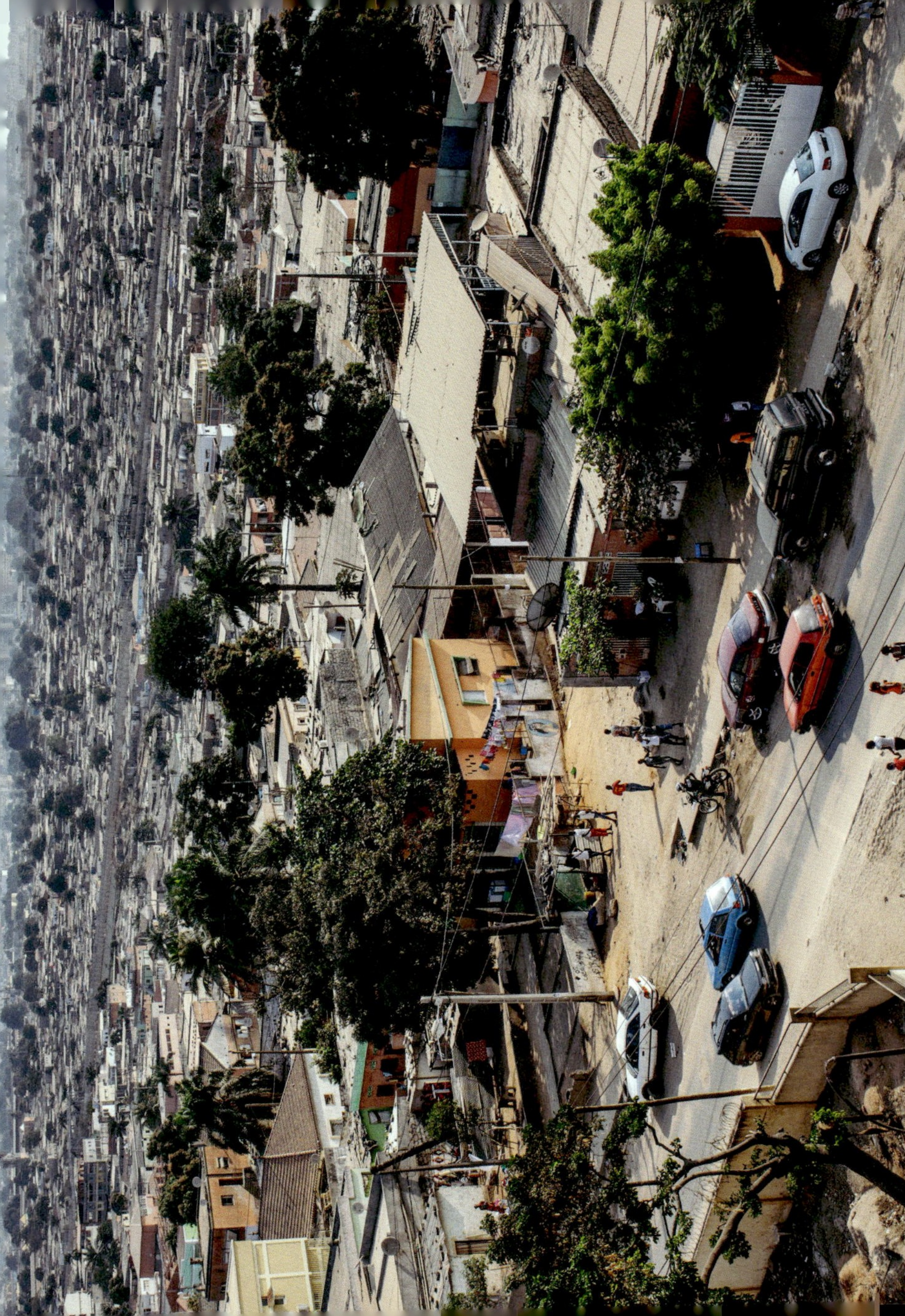

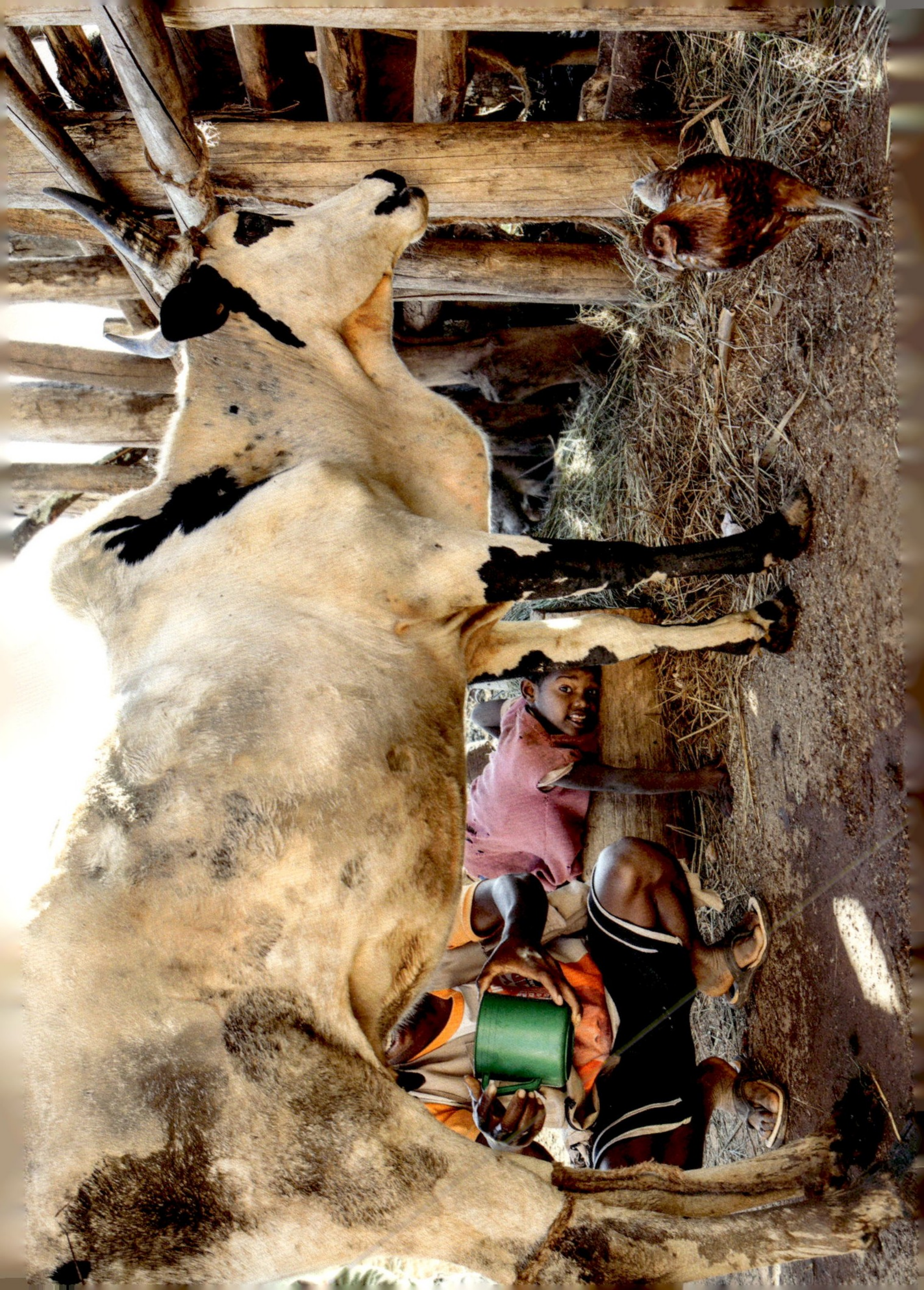

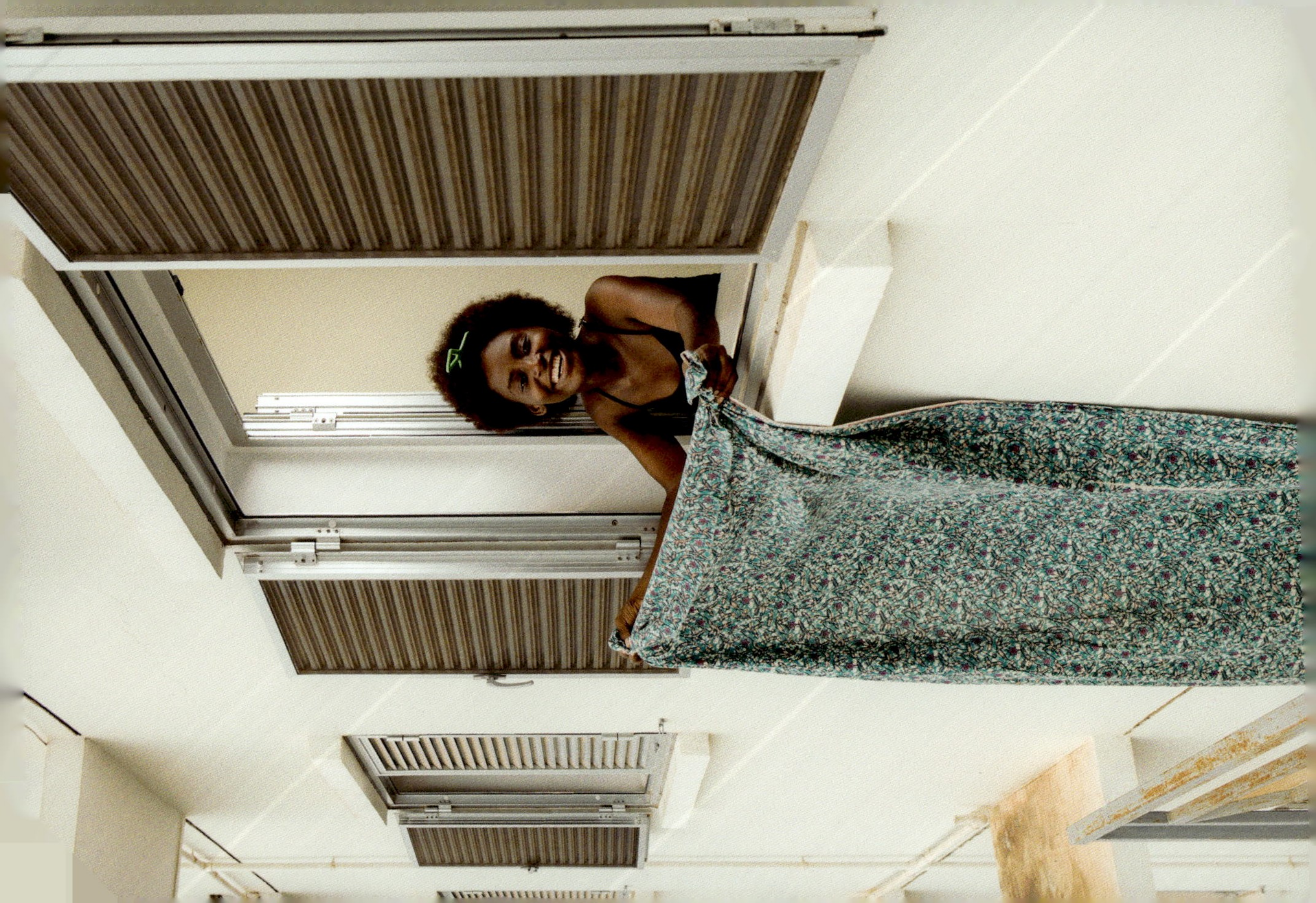

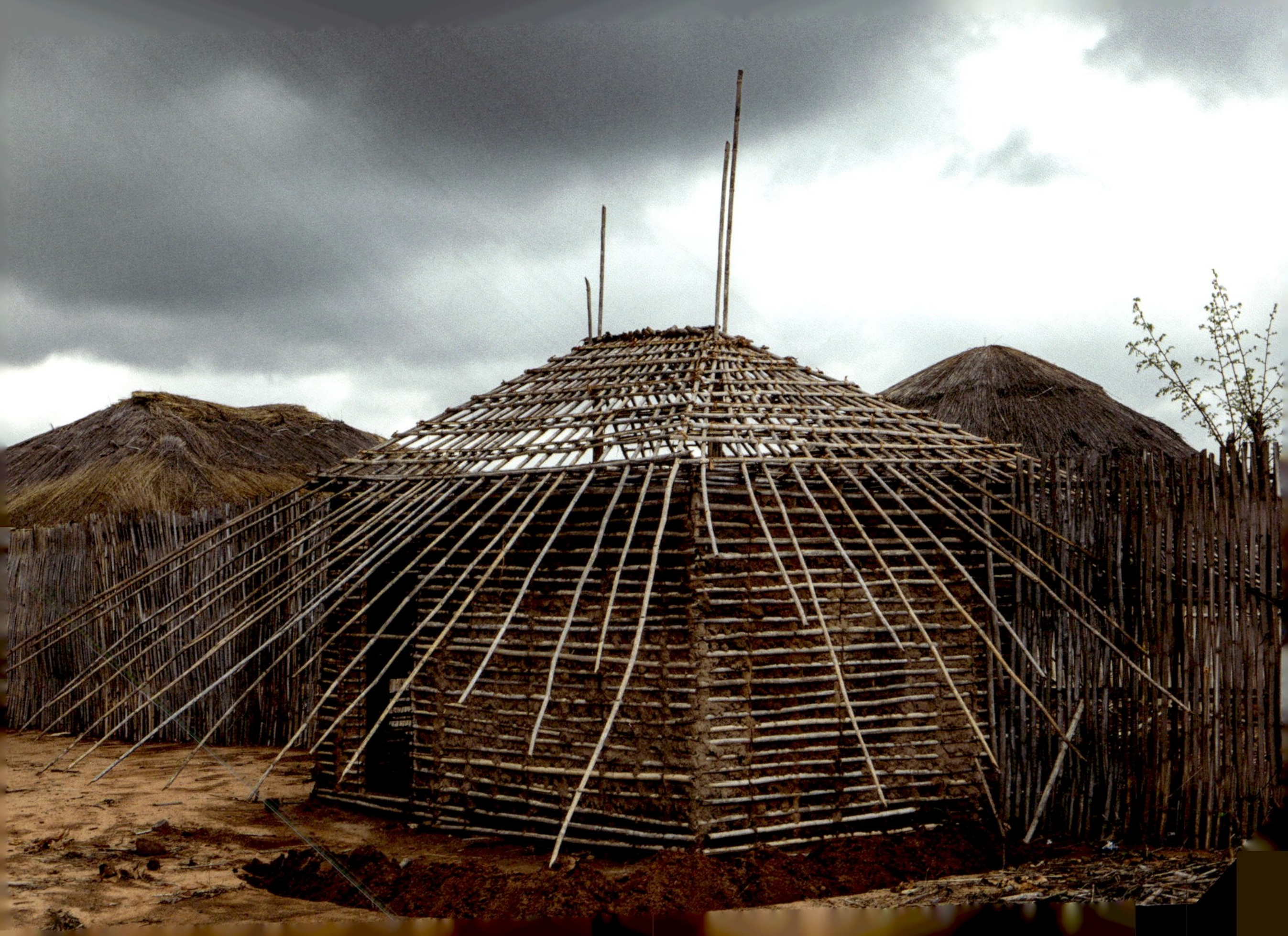

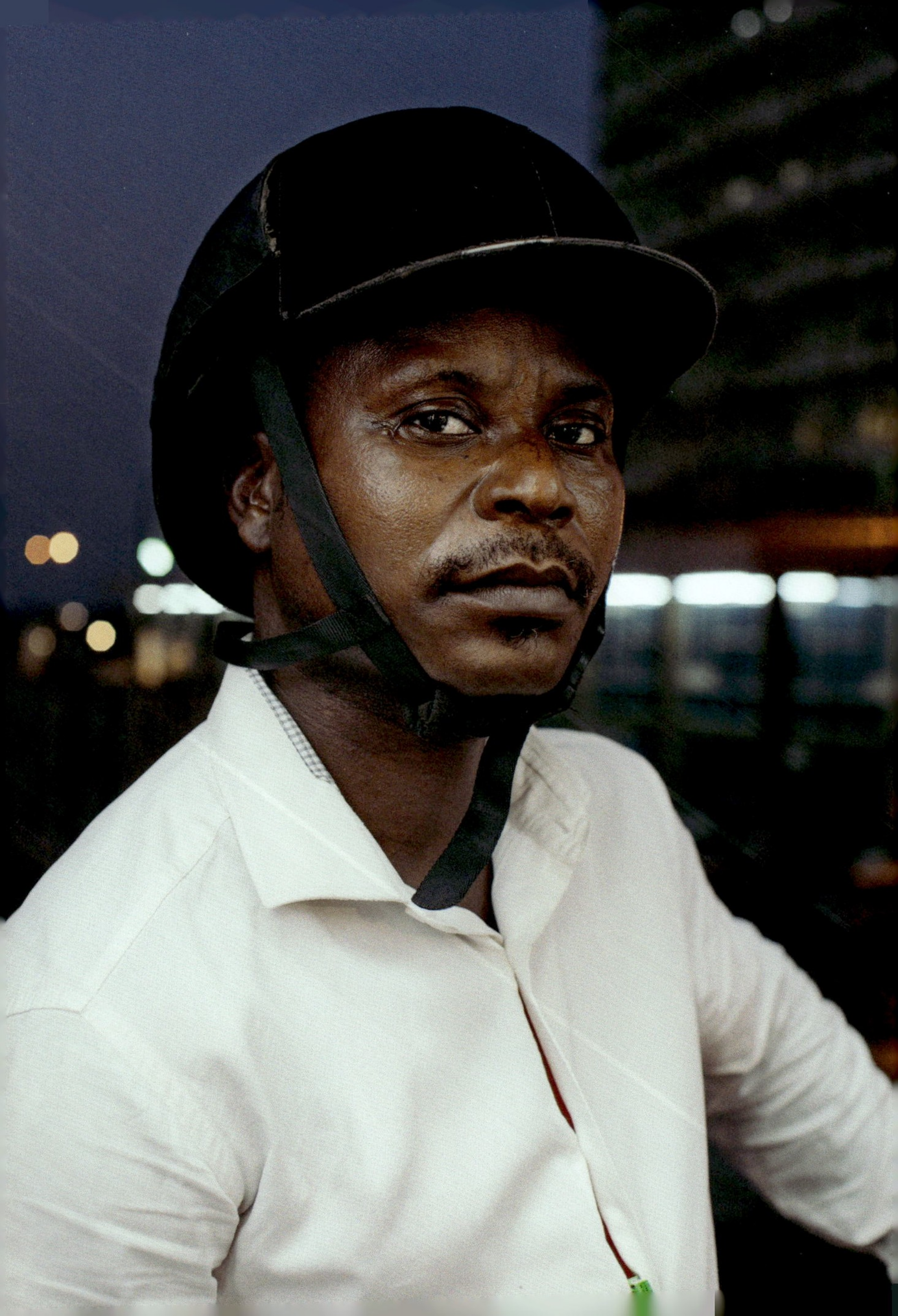

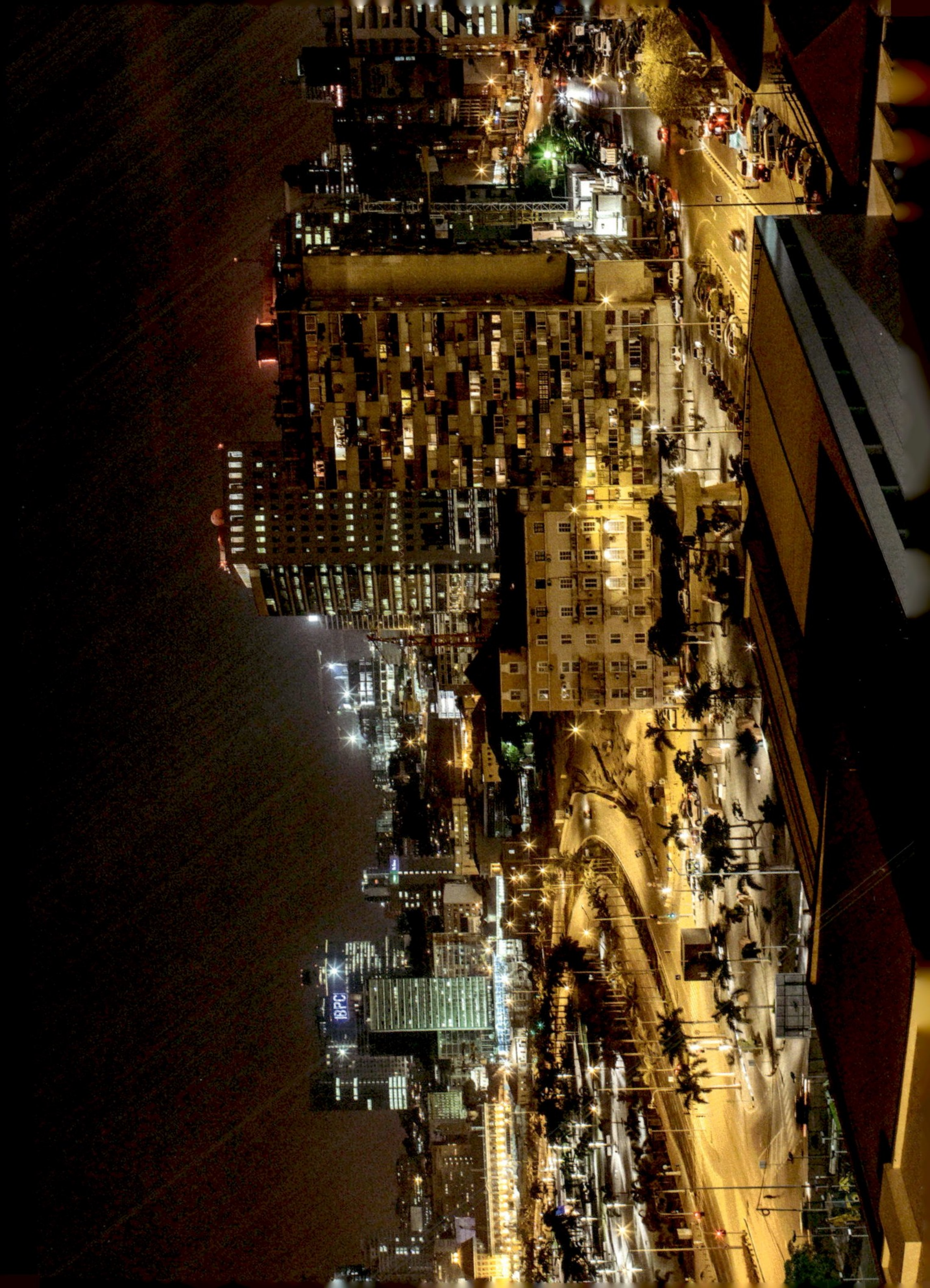
BPC

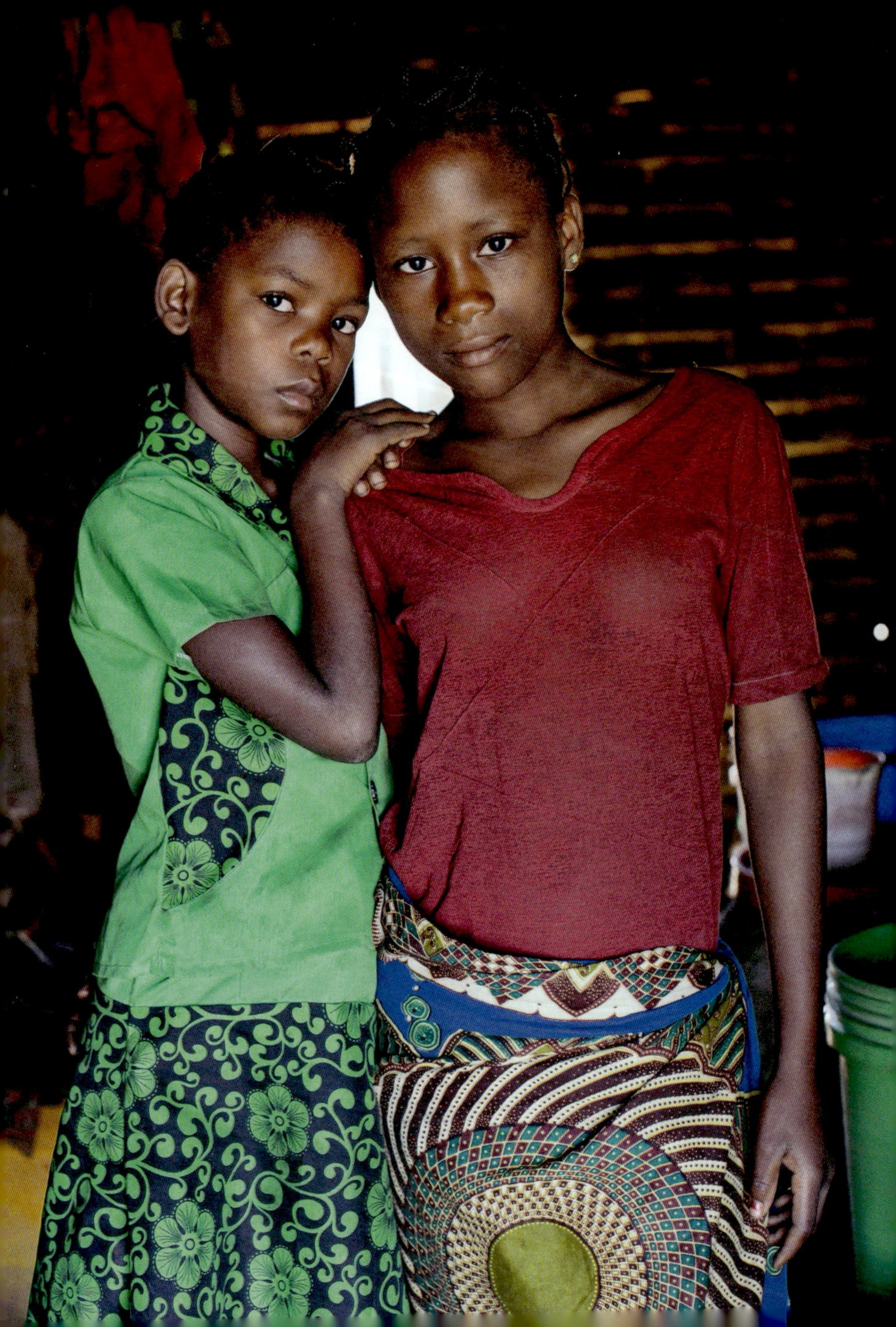

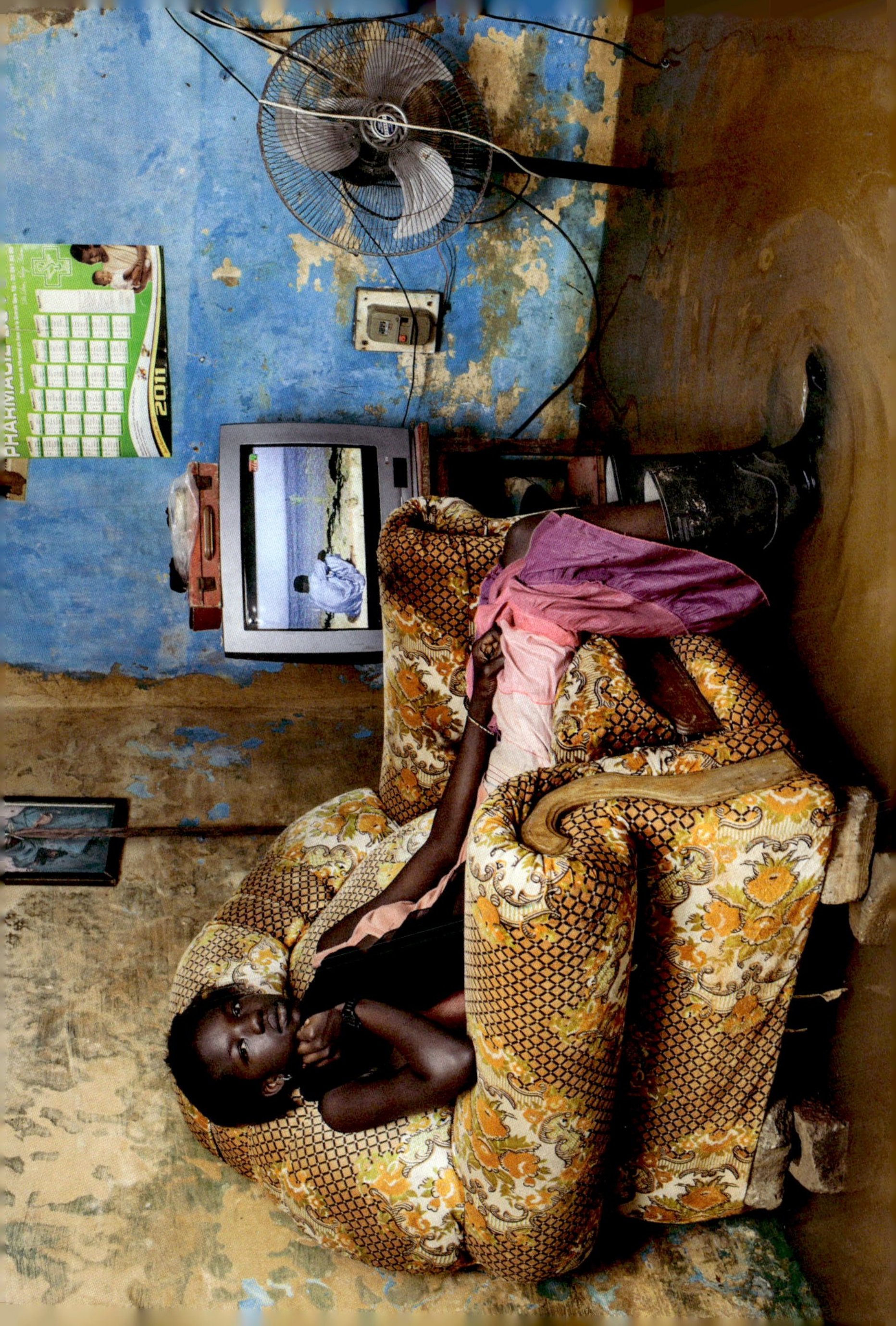
PHARMACIE
2011

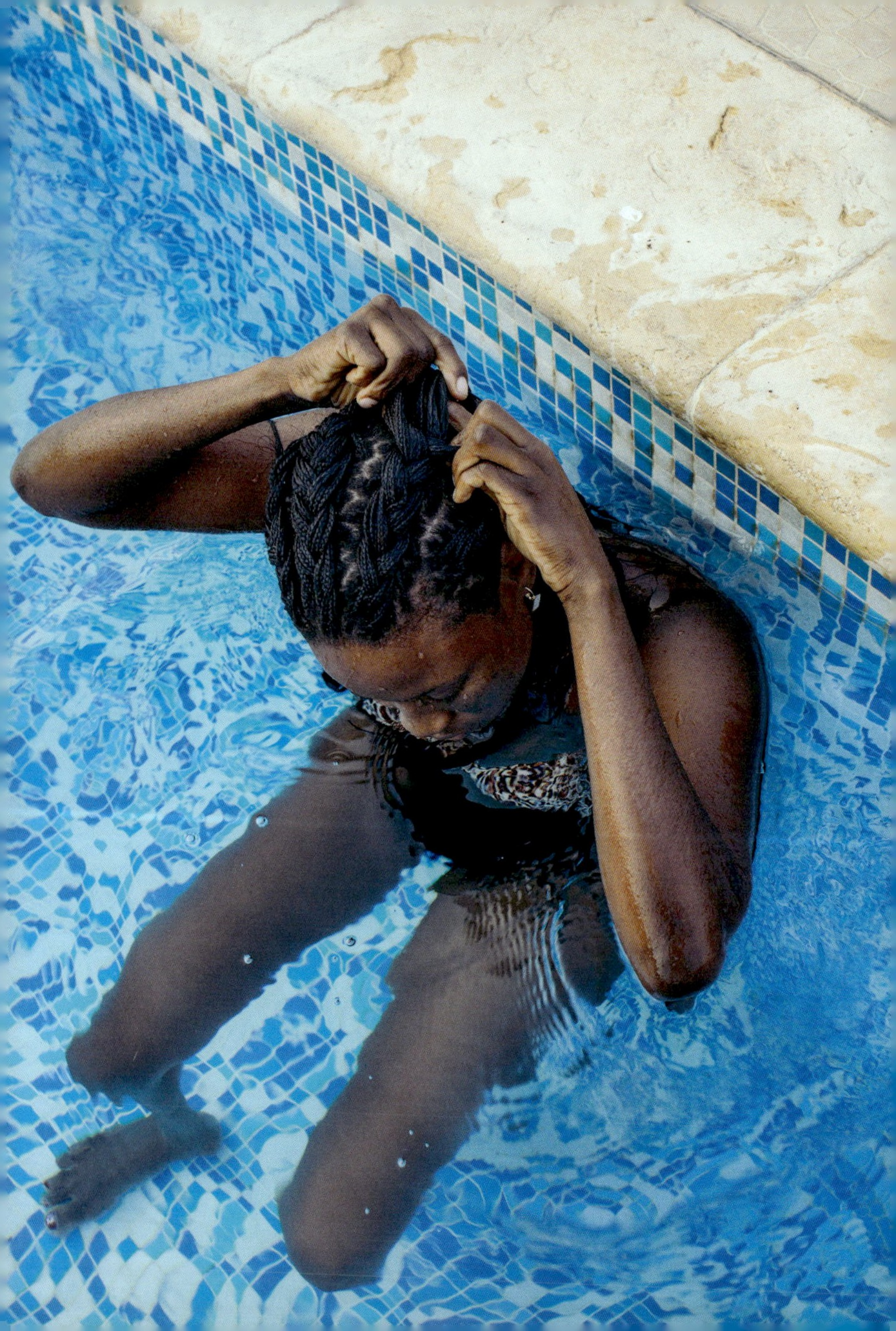

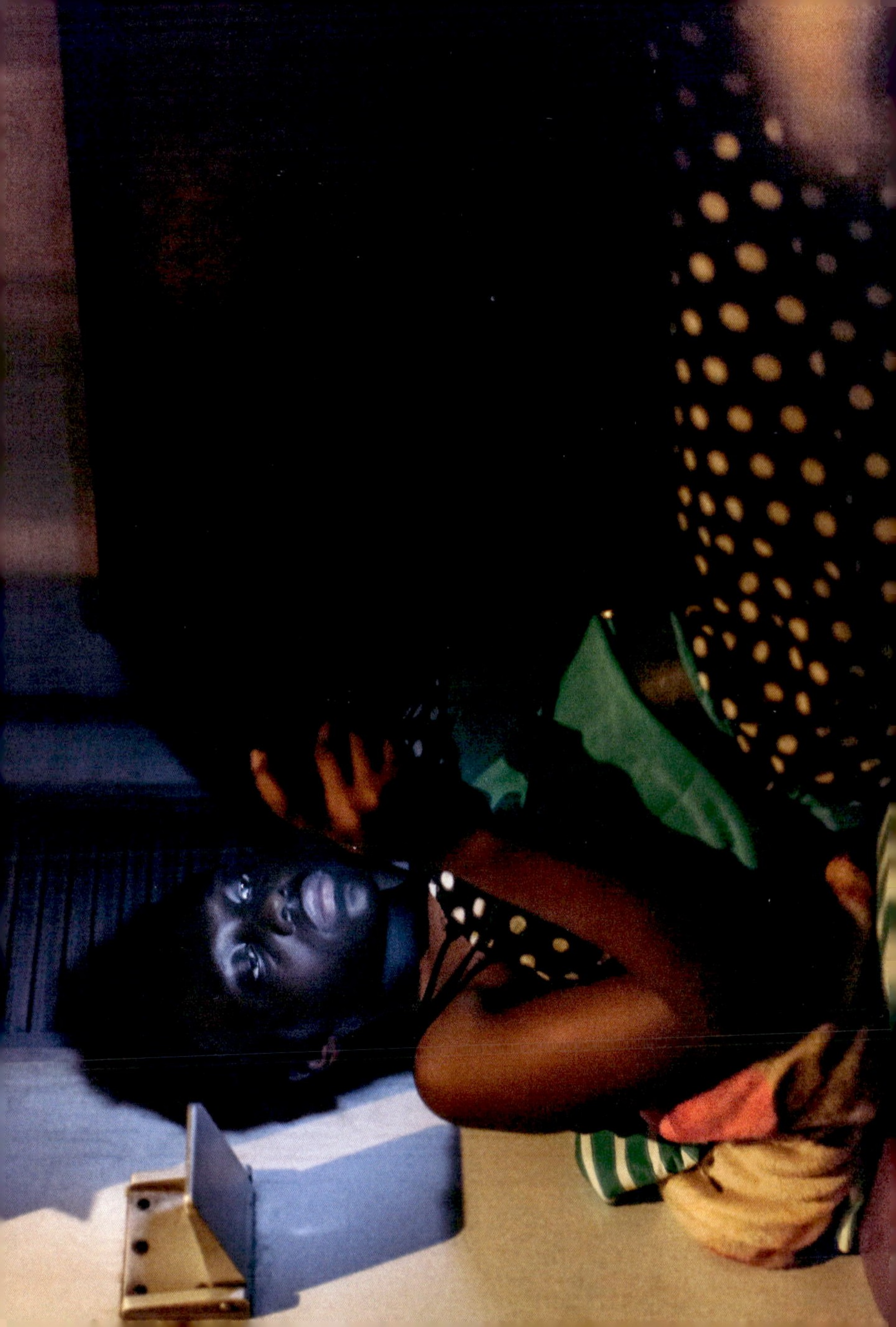

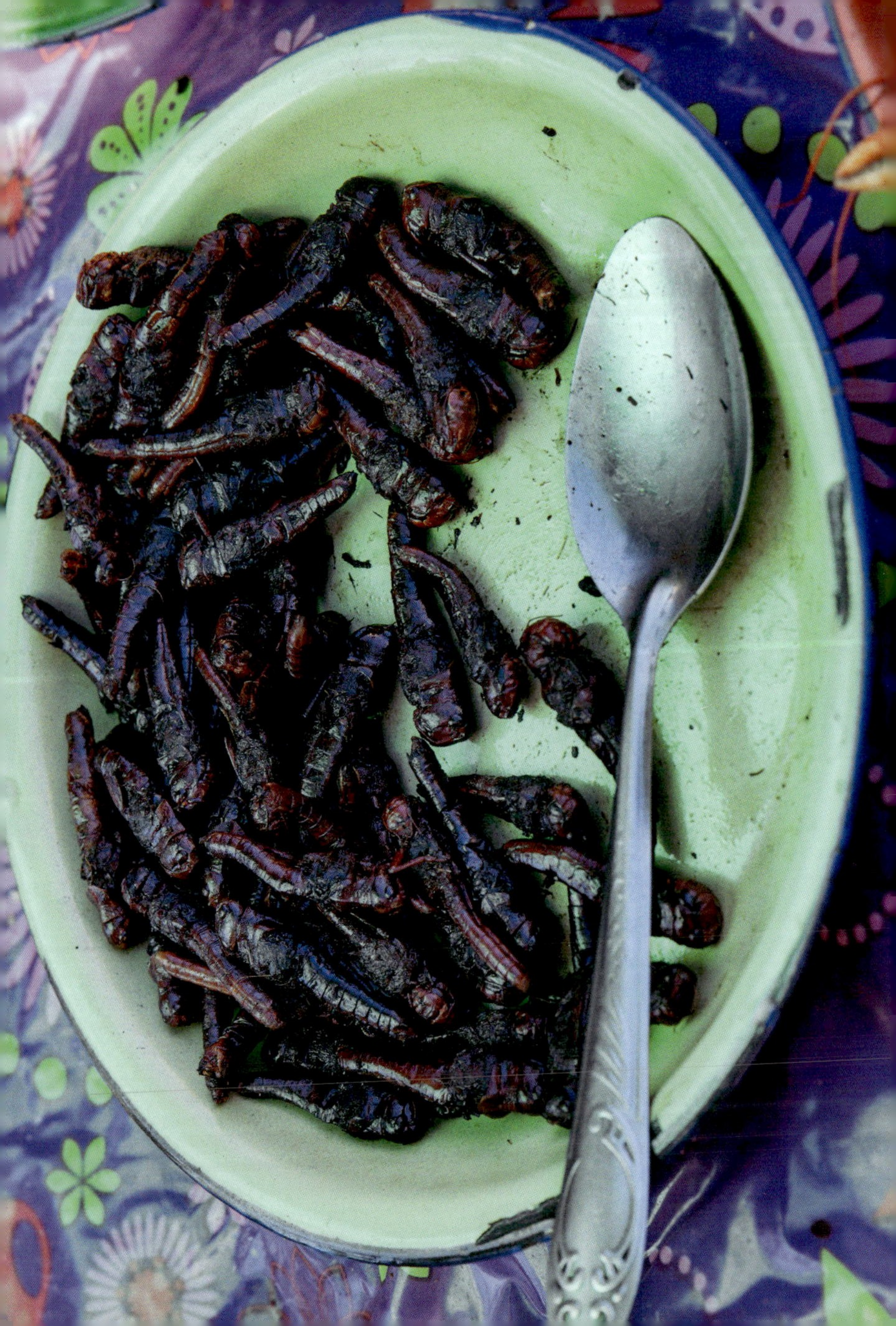

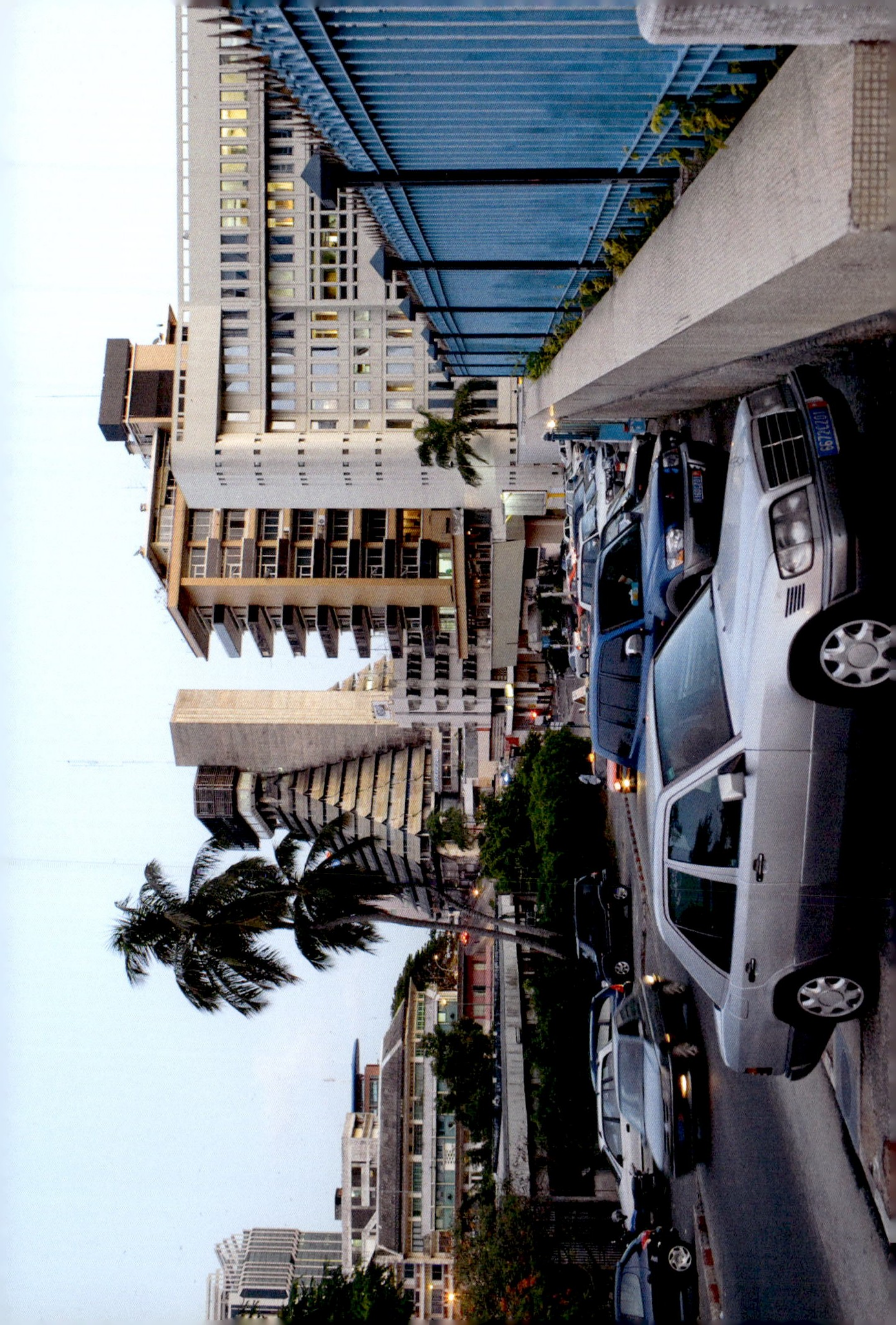

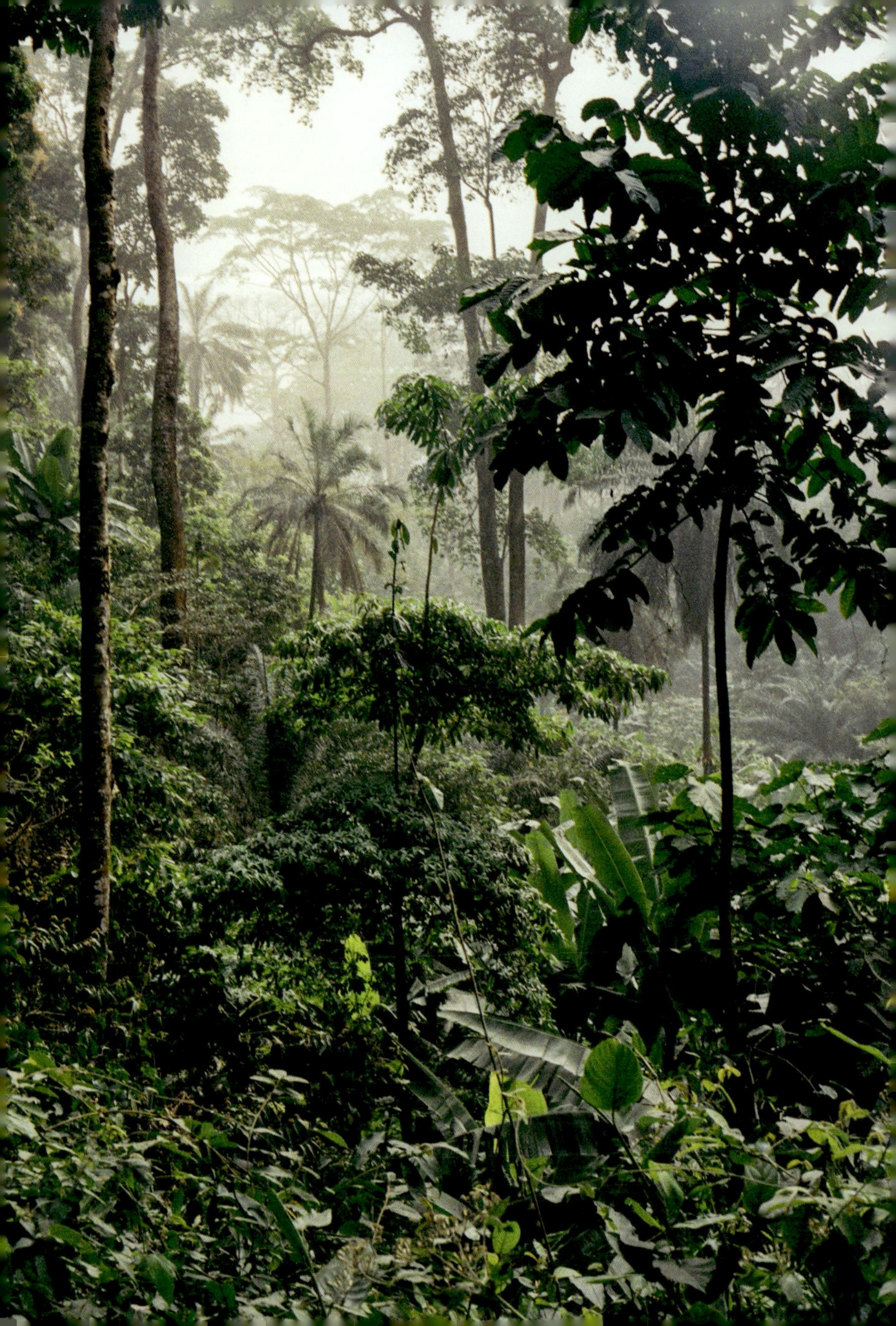

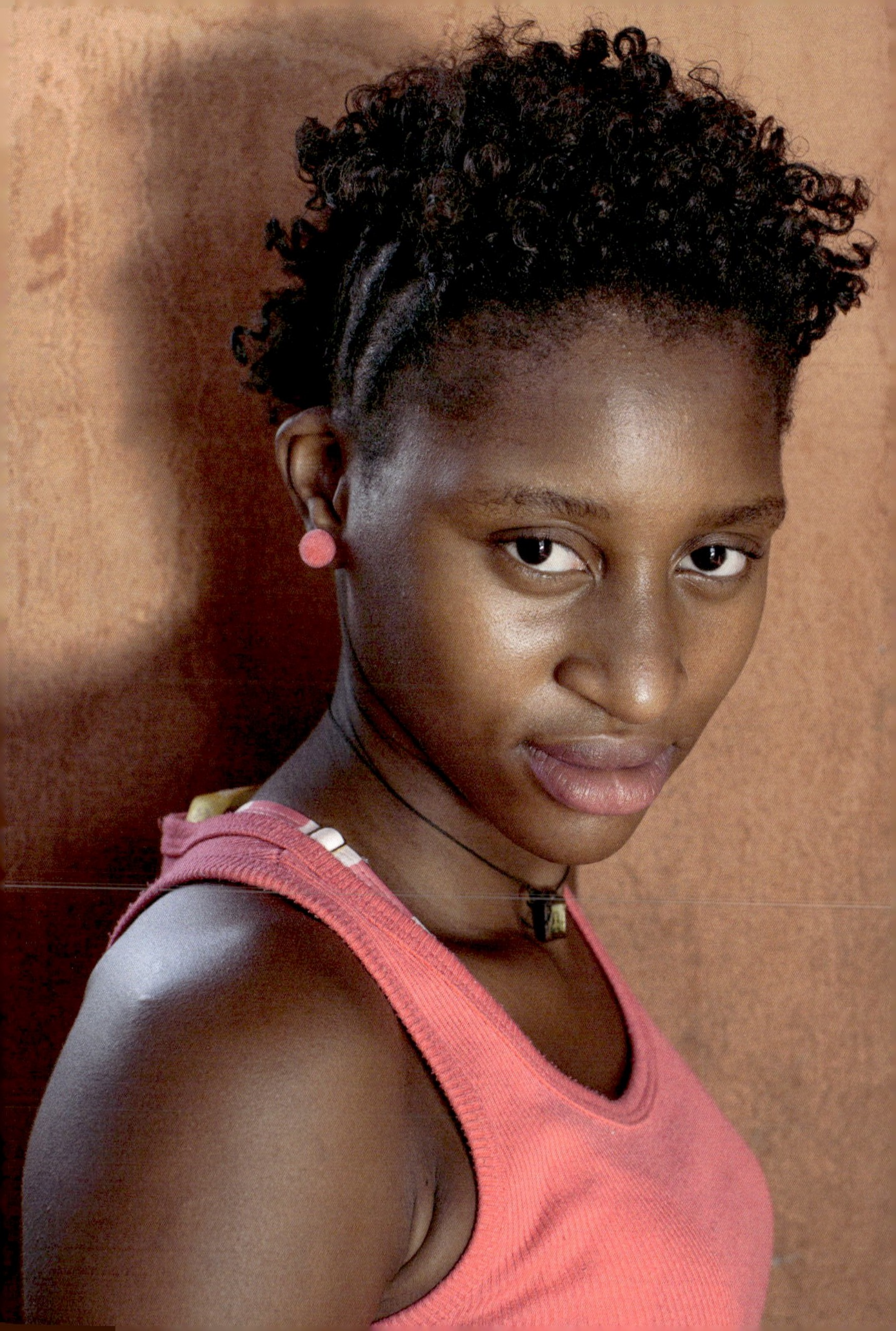

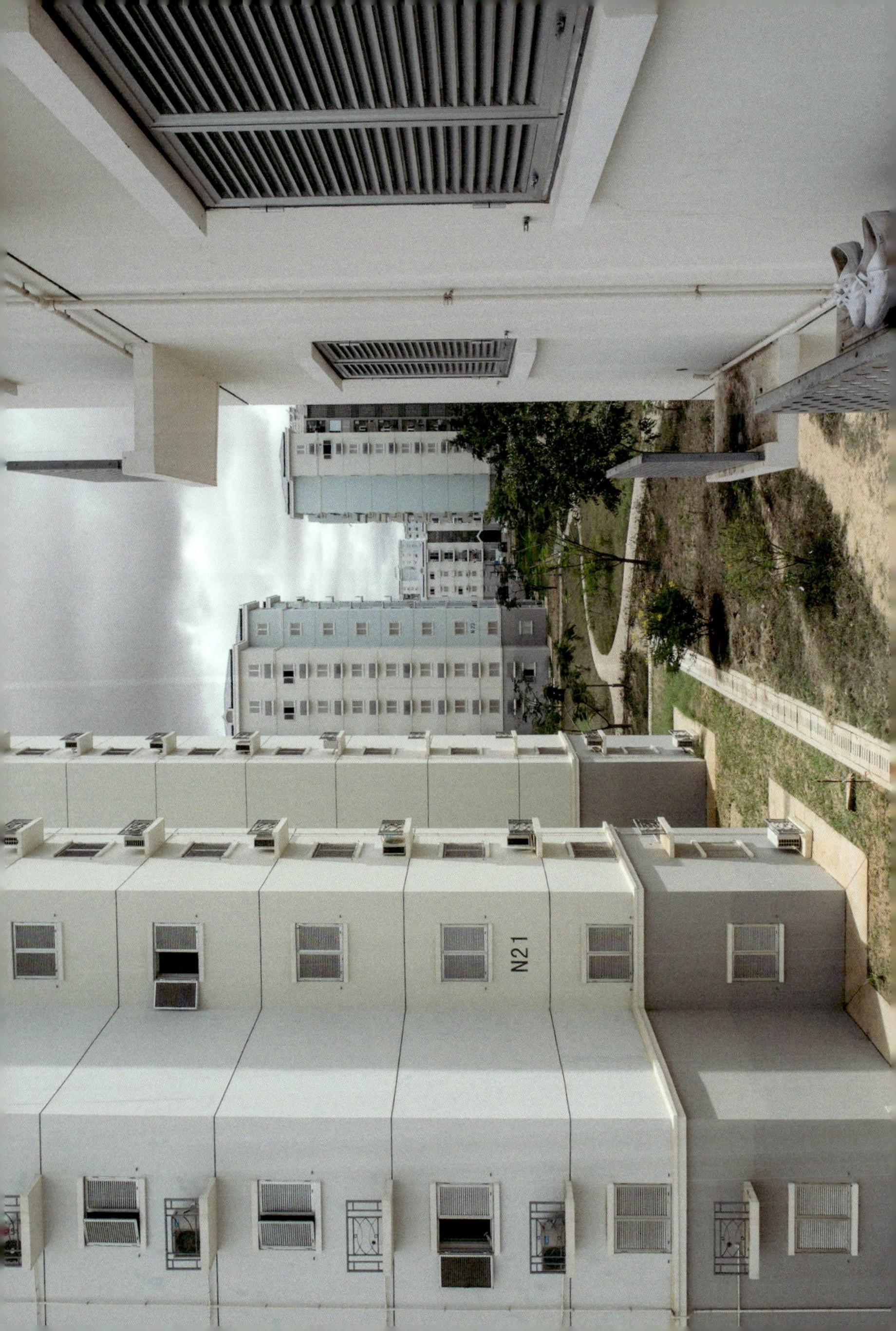
N21

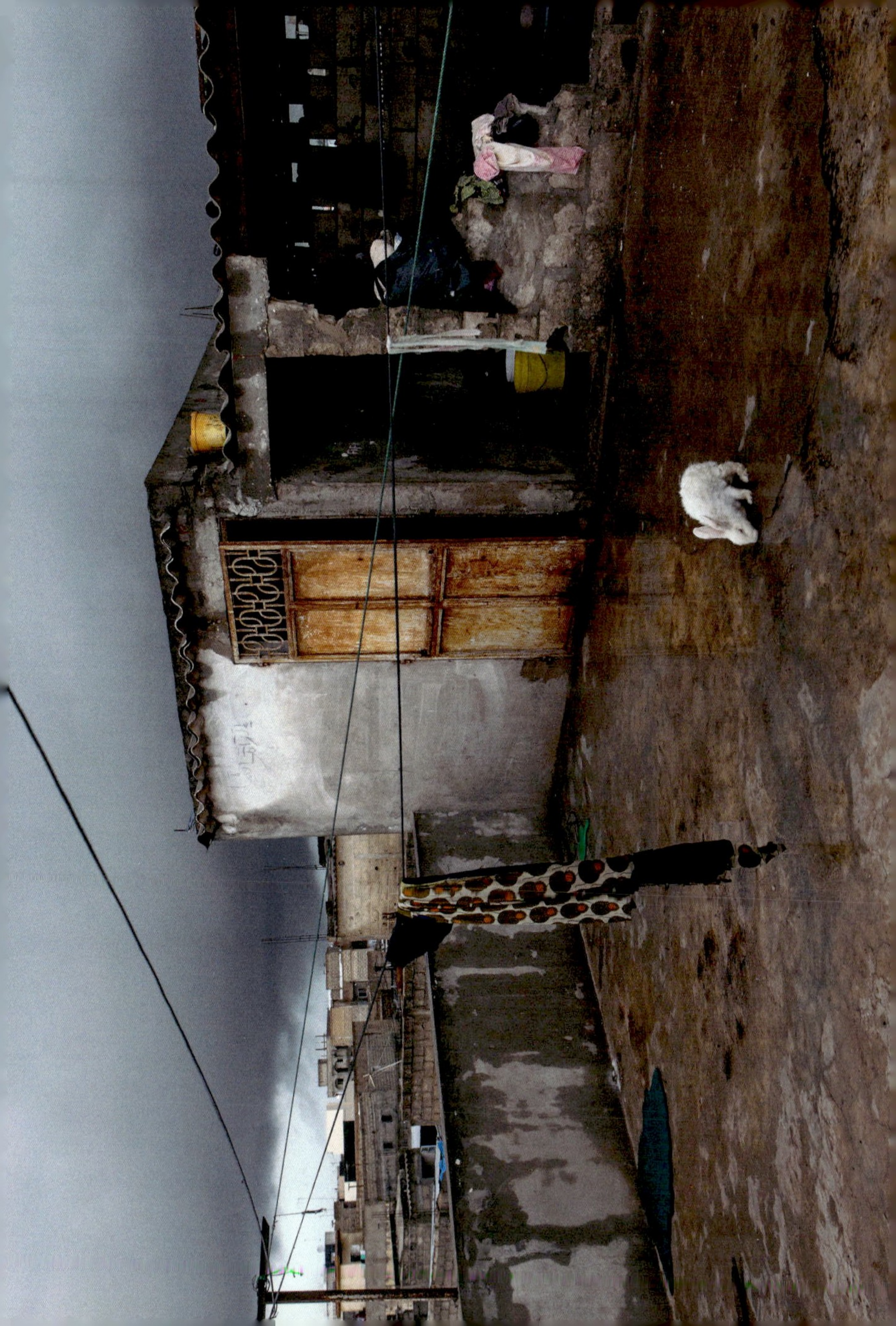

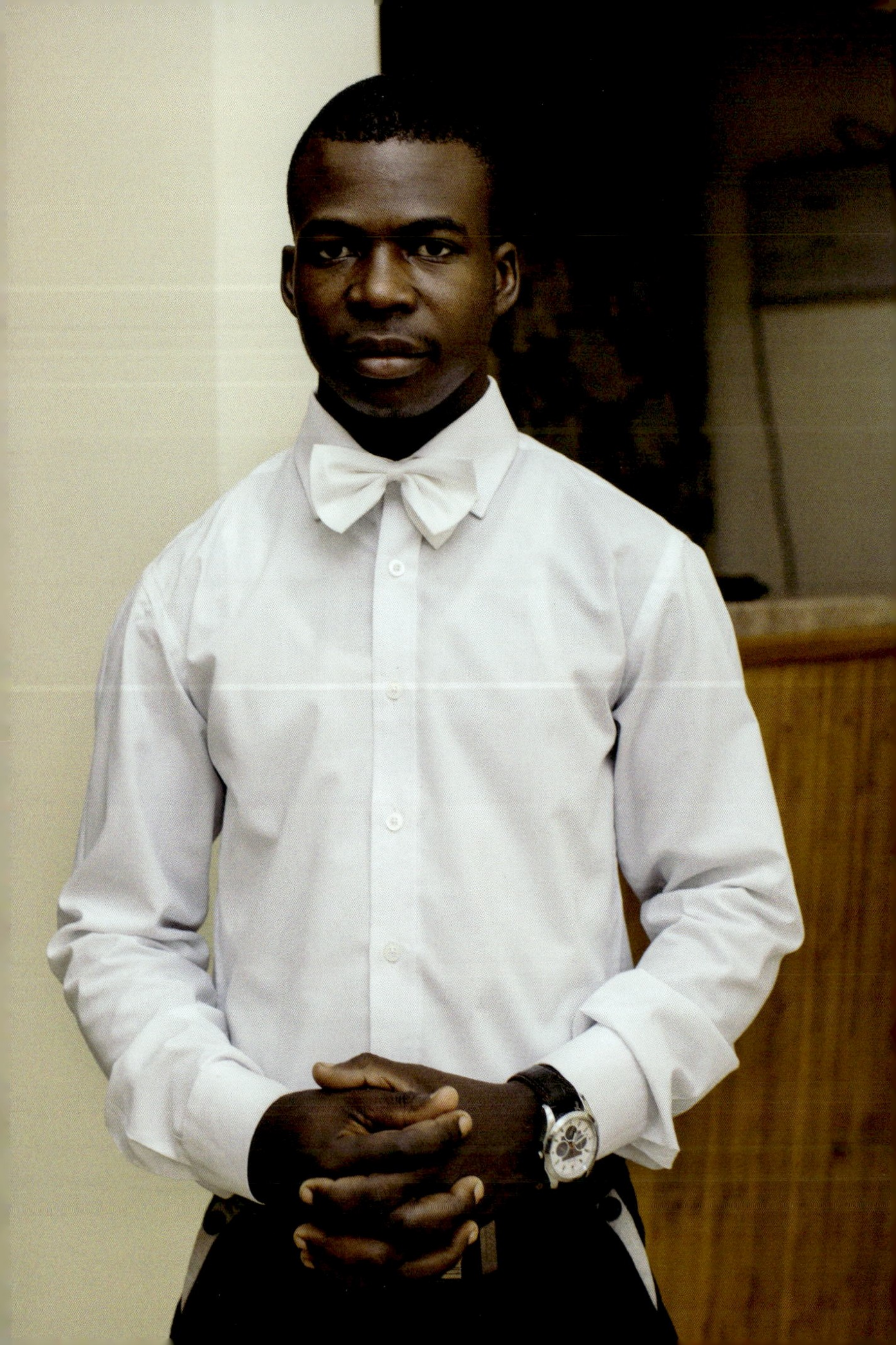

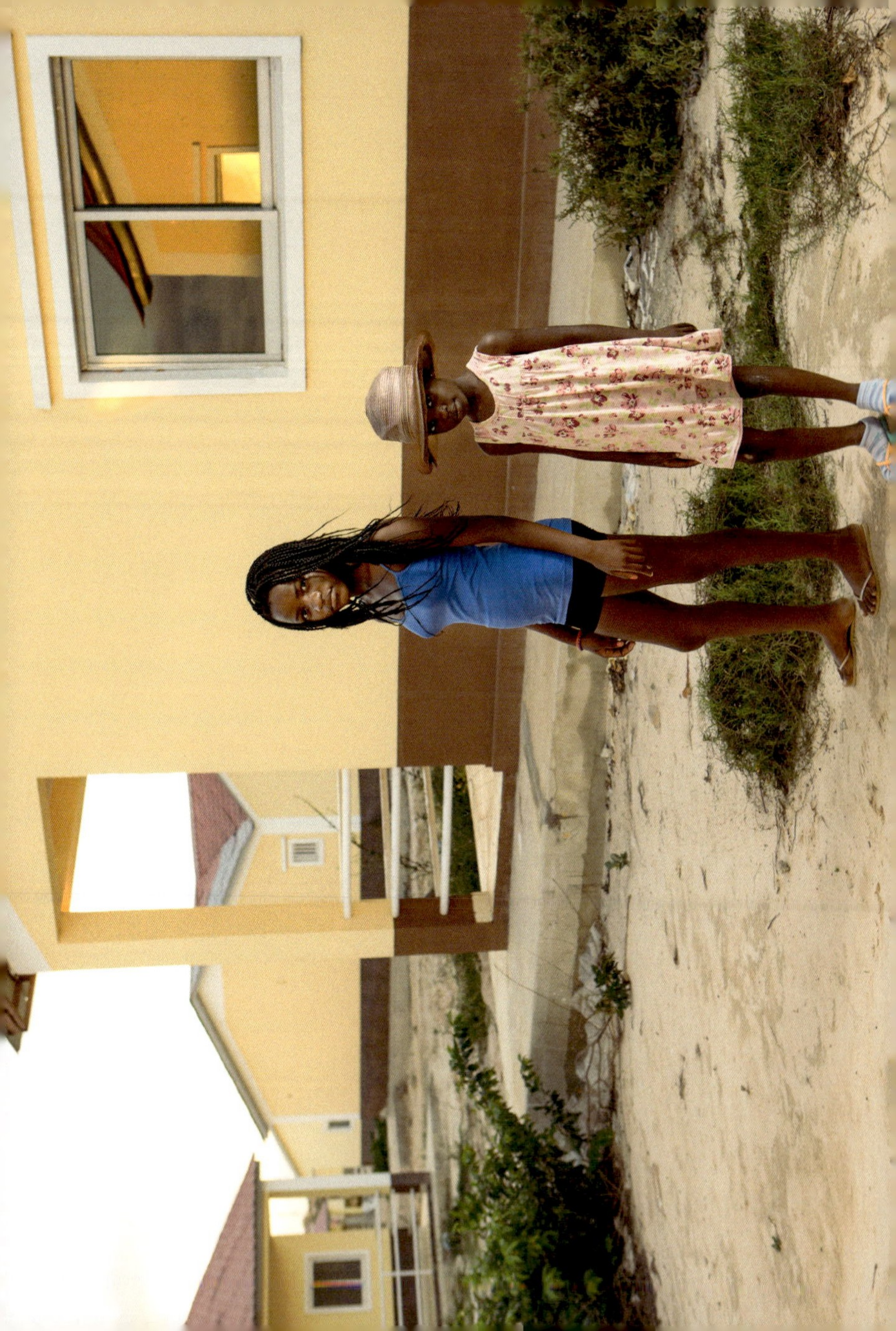

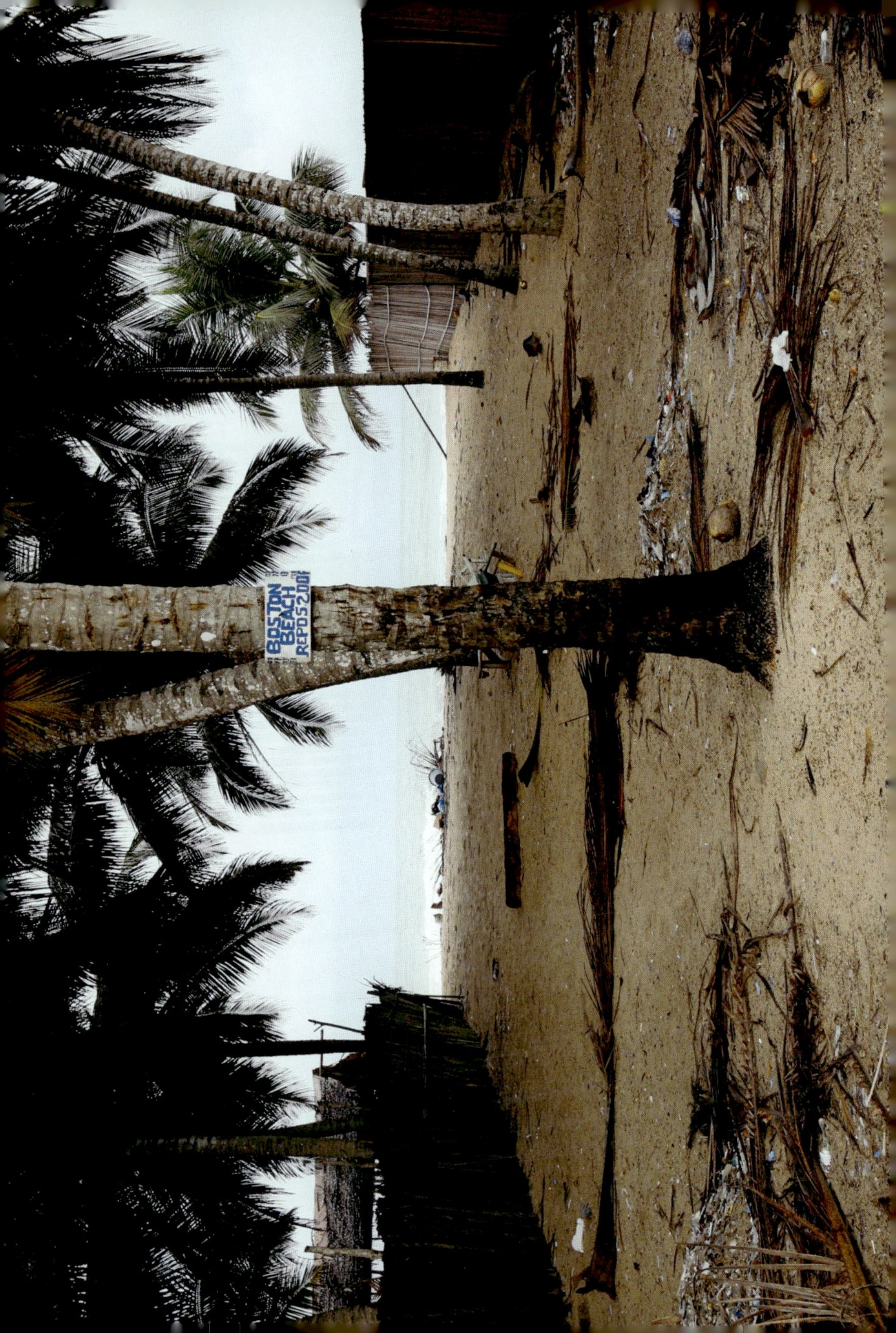
BOSTON
BEACH
REPOS 2.00F

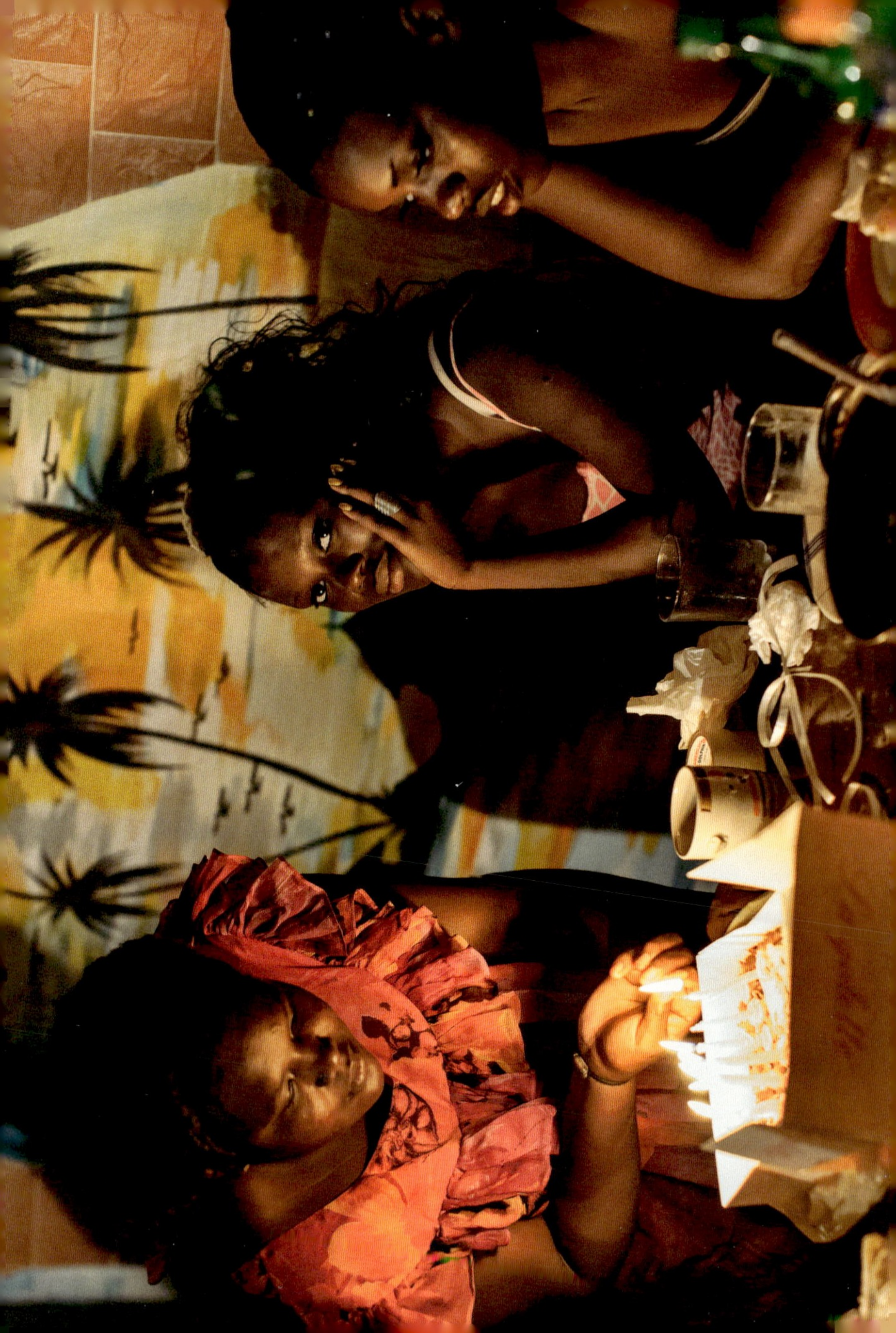

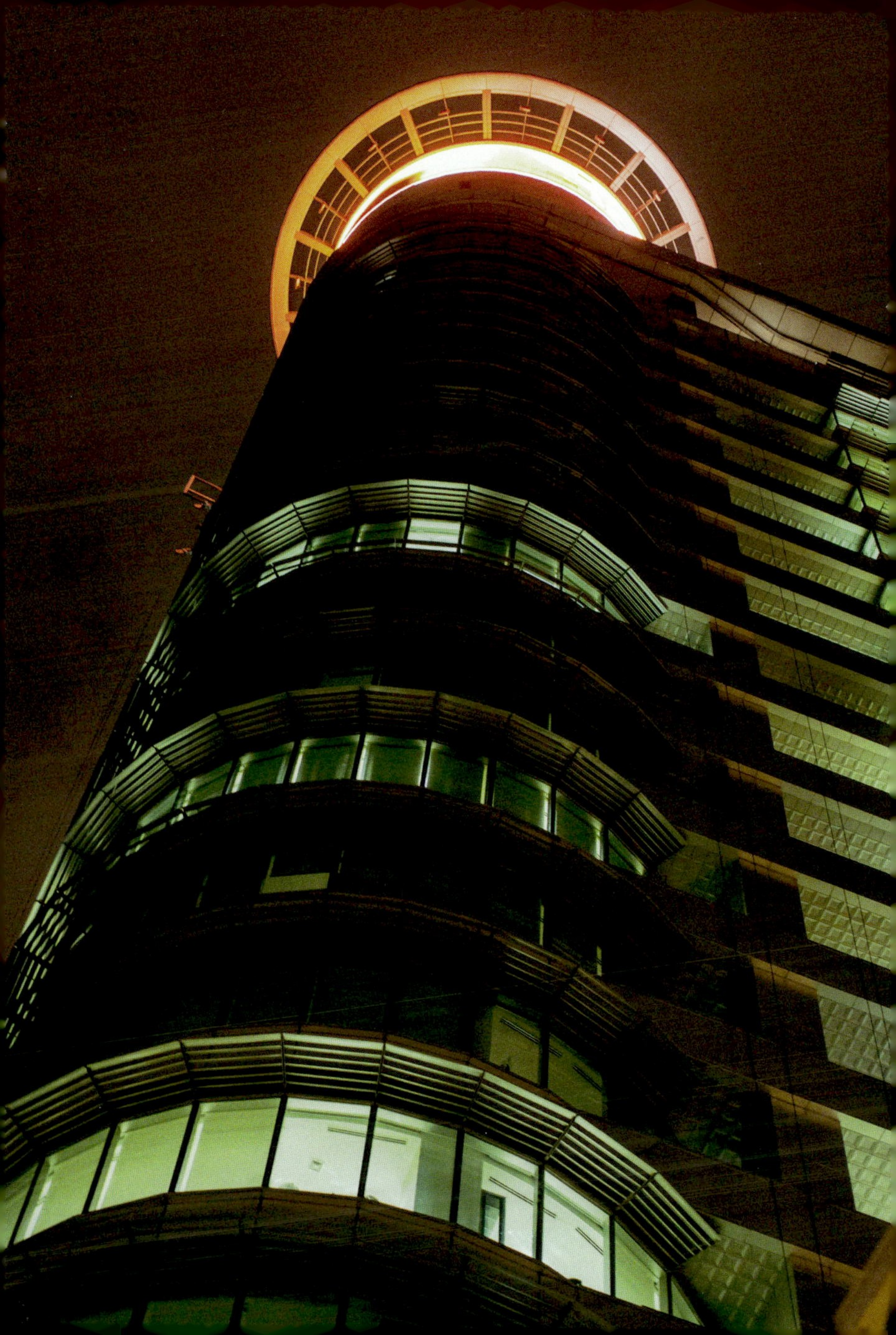

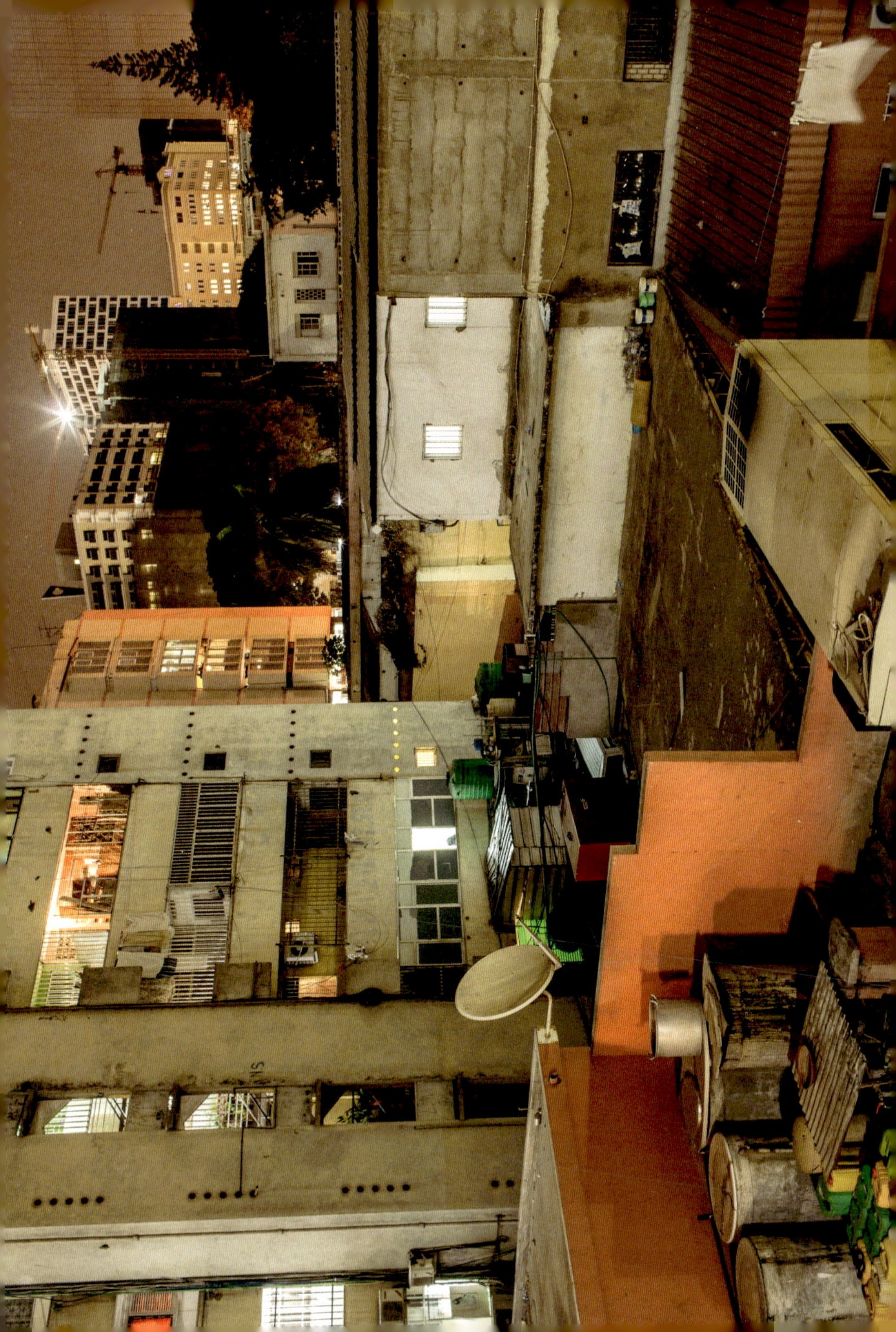

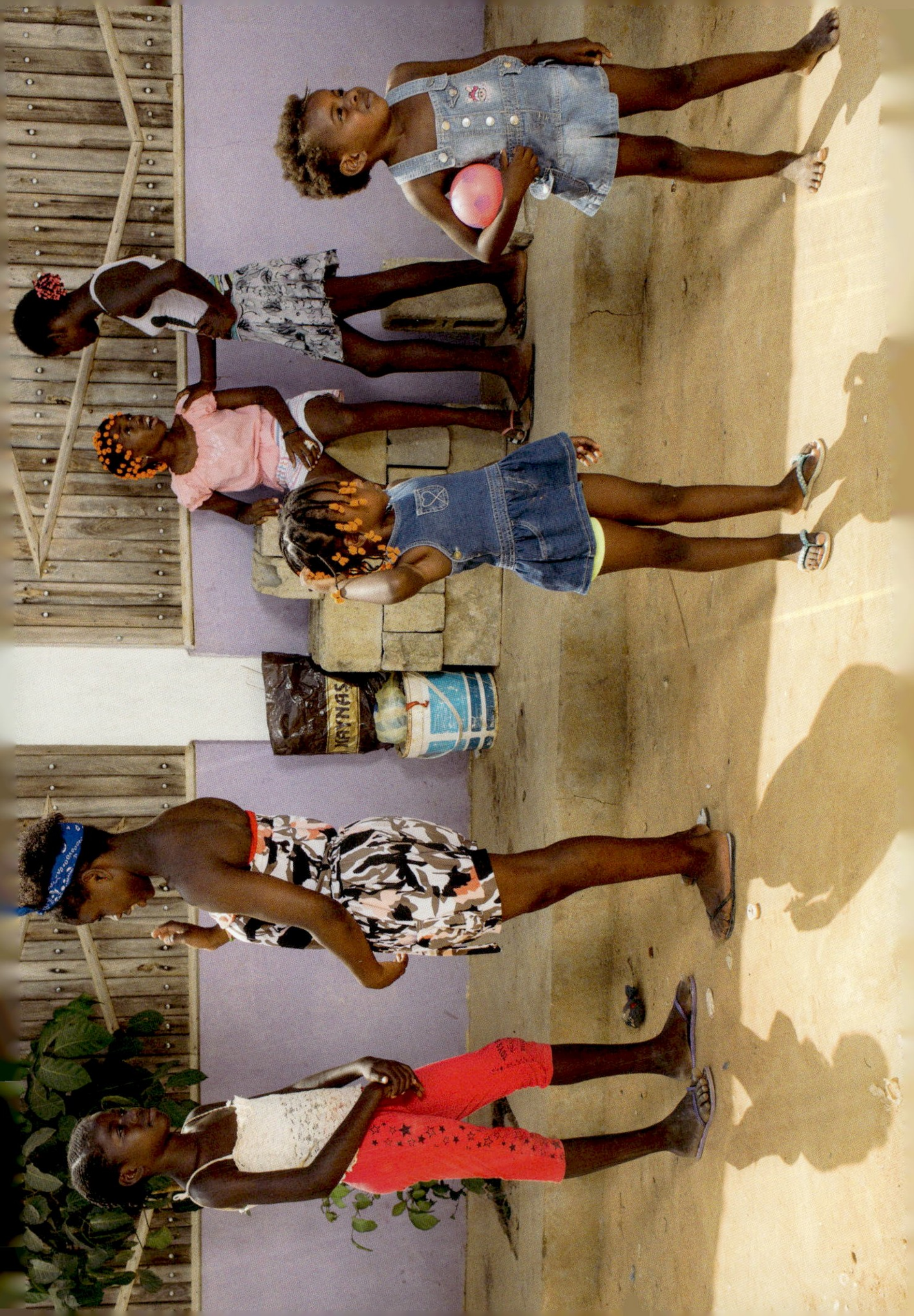

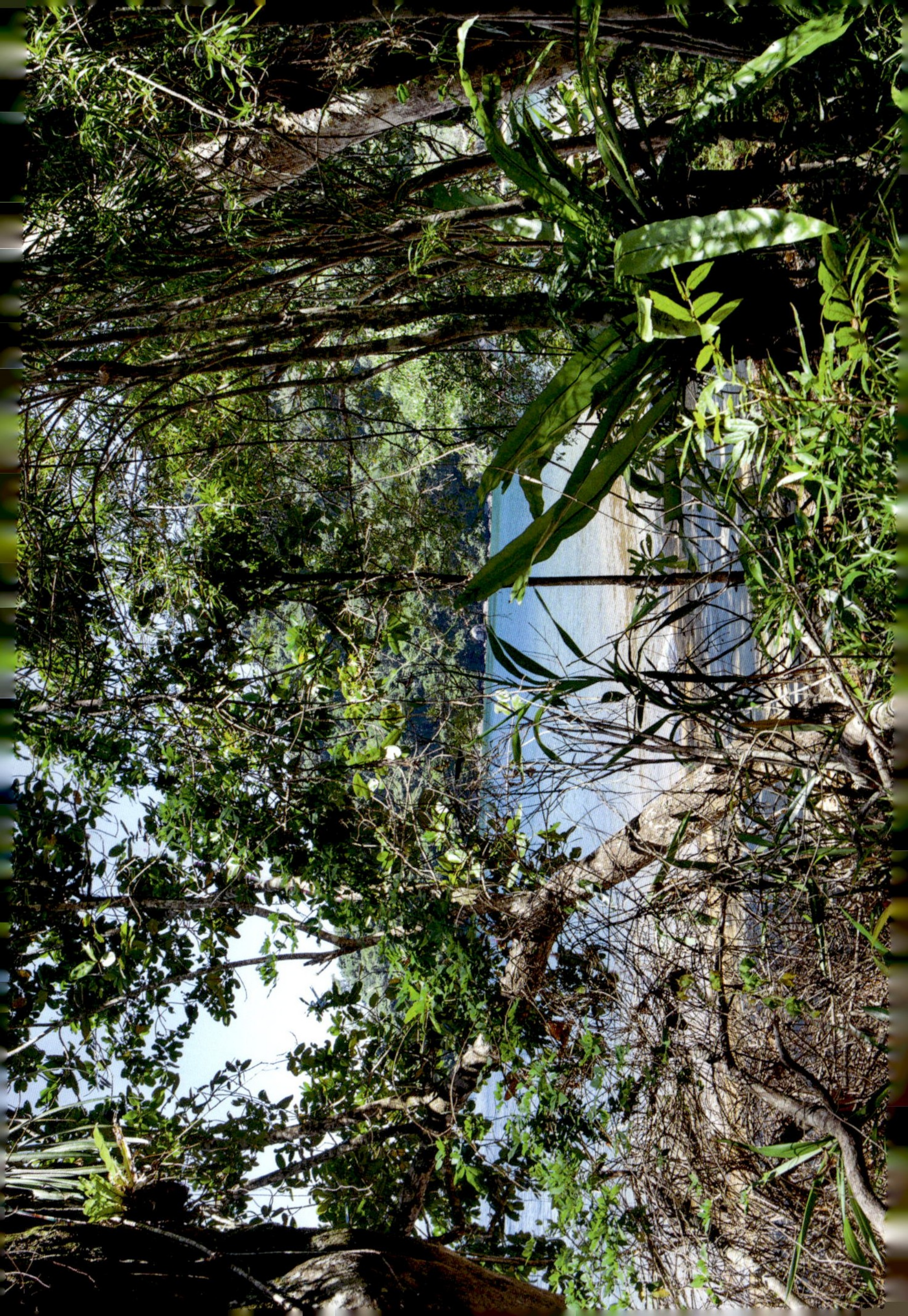